THE BURDENS OF P

Adjudicative tribunals in both criminal and noncriminal cases rely on the concept of the "burden of proof" to resolve uncertainty about facts. Perhaps surprisingly, this concept remains clouded and deeply controversial. Written by an internationally renowned scholar, this book explores contemporary thinking on the evidential requirements that are critical for all practical decision making, including adjudication. Although the idea that evidence must favor one side over the other to a specified degree, such as "beyond reasonable doubt," is familiar, less well understood is an idea associated with the work of John Maynard Keynes, namely, that there are requirements on the total amount of evidence considered to decide a case. The author expertly explores this distinct Keynesian concept and its implications. Hypothetical examples and litigated cases are included to assist understanding of the ideas developed. Implications include an expanded conception of the burden of producing evidence and how it should be administered.

DALE A. NANCE is the John Homer Kapp Professor of Law at Case Western Reserve University.

THE BURDENS OF PROOF

Discriminatory Power, Weight of Evidence, and Tenacity of Belief

DALE A. NANCE

CAMBRIDGE
UNIVERSITY PRESS

University Printing House, Cambridge CB2 8BS, United Kingdom

One Liberty Plaza, 20th Floor, New York, NY 10006, USA

477 Williamstown Road, Port Melbourne, VIC 3207, Australia

314-321, 3rd Floor, Plot 3, Splendor Forum, Jasola District Centre, New Delhi - 110025, India

79 Anson Road, #06-04/06, Singapore 079906

Cambridge University Press is part of the University of Cambridge.

It furthers the University's mission by disseminating knowledge in the pursuit of education, learning and research at the highest international levels of excellence.

www.cambridge.org
Information on this title: www.cambridge.org/9781107570481

© Dale A. Nance 2016

This publication is in copyright. Subject to statutory exception and to the provisions of relevant collective licensing agreements, no reproduction of any part may take place without the written permission of Cambridge University Press.

First published 2016
First paperback edition 2018

A catalogue record for this publication is available from the British Library

Library of Congress Cataloging in Publication data
Names: Nance, Dale A., author.
Title: The burdens of proof : discriminatory power, weight of evidence, and tenacity of belief / Dale A. Nance.
Description: Cambridge, United Kingdom : Cambridge University Press, 2016. | Includes bibliographical references and index.
Identifiers: LCCN 2015039553 | ISBN 9781107124189 (hardback)
Subjects: LCSH : Burden of proof. | Evidence. | Proof theory. | Keynes, John Maynard, 1883–1946.
Classification: LCC K2263.N36 2016 | DDC 347/.06–dc23
LC record available at http://lccn.loc.gov/2015039553

ISBN 978-1-107-12418-9 Hardback
ISBN 978-1-107-57048-1 Paperback

Cambridge University Press has no responsibility for the persistence or accuracy of URLs for external or third-party internet websites referred to in this publication, and does not guarantee that any content on such websites is, or will remain, accurate or appropriate.

CONTENTS

Preface   *page* ix
Acknowledgments   xiii

1. Introduction   1

2. Discriminatory Power: Adjudication as Practical Reasoning   15

   2.1   Practical Reasoning in the Adjudicative Context   16

   2.2   The Decision-Theoretic Formulation   21

       2.2.1   The Utility Ratio and the Standard of Proof   31

       2.2.2   The Fact-Finder's Assessment of Odds   42

       2.2.3   The Significance of Second-Order Uncertainty   57

   2.3   Competing Theories of Discriminatory Power   63

       2.3.1   The Standard of Proof and the Regulation of Substantive Conduct   64

       2.3.2   Relative Plausibility and the Best Explanation   73

   2.4   Free Evaluation versus Structured Analysis of Evidence   84

   2.5   The Importance and Sources of Background Information   95

   2.6   Concluding Remarks   101

3. Keynesian Weight and Decision Making: Being Prepared to Decide   103

   3.1   Motivation: Paradoxical Cases of "Naked Statistical Evidence"   104

   3.2   The Nature and Importance of Keynesian Weight: A First Look   111

- 3.3 Adequacy of Keynesian Weight as a "Preferential" Requirement   124
- 3.4 Keynesian Weight and the Importance of Informal Reasoning   137
- 3.5 The Quantification of Keynesian Weight   147
- 3.6 Keynesian Weight and "Holistic" Accounts of Epistemic Warrant   156
- 3.7 Decision Making with Non-Bayesian Belief Functions   167
- 3.8 Keynesian Weight and the Goals of Adjudication   178

4. **Keynesian Weight in Adjudication: The Allocation of Juridical Roles**   184
   - 4.1 The Law's Management of Keynesian Weight   186
     - 4.1.1 Discovery and Relevance: Adversarial Duty and Privilege   188
     - 4.1.2 Discovery Sanctions and Related Preemptive Rulings   193
     - 4.1.3 Admissibility Rules   195
     - 4.1.4 The Burden of Production   201
     - 4.1.5 Recognizing the Forest and Cultivating the Trees   212
   - 4.2 The Fact-Finder's Role in Monitoring Keynesian Weight   227
   - 4.3 Allocating Responsibility for Curing Deficiencies in Keynesian Weight   243
   - 4.4 Final Observations   249

5. **Tenacity of Belief: An Idea in Search of a Use**   251
   - 5.1 The Relationship between Keynesian Weight and Resilience of Probability   253
   - 5.2 The Dubious Value of a Distinct Resiliency Requirement   270
   - 5.3 Tenacity of Categorical Belief   278

6. **Conclusion**   292

    6.1   A Brief Summary   292

    6.2   Further Applications of the Theory: International Tribunals   294

    6.3   Postscript   303

References   305
Index   327

PREFACE

Adjudication is a conspicuous example of decision making under uncertainty, with "burdens of proof" employed to structure the decision. At the center of the following discourse is a set of ideas that collectively constitute the burdens of proof. These ideas inhabit the intersection of diverse disciplines, including law (its principal subject), epistemology, and decision theory. My goal is to elucidate this fascinating interplay of ideas. This work's focus is not heavily doctrinal or historical, although doctrine plays an important part, as does the history of ideas. It is, ultimately, an elaboration of a philosophy of factual adjudication.

In evidence law scholarship, much more attention has been paid to the rules of admissibility over the last two centuries, perhaps because rules regarding the "sufficiency" of evidence have languished: many that had once existed have disappeared, and the few that remain can be learned easily, at least at a superficial level. But among those who are concerned with the process and logic of proof, in the context of evidence that has passed the hurdles of admissibility, the rules that structure the decision take on great significance. And despite a recent surge of scholarly interest in the subject of legal proof, it remains decidedly undertheorized.

It will be widely agreed that adjudication of disputed facts is properly based on the *weight* of evidence. But "weight" can mean many things. For most lawyers, the weight of evidence is understood as the degree to which the evidence favors one side of the dispute over the other, what I will call its "discriminatory power." In modern legal scholarship, however, there has been considerable interest in the weight of evidence in a sense developed, most prominently, by John Maynard Keynes – which refers to the total amount of relevant evidence considered, regardless of which side is favored thereby. The interest in this subject has been limited to a relatively small number of theorists, to judge by the impact that it has had on mainstream evidence scholarship. Perhaps this is because there remains significant disagreement about what lessons to take from the conversation.

This is an unfortunate state of affairs, I believe, because these lessons are of considerable theoretical and practical import.

I argue that the interest in a Keynesian sense of weight (hereafter, "Keynesian weight") is well founded, in that recourse to such an idea is necessary for a full account of the burdens of proof. Although the genesis of this idea goes back to articles I wrote in the 1980s and 1990s, I have sketched its broader themes only more recently. See Dale A. Nance, "The Weights of Evidence," 5 *Episteme* 267 (2008). The present book develops these arguments at greater depth and relates them more fully to the work of others. That said, I should also disclaim any attempt at comprehensiveness of treatment. Despite its underdeveloped character, the volume of sophisticated writings on the burdens of proof and related ideas in both legal and nonlegal disciplines is still such that a comprehensive exposition of all significant contributions would be unbearable for all but the most determined reader. Consequently, many qualifications and subtleties are passed over in the interest of a readable overall presentation. I hope to have achieved a reasonable balance of depth and breadth.

The reader will see that, at least in some parts of this book, I have not shied from the use of mathematical formulas. This reflects two considerations: (1) inference invokes probabilities, as to which an important body of mathematical theory is available, though it cannot tell the whole story, and (2) the formalization involved in the use of mathematics permits a high degree of precision in one's communication, a commodity that is greatly needed in a subject matter where important terms, such as *burden of proof* and *weight of evidence*, are subject to considerable ambiguity and where, as a consequence, the meaning underlying the use of such terms can so easily shift (often without notice) from one context of expression to another. Nevertheless, the reader uncomfortable with mathematics in general or probability theory in particular ought not to be deterred from proceeding. Much of the argument presented here can be understood without engaging the mathematics at any depth, and I have signaled at places where the reader can even skip particular sections without losing the thread.

I emphasize two main conclusions, each of which runs contrary to prevailing opinion among legal theorists who have addressed the topic of Keynesian weight, whether or not by that name. First, the Keynesian weight requirement should be, and generally is, subject to an excusable preference structure: what should be required is limited by what can be obtained. Second, generally speaking, the adequacy of Keynesian weight should not be, and generally is not, a matter for consideration by the trier of fact but rather something to be considered by the court. In lawyers' jargon, it is a "question of law." Thus, repeated efforts made by theorists to include an assessment of weight in the burden of persuasion applied by the trier of fact are generally misguided. These claims have broad implications.

Format and style notes: Citations are in footnotes to avoid cluttering the text. Primary legal authorities are cited in full in the footnotes. Abbreviated citations are used in the footnotes for books, articles, and secondary legal authorities (treatises, compendia of jury instructions, and so forth); full citations for these are found in the References at the end of the book. For stylistic consistency, letters used as abstract persons or propositions, variables, or functions are italicized throughout, even in direct quotations from works that do not italicize in this manner.

ACKNOWLEDGMENTS

This project could not have been completed without either the generous support of research provided by Case Western Reserve University School of Law or the enthusiasm for this time-consuming project shown by my loving wife, Melani. I specifically want to thank Peter Gerhart for his steady encouragement, Jane Moriarty for her generous friendship through difficult times, Paul Giannelli for his always patient and helpful responses to my "off the wall" questions, and Andrew Pollis for his detailed comments after a careful reading of a draft of the manuscript. I am also grateful for research assistance from several students over the gestation period of this book, especially Shannon Pagano, Ashley Sheroian, and Adam Rosen, and for technical and clerical support in the final stages from Megan Allen and Kimberly Peterson. Finally, I have an enormous intellectual debt to those who have preceded me in the exploration of the epistemology of decision making, especially those who have attempted to apply knowledge developed in other fields to the context of adjudication. Many, though not all, of these intellectual explorers will be discussed in the following pages, and in my effort to find the clear path, and to be clear about the path I am taking, I am often critical of prior work. In every case, however, my comments should be understood in the context of the great respect I have for the work of these fellow travelers.

1

Introduction

In adjudication, facts matter. Cases are often disputes over conflicting versions of the facts. In both civil and criminal cases, certain important, so-called ultimate facts are specified as determinative by the applicable substantive law.[1] When there is uncertainty about these facts, and trials become necessary to resolve the dispute, burdens of proof structure the tribunal's factual assessments. In American civil cases, for example, the ultimate facts that define a cause of action or defense usually must be shown by the plaintiff to be true "by a preponderance of the evidence," and in criminal cases, the ultimate facts must be shown by the prosecution to be true "beyond reasonable doubt."[2] The epistemic components of these requirements reflect the fact that they do not involve a surrender to some kind of pure proceduralism, in which the quest for accuracy is ignored in favor of whatever results from fair procedures.[3] Instead, they reflect the necessity of judgment under uncertainty and the need to exercise that judgment in a way that makes the best use possible of our unavoidably fallible assessments of the facts. This, at any rate, is the premise on which the following account will build.

But what exactly does it mean to prove a civil case "by a preponderance of the evidence"? Or to prove a criminal case "beyond reasonable doubt"? Much appellate ink has been spilled, and many issues settled, on how to formulate these standards verbally, on which standard applies in which kinds of cases, and on the applicability of yet other intermediate standards to some classes of cases.[4] Nevertheless, fundamental questions

---

[1] More precisely, ultimate facts are the facts constituting necessary components of a set of facts sufficient to instantiate a cause of action or affirmative defense. They are distinguishable from other facts that, once evidenced, can be the basis for inferring an ultimate fact. Cf. Wigmore (1937) at 9–11 (distinguishing between a "factum probans" and a "factum probandum," the former used to draw an inference to the latter).
[2] 2 McCormick (2013) §§ 339, 341.
[3] See Rawls (1971) at 85–6. For a discussion of the challenges of pure proceduralism in the adjudicative context and its associated fact skepticism, see Kaptein (2009).
[4] Most American jurisdictions have an intermediate standard applicable to certain civil cases or certain issues in civil cases, a standard often characterized as requiring "clear and

about what these standards mean remain deeply controversial.[5] In this book I address a set of issues critically important to answering these questions. Specifically, I explore the relationships among three ideas that infuse modern scholarship regarding the burdens of proof. Clarification of these ideas and their relationships promises significant advances in our understanding of the proof process.

Before stating these ideas, a few preliminary comments are in order. The present discourse concerns proof of "adjudicative" facts, facts concerning the conduct of parties to litigation that trigger the applicability of substantive legal rules – such as the fact that the defendant's conduct caused the injury to the plaintiff or the fact that the accused had the intent to kill the deceased. Courts sometimes must assess a different category of facts, so-called legislative facts, facts that are pertinent to determining the content of the legal rules (whether substantive or procedural) that are to be applied in the litigation. For example, if a court is choosing between two possible common-law rules (or two possible interpretations of a statutory rule), one factual matter that it might consider is a comparison of the consequences that can be expected to flow from one or the other rule candidate. These are matters not submitted to the trier of fact at all. There is little regulation in terms of the burdens of proof in the latter context, and I shall not address this important question here.[6]

As is well known, the "burden of proof" on ultimate adjudicative facts has two aspects, at least in Anglo-American procedure. The "burden of persuasion" is that aspect of the burden of proof that, while specified by law, is applied by the trier of fact. It poses the question whether the standard of proof (such as "beyond reasonable doubt") has been satisfied. This is to be distinguished from the "burden of production," that aspect of the burden of proof that is applied (almost exclusively) by the court.[7]

---

convincing evidence." See 2 McCormick (2013) § 340. In other common-law jurisdictions, the matter is more complicated and ambiguous, but standards exist that are also clearly considered intermediate between that applied in the ordinary civil case and that applicable to the prosecution in criminal cases. See Redmayne (1999).

[5] See, e.g., Stein (2005); Laudan (2006); Ho (2008); and Clermont (2013).

[6] See 2 McCormick (2013) § 331 (discussing standards for taking judicial notice of legislative facts). I also do not address the standards involved in circumventing the usual proof process by the taking of judicial notice of adjudicative facts. See Id. §§ 329–30.

[7] Id. §§ 336, 338. The main reason for the qualifier ("almost exclusively") is that the assistance of the jury is sometimes enlisted in applying presumptions that shift the burden of production by requiring the jury to determine whether or not the "basic facts," those that trigger the presumption, are true. Id. § 344. As we will see, there is another complication. See § 4.2, infra.

INTRODUCTION 3

Under various circumstances, that burden requires the court to determine whether the evidence that has been produced at trial is good enough to warrant a determination by the trier of fact.[8] Our initial puzzle obviously relates to the burden of persuasion, but we will see that the burden of production is inevitably brought into the discussion.

One component of the burden of persuasion is the *allocation* question: which party is to bear the burden, however heavy that burden may be? This is functionally equivalent to the question of which ultimately determinative facts will be assigned to the complainant as part of that party's affirmative case and which will be assigned to the defendant as elements of an affirmative defense. It also determines the "default" rule; that is, it specifies which party is to be awarded the verdict if the fact-finder is unable to determine whether or not the burden of persuasion with respect to those ultimate facts has been satisfied. The case law and commentary have identified a variety of factors that supposedly control the decision about this allocation question. Some of them are more coherent than others.[9] They include

1. The policy of placing the burden on the party who seeks to change the status quo (unhelpful without an explanation of why, in cases that are litigated, the status quo is presumptively just or otherwise desirable);
2. The policy of placing the burden on the party whose actions necessitate engaging the public machinery of adjudication and the associated litigation costs (also unhelpful, in light of the fact that *either* party could act to avoid such engagement – the complainant by not filing a complaint and the defendant by settling without litigation);
3. The policy of placing the burden on the party asserting an occurrence rather than on the party asserting a nonoccurrence (an arbitrary dictum that explains nothing because it depends entirely on how the matter is stated – for example, stated affirmatively as a party's "breach of duty" or stated negatively as the party's "failure to exercise ordinary care" or "failure to honor a contractual commitment");
4. The policy of placing the burden on the party to whose case the element is essential (an unhelpful tautology);[10]

---

[8] Unfortunately, the terminology used to mark this distinction is not uniform, even among common-law countries. What in the United States is usually called the "burden of persuasion" is elsewhere sometimes called the "legal burden"; what in the United States is usually called the "burden of production" is elsewhere sometimes called the "evidential burden." See, e.g., Tapper (1995) at 119–25.

[9] See 2 McCormick (2013) § 337; see also Bolding (1960) at 23–7 and Nance (1994) at 659–69.

[10] The seeming plausibility of this principle arises when and because it is offered not as an explanation or justification for the allocation but as guidance to someone, such as a student

5. The policy of handicapping a substantively disfavored claim, one the very making of which is to be discouraged (sometimes plausible and often overlapping with rationale 8);
6. The policy of placing the burden on the party with presumptively superior access to evidence (seemingly plausible but inconsistent with many conventional allocations because plaintiffs often must prove what defendants did, and with what mental state, and vice versa);
7. The policy of placing the burden on the party whose allegations are *a priori* less likely to be true (also seemingly plausible but ultimately unnecessary unless understood as imposing a judicial evaluation of the strength of evidence on a jury that might be otherwise disposed); and
8. The policy of placing the burden on a party who asserts that an opponent has violated a serious social norm (a useful criterion when disputes involve such allegations, but not in no-fault disputes).

For present purposes, it is unnecessary to develop a unified solution to this question, if indeed any exists.[11] Part of the difficulty in doing so is that there are really two issues being decided with reference to such factors, at least for Anglo-American adversarial trials. The allocation of the burden of persuasion generally determines the allocation of the initial burden of production with respect to the same ultimate facts.[12] This is understandable because inevitably *one* of the parties must start the process, and requiring the other party to present evidence would be wasteful if the party bearing the burden of persuasion cannot establish a prima facie case.[13] From this perspective, policies 6 and 7 make more sense than they otherwise would because they speak more to the allocation of the burden of producing evidence. In fact, allocating the initial burden of production may be the more

---

or practitioner, who is trying to discern where the burden has been placed, after it has been so placed for other reasons. See, e.g., Park et al. (2011) at 87 n. 23 and accompanying text.

[11] See Wigmore (1981) § 2486 at 291 ("The truth is that there is not and cannot be any one general solvent for all cases. It is merely a question of policy and fairness based on experience in the different situations.").

[12] In the unusual case where the burden of raising an issue is separated from the risk of non-persuasion on that issue, it can be difficult to say whether the matter is part of the claimant's affirmative case (conditional on its being raised by the opponent) or, rather, a true affirmative defense. Neither characterization seems entirely satisfactory. For example, in a minority of American jurisdictions, the burden to plead (and to present some evidence on) the question of insanity rests on the accused, but the burden to prove sanity then rests on the prosecution. See 1 LaFave (2003) § 8.2.

[13] See Posner (2001) at 1502–4 and Lempert (2001) at 1662–3. Elaborate explorations from a game-theoretic perspective, using simplifying assumptions, can be found in Hay (1997) and Sanchirico (2008).

important of the two tasks. In any event, my focus here is on the question of what it takes to satisfy these burdens once they have been allocated to a party. So the allocation of material facts as between the plaintiff's (or prosecution's) case and affirmative defenses will be taken as given.

The same considerations generally apply in thinking about the burdens placed on the defense – affirmative defenses – as apply in thinking about the burdens for the plaintiff's or prosecution's case. Therefore, to simplify matters, unless otherwise indicated, discussion will proceed in terms of the context of a burden of persuasion placed on the plaintiff or prosecution. Hereafter, when it is unnecessary to distinguish between civil or criminal cases, I will use the generic term *claimant* to refer to either the plaintiff or prosecution.

With these preliminaries out of the way, it is time to articulate the three ideas around which the present discourse is organized. First is the idea of balancing the evidence favoring one side of a case against the evidence favoring the other side. The metaphor of "weighing" the evidence is a powerful one. Thus, in explaining the preponderance-of-the-evidence standard, Pennsylvania's pattern jury instruction advises as follows:

> Think about an ordinary scale pan on each side to hold objects. Imagine using a scale as you deliberate in the jury room. Place all the evidence favorable to the plaintiff in one pan. Place all the evidence favorable to the defendant in the other. If the scales tip, even slightly, to the plaintiff's side, then, you must find for the plaintiff.[14]

Of course, the metaphor can be questioned. For example, it would be more accurate to speak of comparing the degree to which the evidence *as a whole* and the inferences rationally drawn therefrom support one side as compared to the other. Evidence does not always neatly divide into that which favors one side and that which favors the other. In particular, whereas adversarial trials divide evidence into that which is *presented* by one side and that which is *presented* by the other, the evidence presented by one side may, of course, actually favor the other, and it is the net effect of all the evidence that matters.[15]

---

[14] Pennsylvania Suggested Standard Civil Jury Instructions § 1.42 (3d ed., 2005).

[15] A standard jury instruction for civil cases reads

> In determining whether any fact in issue has been proved by a preponderance of the evidence, unless otherwise instructed you may consider the testimony of all witnesses, regardless of who may have called them, and all exhibits received in evidence, regardless of who may have produced them.

3 O'Malley et al. (2006) § 104.01. See also United States v. Keuylian, 602 F.2d 1033, 1040–41 (2d Cir. 1979) (applying the widely recognized rule, adapted from civil cases, that evidence

Still, the metaphor has undeniable appeal. And it suggests something important, especially when considering cases not governed by the preponderance-of-the-evidence standard.[16] Though a simple scale may not be able to measure it, we know that the physical weight that is involved in the use of ordinary scales can be measured; with appropriate measuring devices, one can say just how much more one object weighs than another, and *a fortiori*, one can measure the ratio of the weights of the objects in the two pans. Does such a strategy carry over to adjudication? By some accounts, the balance of evidence is quantifiable as a ratio of probabilities, for example, "Given the evidence, claimant's case is twice as likely as defendant's." By some accounts, no such quantification is possible: whereas we might say, at least in some contexts, that claimant's case is stronger than defendant's, we cannot quantify *how much* stronger.[17]

In using the phrases "claimant's case" and "defendant's case," I have deliberately abstracted to avoid certain difficulties in defining what it is, precisely, that the claimant or the defendant tries to prove or is required to prove. In particular, one needs to distinguish between an alleged cause of action (or defense) and the specific factual story (or "theory of the case") advanced by a party to show that a cause of action (or defense) is instantiated or that it is not instantiated. This distinction is important in understanding any theory of the burdens of proof, and we will pay attention to it in what follows. And both these ideas must be distinguished from whatever pleading requirements are in place. In civil and criminal cases, most jurisdictions follow pleading requirements that are demanding enough to do somewhat more than just identify the cause of action or affirmative defense relied on but still permissive enough not to require the articulation of a detailed theory of the case.[18]

Quantifiable or not – and abstracting for the moment from exactly what it is that must be compared – this sort of comparative assessment is surely what most lawyers in the common-law tradition regard as the weight of the evidence.[19] Thus, "[i]n civil actions, the burden of persuasion

---

presented by the defense may cure what otherwise would be a defect in the state's evidentiary case, so a motion for directed verdict by the defense must be decided taking into consideration not only evidence presented by the state but also any evidence presented by the defense that might fill any gap in the state's evidence).

[16] See Walton (2002) at 13–14 (using the image of the "teeter-totter" to illustrate the difference between the criminal and civil standards).
[17] See, e.g., Haack (2014) at 47–77.
[18] See, e.g., Fed. R. Civ. P. 8 & 9 and Fed. R. Crim. P. 7(c)(1).
[19] "[W]eight of the evidence: the persuasiveness of some evidence in comparison with other evidence" declares the standard legal dictionary. Black's (1999) at 1588.

INTRODUCTION   7

is usually described as a requirement that there must be a *preponderance of the evidence*, or that the *greater weight of the evidence* must exist in favor of the party having the burden of persuasion."[20] Indeed, the two modes of expression are often used interchangeably within the same jurisdiction. For example, one standard jury instruction for federal civil cases reads

> The party who has the burden of proving a fact must prove it by the [(greater weight) or (preponderance)] of the evidence. To prove something by the [(greater weight) or (preponderance)] of the evidence is to prove that it is more likely true than not true.[21]

The committee comments that accompany this instruction indicate that the choice presented in the brackets is a matter of the preference of the individual judge, confirming that the authors see no material difference between the two wordings; to prove by the preponderance of the evidence is just to prove by the greater weight of the evidence.[22] Moreover, the instruction makes clear that what both these ideas mean is proving that a fact is more likely than not, invoking the concept of probability. Several American jurisdictions state this "more probable than not" standard for the typical civil case.[23]

This notion of case weight involves an "apportionment" between the parties. The more the evidence favors the claimant, the less it favors the defendant. What matters to the decision is which of the contending hypotheses is more favored by the evidence and by what margin or to what degree. The margin required to support a verdict depends on the nature of the case. In particular, it is generally thought that a wider margin is required to warrant a conviction in a criminal case than is required to warrant a verdict for the plaintiff in a civil case.[24] I will refer to this sense of

---

[20] Teply & Whitten (1994) at 828 (emphasis in original).
[21] Manual of Model Civil Jury Instructions for the District Courts of the Eighth Circuit, Instruction No. 3.04 (1999). This model instruction has since been simplified to eliminate the phrase "preponderance of the evidence"; now it equates proving by "the greater weight of the evidence" with proving "more likely true than not true." Manual of Model Civil Jury Instructions for the District Courts of the Eighth Circuit No. 3.04 (2013).
[22] See also Connecticut Civil Jury Instructions 3.2-1 (2011) ("The party who asserts a claim has the burden of proving it by a fair preponderance of the evidence, that is, the better or weightier evidence must establish that, more probably than not, the assertion is true.")
[23] See, e.g., State Bar of Arizona, RAJI (Civil) 4th, Std. 2 (2005) and Judicial Council of California Civil Jury Instructions (CACI) No. 200 (2011). See also 3 O'Malley et al. (2006) § 101.41 (presenting pattern instruction for federal civil cases). On the evolution of the various versions of the usual standard of proof for civil cases, see Leubsdorf (2013).
[24] 2 McCormick (2013) § 341. Continental European countries in the "civil law" tradition often do not explicitly distinguish criminal from noncriminal cases in terms of the standard

weight as the *discriminatory power* of the evidence because it reflects the extent to which the evidence, placed in the context of background information that the trier of fact is entitled to use, discriminates between the two sides of the dispute.

The second idea of concern here is, roughly speaking, the amount of evidence relating to the contending hypotheses that has been developed and taken into consideration. In *very* rough terms, if discriminatory power entails an apportionment, it is plausible to focus on and attempt to measure or otherwise assess that which is being apportioned. Returning to the metaphor of the scales, one can imagine placing a measurable amount X of evidence in the pan favoring the claimant and a measurable amount Y in the pan favoring the defendant. In these terms, discriminatory power compares X to Y by looking, for example, to the ratio of X to Y. But one can also consider combining X and Y, representing the total amount of evidence that is considered by determining, for example, the sum $X + Y$. This idea is also commonly called the "weight" of the evidence by several theorists, following the terminology of John Maynard Keynes.[25] I would follow this simple usage, but for the fact that the term *weight* by itself is so commonly associated by lawyers with what I have here called "discriminatory power." To avoid confusion, this second conception of weight will be referred to as the "Keynesian weight" of evidence.[26]

This notion of weight will be refined in Chapter 3, but even with the relatively crude articulation just provided, an important observation can already be made. Keynesian weight is not comparative in the sense described earlier. It is incoherent to ask how the weight of evidence, in Keynes's sense of the term, differs as between contending hypotheses. This is so because the weight of the evidence with respect to a hypothesis is always the same as the weight of the same evidence with respect to the competing hypothesis. Keynesian weight, however, is comparative in a different sense (one that it

---

of proof to be applied, a curious fact (at least to the Anglo-American legal mind) that calls for explanation. See, e.g., Clermont & Sherwin (2002).

[25] Keynes (1921) at 71.

[26] In a previous paper I distinguished these ideas by using the term Δ-*weight* for discriminatory power and the term Σ-*weight* for Keynesian weight. See Nance (2008) at 269. The reasons for this nomenclature may already be obvious. The verbal characterizations used here may be easier for readers to keep straight. It comes, however, with its own potential for confusion: what I call the discriminatory power *of the evidence in a particular case* ought not be confused with what forensic scientists call the discriminating power *of a particular test*. The latter measures the relative usefulness of various forensic tests across a group of cases, as distinct from the value of the result of any test in any particular case. See Aitken & Taroni (2004) at 129–41.

shares with discriminatory power): one can, at least sometimes, meaningfully compare Keynesian weight (or, for that matter, discriminatory power) *for different states of the evidence.* To illustrate in terms of our admittedly clumsy metaphor of evidence in the pans of the scales of justice, suppose that one were to double the amount of evidence favorable to the claimant and likewise double the amount of evidence favorable to the defense. Then the ratio of the amount of evidence favoring the claimant to the amount of evidence favoring the defendant would remain unchanged, but the total amount of evidence allocated between them would double. If we use the indicated ratio to measure discriminatory power and the indicated sum to measure Keynesian weight, then discriminatory power is unchanged, whereas Keynesian weight is doubled.

The third idea to be addressed is the *tenacity* with which one holds one's belief that a hypothesis is correct, that is, how difficult it is for one to be persuaded to abandon that belief.[27] The belief in question may be either categorical or partial. (Categorical belief is dichotomous: if *p* is a proposition of fact, then one believes that *p* or one does not. Partial belief is gradational: one can believe more or less that *p* from an extreme of certainty that *p* is false to an extreme of certainty that *p* is true.) Especially in the context of a partial belief that is graded in terms of probability, tenacity is sometimes referred to as "resilience." Thus theorists have referred to the resilience of probabilities.[28] As explained later, these ideas are, or at least can be, related to Keynesian weight, but the relationship is complex.

In modern legal scholarship, the question has been posed whether the burden of persuasion requires anything more than, or something completely different from, a comparison of the assessed discriminatory power of the evidence to the standard of proof appropriate to a particular kind of case. For example, if the civil standard is articulated as requiring that a fact be proved more likely than not – as it often is – then the question becomes, what more (if anything) is required for a verdict favoring the burdened party (usually the plaintiff) than a determination by the trier of fact that the odds favor the burdened party, that is, that the probability that the plaintiff's claim is true is greater than the probability that it is not? Most lawyers, certainly most lawyers practicing before common-law courts, would reflexively say that nothing more is required, and there is considerable support for this intuition in recognized authority.[29]

---

[27] See, e.g., Harman (1986) at 22 and Owens (2000) at 144.
[28] See, e.g., Logue (1995) at 78–95 and Stein (2005) at 82.
[29] See, e.g., 3 O'Malley et al. (2006) § 104.01 (providing a standard jury instruction): "'Establish by a preponderance of the evidence' means to prove that something is more

Nevertheless, there have been dissenting voices. Occasional judicial opinions seem to balk, although it is often difficult to discern in such cases whether the court is simply opposed to probabilistic judgments or is rather concerned that, in the context of the particular case, a probabilistic judgment cannot by itself encapsulate the totality of the standard of proof, or rather that the probability threshold simply has not been set high enough.[30] Picking up on these qualms, several scholars have maintained that an assessment of discriminatory power must be *supplemented with* an assessment of something else, that satisfying the burden of persuasion requires both attainment of the necessary margin of discriminatory power in the evidence and attainment of a certain degree of (what I have called) Keynesian weight.[31] For at least one important scholar, the argument goes so far as to suggest that an assessment in terms of Keynesian weight should be *substituted for* any assessment in terms of conventional probabilities.[32]

Similarly, there are those who have maintained that the assessment of discriminatory power, when conceived in probabilistic terms, must be supplemented with an assessment of, and test for, the resilience of those probabilities.[33] For the most part, those who make this argument do not distinguish it from, and appear to believe that it is the same as, the preceding argument, namely, that the assessment of discriminatory power should be coupled with a separate assessment of Keynesian weight. In some cases, once again, this argument goes so far as to dispense (seemingly) with discriminatory power entirely so that the burden of persuasion consists of the

---

likely so than not so"; 2 McCormick (2013) § 339 at 661 ("The most acceptable meaning to be given the expression, proof by a preponderance, seems to be proof which leads the jury to find that the existence of the contested fact is more probable than its nonexistence. Thus the preponderance of the evidence becomes the trier's belief in the preponderance of the probability.")

[30] See, e.g., Sargent v. Massachusetts Accident Co., 29 N.E.2d 825 (Mass. 1940) and Lampe v. Franklin American Trust Co., 96 S.W. 2d 710 (Mo. 1936). Not all the cases are older ones. See, e.g., Spencer v. Baxter Int'l, Inc., 163 F. Supp. 2d 74, 80 n.7 (D. Mass. 2001) (noting Massachusetts law). See also Sienkiewicz v. Greif (UK), Ltd. [2011] UKSC 10 (9 March 2011) (expressing reservations about overtly and exclusively statistical proof that meets such a quantitative standard).

[31] See, e.g., Brilmayer (1986) at 681–5; Davidson & Pargetter (1987) at 183–5; Friedman (1996) at 1819–20; and Stein (2005) at 120.

[32] Cohen, J. (1977). By "conventional probabilities" here, I refer to probabilities that are numbers conforming to the familiar Kolmogorov axioms, what Cohen refers to as "Pascalian" or "mathematical" probabilities. Cohen constructed a different kind of probability, which he called "Baconian" or "inductive," which follows a different logic and which Cohen thought cohered better with standards of proof in adjudication.

[33] Davidson & Pargetter (1987) at 183–5 and Stein (2005) at 47–8, 120. See also Cohen, N. (1985).

requirement that the trier of fact categorically believe the allegations of the burdened party. For such scholars, the variable indexed by phrases such as "preponderance of the evidence" and "beyond reasonable doubt" is simply the tenacity with which the trier of fact holds this categorical belief.[34]

None of these ideas can be ruled out simply on the grounds of the conventional understanding of particular words, such as the term *weight*. A standard legal articulation of the phrase *weight of evidence* is that it refers to the "persuasive effect" or the "persuasive force" of evidence.[35] The primary juridical function of this kind of articulation, however, is to differentiate between questions of admissibility of individual items of evidence and questions of the sufficiency of the evidence as a whole, that is, its adequacy when measured against the appropriate standard of proof. The exact relationship between weight and sufficiency often is not front and center in the lawyer's use of the term *weight*. Indeed, the idea of "persuasive force" admits of several glosses. Some might incorporate only discriminatory power, while some might include components of Keynesian weight or resiliency.[36] In order to resolve the debates, one must move beyond analysis of the conventional meanings of words and conventional expressions of legal doctrine. One must examine how these ideas work together to create a coherent whole. One must articulate a theory of factual adjudication.

The theory presented here is neither wholly descriptive nor wholly prescriptive. Rather, it is interpretive: I ask how the proof standards *ought* to be understood, which need not be the same thing as how they *are* understood by courts on a day-to-day basis, nor the same as how they *were* understood by those who announced them. As an interpretive theory, it need not match in all particulars the law's current workings, including the details of the psychological processes of decision makers and the intricacies of every rule, statutory or common law, that regulates the process. Of course, in working out such a theory, it is necessary to advert to the prevailing understanding of many ideas that condition and are affected by the burden of proof. Still, such a theory need only illuminate how the law works and how it can work better while remaining faithful to the basic assumptions and commitments that are implicit in the law.[37] This point is worth emphasizing because, as will be seen, I make some use of results coming out of formal decision theory. In some ways, my theory is an attempt to discern

---

[34] Ho (2008) at 121–43, 185–229.
[35] See Wigmore (1983) § 29.
[36] Schum (1994) at 200–69.
[37] See Dworkin (1986) at 45–86.

in what respects a "rational actor" hypothesis can shed light on prevailing practices and to suggest how they can be improved. In this, I am not committed to the existence of a fully quantitative theory, either as a description of prevailing practices or as a very precise or infallible normative guide.

My analysis proceeds as follows: in Chapter 2, I explore the idea of discriminatory power. I give considerable attention to the decision-theoretic interpretation of that idea and to two prominent competing theories that shed additional light on the nature of discriminatory power. I emphasize, however, that the principal theses of this book concern Keynesian weight and its relationship to discriminatory power. Getting the theory of discriminatory power precisely correct is not critical to my present enterprise. Nevertheless, it is important to have some working conceptions about how one might fill out the requirement of discriminatory power in order to set the stage for the crucial discussion of Keynesian weight. The decision-theoretic formulation is useful in this regard for several reasons. First, it provides an unusually clear articulation of the rationale of various standards of proof, in the context of which Keynesian weight can itself be clearly articulated. Second, it has received discernible endorsement by the United States Supreme Court in articulating the proof requirements mandated by the federal constitution. And third, no competing theory has been developed that is as useful and analytically powerful.

In the pivotal Chapter 3, I argue that there is *something* that the burden of proof should be understood to require besides an assessment of discriminatory power, in whatever plausible way discriminatory power is properly understood. That something is a practical optimization of Keynesian weight. In addressing this, for the most part the discussion will abstract from the details of how one goes about achieving such optimization. In particular, it will treat the adjudicative system as a corporate actor with undifferentiated roles. The most important conclusions are these:

1. The practical optimization of Keynesian weight is analytically distinct and (to a large extent) functionally separable from determinations regarding the degree of discriminatory power necessary to warrant a verdict;
2. Practical optimization of Keynesian weight has a payoff in terms of increasing the expected gains from decisions made under conditions of uncertainty; and
3. This practical optimization involves an "excusable preference" structure that ordinarily requires only what can reasonably be obtained as opposed to a "strict" requirement that, indifferent to the availability of

evidence, demands that Keynesian weight exceed some predetermined threshold.[38]

Each of these claims can be found by itself in diverse scholarship on decision making under uncertainty, though not without some opposition. Extant legal scholarship in particular has so far failed to internalize them fully or to integrate them into a theory of adjudication.

Chapter 4 turns to the practical side of the theory by differentiating among the roles of the various actors in the law's adjudicative systems. In contrast to the views commonly expressed by others who have recognized an important role for Keynesian weight, I argue that, generally speaking, effectuating (or monitoring the effectuation of) the adequacy of Keynesian weight is, and ought to be, a judicial function, not one to be performed by the fact-finder. (In discussing Anglo-American courts hereafter, when it is unnecessary to differentiate, the trier of fact is called the "fact-finder," whether that be a petit jury or a judge acting as trier of fact in a bench trial.) This exploration involves placing in perspective a wide variety of doctrinal tools now in use in Anglo-American courts. The use of these tools demonstrates pervasive judicial management of Keynesian weight. With this in clear view, fact-finder assessment of Keynesian weight will be understood as aberrational and potentially counterproductive. This, however, leaves open the question whether the judiciary adequately performs its function in monitoring cases for adequacy of Keynesian weight and whether, therefore, the fact-finder may need to perform a "backup" role in this regard.

Chapter 5 turns to the question of theories of the burden of proof that are built on the idea of tenacity of belief. While Keynesian weight is related to tenacity of belief, they are not the same thing. It is generally hoped, and it often happens, that decisions to increase Keynesian weight by demanding additional evidence will have the effect of increasing tenacity of belief or resilience of probability assessments. But increases in Keynesian weight

---

[38] The phrase "available evidence" appears in many discussions in the literature, but unfortunately, that phrase is ambiguous, and one must often attempt to determine from context what is meant by any particular author. It could refer to evidence that is in fact (properly) before the tribunal, admitted evidence that is thus "available" for the tribunal to use in drawing inferences, or it could refer to evidence that is not before the tribunal but might be brought before it and is thus "available" to be admitted for the tribunal in order to use it, or it might be used in a sense broad enough to include both these categories of evidence. Compare, e.g., Kaplow (2014) at 2, 6 (apparently using the phrase in the first sense) with Cohen, N. (1987) at 85 (more clearly using the phrase in the third sense). A focus on Keynesian weight necessitates discussion of the second and third senses of the phrase.

do not necessarily have this effect, nor are they undesirable just because they do not. The important implication is this: assuming that robust institutional mechanisms are in place to optimize Keynesian weight, there is no reason to have a separate requirement that the fact-finder consider the resilience of its probability assessments or the tenacity of its beliefs.

Chapter 6 summarizes the argument and concludes by illustrating the importance of the distinction between Keynesian weight and discriminatory power in assessing adjudicative systems that are not as effective qua fact-finding institutions as many modern municipal legal systems. Specifically, the distinction is offered as a lens through which to assess adjudication before international tribunals.

2

Discriminatory Power

Adjudication as Practical Reasoning

> *The conduct of our Lives, and the management of our great Concerns, will not bear delay: for those depend, for the most part, on the determination of our Judgments in points, wherein we are not capable of certain and demonstrative Knowledge, and wherein it is necessary for us to embrace the one side, or the other.*
>
> – John Locke (c. 1690)[1]

In this chapter, I explore what is involved in the idea of the "discriminatory power of the evidence" and what determines the margin by which that power must favor the claimant (assumed here to be the party bearing the burden of persuasion) in order to warrant a positive verdict. To do this, we consider the nature of a verdict itself and its relationship to the goals of adjudication (§ 2.1). This will lead naturally to the well-known decision-theoretic model specifying the degree of discriminatory power necessary for a verdict (§ 2.2). By briefly examining two competing theories of discriminatory power, I will show how certain contemporary debates about the viability of the decision-theoretic model are largely tangential to the issues addressed in subsequent chapters, though they place those issues in clearer context (§ 2.3). Theories of discriminatory power are also related to complex questions about how the inference process can be understood, modeled, or described (§ 2.4), and they must recognize the importance of background information, information that is not part of the evidence formally presented (§ 2.5). I explore these ideas and hope thereby to contribute to our understanding of discriminatory power. But I emphasize that this is not my primary purpose. Rather, these ideas simply serve as a backdrop for the critical discussion of Keynesian weight in the following chapters.

---

[1] Locke (1690) at 659.

2.1 Practical Reasoning in the Adjudicative Context

Verdicts seem declaratory in the sense that they declare certain facts to be true or false. But these declarations are not made in a vacuum; they are not idle speculations. The facts declared in adjudication very often, though not always, entail the attribution of the breach of serious social obligation, and almost always, serious consequences attach to them. So it would be more precise to say that verdicts declare that certain facts are to be *taken as true* for the serious purposes of such application. Such verdicts are essentially *performative* in that they license (or deny) the application of rules of law that change persons' legal relationships and, ultimately, may license (or deny) the application of the state's coercive powers.[2] In a world of imperfect information, verdicts involve risks of factual error and the harmful consequences that attend such errors. "False-positive" and "false-negative" verdicts impose social costs, whereas "true-positive" and "true-negative" verdicts entail social benefits.[3] At least one may take this to be true as long as one assumes the substantive law to be properly drawn. For purposes of designing adjudicative procedures, one generally ought to do so out of respect for the authority of legitimate lawmaking institutions.

As a result, adjudicative processes are exercises in the management of risk arising from unavoidable factual uncertainty and the necessity of judgment. In particular, unlike many scientific investigators, adjudicators do not have the luxury of declaring the matter unresolved pending further investigation. At least they cannot do so indefinitely, or even for very long.[4] This is strictly so as regards the fact-finder, especially a jury, which has no authority to delay a verdict beyond the time required for deliberation. Pursuant to the principle of promptness of adjudication, adjudicators must decide the case, one way or the other,[5] as long as the parties

---

[2] For an extended but somewhat diverging discussion of these and other aspects of the verdict, see Ho (2008) at 12–32.

[3] A "true-positive" verdict here means a verdict for the claimant (hence "positive") when, under the true facts (were they known), the claimant is entitled to the verdict (hence "true"). A "true-negative" verdict means a verdict against the claimant (hence "negative") when, in truth, the claimant is not entitled to a verdict (hence "true"). Similarly, a "false-positive" verdict means a verdict for the claimant when, in truth, the claimant is not entitled to the verdict, and a "false-negative" verdict means a verdict against the claimant when, in truth, the claimant is entitled to a verdict.

[4] See Hart & McNaughton (1958) at 45.

[5] The exposition in the text assumes the conventional "winner take all" approach to liability in which compromise verdicts, at least those based on doubts about the facts, are not allowed. See, e.g., Coons (1964) (assessing the usefulness of a rule that, in civil cases where

bring the case to trial within the time periods specified by law.[6] Moreover, the decision generally has permanent legal consequences pursuant to the principles of finality of adjudication.[7] As emphasized by Justice Blackmun, speaking for the Court in the well-known *Daubert* decision: "[T]here are important differences between the quest for truth in the courtroom and the quest for truth in the laboratory. Scientific conclusions are subject to perpetual revision. Law, on the other hand, must resolve disputes finally and quickly."[8] This point will recur throughout, so let me state it clearly: as far as the fact-finder is concerned, when a verdict is required, "not deciding" is *not* an option.[9]

Of course, it is not that legal decisions, once reached, can never be modified. Putting aside decisions (such as child-custody rulings) that may involve a court's retaining continuing jurisdiction to modify rulings based on changed circumstances, the law does have certain mechanisms for "relief" from otherwise final judgments. But two points must be emphasized. First, such relief is allowed only under very limited conditions, especially when the claim is that relief should be granted based on the discovery of new evidence that would suggest the initial judgment was in error.[10] And

---

the evidence equally favors either side, the amount in controversy be split equally between the parties) and Levmore (1990) (identifying special contexts in which "winner take all" may be suboptimal).

[6] Statutes of limitations apply in most contexts to require actions to be commenced within designated time periods after the litigated events. See, e.g., 28 U.S.C. § 1658 (four-year default limitation on commencement of civil actions arising under federal statute) and 18 U.S.C. § 3282 (five-year default limitation on commencement of noncapital criminal prosecutions arising under federal law). And further rules limit how long the case can be pending, once initiated, before it is brought to trial. See, e.g., Fed. R. Civ. P. 41(b) (providing for dismissal of civil actions, on motion of defendant, for want of prosecution); Fed. R. Crim. P. 48(b) (providing for dismissal of criminal prosecutions for unnecessary delay in bringing the accused to trial); and 18 U.S.C. §§ 3161–2 (the "Speedy Trial Act," detailing time limits for federal criminal prosecutions).

[7] See, e.g., Fed. R. Civ. P. 60(c)(1) (limiting to at most one year from judgment the time during which relief from judgment can be granted under Rule 60(b)(2) on the basis of newly discovered evidence in a federal civil case) and Fed. R. Crim. P. 33(b)(1) (limiting to three years from verdict the time during which a new trial may be granted on the basis of newly discovered evidence in a federal criminal case).

[8] Daubert v. Merrell Dow Pharm., Inc., 509 U.S. 579, 596–7 (1993).

[9] A "hung jury" is different: when the requisite number of jurors (unanimous or otherwise) is unable to agree on a verdict, a mistrial results, with the possibility of retrial. See Marder (2005) at 172. What is addressed in the text is a situation in which the requisite number of jurors agree, but what they agree on is that they are not yet able to determine the ultimate factual issue one way or the other.

[10] See, e.g., Johnson Waste Materials v. Marshall, 611 F.2d 593 (5th Cir. 1980) (describing the heavy burden borne by a party to a civil case initiating an equitable action for relief

second, pending such extraordinary relief, the judgment has full force and effect: people's lives are affected, often in very serious ways. As Alex Stein put it: "Adjudicative factfinding instantiates practical reasoning. This goal oriented reasoning aims at producing the best decision available, not at finding the truth for its own sake."[11]

Some commentators deny this. For example, in his elaborate 2008 monograph on the theory of Anglo-American evidence law, Hock Lai Ho emphasizes that the fact-finder is not encouraged or even permitted to make the best decision, all things considered, because fact-finders must take the substantive law as given to them. Instead, the fact-finders' special role is simply to declare the facts to which those substantive laws are applied (and, of course, in many contexts to do the application of the law as well), a declaration that is based on their justifiable beliefs.[12] From this conventional narrowing of juridical role, Ho concludes that a fact-finder's decision is not a matter of practical reasoning but rather one of theoretical reasoning, not one of "betting on the truth" by "acting on probabilities" but rather one of declaring justified beliefs.[13] He explains the distinction concisely as follows:

> [P]ractical reasoning is reasoning about what to do; theoretical reasoning is reasoning about what to believe. The reasoning a driver uses in deciding whether to take a safer route or a more scenic one is largely practical; she must choose between her interests and desires. The reasoning she uses in determining which of two routes is safer or more beautiful is ultimately theoretical; she is seeking the truth on the matter.[14]

For Ho, an additional aspect of the fact-finders' theoretical role is that they are to deliver verdicts based on categorical beliefs about the determinative facts of each case, which (in Ho's view) helps to resolve certain familiar paradoxes of proof. Using such categorical belief judgments, there are just three distinct options, corresponding to three doxastic positions: to declare the fact true if it is justifiably believed to be true, to declare the fact

---

of judgment, under Fed. R. Civ. P. 60(d)(1), on the basis of evidence discovered after a judgment is entered, when relief is not available under the one-year rule of Fed. R. Civ. P. 60(c)(1)) and Mankarious v. United States, 282 F.3d 940, 945 (7th Cir. 2002) (holding that motions under 28 U.S.C. § 2255 to vacate or set aside a criminal conviction based on newly discovered evidence are subject to the same standards and three-year limitation applicable to motions for new trial under Fed. R. Crim. P. 33(b)(1)).

[11] Stein (2005) at 34.
[12] Ho (2008) at 1–171.
[13] Id. at 131, 142, and 185–99.
[14] Id. at 190.

false if it is justifiably believed to be false, or else to suspend judgment on the matter.[15]

Ho's argument is interesting and elaborately developed. It rests on two ideas – theoretical reasoning and categorical beliefs – that are not necessarily tied together.[16] I will address at some length the role of categorical beliefs later (§ 5.3). (One can already see a serious problem, however: when a verdict is required, a fact-finder cannot suspend judgment.) For the moment, I focus on the claim that fact-finders are to engage in theoretical reasoning. There is an understandable appeal in the claim that fact-finders are expected to simply "find the facts" as opposed to, say, "do justice" or "do the best thing for all concerned" or even "decide who should win." Inevitably, however, Ho must and does acknowledge that pragmatic considerations affect the fact-finders' supposedly theoretical inquiry. A verdict must be given knowing that it will determine public action but without certainty regarding the truth or falsity of the parties' claims: "[T]he practical aspect infringes on the theoretical aspect by affecting the amount of justification needed for judging as true, and thus believing, a contested proposition of fact."[17] In fact, Ho accepts that the practical realities of what is at stake and the associated risks of potential error affect (what Ho calls) the "degree of caution" and the "distribution of caution" that fact-finders should use in deciding whether the claim is worthy of (categorical) belief.[18]

Given this concession, what rightly remains of Ho's argument that fact-finding is an exercise in theoretical reasoning is the correct but largely uncontroversial conclusion that, in the usual case (i.e., the possibility of legitimate "jury nullification" aside), a fact-finder ought not to declare a

---

[15] Id. at 124. To be precise about the sense of "justifiable belief" here, Ho develops at length the thesis that

> [t]he fact-finder must find that *p* only if (i) one would be justified in believing *sufficiently strongly* that *p* *if one were to take into account only the admitted evidence, ignore any inadmissible evidence to which one might have been exposed, and avoid reliance on any line of evidential reasoning that the law might forbid in the case at hand*; and (ii) if one found that *p*, one would find that p at least in part because one would be justified in believing that *p* under (i).

Id. at 93.

[16] This is illustrated by various probabilistic accounts of scientific reasoning and inference that employ partial beliefs. See, e.g., Horwich (1982) and Howson & Urbach (1993).

[17] Ho (2008) at 197.

[18] Id. at 201–28. Ho's distinction between degree of caution and distribution of caution roughly parallels the distinction between Keynesian weight and discriminatory power. See infra § 5.3.

litigated fact to be true (or taken to be true or adequately proved) based simply on her own assessment that such a declaration and its anticipated consequences will lead to the better (or more just) overall state of affairs in the world. Rather, the declaration should be based on the fact-finder's epistemic assessment, the conditions of which are regulated by institutional arrangements and the significance of which is determined by the allocation of risks of error prescribed by the legally established standard of proof.[19] True, the fact-finder's special role within that system can be separately characterized as involving something that is closer to theoretical reasoning than many judgments in everyday affairs. (Importantly, one task that would be theoretical in Ho's sense is simply the assessment of the probability that the claim is true.) So one could, without going too far afield, describe the fact-finding component of adjudication either as theoretical reasoning subject to considerable institutionalized pragmatic encroachment or, alternatively, as participation in practical reasoning that involves specialized institutional roles. One factor tips the balance toward the latter characterization: the critical reality that the point of the entire process is to act on the parties by declaring their rights and remedies and, if necessary, enforcing them. As a whole, this is surely practical reasoning in the course of decision making. And it requires that fact-finders in some way incorporate – or be made to reflect – an appropriate balancing of the risks of false-positive and false-negative verdicts, a decidedly practical aspect of reasoning.

Specifying the margin of discriminatory power needed for a verdict is, of course, how this is done. The degree to which this comparative assessment must favor the party bearing the burden of proof, in order to warrant a positive verdict, is easily understood as implementing the weighting of the risks of false-positive and false-negative verdicts. The higher the margin required for the claimant to succeed, the greater relative emphasis is placed on avoiding false-positive verdicts; the lower the margin required for the claimant to succeed, the greater relative emphasis is placed on avoiding false-negative verdicts. Indeed, a line of United States Supreme Court decisions, regarding constitutional requirements on the standard of proof, has emphasized this point: the Court has explicitly considered the relative costs involved in deciding what standard of proof is constitutionally required.

---

[19] Cf. Picinali (2013) (arguing that adjudicative fact-finding is a theoretical enterprise, but one that is structured by the standard of proof that is itself generated by an exercise of practical reason).

The seminal case is *In re Winship*,[20] which held that proof beyond reasonable doubt is constitutionally required in criminal cases for the proof of the prosecution's affirmative case and extended that rule to nominally civil adjudications of juvenile delinquency. In his important concurring opinion, Justice Harlan stated that "the choice of the standard for a particular variety of adjudication does, I think, reflect a very fundamental assessment of the comparative social costs of erroneous factual determinations" and that "the choice of the standard to be applied in a particular kind of litigation should, in a rational world, reflect an assessment of the comparative social disutility of each."[21] Later cases applying this framework include *Addington v. Texas*,[22] which held that proof by the intermediate standard of clear and convincing evidence is constitutionally required to establish grounds for noncriminal involuntary commitment; *Santosky v. Kramer*,[23] which held that proof by clear and convincing evidence is constitutionally required for permanent termination of parental rights; and *Rivera v. Minnich*,[24] which held that proof by clear and convincing evidence is *not* constitutionally required for the establishment of paternity in an action for child support. In each of these cases – despite some infelicities of expression and contestable judgments – the Court assayed the potential costs to the parties, and to society more generally, that are thought to be associated with erroneous decisions in either direction and assessed comparatively the significance of those costs in determining what standard of proof is constitutionally required.

In the following sections of this chapter, I develop competing conceptualizations of discriminatory power. The emphasis throughout is on the fact that discriminatory power, however it is worked out in detail, is essentially comparative in nature – a comparison between the competing claims based on the available evidence. I focus on three distinctly different theories that attempt to make sense of the comparative assessments that the law prescribes.

2.2 The Decision-Theoretic Formulation

The traditional decision-theoretic formulation, in a single-cause-of-action case between two parties, with no affirmative defenses, is that minimizing

[20] 397 U.S. 358 (1970).
[21] 397 U.S. 358, 370–1 (1970) (Harlan, J., concurring).
[22] 441 U.S. 418 (1979).
[23] 455 U.S. 745 (1982).
[24] 483 U.S. 574 (1987).

the expected error costs requires a decision for the claimant if and only if the expected loss from such a decision is less than the expected loss from the alternative decision (a decision for the opponent). To be clear about the formal result, we start with some definitions:

> C denotes the proposition that the ultimate facts are so as to instantiate the substantive elements of the alleged cause of action (hereafter, simply the "claim"), whereas not-C denotes the proposition that the ultimate facts are not so as to instantiate that claim.
> E denotes the totality of the formally admitted evidence before the court.[25]
> P(C|E) denotes the probability that the claim C is true given E.
> $D_{(+)}$ denotes the magnitude of the utility loss attributable to a false-positive decision, that is, an erroneous decision for the claimant.
> $D_{(-)}$ denotes the magnitude of the utility loss attributable to a false-negative decision, that is, an erroneous decision against the claimant.

The magnitude of the *expected loss* from a decision for the claimant is just the magnitude of the loss associated with a false-positive decision weighted by the probability that the claim is false, or $P(\text{not-}C|E) \times D_{(+)}$. Similarly, the magnitude of the expected loss from a decision against the claimant is just $P(C|E) \times D_{(-)}$. Thus the standard result prescribes a decision for the claimant just when

$$P(\text{not-}C|E) \times D_{(+)} < P(C|E) \times D_{(-)}$$

Doing a little algebra, we can restate this as prescribing a verdict for the claimant if and only if

$$O(C|E) > D_{(+)}/D_{(-)} \qquad (2.1)$$

where $O(C|E)$ is the odds that the facts are so as to instantiate the substantive elements of the claim C given the evidence E; that is, by definition,

$$O(C|E) =_{\text{def}} P(C|E)/P(\text{not-}C|E)$$

---

[25] For the most part, E will consist of testimonies, and one must differentiate between the giving of testimony and the factual proposition asserted by the testimony. See Schum (1994) at 16–19. When, therefore, a conditional probability posits that E is "given," this means only that the court is given certain testimonies, that is, that such testimonies occur in court; it does *not* mean, as to any of these testimonies, that the facts asserted therein are to be taken as true, although it may be useful to assume this to be so for the purpose of some particular analysis.

As one would expect, criterion (2.1) tells us that the margin of the odds required for a verdict in favor of the claimant is directly proportional to the magnitude of the utility loss of a false-positive verdict (i.e., the higher that magnitude, the higher is the required margin of discriminatory power) and inversely proportional to the magnitude of the utility loss of a false-negative verdict (i.e., the higher that magnitude, the lower is the required margin of discriminatory power). The translation from odds to probability is probability = odds/(odds + 1). Criterion (2.1) therefore can be stated as prescribing a verdict for the claimant if and only if

$$P(C|E) > 1 \Big/ \Big[1 + \big(D_{(-)} / D_{(+)} \big) \Big] \tag{2.1'}$$

This is the version appearing in John Kaplan's classic article.[26]

Although I will work with both the odds form and the probability form of the criterion as the context requires, it is worth noting right away the fact that criterion (2.1) is, in an obvious way, "simpler" than criterion (2.1'). This is of no small importance, to the extent that these criteria are to be used by practical policy makers and decision makers. It does not require the citation of psychological research to recognize that assessment in terms of odds is a more natural framework for decision makers than assessment in terms of probabilities: it is more plausible to think of a fact-finder saying that the odds are 2:1 in favor of the plaintiff's case than saying that the probability of the plaintiff's claim is 0.67.[27] The difference arises not because 0.67 involves two figures after the decimal but because it is easier for people to think in comparative terms (how much one thing is greater than another) than in terms of absolute magnitudes (how great one thing is on some scale). Beyond this, the quantity that is to be compared with either of these epistemic measures, that is, the quantity on the right side of each inequality, is also significantly simpler algebraically in criterion (2.1) than in criterion (2.1'). If a false-positive result is three times worse than a false-negative result, it is simple enough to think in terms of whether the odds on the claim are larger than 3:1.

Unfortunately, both right-hand sides of these criteria are a bit *too* simple. As a number of scholars have noted, each of the preceding versions of the decision-theoretic result is incomplete in that it fails to take into

---

[26] See Kaplan, J. (1968), cited approvingly by Justice Harlan in his concurrence in *Winship*. 397 U.S. at 369–72.
[27] For the skeptic, here is the requisite citation: Miller (1956) at 90.

account the positive changes in utility associated with accurate decisions.[28] To improve the formulation, we must add two definitions.

$U_{(+)}$ denotes the magnitude of the utility gain attributable to a true-positive decision, that is, an accurate decision for the claimant.

$U_{(-)}$ denotes the magnitude of the utility gain attributable to a true-negative decision, that is, an accurate decision against the claimant.

With these additions, and a fresh algebra exercise, the criterion becomes: decide for the claimant if and only if

$$O(C|E) > \left(U_{(-)} + D_{(+)}\right) / \left(U_{(+)} + D_{(-)}\right) =_{\text{def}} O^* \qquad (2.2)$$

In what follows, reference sometimes will be made instead to a critical probability P^* when the context makes this appropriate. Thus the decision criterion in probability terms is: decide for the claimant just when

$$P(C|E) > P^* =_{\text{def}} O^* / (O^* + 1) \qquad (2.2')$$
$$= \left(U_{(-)} + D_{(+)}\right) / \left[\left(U_{(-)} + D_{(+)}\right) + \left(U_{(+)} + D_{(-)}\right)\right]$$

The decision-theoretic result thus presents the possibility of identifying the discriminatory power of the evidence with the odds $O(C|E)$ or (if one prefers to think in terms of probabilities) the probability $P(C|E)$. Stated either way, when the expected utilities of the two decisions are equal or at least indistinguishable – that is, when $O(C|E) = O^*$ and $P(C|E) = P^*$ – a default rule favors the defendant, and this is so for whatever reasons support the allocation of the burden of persuasion to the claimant (see Chapter 1).

In the derivation presented earlier, unlike many derivations that appear in the literature, the utility gains and losses are all relative to the

---

[28] See, e.g., Tribe (1971) at 1378–81, 1383 n. 168; Friedman (1997a) at 277–8; Nance (1999) at 290–2; Redmayne (1999) at 169–70; and Lillquist (2002) at 107–8. Occasionally, courts do make reference to what is identifiably the potential gains from an accurate determination. For example, in one of the leading due process decisions, the issue was whether a state may terminate the parental relationship on a showing of permanent neglect, established by a "fair preponderance of the evidence." Santosky v. Kramer, 455 U.S. 745 (1982). In the course of arguing that this standard of proof was constitutionally adequate, the four dissenting justices emphasized the difference between the benefits associated with a true-positive result – freeing the child not only from neglectful parents but also from the unstable world of foster care – and the benefits associated with a true-negative result – leaving the child in the limbo of foster care with only the potential to be returned to natural parents already found to have been abusive, if not permanently neglectful. See id. at 785–91 (Rehnquist, J., dissenting).

```
                    Utility
                       ↑
                       |   •
                       |
                       |  U₍₊₎
                       |         U₍₋₎
Ex ante      ----------|----|----|----------
decision               |    |    |
                       |   D₍₋₎  |
                       |        D₍₊₎
                       |    •
                       |         •
```

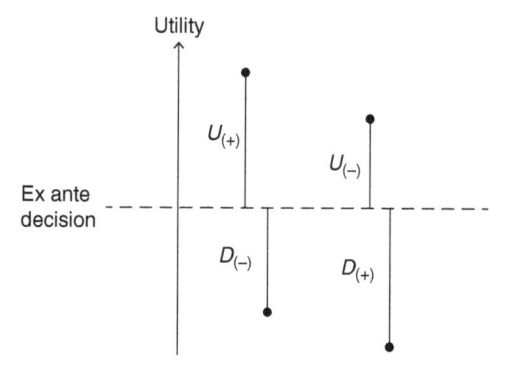

Figure 1. The utilities of decision.

status quo ante decision. Inspecting the denominator of the fraction in criterion (2.2), it is easy to see that $(U_{(+)} + D_{(-)})$ is just the difference in resulting social utility between the end-result situation in which a true claim is correctly accepted by the law and the end-result situation in which such a true claim is erroneously rejected (see Figure 1). Similarly, the numerator $(U_{(-)} + D_{(+)})$ is the difference in social utility between the end-result situation in which a false claim is correctly rejected and the end-result situation in which such a false claim is erroneously accepted. The decision criterion is often expressed in terms of these differences,[29] and in what follows, I will (for simplicity) refer to the ratios in criteria (2.1) and (2.1′), as context requires, as ratios of "utility differences" or simply "utility ratios."[30]

This kind of decision-theoretic model, based on the idea of maximizing expected utility, has been around for a long time and has been discussed,

---

[29] See, e.g., Tribe (1971) at 1383 n. 168; DeKay (1996) at 110–11; and Lillquist (2002) at 107–8. Unlike such previous accounts, I have used *magnitudes* of gain and loss because I have assumed that the net effect on utility of either a true-positive a true-negative verdict is positive, while the net effect of a false-positive or false-negative verdict is negative. These assumptions respect the legislative judgment that a positive judgment is desirable if the claim is true and a negative judgment is desirable if the claim is false.

[30] Criteria (2.1) and (2.2) are equivalent only if one makes certain dubious assumptions. However, formulations such as Kaplan's that read like criterion (2.1) might have been intended, contrary to appearances, to refer to disutilities of errors as differences relative to the correct verdict on the *same* assumption about the true state of the facts. That is, what Kaplan might have meant by the disutility of a false positive is the magnitude of the difference in utility between a true negative and a false positive, the difference in utility between correctly denying the claim and incorrectly accepting the claim. Thus construed, the two criteria – (2.1) and (2.2) – are the same, but then one must be mindful that the assumed benchmark for assessing the disutility of a false positive is not necessarily the same as the assumed benchmark for assessing the disutility of a false negative.

criticized, and defended more generally, that is, in contexts much broader than legal adjudication.[31] Its employment as a tool for understanding standards of proof for adjudication has been equally controversial.[32] It makes a difference, of course, whether one is using the model as a pure description of our institutional arrangements and processes (or perhaps as an approximating substitute for such a detailed description), as a prescriptive analysis, or a combination of the two. As indicated in Chapter 1, the present enterprise is interpretive in the sense that it seeks a model that can be used to understand what the law is at least *trying* to do with its rules regarding the burden of proof and to rationalize those purposive efforts. Again, the interpretive enterprise requires some degree of abstraction from institutional details, though it must remain grounded in a generally accurate description of the practices being interpreted.

Some of the arguments that can be raised against the use of this model in the adjudicative context concern the problem of giving meaningful content to the terms of the decision criterion, the probabilities and utilities in criterion (2.2), and attention will be given to these issues in the following subsections.[33] But other objections to the model proceed from the premise that adjudication ought not to handle the risk of error by reference to changes in utilities, however the utility functions are worked out in detail, but rather should attempt to do other things. Thus it has been argued that the law's policy should attempt to achieve a given ratio of false-positive to false-negative verdicts. For example, in civil cases, the usual argument is that errors should be made as often for plaintiffs as for defendants. And for criminal cases, the argument is that the law should strive for a certain ratio of erroneous acquittals to erroneous convictions. To summarize a complex argument made elsewhere, the problems with such suggestions are two: (1) they require some coherent normative basis (which is not easily identifiable) for diverging from the decision criterion

---

[31] See, e.g., Schoemaker (1982) and Kaplan, M. (1996).
[32] See, e.g., Allen (1997); Kaye (1999); Allen (2000); and Kaye (2000).
[33] Note that the decision-theoretic solution prescribes how to minimize *expected* error costs or, more generally, how to maximize *expected* utility. Whether this will minimize *actual* error costs (or maximize *actual* utility), even in the long run of cases, depends on many factors that are unknown at the point when the decision is made; if they were known, they would be incorporated into the decision. Thus it is pointless to say that if (unbeknownst to the decision maker) certain facts (e.g., base rates of legitimate claims) turn out to have a specific configuration, then decision according to criterion (2.2) will fail to minimize actual error costs. Obviously, what one can learn about what happens in the operation of the litigation system and, more broadly, in society as a consequence of adjudication can and should have an impact on one's probabilities or the ratio of utility differences that is deemed necessary to warrant a verdict. See Kaye (1999).

that will maximize expected utility, and (2) they require access to information about the base rates of liable (or guilty) individuals who go to trial and about the accuracy of the trial system – information that is not now, or likely to become, available.[34]

Another common objection to the use of the decision-theoretic model is that the standard of proof in adjudication is multidimensional, with too many factors that must be considered and that cannot be reduced to a simple comparison of posterior odds with some threshold value. A large part of this concern derives from confusions regarding the role of Keynesian weight, confusions that I will try to resolve in Chapter 3. Otherwise, this concern grows out of varying understandings of the ideas of social utility and probability that are employed. A sympathetic yet critical understanding of the decision-theoretic criterion requires us to interpret exactly what is on each side of the inequality stated in criterion (2.2). To apply the model, we take the fact-finder's assessed odds on the claim $O(C|E)$ as a measure of the discriminatory power of the evidence, which measure the fact-finder compares to the critical value, represented by O^*. Of course, I refer here to the fact-finder's assessed odds only as a convenience. In jury trials, I do not mean to suggest that jurors necessarily agree on specific odds in the case. They might, for example, each make their own assessments, and those assessments might all be different. As long as the requisite number of jurors believe that $O(C|E) > O^*$, a verdict for the claimant would be appropriate. But this simple statement requires both elaboration and qualification.

Were the fact-finder engaged in pure practical reasoning, one might expect the value of O^* – that is, the ratio of utility differences – to be that which the fact-finder supplies based on its own values. This, indeed, might seem to be the effect of the traditional, and still largely prevailing, Continental European refusal to specify a standard of proof other than to say that the fact-finder must be convinced.[35] In common-law adjudication, as already noted, the fact-finder's institutional role in practical reasoning is more constrained. In particular, the specification of the relative values of the utilities in criterion (2.2), and thus O^*, is understood as a policy issue

---

[34] See DeKay (1996). The importance of these issues may well be exaggerated. Under some circumstances (e.g., if (a) changes in social utility are an approximately linear function of the number of erroneous verdicts or (b) the diagnostic power of trials – the ability of trials to produce evidence that separates the guilty from the innocent – is high), a policy of achieving a certain ratio of errors is equivalent to a policy of maximizing social utility with the same ratio for O^*. Id. at 107, 117–26.

[35] There is, of course, variation among Continental European countries regarding the required standard of proof, but the description in the text is reasonably accurate. See, e.g., Taruffo (2003) at 666–9 and Brinkmann (2004) at 878–81.

that, accordingly, is determined by lawmaking authority, at least to a large extent. Doing so serves an important principle of procedural equality by helping to ensure that equivalently situated parties are subject to the same standard of proof.[36] Pragmatic considerations (i.e., consideration of the utility differences) are thus incorporated into the fact-finder's verdict by way of the required odds O^*. The fact-finder *accepts* (or not) the claim C and *declares* the claim C to be true (or not) based on its determination of whether criterion (2.2) is satisfied.[37] This does not necessarily mean that the fact-finder, in failing to act entirely on its own ratio of utility differences, acts irrationally. Rationality is a broader concept than this presupposes. The fact-finder rationally pursues the goal of doing justice according to law by respecting the public policies embedded in O^*.[38]

This difference between the civil-law and common-law systems has become a matter of tension in international adjudication. Courts such as the International Court of Justice, staffed by judges purposefully selected to reflect both legal traditions, are experiencing a struggle between those who, following the common-law philosophy, believe that standards of proof must be objectively stated and those who, adhering to the civil-law philosophy, believe that no such standards need be publicly stated, that the standard should be internal to the judge and flexible, depending on the particulars of the case.[39] On this particular debate, the common law would seem to have the better argument. At stake is something broader and more fundamental than predictability or certainty for parties to litigation. It is the rule of law itself, because no substantive rule of law or allocation of the burden of persuasion with respect thereto has much serious meaning if the standard that determines the adequacy of proof is wholly within the discretion of the fact-finder.[40]

---

[36] See DeKay (1996) at 114–15.
[37] Cf. Cohen, J. (1992) at 108–25.
[38] See Posner (1998) at 1551 (explaining "rationality" as "choosing the best means to the chooser's ends").
[39] See Riddell & Plant (2009) at 123–37.
[40] See id. at 136. Indeed, predictability may not be such a serious issue. Defenders of the civil-law system will point out that ad hoc subjectivity is controlled by the various institutions regulating the judiciary, including the required background and training of judges as well as the rights to de novo appeal on questions of fact. Such vectors may account for a degree of convergence in the applications of European standards in noncriminal cases. Compare Clermont & Sherwin (2002) (arguing that its convergence on a standard that is roughly the equivalent of the "beyond reasonable doubt" standard for common-law criminal cases raises serious questions about the legitimacy of civil-law adjudication because it imposes a standard that is too high) with Taruffo (2003) at 673 (arguing that civil-law courts converge on a standard not unlike Anglo-American standards because "the court cannot but choose the 'relatively more probable' version of the facts") and Brinkmann

To illustrate, suppose that the nominal substantive legal regime is that the burden of persuasion in a negligence case is on the plaintiff; ostensibly, the plaintiff bears the risk of nonpersuasion on the issue of defendant's negligence. This allocation will be essentially meaningless, however, if the fact-finder is at liberty to decide that the critical probability for proof of negligence is just 0.01 because in such a case, for all practical purposes, the defendant will have to eliminate the possibility of negligence to avoid liability. Similarly, if one were to suppose a nominal regime that specifies that contributory negligence is a complete defense, which must be proved by the defendant, if the fact-finder is free to select 0.01 as the critical probability that will suffice for a finding that the plaintiff was negligent, then the allocation of the burden of proving plaintiff's contributory negligence will be practically meaningless.[41] By such ad hoc selections of the standard, the fact-finder can effectively change a regime of negligence liability with an affirmative defense of contributory negligence into any of the following: (1) a regime of strict liability, (2) a regime of strict liability with an affirmative defense of contributory negligence, or even (3) a regime of strict nonliability for negligence in tort. In the end, the goals of the rule of law that entail the public announcement of the rules of substantive law and implicate the allocations of the burdens of proof with respect thereto require as well publicly stated standards of proof. This is not to suggest that private parties commonly rely on standards of proof in conducting their affairs outside the courtroom (see § 2.3.1), though at the illustrated extremes they might. It is only to say that the expectations of the community as a whole, arising from the articulation of substantive norms, ought not be so susceptible to being undermined by ad hoc, idiosyncratic imputations of standards of proof.[42]

(2004) at 882–7 (arguing that such convergence results in a floating standard that is not unlike that used by Anglo-American courts).

[41] Somewhat similar arrangements may be wise and are sometimes encountered. For example, some jurisdictions require defendants in criminal cases merely to raise particular defenses, such as self-defense, by presenting some evidence in support thereof, after which the burden of persuasion on that issue is placed on the prosecution. See 1 LaFave (2003) § 1.8. But such arrangements are still publicly announced rules, not simply the result of ad hoc fact-finder discretion.

[42] See Clermont (2013) at 259 (referring to the civil law's "lawlessness of applying an ad hoc standard of proof"). Indeed, both the allocation of the burden of persuasion and the required standard of proof are generally regarded in Anglo-American law as part of the substantive law itself and not merely adjectival or procedural attendments. See, e.g., Park et al. (2011) at 84, 86. Of course, the substance/procedure dichotomy is notoriously context dependent, but so outcome determinative is the burden of persuasion that it is treated as substantive for purposes of "vertical" choice of law under the *Erie* doctrine: federal courts using federal procedures

But why, then, in jury trials does not the jury simply state its odds as its finding, allowing the judge to apply the law on the burden of persuasion using a publicly announced standard of proof? Several reasons for the law's preference seem to be involved. Most important, jurors may more readily be able to agree that criterion (2.2) is satisfied (or not) than to agree on a specific value to report as the odds on the claim. Also, the law usually allows for some flexibility, some tailoring by the jury, indeed by individual jurors, of the value of O^*, notwithstanding the concern articulated earlier. Further, there is the desire – certainly among the judiciary – that jurors take responsibility for the verdict, which may encourage jurors to perform their task seriously.[43] Yet other reasons for the practice can be imagined. For example, there may be an official desire, however admirable, to avoid publicly acknowledging the (inevitably) probabilistic nature of the decision.[44]

However the practice is explained, it does bring in train a number of difficult practical problems. Specifically, there is the difficulty of how to communicate to fact-finders appropriately the publicly established value (or perhaps range of permissible values) for O^*. It has been frequently observed that the standards, as usually expressed in jury instructions, sometimes focus on the quantity or quality of the evidence (as in proof by "a preponderance of the evidence" or proof by "clear and convincing evidence") and sometimes focus on the required mental state of the fact-finder (as in proof "beyond reasonable doubt"). The former have been criticized as not giving meaningful guidance about the needed degree of belief,[45] whereas the latter have been criticized (rather more recently) as not giving meaningful guidance about how to go about assessing the evidence.[46] These are important debates, and there is something to be said for both sides of the issue. The best instructions will speak to both questions without being

---

to adjudicate substantive claims that are based on state law must use the state's rules regarding the burden of persuasion. See Cities Service Oil Co. v. Dunlap, 308 U.S. 208 (1939) and Raynor v. Merrell Pharms. Inc., 104 F.3d 1371, 1376 (D.C. Cir. 1997). The treatment of the issue in "horizontal" choice-of-law contexts has been more clouded in part because many Anglo-American judges have confused the substance/procedure distinction with the right/remedy distinction. See Risinger (1982). But the trend here as well is to recognize the "substantive" risk-allocating character of the burden of persuasion. See Felix & Whitten (2011) at 226–8. To the extent that burdens of proof are given content in civil-law jurisdictions, this trend is transnational. See Garnett (2012) at 198–201.

[43] The history of proof standards in criminal cases involves considerable effort by the judiciary to shift as much responsibility to juries as possible. See Whitman (2008) at 125–57.
[44] See Nesson (1985).
[45] See, e.g., Morgan (1933) at 63–7 and McBaine (1944).
[46] See, e.g., Cohen, J. (1986) at 646, 648 and Laudan (2006) at 32–54.

inconsistent and without unduly constraining fact-finders' epistemic freedom to evaluate the evidence.[47]

The following subsections consider the components of the decision-theoretic model – utilities and probabilities – in more detail. While this material is useful to fill out an understanding of how to apply the model, readers who are already comfortable with the model may want to skip to § 2.3. This can be done without too much loss of continuity.

2.2.1 The Utility Ratio and the Standard of Proof

Given that the determination of O^* is primarily, if not exclusively, a legislative function, even when arising out of common-law rule making, how ought policy makers think about the matter? The issues here are puzzling and controversial. I do not pretend to be able to give definitive answers that would specify critical odds for every class of case. What I propose to do, however, is to suggest a variety of considerations – both consequentialist and deontological – that ought to be taken into account in that judgment of political morality.[48] For ease of reference, recall that

$$O^* = \left(U_{(-)} + D_{(+)}\right) \big/ \left(U_{(+)} + D_{(-)}\right)$$

$$= \frac{\left(\text{true-negative gain} + \text{false-positive loss}\right)}{\left(\text{true-positive gain} + \text{false-negative loss}\right)}$$

---

[47] A decent effort for the usual standard in civil cases is the following:

"Establish by a preponderance of the evidence" means evidence, which as a whole, shows that the fact sought to be proved is more probable than not. In other words, a preponderance of the evidence means such evidence as, when considered and compared with the evidence opposed to it, has more convincing force, and produces in your mind's belief that what is sought to be proved is more likely true than not true.

3 O'Malley et al. (2006) § 104.01. Notice that by the explicit adoption of a "more probable than not" meaning for "preponderance of the evidence," the court ostensibly ties the fact-finder to a specific P^* of 0.5. While this seems to limit the fact-finder's discretion to make retail adjustments, it could be thought necessary to anchor such adjustments to something at least close to 1:1 odds. At the same time, the reference to "convincing force" of the evidence reminds the jury that odds that exceed 1:1 only because of bias or prejudice will not suffice. The considerations that necessarily go into crafting useful instructions are many and complex but of little importance to the theoretical issues of primary importance here. See, e.g., Stoffelmayr & Diamond (2000) (developing criteria and suggesting appropriate language to meet these criteria) and Weinstein & Dewsbury (2006) (favoring a combined quantitative and qualitative description of the burden in criminal cases).

[48] One of the more difficult issues is whether, and to what extent, social utility variables can meaningfully incorporate nonconsequentialist values and concerns. See, e.g., Kaplow &

Also recall that the numerator can be associated with a claim that is in fact false: it is just the difference in end-state utility between a correct negative verdict on such a claim and an incorrect positive verdict. Similarly, the denominator can be associated with a claim that is in fact true: it is just the difference in end-state utility between a correct positive verdict on such a claim and an incorrect negative verdict.

For civil cases, authorities generally opine that the disutility of a false-positive verdict (for the plaintiff) is not significantly different from the disutility of a false-negative verdict (for the defendant).[49] Presumably, the same will generally be said of the gains associated with true-positive and true-negative verdicts. This symmetry yields the critical odds O^* of 1:1, which correspond to a P^* of 0.5. The plaintiff's claim must be more probable than not in order to warrant an affirmative verdict. This result reproduces the standard endorsed for most civil cases, at least as it is understood in many jurisdictions. On closer consideration, though, this result is too simplistic. The reasons relate to the fact that, in some cases, indeed some classes of cases, the numerator of O^* may well not be equal to the denominator.

The symmetry claim is most plausible in "no fault" disputes, such as when the dispute is one over the ownership of property where the facts that determine ownership (such as whether one person survived another) do not entail any wrongdoing by either party to the litigation. In such cases, there is no reason to think that one type of error is worse than the other, as there is no reason to think one type of correct verdict is better than the other. Similarly, were a dispute to arise between two sets of parents as to which of two children born the same day in the same hospital belongs to which couple and should be delivered thereto, what standard of proof would be appropriate other than the "more likely than not" rule?[50] These conclusions, to be clear, are heavily laden with judgments of political morality. They assume that civil parties are entitled to equal consideration

---

Shavell (2002) (arguing that a robust notion of social welfare can account for justice concerns). I make no attempt to resolve this issue but present in the text all manner of considerations affecting and constraining social utilities.

[49] See, e.g., In re Winship, 397 U.S. 358, 371 (1970) (Harlan, J., concurring); Ball (1961) at 816–17; and Kaplan, J. (1968) at 1072 (stating qualifications as well).

[50] See Bolding (1960) at 21 (contrasting such a case with a case in which the parentage controversy arose only after the children had lived with their supposed parents for several years, at which point the potential disruption of family bonding becomes a serious consideration). Of course, the availability of modern DNA tests would no longer make it likely that $P(C|E)$ would be anywhere close to 0.5 in either contemplated case, but this does not change the appropriate standard of proof. It would, however, affect the quite different question of whether either case should be decided in the absence of the results of appropriate DNA tests. This is just where Keynesian weight comes in, as will be discussed in Chapter 3.

regardless of their surrounding circumstances, such as party wealth, social status, and power, considerations that might well matter in an "all things considered" assessment of the social utility of potential outcomes. Jurors are generally instructed to ignore such matters,[51] and we may take that as a norm of political morality controlling the setting of O^*.

This "even odds" idea is invoked by a different constraint, applicable as well to claims based on the assertion of a breach of duty. It arises from principles governing the rule of law itself, in particular, the principle that requires a reasonable degree of congruence between the law as announced and the actions of courts and other officials.[52] When the law's commitment to those it governs is that a legal sanction will not be imposed unless certain events have occurred, this carries an important message. At an epistemic level, this will be rightly understood by the citizenry as a commitment that there must (at least) be *good reason to believe* that those events occurred before the sanction is imposed. This imports a constraint: for evidence E to provide good reason to believe the claim C, it must be the case that, in light of E, C is more likely true than false, which is to say that P^* cannot be less than 0.5.[53] None of this means that the utility ratio in criterion (2.2′) is irrelevant. But it does mean that some limits are placed on the permissible values of P^*. In fact, one does not encounter standards of proof for final verdicts (as opposed to "probable cause" and other intermediate determinations) that involve a P^* that is demonstrably less than 0.5.

Relatedly, when the claim involves the proposition that the defendant has committed the breach of a serious social obligation (i.e., when it is *not* a "no-fault" determination), it would be unjust to impose the legal stigma, and any associated sanction, for the violation of such an obligation if the fact-finder cannot justifiably believe that the claim of such a breach is more likely than not true regardless of what values might be attributed otherwise to the utilities and disutilities of criterion (2.2).[54] This limitation

---

[51] See, e.g., 3 O'Malley et al. (2006) §§ 103.11, 103.12. There is empirical evidence to support the idea that it is what jurors are inclined to do anyway. See Mitchell & Tetlock (2006).

[52] Fuller (1968) at 38–9, 81–91.

[53] This is a necessary, not a sufficient condition. See Achinstein (2001) at 115–16 (arguing that this necessary condition follows from two defensible assumptions: (1) that for E to be good reason to believe C, it must be the case that $P(C|E) > k$, for some number k greater than or equal to zero, and (2) that for any E and any C, if E is a good reason to believe C, then E cannot be a good reason to believe not-C). Achinstein himself defends a "threshold" concept of belief, which is categorical but premised on probabilities, one that is not inconsistent with thinking in terms of degrees of belief. Id. at 118–20.

[54] Cf. Weinrib (2011) at 210 (noting that Kant described the plaintiff's burden of proof "as an aspect of the defendant's innate right to be considered beyond reproach in the absence of an act that wrongs another").

is associated with the presumption, which all citizens share, that they do not violate such serious social obligations, what I have called the "principle of civility."[55] Moreover, when the civil case involves such an alleged breach of serious social duty, there are reasons to believe that the disutility of a false-negative verdict is not as large as the disutility of a false-positive verdict: the latter entails the erroneous imputation of wrongdoing, whereas the former (in most cases) does not: a negative verdict may indicate (and may be understood to indicate) the occurrence of an accidental harm that would impute wrongdoing to neither party. A proper reluctance to impute wrongdoing to someone helps to explain a variety of observations, including (1) the fact that a higher standard, that of "clear and convincing evidence," is often used when the allegations involve serious immorality (such as fraud) and (2) the fact that people (especially laypersons) often quantify the more usual "preponderance of the evidence" test as a probability significantly higher than 0.5.[56] A similar point applies to civil cases where the claim, if true, would impute incompetency or insanity to a person, such as an involuntary commitment proceeding,[57] or would cause serious disruption of family relations.[58]

Complementary considerations that may drive up the de facto odds required by a fact-finder in civil cases arise from findings in behavioral economics. Because decision makers tend to display "omission bias," by which they are more willing to accept a risk as the result of inaction than the same objective risk as the result of action, there is a psychological preference for inaction that favors the defense.[59] Whether policy makers should endorse this bias is another matter. Arguably, the law ought to set standards so as to counteract such preferences as irrational.[60] Similarly, because people tend

---

[55] See Nance (1994). Manifestations of this presumption are not hard to find and include the following standard jury instruction for federal civil cases:

> Unless outweighed by evidence to the contrary, you may find an official duty has been regularly performed, private transactions have been fair and regular, ... and the law has been obeyed.

3 O'Malley (2006) § 104.21.

[56] See Nance (1994) at 659–72. Such considerations undermine the plausibility of theories of the standard for civil cases that rely on a broadly applicable assumption of symmetry between plaintiff and defendant. See, e.g., Cheng & Pardo (2015) (making the symmetry assumption at 202 n. 40).

[57] See Addington v. Texas, 441 U.S. 418 (1979).

[58] See Santosky v. Kramer, 455 U.S. 745 (1982).

[59] Zamir & Ritov (2012).

[60] See Clermont (2013) at 22.

to attribute greater disutility to the *loss* of a certain thing than they attribute to the *failure to acquire* that same thing (called "loss aversion" or the "endowment effect"), there is some reason to think that the litigants' subjective utilities and disutilities associated with the decision are not symmetrical. Plaintiff will not value the (correct or erroneous) obtaining of X via litigation as much as the defendant will (dis)value the (correct or erroneous) requirement that she give up X. To the extent that these subjective utilities are part of the public's assessment of O^*, an asymmetry is introduced that should favor the typical defendant, who is asked to give up something to the plaintiff. Again, as a normative factor, this argument presupposes that the public should endorse this asymmetrical evaluation by including these special psychic costs in the determination of O^*, or at least permit the fact-finder to do so.[61] Unless and until such biases can be shown to possess some subtle, context-appropriate function, rational decision making arguably calls for a policy that ignores or even attempts to offset such biases.

A familiar efficiency argument can be made that would favor defendants without regard to such subjective utilities of the fact-finder or the parties. There are certain assessment and enforcement costs associated with a verdict for the plaintiff that do not arise, in the typical case, out of a verdict for the defendant. If the verdict goes for the plaintiff, then the tribunal must concern itself with the issue of remedies (e.g., the assessment

---

[61] Unlike the omission bias, the loss-aversion argument obviously presupposes an interpersonal comparison of utilities, which makes it even more vulnerable as a normative principle. It also assumes that the public should endorse the proposition (which has some empirical support) that litigants treat the status quo ante, relative to which one determines what is a subjective loss and what is a subjective gain, as the situation when the litigation is commenced rather than the situation before the alleged breach of duty (if any) occurred. Relative to the earlier reference point, loss aversion can produce the opposite result (a lowered standard of persuasion) or leave the standard unchanged by the subjective utilities depending on what one assumes about the nature of the claim. If the claim is for the return of property, for example (and abstracting away litigation costs), a positive verdict imposes no loss on the defendant and no gain for plaintiff, whereas a negative verdict imposes a loss on the plaintiff and confers a gain on the defendant, thus producing a lowered standard of proof and a preference for positive verdicts insofar as subjective utilities are concerned. But a claim for damages, which must be suffered by one party or the other, works differently: the effect of potential losses for the plaintiff associated with a negative verdict offsets the effect of potential losses for the defendant associated with a positive verdict. Thus, if the public chooses to endorse this earlier reference point, at least for the purpose of determining what is a gain and what is a loss in parties' subjective utilities, this particular argument for increasing O^* fails. Interestingly, Zamir and Ritov found less support for the theory that loss aversion raises the de facto standard of proof than the theory that omission bias raises that standard. Zamir & Ritov (2012) at 189–93.

of damages and, possibly, the enforcement of a judgment) that need not be addressed on a verdict for the defense.[62] If these costs are to be included in the social-utility calculus – a plausible but not quite inevitable conclusion – then any symmetry otherwise existing between positive and negative verdicts is disturbed, and this suggests some discrete margin in favor of the plaintiff that must be achieved to warrant a plaintiff's verdict.[63] The extent of this margin will vary considerably from case to case depending on the amount of costs at issue and their relationship to the amount in controversy (or some other measure of the importance of the controversy). In most cases, the relatively small differential in litigation costs attending a positive verdict can do little more than provide a reason to break the tie when the odds are approximately equal to O^*, where O^* is determined without regard to such marginal litigation costs.[64] Still, the case may arise where this is not so. If, for example, in the case of a decision for the plaintiff that would require injunctive relief with considerable long-term judicial administrative costs (institutional reform class actions come to mind), then perhaps O^* might need to reflect a noticeable differential.[65]

In the aggregate, these considerations explain some of the controversy that surrounds the question of whether $P^* = 0.5$ is the proper standard for all civil cases. They also explain reasonably well the divergences that one sees in the doctrines on the matter. Criminal cases, however, are more difficult. Clearly, the floor on the value of P^* applies here as well; it may

---

[62] Cf. Lee (1997) at 12 (noting "remedy construction costs, enforcement costs, and transaction costs associated with payment" as justifications for the default rule favoring the defendant).

[63] The differential costs at issue apply whether the verdict for the plaintiff is a true positive or a false positive. They will decrease the magnitude of gain for a true positive and increase the magnitude of loss for a false positive. If the utilities are otherwise symmetrical, this can be modeled by setting $U_{(+)} = U_{(-)} - L$ and $D_{(+)} = D_{(-)} + L$, where L is the indicated litigation cost differential. In this case, we have $O^* = (U_{(-)} + D_{(-)} + L)/(U_{(-)} + D_{(-)} - L) > 1$.

[64] To get some sense of the magnitude of the effect, we can use the formula from the preceding footnote and add the assumption that the non-litigation-cost (dis)utilities involved are on the order of the amount in controversy, say, $U_{(-)} + D_{(+)} = U_{(+)} + D_{(-)} = \$100,000$, as well as the assumption that the cost differential for assessing and enforcing damages is $5,000. This would yield an O^* of $(100,000 + 5,000)/(100,000 - 5,000) = 11:10$, or a critical probability P^* of just 0.53. The difference between a critical probability of 0.50 and one of 0.53 would be barely discernible by the practical decision maker.

[65] Using the example from the preceding footnote, suppose that we change the enforcement cost figure to $40,000. Then the critical probability rises to 0.70. Case law does reflect a reluctance to grant injunctive relief, especially when that remedy involves costly judicial oversight. See, e.g., American Chocolate Cookie Co., Inc., v. River Valley Cookies, Ltd., 970 F.2d 273, 277 (7th Cir. 1992). This reluctance is generally expressed, however, not by a nominally higher standard of proof but rather by a preference for the granting of nonequitable remedies such as damages. See generally 11A Wright et al. (1982) § 2942.

not be set below 0.5. It follows, for example, that it would be improper to attempt to deter wrongdoing, in the civil or criminal context, by the imposition of a sanction on a person when it is known that such person has not violated the subject behavioral norm, even if the broader public is unaware that the imposition of the sanction is undeserved and such imposition would, on balance, serve consequentialist goals. Beyond this, the conventional claim is that the disutility of a mistaken conviction is much larger than the disutility of an erroneous acquittal, and thus the critical probability approaches 1 in the opinion of most commentators. Often cited as authority for such claims are statements by esteemed eighteenth- and nineteenth-century writers. For example, Blackstone famously stated, "the law holds, that it is better that ten guilty persons escape, than that one innocent suffer."[66] Interpreting this as a claim that a false conviction is ten times worse than a false acquittal ($D_{(+)} = 10 \times D_{(-)}$), then criterion (2.1) yields the critical odds of 10:1, or a critical probability of 0.91.[67] Other such authorities have given different values for this ratio. Hale, for example, put it at 5:1, which yields a critical probability of 0.83,[68] and Starkie seems to put the ratio at 99:1, or a critical probability of 0.99.[69]

---

[66] 4 Blackstone (1769) at 352.

[67] Such an interpretation is plausible, although it is not exactly what Blackstone said. See DeKay (1996) at 103–10, 129–30.

[68] 2 Hale (1847) at 289. Hale's tradeoff was often relied on in important trials of an earlier era. For example, Aaron Burr relied on Hale's ratio in his argument to the jury for the defense in the Manhattan Well Mystery case, tried in 1800. See Kleiger (1989) at 163.

[69] See Schlup v. Delo, 513 U.S. 298, 325 (1995) (citing Starkie's treatise approvingly on this point). What is sometimes neglected in references to Starkie, including the Supreme Court's citation, is the context of Starkie's comment. His passage, which concerns circumstantial evidence, actually shows little respect for the number 99:

> Whenever, therefore, the evidence leaves it indifferent which of several hypotheses is true, or merely establishes some finite probability in favour of one hypothesis rather than another, such evidence cannot amount to proof, however great the probability may be. To hold that any finite degree of probability shall constitute proof adequate to conviction of an offender would in reality be to assert, that out of some finite number of persons accused an innocent man should be sacrificed for the sake of punishing the rest; a proposition which is as inconsistent with the humane spirit of our law as it is with the suggestions of reason and justice. The maxim of law is, that it is better that ninety-nine (i.e. an indefinite number of) offenders should escape than that one innocent man should be condemned.

1 Starkie (1832) at 506. Making sense of this seemingly "humane" argument is no easy task. Unless we are to believe that convictions are only the result of certainty or that whatever uncertainty remains cannot rationally admit the assignment of a finite probability of innocence, at best it says simply that we should avoid admitting openly what we are in fact (and inevitably) doing.

Although such high critical probability norms have a strong hold on the modern legal mind and are supported by a variety of utilitarian and nonutilitarian considerations,[70] they have been seriously questioned by some scholars, especially when applied to crimes that are not very serious in nature.[71] Even in the case of serious crimes, and perhaps especially in such cases, the dangers to the public that follow from erroneous acquittals, in terms of blunted specific deterrence of the prosecuted individual and decreased general deterrence of those who become aware of the error, cannot be ignored. They tend to be downplayed in many discussions, plausibly because the losses are so diffuse. In any event, the ratio of disutilities associated with erroneous verdicts becomes less determinative of the critical odds once one begins to consider seriously the utility gains of true convictions $U_{(+)}$ and true acquittals $U_{(-)}$. After all, regretting mistakes is not the only concern in decision making.[72] There is much to suggest that the critical probability may not be so high as Blackstone's ratio would suggest.

Even if $U_{(+)}$ is equal to $U_{(-)}$, this has an impact, lowering O^*. For example, starting with the Blackstonian ratio, suppose that $D_{(+)} = 10$ and $D_{(-)} = 1$. Ignoring positive utilities produces critical odds of 10:1, to be applied according to criterion (2.1). But suppose now that even modest positive utilities of correct verdicts are added; using criterion (2.2), suppose that $U_{(+)} = U_{(-)} = 2$. Then the critical odds are significantly reduced, becoming (2 + 10):(2 + 1), or 4:1 (or a critical probability of 0.80). Moreover, at least for many contexts, a true-positive verdict will entail much of the utility associated with a true-negative verdict. For example, if there are five plausible suspects in a crime committed by a single person, correctly acquitting one of them leaves the guilty person at large and three innocent persons at some potential risk of conviction. But correctly convicting the guilty person necessarily leaves all four innocent individuals effectively free of legal liability.[73] In such cases, $U_{(+)}$ can be expected to be larger than $U_{(-)}$, which drives O^* down further.[74]

---

[70] See Kitai (2003).

[71] See, e.g., Laudan (2006) at 55–61 (arguing that the possibility of capital punishment adversely affects reasoned discourse on the subject).

[72] See, e.g., Allen & Laudan (2008) and Laudan & Saunders (2009).

[73] See Hamer (2004) at 86.

[74] Continuing the example, suppose that the utility gain from a true acquittal $U_{(-)}$ is twice the loss from a false acquittal $D_{(-)}$ and that the utility gain of a true conviction $U_{(+)}$ is twice the utility gain of a true acquittal $U_{(-)}$. Then O^* becomes (2 + 10):(4 + 1) = 2.4, and P^* becomes 0.71. (A parallel adjustment starting from Hale's less demanding 5:1 ratio yields an O^* of (2 + 5):(4 + 1) = 1.4, or a P^* of 0.58.) Note that these assumptions about utility gains are extremely modest. Under Blackstone's ratio, they are barely large enough to have an

Nevertheless, one set of factors, suggested by our discussion of civil cases, deserves emphasis, involving considerations that were largely irrelevant in Blackstone's day, when convictions for even modestly serious crime often led to prompt execution.[75] While the postverdict enforcement costs are comparatively minor for civil cases, the same cannot be said for criminal cases, at least not in the modern era. In criminal cases, at least serious ones, a conviction carries in train huge public and social costs associated with incarceration or, when it is at issue, execution. These include the costs of feeding, clothing, and providing healthcare and even educational and recreational opportunities for inmates.[76] Then there are the opportunity costs associated with the fact that at least some of the persons incarcerated (whether guilty or not) would, if not incarcerated, earn honest incomes, pay taxes, and so forth.[77] In addition, there are the considerable costs to families, especially the children of the incarcerated.[78] Finally, a factor that is probably as important as the others, there are the costs associated with the brutalization of inmates and the inculcation of illegal behavior that is ultimately foisted on the public when the convicts are released (or the increased costs associated with the measures that would be required to avoid such results).[79] For such reasons, accumulating opinion expresses serious and justifiable reservations about the very practice of incarceration, especially long-term incarceration.[80]

As long as our collective imagination cannot find meaningful alternatives to long-term incarceration,[81] we are stuck assessing the critical odds for conviction in light of these harsh realities, at least when imprisonment is at stake in a category of cases. And the striking feature of the indicated incarceration costs is that they both reduce the (otherwise attainable) gain

---

expectation of a net gain in social utility from a positive verdict when $P(C|E)$ exceeds P^*. For example, if $P(C|E) = 0.72 > P^*$, then the expected gain from a guilty verdict is just $(0.72)(4) - (0.28)(10) = 0.08$.

[75] "It was not until the nineteenth century that long-term imprisonment developed as a feasible alternative to the death penalty." Simon & Blaskovich (2002) at xiii.

[76] "The fee to cover the average cost of incarceration for federal inmates in Fiscal Year 2013 was $29,291.25 ($80.25 per day).... The average annual cost to confine an inmate in a Residential Re-entry Center for Fiscal Year 2013 was $26,612.15 ($72.91 per day)." 79 Fed. Reg. 26996 (May 12, 2014).

[77] See Hamilton & Urahn (2010).

[78] See Herman-Stahl et al. (2008).

[79] See Gibbons & Katzenbach (2006).

[80] See, e.g., Sommer (1976), Forer (1994), Sowle (1994), Durlauf & Nagin (2011).

[81] For arguments in favor of a restitutionary alternative, see Barnett (1980) and Abel & Marsh (1984).

in utility of a true conviction and increase the magnitude of the (otherwise incurred) loss from a false conviction because for the most part these costs are incurred regardless of the guilt of the accused. Both the guilty and the innocent must be housed and fed; both the guilty and the innocent are unable to work or otherwise provide for any families they have; both the guilty and the innocent will be subjected to an environment that is unlikely to make of them model citizens on their release. This set of effects drives up the assessed odds necessary for conviction under criterion (2.2): it both increases the numerator and shrinks the denominator of the ratio of utilities, whether or not to the same degree. It thus suggests a fairly high standard of proof, certainly higher than what is required for the vast majority of civil cases.[82]

Conceivably, there are various additional deontological constraints at work in the criminal-law context as well. The fundamental legal norm requiring that like cases be treated alike permits judgments that certain differences between defendants ought not to affect the standard of proof, even if they would affect the ratio of utilities. For example, it would be inappropriate to specify a lower O^* for the trial of an alleged crime just because the crime is high profile and will receive more public attention such that a conviction would produce a greater deterrent effect among third parties.[83] Other considerations may require ignoring particular anticipated gains or losses, real though they may be.[84]

In the end, for both civil and criminal cases, the appropriate standards to apply should be the result of informed political discourse that attempts to take all these factors into account, and they should, in the first instance, be publicly settled. However determined, the applicable critical value O^* must then be communicated to the fact-finder in appropriate language. Current practice generally avoids explicit quantification of O^*, and there is an extensive literature concerning the question of whether the relatively vague verbal formulations of the standards of proof should be replaced

---

[82] Continuing the preceding example in the text and footnote, suppose that the utility gain of a true positive is cut in half and the utility loss from a false positive is increased by the same amount, both due to incarceration effects. This would produce an O^* of $(2 + 12):(2 + 1) = 4.67$, or a P^* of 0.82. This, as indicated, starts from Blackstone's 10:1 ratio. Even if one starts, instead, with Hale's more crime-control-oriented 5:1 ratio, the resulting modified calculation yields an O^* of $(2 + 7):(2 + 1) = 3$, or a P^* of 0.75.

[83] Cf. Lempert (2001) at 1664.

[84] For example, in considering the utility losses associated with (unintentionally) convicting the innocent, is it appropriate to reduce the magnitude of that loss by the positive deterrent effects it may nonetheless cause among those who do not know that the accused is innocent?

with specific probability standards.[85] One important explanation of the reluctance to quantify the various standards of proof is this: there are reasons to think they cannot be fixed by lawmaking authorities at specific values that are appropriate for all cases or even all cases of a broad category, such as "all civil cases" or "all criminal cases" or even "all felony cases." The most obvious reason, readily explained using criterion (2.2), is that the ratio of utilities will depend on the situation of the individual case. Even if it is true that the average civil case calls for a standard of approximately 1:1 odds, or a critical probability of about 0.5, specific civil cases may not. Marginal or "retail" adjustment by the fact-finder may be appropriate in many cases, civil or criminal, just as fact-finders often are called on to tailor the requirements of substantive law under standards that delegate to them the responsibility of determining whether conduct has been "reasonable."[86] Of course, the downside of permitting such adjustment is the possibility that the fact-finder will be tempted to violate important deontological constraints or ignore important utility impacts that are plain to law-makers.

Although the matter is contested, for good or ill, the operative language of proof rules reflected in jury instructions often allows for some degree of retail adjustment.[87] This is conspicuous for the criminal-law standard, by which the fact-finder seems to be invited to determine case by case what degree of doubt it is "reasonable" to entertain and yet still give a verdict of guilty.[88] But it is recognizable as well within articulations of the civil-law

---

[85] See, e.g., Kagehiro & Stanton (1985) (reporting experiments that show quantification of standards produces the kinds of differences that are supposed to exist, but do not, in verdicts based on qualitatively distinct standards) and Weinstein & Duesbury (2006) (arguing for a combination of qualitative and quantitative description of the standard in criminal cases).

[86] See Kaplan, J. (1968) at 1072–7.

[87] Compare, e.g., Lillquist (2002) (arguing in favor of allowing retail adjustment of the general standard in the criminal context) with Saunders (2005) (arguing that legislatures must set the standard of proof for criminal cases and do so fairly precisely) and Redmayne (1999) at 180–4 (arguing against such retail adjustments in the civil context).

[88] Federico Picinali rejects the idea that the present "reasonable doubt" standard is sensitive to the ratio of utility differences because he considers the fact-finder's task to be a matter of theoretical reasoning. Picinali (2013). This might be taken to mean, and Picinali seems to assume, that the fact-finder does not have the kind of "adjustment" role described in the text. However, such a conclusion would ignore the possibility that the authority to make such adjustments is part of the message conveyed by the standard itself in that "reasonable doubt" incorporates an element of practical reasonableness. Such an understanding of the standard would render it unnecessary to reject, as Picinali does, the continuing relevance of the history of the standard, a history that reveals a connection to the exercise of practical reason by the fact-finder. See id. at 867–8. It also would avoid the necessity

standard in terms of "clear and convincing evidence" or even a "*fair* preponderance of the evidence."[89] Surely, jurors perceive some "wiggle" room in both contexts.[90] The potential implications of such a practice for the rule of law have already been noted (§ 2.2), but it is worth emphasizing that the law is not faced with an inescapable dilemma between choosing either a precise and uniformly applicable standard for a whole class of cases or else permitting largely unfettered ad hoc fact-finder discretion for each case. Even if one believes that no single critical probability can be assigned to a category of cases in advance of deliberation, this does not necessarily mean that standards cannot be quantified to any extent. It is entirely possible, for example, to quantify a given standard by reference to a *range* of values, a range within which the fact-finder would be free to select a specific value thought to be appropriate.[91] For example, arguably both the "preponderance of the evidence" standard and the "beyond reasonable doubt" standard are properly understood as quantifiable to the extent that they both require a probability in excess of 0.5. This itself is a meaningful public constraint, and considerably more may be possible and appropriate in this regard.

2.2.2 *The Fact-Finder's Assessment of Odds*

If fact-finders are to assess the odds on a claim, they are necessarily working with probabilities, at least relative probabilities. As Justice Harlan observed, "all the fact-finder can acquire is a belief of what *probably* happened."[92] But the nature of the probabilities involved is a complex matter.

of distinguishing, as Picinali does, between the law's supposedly limited message and the broader message that juries appear to receive. See id. at 871 n. 86.

[89] See, e.g., Connecticut Civil Jury Instructions 3.2-1, 3.2-2 (2011) (emphasis added).

[90] Indirect evidence of this comes from the various attempts to assess how jurors, judges, and others translate the verbal standards provided by jury instructions into probabilities. Some of these studies reveal a sensitivity of the subjects to the nature and details of the case. See Hastie (1993) at 100–8 (summarizing studies). In later studies, using a methodology that identifies at what level of probability jurors are likely to convict, a difference can be discerned between, for example, the probability necessary to convict for (stranger) rape and that necessary to convict for robbery. See Nance & Morris (2005) at 407 (estimating the minimum predeliberation probability for a rape conviction in the specific case as falling between 0.75 and 0.85) and Kaye et al. (2007) at 818–24 (estimating the minimum predeliberation probability for a robbery conviction in the specific case at 0.68).

[91] See Tillers & Gottfried (2006) at 144–6 (noting that quantification of the proof standard does not entail a single, invariant probability). This article is a useful antidote for a variety of senseless challenges that can be, and have been, made against any attempt to quantify burdens of persuasion.

[92] In re Winship, 397 U.S. 358, 370 (1970) (Harlan, J., concurring).

There are several vigorously contested theories of the nature and meaning of probabilities. These are entirely distinct from a mathematical theory of probability, which consists of a set of abstract entities and a function stipulated to obey certain axioms, from which one can deduce theorems that relate hypothetically given probability values to other probability values of potential interest.[93] In principle, such a mathematical theory might exist as a conceptual plaything without any significant application in human affairs. Of course, we know that this is not true in the case of conventional mathematical probability theory.[94] Its useful applications are diverse and powerful. Although applications of the mathematics often proceed without being self-conscious about the matter, any such application presupposes an interpretation of the mathematics, in particular, an interpretation of what it means to ascribe probabilities to real world events.

Among the variety of interpretations there are so-called frequency theories, propensity theories, subjective theories, intersubjective theories, logical theories, and other variants.[95] For our purposes, the following categorization will suffice:

1. *Empirical* theories take probability to be a property associated with objectively observable phenomena. Thus conceived, probabilities are often unknown quantities, subject to empirical testing. Such probabilities are sometimes called "chances."
2. *Rationalist* theories identify probability with degree of rational belief or degree of justification of belief. Such probabilities are often called "epistemic." It is sometimes assumed that given the same evidence, all rational human beings will entertain the same degree of belief (or justification of belief) in a hypothesis. In such a case, probabilities can be

---

[93] See Fine (1973) at 15–84.

[94] There are different versions of the axioms of that conventional theory that lead to the same basic system. The following is fairly straightforward: if (1) Ω is a nonempty set, (2) B is collection of subsets of Ω that contains the empty set $\emptyset$ and is closed under the formation of complements and of finite or countable unions of its members, and (3) P is a nonnegative function defined on B such that $P(\Omega) = 1$ and P is countably additive in the sense that $P(U_i A_i) = \Sigma_i P(A_i)$ for any sequence $A_1, A_2, \ldots$ of mutually exclusive members of B, then P is a probability measure over the set of "events" B. See, e.g., Lamperti (1996) at 1. From this definition follows the usual properties of mathematical probabilities, such as

   a. $0 \leq P(A) \leq 1$, for any event A;
   b. $P(\text{not-}A) = 1 - P(A)$, for any event A; and
   c. $P(A \text{ or } B) = P(A) + P(B) - P(A\&B)$, for any events A and B.

Such rules were, of course, used in deriving criterion (2.2).

[95] There are several excellent general introductions. See, e.g., Gillies (2000) and Mellor (2005).

unknown only through ignorance or logical incompetence; such probabilities are usually called "logical" probabilities.
3. *Subjective* theories identify probability with the degree of belief of a particular individual. It is not assumed that all rational human beings with the same evidence will have the same degree of belief in a hypothesis or prediction, though "convergence" in beliefs may arise from one of several sources. By most accounts, such probabilities can in no event be unknown, though they may be subject to modification in order to ensure that they comport with the axioms of mathematical probability. Such probabilities are sometimes called "credences."

Although some theorists who have developed or endorsed one kind of theory have been firm, even strident, in denying the usefulness or coherence of any other kind, most philosophers today are rather more eclectic or pluralist: while some theories may be simply incoherent or mistaken, the applicability of others may be context dependent. Moreover, the theories are not necessarily mutually exclusive, even in a particular context, but may instead be coextensive and interrelated. For example, one's subjective assessment of the probability of an event will be affected by empirical information one knows about its chances.

What these theories are *not* is theories about *how one quantifies* probabilities. The latter subject concerns the important issue of how to measure or otherwise determine a real-world probability of whatever kind. This process provides the connection, when such a connection is possible, between the world of applications and the mathematical theory. To illustrate this important distinction, it is worth observing that one particular empirical theory was developed without careful attention to it. Specifically, some theorists have sought to define probability in terms of long-run frequencies of occurrence (i.e., how many times a given event occurred in a long series of similar trials). The so-called frequency theory of probability was built on this idea.[96] But it was recognized that *defining* probability in such terms would not allow one to speak coherently, except perhaps in a metaphorical way, about the probability of a single event, even random events such as the probability that a coin tossed will land heads on a particular occasion. To deal with this problem, Karl Popper introduced a different empirical theory, the "propensity" theory, by which probability is understood as a property of the chance setup and is well defined for individual events. Of course, the obvious way to *measure* or *estimate* the quantitative aspect of such a propensity is to count up

---

[96] See Gillies (2000) at 88–112.

the results of a long series of similar trials, and this no doubt accounts for the initial attractiveness of a frequency theory. The mistake of frequency theorists was to insist, in true positivist fashion, that there is no difference between the theoretical construct, here "probability," and the quantity used for its practical measurement, here the "long-run frequency of occurrence."[97] The propensity theory avoids this conceptual error.

In the legal context, probabilities that are the target or end product of fact-finding – those reflected in criterion (2.2′) – are "epistemological," in that they grade partial beliefs or degrees of justification rather than grading features of the physical world (such as the probabilities associated with radioactive decay) that are, in an important sense, independent of what humans believe. This means that law's decisional probabilities are to be found more in the conceptual neighborhood of rationalist or subjective theories of probability and less in the conceptual neighborhood of empirical theories of probability.[98] This does not mean, however, that the latter, more "objective" probabilities to be found in the world (such as a random-match probability for DNA evidence) are irrelevant to the epistemological probabilities that fact-finders form. Their relevance will be context dependent and determined by their rational influence on epistemological probabilities.[99]

It is sometimes said that adjudication is (mostly) about past events, events that either happened or not. As to these events, it is claimed, probability makes no sense, or rather, the only probabilities that make sense are 1 (it happened) and 0 (it did not happen).[100] The claim might be true if the relevant probabilities are understood as empirical: examination will reveal whether the event occurred or not, and *its* "chanciness" has been resolved (by the occurrence of the event) even before that examination occurs. But this kind of thinking overlooks the fact that uncertainty can exist as to past

---

[97] Id. at 113–36. As Richard Cox nicely put it, "Measurement, however, is always to some extent imposed upon what is measured and foreign to it." Cox (1961) at 1.

[98] See Gillies (2000) at 1–2, 18–22 (categorizing logical and subjective theories as "epistemological," in that they are concerned with the knowledge or belief of human beings, whereas frequency and propensity theories are "objective" interpretations that take probability to be a feature of the objective material world).

[99] For example, considerable thought has been given to articulating and defending a "principle of direct inference," which stipulates how knowledge of chances or empirical probabilities should be used to determine one's epistemic judgments about the outcomes of trials. Levi (1984) at 192–213; Plantiga (1993) at 151–8 (critically assessing Kyburg's extensive contributions to this topic).

[100] For an illustration of this assertion, see the opinion of Lord Justice Toulson in Nulty et al. v. Milton Keynes Borough Council [2013] EWCA Civ 15 at ¶ 37.

facts, just as it does as to future ones, and this uncertainty can be the subject of probability ascriptions. This is most easily illustrated by reference to observable events with a random element. Suppose that someone flips what is known to be a fair coin, it lands, but the coin is behind a screen such that you cannot see how it landed. (Assume that you have complete confidence that no one is "gaming" you by fixing the result behind the screen or otherwise.) In such a case, it makes just as much sense for you to say that the probability that the coin landed heads (past tense) is 0.5 as it does to say that the probability of the next (future) flip landing heads is 0.5. In each case, the figure 0.5 grades one's degree of certainty about the proposition that when a factual condition has changed (in one case, the removal of the screen; in the other, the observation of the result of the next flip), the coin will show heads. And this is so even though it is true in the one case, we may assume, that the coin in fact landed either heads or tails behind the screen.[101]

In this example, the objective propensity of the coin to land heads is one factor – a controlling one under the posited conditions – in the determination of your epistemological probability that the coin landed heads. The matter becomes more controversial when the uncertainty in question arises from a source that is not (or not entirely) a random or chance process. When the truth or falsity of some proposition regarding a past event, however deterministic, is at issue, does it still makes sense to speak of the probability that the proposition is true? Suppose that there is a coin that is known by you with certainty to be either heads on both sides or tails on both sides; with no reason to believe which kind of coin it is, you are asked how strongly you believe (or should believe) that the coin, when flipped, will land heads. Laplace's answer was 0.5.[102] One could just as easily have asked this question about a completed toss: how strong is your credence, before observing or being informed about how it landed, that the coin landed heads? Again, Laplace would answer, 0.5. Under either version of the question, the propensity of the coin to land heads (which is either 0 or 1) is not equal to the degree of credence. What matters in this context, given the paucity of information about which

[101] See Beebee & Papineau (1997) (arguing that from the prudential perspective, "the correct degree of belief in an outcome is not necessarily equal to its single-case probability, but rather to its relative probability, ... the objective probability of that outcome relative to the features of the situation which the agent knows about" (p. 218)).

[102] The hypothetical in the text is an extreme case of a famous example used by Laplace, who supposed that a coin that was known to be biased toward either heads or tails, but the direction of the bias was unknown. Laplace (1814) at 56.

kind of coin was used, is the perennially controversial "principle of indifference" or "principle of insufficient reason," which prescribes (under certain conditions) equal probabilities to mutually exclusive and exhaustive events as to which the evidence provides no basis to favor any one over the other.[103] In other contexts of past events, there will be significant additional evidence to assess. In any event, it makes as much sense to speak of the probability that a meteor of certain size struck the Earth in the past as it does to speak of the probability that a meteor of such a size will strike the Earth in the future, although the evidence that one would gather and consider about the two events, and the resulting probabilities, might be quite different.[104]

Moreover, as in this example, the target probabilities in adjudication are "objective" in a different sense than the one noted earlier: whether and to what extent evidence counts in favor of a hypothesis is not purely "subjective" in the sense that they are merely a matter of individual opinion.[105] Better and worse arguments (such as the principle of indifference) can be made on the matter, and not all epistemic appraisals in such a context are equally sound. Such "epistemic" probabilities are therefore conceptually distinct from (but closely related to) "subjective" or "credal" probabilities that simply grade partial beliefs or degrees of belief.[106] The relationship between them is normative: one's subjective, credal probability that a certain proposition is true *ought* to be set equal to the epistemic probability of that proposition, determined in light of (relative to) the evidence that

---

[103] See Gillies (2000) at 37–49 (providing extensive discussion of the indifference principle, including defenses thereof provided by Keynes and by Jaynes) and Mellor (2005) at 12, 27–9 (doubting the validity of the principle of indifference but nonetheless accepting the plausibility of a credence of 0.5 in the hypothetical presented in the text). See also Schlesinger (1991) at 5–15, 181–202 (providing a spirited defense of the principle, including the claim (at 199) that "even the most elementary kind of inductive argument could not get off the ground without its use") and Franklin (2001) (defending the theory of logical probability against attacks on it that consider the principle of indifference to be unsustainable).

[104] See, e.g., Hacking (2001) at 141–2. Compare Kaye (1979b) at 45 (arguing that the difference between prediction and postdiction is merely a matter of degree) with Hamer (2004) at 79–80 (arguing that this difference is nonetheless significant because of "the absence of a 'criterion' or 'gold standard' for checking postdictions" the way that predictions ordinarily can be tested).

[105] Cf. Gillies (2000) at 169–80 (discussing a spectrum of probability ideas in terms of the degree of subjectivity/objectivity and including "intersubjective" probabilities as falling between the extremes). For a useful overview of the problem of objectivity in the assessment of adjudicative probabilities, see Redmayne (2003).

[106] See, e.g., Mellor (2005) at 5–13 (distinguishing "epistemic probability" from both "chances" and "credences").

one has for it.[107] Unless one is irrational, the point of forming a subjective probability is to have available a measure of uncertainty that aligns with epistemic probability. Thus the well-known but relatively minimalist ("coherence") condition on a person's subjective degrees of partial belief – that, to be rational, they must conform to the axioms of mathematical probability[108] – reflects only part of what one is aiming at in forming such partial beliefs.

It remains controversial whether epistemic relations between evidence and hypotheses can be understood as mathematical probabilities.[109] But a powerful case, based on a variety of convergent arguments by various scholars, suggests that they can.[110] As nicely stated by D. H. Mellor: "It is as hard to deny that evidence can give these propositions [e.g., 'The butler did it' or 'The defendant is innocent'] epistemic probabilities as it is to identify those probabilities with frequencies."[111] This is not the place to develop in detail these complicated arguments. I mention one, just to give readers a flavor for the kind of argument involved. Mellor gives reasons to accept the following "evidence-to-credence" principle: "The more B confirms A, the greater the degree of belief in A which B justifies." He then argues

> This allows us – although it does not force us – to equate *degrees of confirmation of A* with *justified degrees of belief in A*. By so doing, it lets us use the degree of belief in A which B justifies to measure how far B

[107] See Horwich (1982) at 32–3; Plantinga (1993) at 141; Swinburne (2001) at 152–62; and Mellor (2005) at 79.

[108] The theorem may be stated thus: a person who bets based on his degrees of partial belief will be immune from "sure-loss" bets if and only if his degrees conform to the standard axioms of probability. See Gillies (2000) at 53–65 (discussing the "Ramsey–De Finetti theorem").

[109] See id. at 25–49 (presenting the obstacles to measuring such epistemic relations as mathematical probabilities) and Haack (2012) (presenting opposition to "epistemic probabilism" and its subspecies, "legal probabilism," and indicating similar opposition to be found in the writings of Bentham, Mills, Keynes, and Russell). See also Cohen, J. (1977, 1989) (defending a competing formalism for "inductive" probability) and Stein (2011) (defending a competing "causative" system of probability). The views of Haack, Cohen, and Stein are all addressed at various points in what follows.

[110] See, e.g., Cox (1961) at 1–29 (deriving the mathematics of all probable inferences from two axioms, one for complementation and one for conjunction); Horwich (1982) at 16–50 (developing a rationalist theory of probability and showing why empirical theories presuppose a rationalist theory); Logue (1995) at 150–54 (developing a "strong coherentist subjectivism" about probability that allows for the applicability of the standard probability calculus to juridical proof); Swinburne (2001) at 56–73 (defending the theory of logical probability and its compatibility with the standard axioms of mathematical probability); and Jaynes (2003) (presenting a detailed theory of logical probability reproducing the standard axioms).

[111] Mellor (2005) at 35 (referring to epistemic probabilities that conform to the mathematical axioms).

confirms A. And then, since we already know from [a previous chapter discussing the coherence requirement for degrees of belief] that degrees of belief have a probability measure, this gives us a probability measure for confirmation.[112]

To this point, I would add the following complementary consideration: if subjective probabilities, in order to be rational, must conform to the axioms of mathematical probability, and if subjective probabilities ideally should come into line with epistemic probabilities, then epistemic probabilities must, at least, conform to the indicated axioms. Otherwise, we are placing incoherent aspirations on those who would form beliefs, including fact-finders in adjudication.

So the "target" probabilities in criterion (2.2) should be understood as epistemic probabilities. The shudder quotes are a reflection of the fact that fact-finders will inevitably work with their own subjective probabilities. While a rational fact-finder may analytically distinguish between the two, she will not perceive a difference in their values; if she did, she would adjust them so that they coincide. Understanding the target probabilities this way does not require that there must exist a precise, verifiably correct epistemic probability for each proposition, even relative to given evidence. Nor need there be some computational algorithm that would prescribe how such epistemic probabilities are calculated. For practical purposes, such as adjudication, all that is important is to be able to make comparative assertions about inevitably subjective assessments of epistemic probabilities, including rough quantitative comparisons, such as the assertion that $P(C|E)$ is more or less than (roughly) r times $P(\text{not-}C|E)$, for some number r.

Unfortunately, recent work about probability in the context of adjudication often does not reflect much sophistication about these issues. Just as one encounters bad arguments *against* the idea of interpreting the standards of proof in terms of probability thresholds, one also finds bad arguments *in favor* of them. Here is one from Louis Kaplow, attempting to rely on consistency restraints on subjective probabilities:

> [C]onsider a set of cases that are identical except for the probability that the individual before a tribunal committed a harmful act. Take a case in which that probability is p_1 and suppose that, after reflection, the decisionmaker decides that it is appropriate for liability to be imposed. Then consistency demands the imposition of liability in all cases in which the probability exceeds p_1 (for, after all, it was stipulated that the cases in the set differ only in their probabilities). In another case, the probability is at some lower level p_2, and the decisionmaker decides that it is appropriate to exonerate. Then

[112] Id. at 79.

> consistency demands exoneration in all cases in which the probability is less than p_2. As one considers additional cases, with probabilities between p_1 and p_2, further decision will narrow the undecided range. Ultimately, there will, in principle, exist some probability p^* above which the decisionmaker would always find liability and below which it would always exonerate. (If not, then there must exist as least one pair of cases with differing probabilities – and all else equal – such that the decisionmaker would exonerate in the case with the higher probability but find liability in the case with the lower probability, which does not make sense.)[113]

Now, I have no problem with imaginative thought experiments, but this one starts by assuming that there exist members of an empty set. On what basis would any rational person assign different probabilities to claims in cases that are assumed to be identical in terms of the context, evidence, and so on – that is, all the things that determine one's probability that the claim is true? It is akin to assuming a set of circles, all with the same radius but different circumferences.

A possible explanation of this peculiar argument is that Kaplow has equivocated, making an unsignaled shift somewhere in his argument from a focus on probability as a product of the fact-finder's assessment of the evidence to a focus on probabilities that are much more objective, in the sense addressed here, something that is *part of* the evidence itself (such as a DNA random-match probability) and that could plausibly, if hypothetically, be changed while holding other things constant. Alex Stein has identified the nature of the problem as a tendency of those who work in the field of law and economics – including Kaplow – to use a naive frequentist theory of probability.[114] (As noted earlier, such theories are empirical in that they take probabilities to be features of the material world, things that sensibly could be "varied" while other things are "held constant.") Stein illustrates how the economists have done a rather poor job of tailoring epistemic probabilities in contexts for which a decision maker has more to consider than mere aggregate frequencies.

Unfortunately, Stein goes to a different extreme by postulating that the mathematical probability system can be employed *only* when it is based on such frequencies (what he calls "instantial multiplicity") and that it cannot accommodate assessments of probability based on "evidential variety." Thus he writes:

> The metric set by the mathematical language ... treats probability as coextensive with instantial multiplicity and recognizes no other criteria

[113] Kaplow (2012) at 773 n. 62.
[114] Stein (2011).

for probabilistic appraisals. As a result of this definitional constraint, the metric contains no quantifiers for evidential variety or for the degrees of evidential support for event-specific hypotheses. This limitation is profound: it makes mathematical language unfit as a tool for event-specific assessments of probability.[115]

This leads Stein to the conclusion that a different theory of probability – what he calls "causitive probability" – is the sense of probability at work in much practical decision making, including adjudication. Stein's causitive probabilities do not follow the same rules as mathematical probabilities.[116]

In fact, there is no metric built into mathematical probability that presupposes instantial multiplicity or, indeed, any other method of determining probabilities.[117] As we have seen, there *is* such a definitional metric in at least one particular *interpretation* of the mathematics: the frequency theory.[118] And it is correct that law-and-economics theorists often rely on poorly thought-through frequency determinants of probability. More deeply, the problem for such theorists is their tendency to use empirical theories of probability, without adequate attention to the complexities of how such probabilities, or the frequencies that would serve to measure them, figure into appraisals of epistemological probability. Conversely, Stein's problem is his inability to distinguish the mathematical theory from such empirical theories of probability ascription. He does recognize the potential application of subjective probabilities, which he acknowledges should conform to the axiomatic structure of mathematical probability,[119] but he still insists

---

[115] Id. at 216.

[116] Stein relies heavily on the work of Jonathan Cohen, and it becomes clear that his theory of "causitive probability" is closely related to, if not the same as, Cohen's theory of Baconian (or inductive) probability. See id. at 221 n. 60. For further comments on Cohen's theory, see infra § 3.4.

[117] None of the defining axioms of conventional probability refers to instantial multiplicity, though it is true that Kolmogorov had a frequentist or propensity theory in mind when he came up with those axioms. See Schum (1994) at 39–40.

[118] Although propensity theories are not invariably committed to instantial multiplicity as a definitional matter, they are typically constructed to account for random or chance setups in the objective world, and as already noted in the text, they rely on instantial multiplicity – counting the results of repeated experiments – to measure propensities or to test claims about propensity.

[119] Stein (2011) at 213:

> [P]eople basing their decisions upon intuited or "subjective" probabilities must use mathematical language as well. This language introduces conceptual precision and coherence into a reasoner's conversion of her experience-based beliefs into numbers. Those numbers must more or less correspond to the reasoner's empirical situation. A mismatch between the numbers and empirical reality will produce a bad decision.

that this makes practical sense only in the context of statistical aggregates. Indeed, he seems to go so far as to say that single-event probabilities cannot, therefore, be mathematical probabilities.[120] Nevertheless, Stein asserts that "[a] rational person will rely on that probability only when she has no causal information pertaining to her situation and, consequently, has no choice but to gamble."[121]

This way of looking at things creates a strange and counterintuitive discontinuity between contexts in which mathematical probability (which, for Stein, is inherently attached to frequency measures) is admittedly relevant to the rational actor and contexts in which, as soon as any causal information "pertaining to her situation" is taken into account, the previously existing relevance of the frequency information rather mysteriously evaporates, and the rational actor emerges into a world in which (supposedly) she no longer is forced to "gamble" in making hard choices under admittedly continuing conditions of uncertainty. Throughout his article, Stein gives hypothetical cases designed to show that rational actors ignore base-rate frequencies once "causitive" probabilities are in play. Here is a representative example:

> Take a rural road that is virtually never patrolled by the police, and consider the probability of a speeding driver's apprehension on that road. The mathematical probability of that scenario will obviously be next to zero. But what will this probability mean to the same driver tomorrow? Not much, because tomorrow is literally another day. Tomorrow, the police may actually patrol the road. The driver therefore will have to look out for police presence on the road before she decides to speed.... [T]he driver's decision to speed will not rely on the number of past occasions on which the road was free of police presence. Rather, it will rely on the driver's event-specific elimination of the apprehension risk. The driver will reason in the following way: "There are no police cars on this road today. Therefore, the police will not apprehend me." This form of reasoning is what causative probability is about.[122]

---

[120] Id.:

> Proper use of the mathematical probability system thus can only guarantee a particular kind of accuracy: accuracy in ascribing probability estimates to perceived generalities, as opposed to individual events.... The mathematical system offers no event-specific guarantees of accuracy in probability assessments.

To be precise, Stein does not say that taking such "perceived generalities" into account in making event-specific judgments is "irrational," only that "accuracy" in making event-specific probability estimates is "compromised" by doing so. Id. at 214.

[121] Id. at 247.
[122] Id. at 236.

Stein is not stating a purely descriptive psychological thesis here. It is (also) a normative claim about how rational people approach their decision problems.

Putting aside the cynicism embedded in the example (the driver apparently does not consider the law's norm as having any weight in her decision aside from the risk of being cited by the police), the rationality of Stein's driver must be seriously questioned. To be rational even in such a narrow sense, her reasoning would have to presuppose that her capacity to detect police patrols is perfect. Otherwise, her reasoning would include something like the following: "Of course, I may have failed to perceive the patrol, in which case there is the possibility that a patrol is out there anyway, and the likelihood of that is affected by how often this road is patrolled." How serious that likelihood will be, in her decision, will, in turn, depend on how good she thinks she is at spotting patrols when they are present.[123] Apparently, Stein would have us believe that it makes no difference to our rational driver, one who presumably is aware of her imperfect capacity at detecting patrols, whether the road is one that is rarely patrolled or one that is heavily patrolled. It is difficult to recognize this as rational behavior. The bottom line is this: there is no radical epistemic divide between the range of usefulness of mathematical probability and causally informed probability assessments or between mathematical probabilities informed by statistical frequencies and those informed by causal generalizations.[124] Stein's claim ignores approaches to probability that do not depend exclusively on instantial multiplicity and are compatible with considerations of causal assessments based on evidential variety. Such theories permit the synthesis of background aggregate frequencies (base rates) with tendencies informed by causal mechanisms.[125]

---

[123] There are, of course, other possibilities that, at least in principle, she would take into account. Even if she detects a police car, it might be there for some purpose other than monitoring compliance with speed limits. And even if a patrol is detected, there is the question of the proficiency of the patrol in detecting speeders, a proficiency that can be understood as a propensity. Such background information would be pertinent to assessing the risk of apprehension.

[124] See generally Schum (1994) at 140–55 (discussing the relationship between causality and inferential relevance). Schum concludes that "we need not suppose any causal connections between events for evidence about these events to have inferential relevance and force." Id. at 155.

[125] See Gillies (2000) at 114–36 (explaining how various probability theories should address single-event probabilities by making adjustments to available statistical base rates using causal generalizations); Swinburne (2001) at 74–123 (emphasizing causal explanation in articulating a theory of logical probability that conforms to the mathematical axioms); and Gigerenzer (2002) (providing detailed illustrations of the importance of assimilating

Even the most sophisticated attacks on the idea that epistemic warrant as used in adjudication conforms (or can be required to conform) to the axioms of mathematical probability generally accept the gradient nature of standards of proof. For example, in a recent book, Susan Haack denies that epistemic warrant, which she describes as an inherently multidimensional quality, forms a linear ordering of evidentiary states,[126] and she concludes that epistemic warrant need not, and generally does not, conform to the axioms of mathematical probability.[127] Not surprisingly, then, she also concludes that quantifying the varying standards of proof is not possible, and she expresses doubt that they can (or should) be made more precise than they are. But she also accepts that the "beyond reasonable doubt" standard is more demanding than the "clear and convincing evidence" standard, which, in turn, is more demanding than the "preponderance of the evidence" standard. Moreover, Haack accepts the proposition that the criminal law's relative stringency of standard arises from the same consideration on which the decision-theoretic model is built: "the idea that it is much worse to convict someone of a crime he didn't commit than to fail to convict someone of a crime he did commit."[128] This presents a difficult situation: once one tries to come to grips with the question of *how much worse* it is, one ends up dealing in ratios, which presupposes some measure of epistemic warrant with ratio-like characteristics, such as odds.[129] If Haack were right about our inability to place epistemic warrant on a linear scale, we would expect to see instructions telling jurors to make a multidimensional assessment. For example, we might encounter the following instruction on the question of causation in a civil case: "You should find

base rate information in practical decision making). At various points, Stein does seem to acknowledge that frequency data can be integrated with causal analysis – e.g., Stein (2011) at 216–17 – but he asserts that "[o]n balance, the causative system [without such synthesis] outperforms mathematical probability [even with such synthesis] in every area of fact-finding for which it was designed." Id. at 243. It is clear from context that Stein's primary criterion of performance here is inferential accuracy, but he provides no criterion by which to assess such accuracy nor any empirical evidence to support this assertion.

[126] Haack (2014). From the context, it is clear that the phrase "linear ordering" refers to the idea that for any two evidentiary states E_1 and E_2, relative to the hypothesis, C, the epistemic warrant for C in light of E_1 must be *greater than*, *less than*, or *equal to* the epistemic warrant for C in light of evidence E_2. See Enderton (1977) at 170.

[127] Haack (2014) at 56–64. Haack's arguments on this point are discussed further later (see § 3.6).

[128] Id. at 51.

[129] The criminal law's standard is regularly stated as requiring proof "beyond reasonable doubt" not proof "to the exclusion of reasonable doubt." As Reid Hastie observed, "The metaphorical *beyond* in the standard instruction is certainly intended to evoke a geometric image." Hastie (1993) at 101 (emphasis in original).

for the plaintiff only if the evidence showing causation of the plaintiff's injury favors the plaintiff in some respects and is no worse for the plaintiff than for the defendant in all other respects." But nothing remotely resembling such an instruction is to be found in use in our courts.

In the final analysis, for adjudication and many other practical decision-making contexts, the following statement by Glen Shafer may be most apt:

> I do not pretend that there exists an objective relation between given evidence and a given proposition that determines a precise numerical degree of support. Nor do I pretend that an actual human being's state of mind with respect to a proposition can ever be described by a precise real number called his degree of belief, nor even that it can ever determine such a number. Rather, I merely suppose that an individual can make a judgment. Having surveyed the sometimes vague and sometimes confused perception and understanding that constitutes [sic] a given body of evidence, he can announce a number that represents the degree to which he judges that evidence to support a given proposition and, hence, the degree of belief he wishes to accord the proposition.[130]

Not surprisingly, the law employs a variety of norms, rules, and practices that attempt to assist fact-finders in aligning their inevitably subjective probabilities with the target epistemic probabilities. Foremost among these, in the case of jury trials, are norms, communicated in various ways, telling jurors what is evidence that they may consider and telling them not to decide the case based on prejudice or bias against a party,[131] as well as the requirement that juries deliberate and (in most contexts) return a unanimous verdict.[132] The law presumes, and reasonably so, that a juror's subjective probability is more likely to approach an objective measure of the relevant epistemic probability if the juror has paid careful attention to the evidence and engaged other jurors in discussion about the significance to give the evidence.[133] And, as a final check, trial courts have the

---

[130] Shafer (1976) at 20. Shafer's theory of evidence is discussed later (§ 3.7).
[131] See, e.g., 3 O'Malley et al. (2006) § 101.40 (defining evidence and reminding jurors to draw inferences therefrom based on their own experience), § 102.12 (reminding jurors not to rely on media reports of the trial and the reasons for not doing so), and § 103.01 (reminding jurors of their duty not to decide the case on the basis of bias, prejudice, or sympathy toward a party, nor on the basis of public opinion about the case).
[132] Marder (2005) at 147–78 (summarizing important accuracy-enhancing features of jury deliberation).
[133] This is not to deny that extant jury trial procedures can be improved in this regard. See, e.g., id. at 105–17 (discussing the law's gradual exploration of innovations such as juror note taking, juror question asking, and predeliberation jury discussion).

authority to monitor jury assessments to keep them within the realm of the plausible.[134] In the case of bench trials, the norms that would be transmitted to juries are already well known to judges, and the comparable requirement is simply that the trial judge articulate his or her findings of fact and thus be relatively transparent to appellate review.[135] By these and other mechanisms, the law manifests its pervasive aspiration to objectivity, in this context, objective measures of epistemic probabilities.[136]

There are other legal constraints on a fact-finder's probability assessments. They are sometimes necessarily hypothetical in a certain sense. Various rules limit the use of evidence presented in court; they say, in effect, that the fact-finder may use that evidence in one relevant way but not in another.[137] Examples abound. An out-of-court assertion that is not offered to prove the truth of the matter asserted, but only to show the declarant's state of mind, may be admissible for the latter purpose but inadmissible for the former purpose because of the hearsay rule.[138] Evidence of prior bad acts committed by the accused may be admissible to show his knowledge or skills but not to show a propensity to commit bad conduct because of the character-evidence rules.[139] In all such cases, the fact-finders must form their odds, for purposes of testing criterion (2.2), *as if* the evidence did not affect their actual beliefs in the proscribed ways. In the extreme case, there may be no permissible inference from certain "evidence," such as when evidence the fact-finders have heard has been ruled inadmissible for any purpose. Thus, assuming that impermissible inferences cannot be put entirely out of mind, the odds are not necessarily the odds the fact-finders believe to be accurate but rather the odds that the fact-finders would believe to be accurate if they were able to ignore the impermissible inferences from evidence already heard.[140]

Despite these efforts to coax and to restrict the odds fact-finders are to determine, neither the law nor the decision-theory presented earlier speaks at any depth to the question of *how* fact-finders are to determine

---

[134] See 2 McCormick (2013) § 338.
[135] See, e.g., Fed. R. Civ. P. 52(a) and Fed. R. Crim. P. 23(c).
[136] It is therefore a mistake to think that a probabilistic interpretation of proof standards requires a choice between the most objective (empirical) probabilities measured by quantifiable data, on the one hand, and purely subjective probabilities, on the other. See, e.g., Pardo (2013) at 574–96 (describing probability-based evidence theories as caught in such a bind).
[137] See, e.g., Fed. R. Evid. 105.
[138] See, e.g., Fed. R. Evid. 801(c), 802.
[139] See, e.g., Fed. R. Evid. 404(b).
[140] See Ho (2008) at 92–3.

their odds on the claim. In fact, the law – in both Anglo-American and Continental European courts – generally does not instruct fact-finders in any great detail about how they are to go about assessing the discriminatory power of the evidence, a principle known as "free evaluation of evidence." Arguably, there are somewhat greater restrictions on the free evaluation of evidence in modern Anglo-American courts than in modern Continental European courts.[141] Some of these are of little moment, including some very general guidelines that are given to juries, such as, "You may find that a state of affairs, once proved to exist, continues as long as is usual with things of that nature, in the absence of evidence in the case leading you to a different conclusion."[142] One can readily see that such instructions are intended to do little more than remind jurors, lest they think otherwise, that they need not check their common sense at the door of the courtroom. More important are those special situations in which "presumptions" are used to specify certain inferences that a fact-finder should draw, which may be contrary to ordinary or natural inferential inclinations.[143]

Still, the collective influence of such tools is easily exaggerated, and there remains a decided preference, even in Anglo-American courts, not to provide much specific regulatory restriction or official guidance about how to go about assessing the evidence.[144] As a result, little more is needed for the decision-theoretic model to be useful prescriptively and (perhaps) descriptively than for the fact-finder to be able to create a ratio of the extent to which the (admissible) evidence, in the context of background information, favors one side of the dispute as compared with the extent that it favors the other – not a terribly difficult task, if too much precision is not required. Indeed, neither a single fact-finder nor a jury collectively need actually fix on a specific odds ratio; he or she (or they) need only be able to determine that the ratio is larger than, or smaller than, or indistinguishable from the critical value O^*.

2.2.3 *The Significance of Second-Order Uncertainty*

In both legal and nonlegal literature, one finds considerable discussion of the problem of uncertainty about probability. Probability assessments are themselves efforts to come to grips with uncertainty, so the problem

---

[141] See Damaška (1997) at 17–24.
[142] 3 O'Malley et al. (2006) § 104.23.
[143] See 2 McCormick (2013) §§ 342–8.
[144] See Twining (1985) at 66–100.

here is one of "second order" uncertainty. The issues are profound, and I cannot go beyond a brief sketch of the main ones.[145] The concerns of relevance to adjudication that are commonly expressed emphasize, alternatively, (1) the *imprecision* of a decision maker's estimate of what is taken as a specific (but unknown) probability and (2) the availability of more than one probability distribution, each precise in itself, from which the decision maker is unable to select on rational grounds. I consider these in turn.

There are surely practical limits on the degree of precision attainable in fact-finders' assessments. For some time, it has been common for scholars and judges to believe that fact-finders are incapable of very fine gradations of probabilities. In 1944, J. P. McBaine opined (without the benefit of experimental findings) that "[t]he only sound and defensible hypotheses are that the trier, or triers, of facts can find what (a) *probably* has happened, or (b) what *highly probably* has happened, or (c) what *almost certainly* has happened. No other hypotheses are defensible or can be justified by experience and knowledge."[146] In more recent years, Kevin Clermont has found support for such intuitions in the results of psychological research showing that individuals who estimate perceived quantities that exist on a scale – such as sound pitches – have limited abilities to distinguish the levels thereof.[147] According to Clermont, these cognitive limitations account for the rough but discernible convergence of legal standards of decision on various formulations associated with seven distinct "quantum step" levels of likelihood, each representing a portion of the range between certainty that a proposition is false and certainty that it is true[148]:

0--------|----------|----------|---------|------------|-------------|---------1

Slightest Possibility	Reasonable Possibility	Substantial Possibility	Equipoise	Probability (or Preponderance)	High Probability (or Clear and Convincing)	Near Certainty (or Beyond Reasonable Doubt)

---

[145] For a sophisticated treatment of these issues, not, however, focused on adjudication, see Walley (1991).

[146] See, e.g., McBaine (1944) at 246–7. For judicial attitudes on the matter, see the disagreement between the Supreme Court of Illinois and the federal Seventh Circuit Court of Appeals. United States ex rel Bilyew v. Franzen, 686 F.2d 1238, 1247–8 (7th Cir. 1982).

[147] Clermont (1987, 2013).

[148] See Clermont (2013) at 36. The illustration in the text, taken from Clermont's book, might suggest that there are precise dividing lines between the various categories, but this is clearly not Clermont's meaning: elsewhere, he argues that these levels are "fuzzy" so that no precise limits to them can be stated. See id. at 22–3, 156, 166-8.

Noting some of the many divergent judicial utterances, Clermont nevertheless argues that courts are wise not to stray from these standard seven categories of likelihood in formulating standards of proof, as well as other standards of decision that courts are called on to make.[149] Recognizing them, moreover, somewhat simplifies the task of policy makers who must make "gross" assessments of the ratio of utility differences because they need only be precise enough to allow selecting from among these seven categories.[150]

The idea that proof standards are, by virtue of such cognitive limitations, practically limited to a small set of alternative levels of likelihood is not inconsistent with the decision-theoretic model. Indeed, the underlying rationale for the various levels of proof from which policy makers can choose remains largely based on the ratio of utility differences that the decision-theoretic result identifies.[151] For Clermont problems arise to the extent that policy makers try to create more elaborate or refined proof standards than can be accommodated by the conventional seven levels of likelihood. However, we know that in many contexts (betting, for example), ordinary people are quite capable of formulating odds at a great many discrete values on a wide variety of more or less complex factual hypotheses.[152] Indeed, there is an entire industry that assists businesses in refining probability estimates as part of decision making, and there is no reason to think that fact-finders are incapable of similar refinement.[153] As Clermont frequently acknowledges, one ought not to exaggerate cognitive limitations or the clarity of the picture that social science presents regarding such limitations.[154]

The other set of concerns about the application of decision theory proceeds from the observation that decision makers may not be able to settle unequivocally on a single measure of the probability of interest. More specifically, it has been argued that not all probabilities – or, more precisely, probability distributions – are of equivalent epistemic status and that this fact is important to rational decision making.[155] This presents the possibility of probabilities about probabilities. Whether such "second-order

---

[149] See, e.g., id. at 80–1.
[150] Id. at 25–6.
[151] See, e.g., id. at 15–31, 138.
[152] See Tillers & Gottfried (2006) at 147–50 (discussing "the myth of the unquantifiability of degrees of belief"). See generally Kadane & Schum (1996) at 159–69.
[153] For example, Harry Saunders, an advocate of quantifying the standards of proof – see, e.g., Saunders (2005) – is also the founder of one such company, Decision Processes, Inc.
[154] See, e.g., Clermont (2013) at 81–2.
[155] See, e.g., Levi (1980).

probabilities" are intelligible has been the subject of considerable controversy. Some theorists, those who take probability to be meaningful only as measures of subjective degrees of belief (also called "strict Bayesians") have rejected the idea of second-order probabilities entirely.[156] Others, who recognize the applicability of the concept of probability to matters of objective phenomena ("chance" occurrences), may accept that second-order epistemological probabilities make no sense when applied to other epistemological probabilities (e.g., credal probabilities about credal probabilities) but allow for such second-order probabilities when applied to objective probabilities (e.g., credal probabilities about chance probabilities).[157] One can, that is, be uncertain about what objective probability obtains in a particular context, and one's uncertainty about *that* can be understood in terms of epistemological probability. This is a complex debate, and I will not attempt to resolve it here. Suffice it to notice that insofar as what I have called "epistemic probabilities" have a degree of objectivity not true of subjective probabilities, most participants in these debates should concede the possibility of subjective credal probabilities about epistemic probabilities. And even those who operate entirely within the framework of subjective probability – or even insist that nothing more objective exists *qua* probability – can construct decision procedures to take account of uncertainty about probability.

For example, Gärdenfors and Sahlin have argued that decision making is better characterized as a two-step process in which certain probability distributions are rejected as too implausible (though not necessarily impossible), after which the final decision is reached by a "maximin" procedure.[158] That is, rather than using a single probability (or odds) for the decision, the decision maker uses a set of plausible probabilities, computes (however intuitively) the minimum expected utility associated with each act over the set of plausible probabilities, and then selects the act that maximizes this minimum expected utility. Thus Gärdenfors and Sahlin insist on recognizing uncertainty about epistemological probabilities without imposing the calculus of probability on that second level of uncertainty.[159]

The possibilities are many and varied, but the practical effect of such subtleties on the decision-theoretic model can be illustrated by examining the maximin proposal just described, starting with the supposition that the decisionmaker believes that the target probability

[156] See, e.g., De Finetti (1972) at 189ff.
[157] See, e.g., Levi (1982).
[158] See, e.g., Gärdenfors & Sahlin (1982a).
[159] See Gärdenfors & Sahlin (1982b).

DISCRIMINATORY POWER 61

plausibly falls within a certain range, which cannot be further narrowed, but cannot be any more precise about where within that range it falls.[160] If the (second-order) distribution of the plausible probability values were reasonably well known, then expected utility could, in principle, be calculated using weighted averages of expected utility over the range of plausible values.[161] But the suggestion made by many theorists, including Gärdenfors and Sahlin, extends to situations in which no such distribution is known; indeed, nothing is known except, for example, that the probability falls within some given range. In particular, one cannot then say that it is any more likely that the probability of interest lies near the midpoint of that range than that it lies near one of the endpoints.

The maximin decision rule can be incorporated into the decision-theoretic criteria of inequalities (2.2) or (2.2′). For example, a modification of probability criterion (2.2′) involves assuming that the range of plausible probability values is an interval from $M - \Delta$ to $M + \Delta$ for some number M (the midpoint of the range) and some smallest value Δ. If the entire interval ($M - \Delta, M + \Delta$) lies above (or below) P^*, then this modification will not change the decision prescribed by criterion (2.2′); any value within the range will either satisfy (or fail) the criterion. So complexification arises only when P^* falls within the interval. In this case, under the indicated maximin strategy, the expected utility of a positive verdict is calculated using its minimizing probability $M - \Delta$, whereas the expected utility of a negative verdict is calculated using its minimizing value $M + \Delta$. The result is a criterion that specifies a verdict for the claimant if and only if

$$M > P^* + \Delta R \qquad (2.3')$$

where

$$R = \frac{\left(U_{(+)} - U_{(-)}\right) + \left(D_{(+)} - D_{(-)}\right)}{\left(U_{(-)} + D_{(+)}\right) + \left(U_{(+)} + D_{(-)}\right)}$$

Notice that this is a requirement on the midpoint of the range of plausible probabilities; if $\Delta = 0$, then $P(C|E) = M$, and criterion (2.3′) reduces to criterion (2.2′); if $\Delta \neq 0$, the adjusted critical probability – the right-hand side of the inequality – can be larger or smaller than P^* depending on the sign of the numerator of R. Under plausible assumptions, both differences in the numerator will yield positive results, so the right-hand side will be

---

[160] See, e.g., Kyburg (1983) at 153–7, 204–18.
[161] For more on what should happen in such a case, see infra § 5.1.

greater than P^*. The extent of the "correction," as compared to criterion (2.2′), is proportional to the width of the interval 2Δ and to R.[162]

The important question is whether such complexification is worth the trouble in terms of an interpretive model of practical adjudicative decision making. Its inherent risk aversion is unnecessary when a meaningful measure of the distribution of the target probability over the interval in question is available. For example, when the fact-finder conceives of the interval $(M - \Delta, M + \Delta)$ as one that places $P(C|E)$ near the middle of that interval, the fact-finder has revealed something significant. It is natural to assume that, ordinarily, if someone expresses a belief that a specific but unknown value lies in a certain range, that range has been stated so as to symmetrically bracket the person's most likely estimate of the value. And even in situations for which no information about the probability is available, except that it lies in the indicated interval, it may be possible to apply the principle of indifference, which prescribes a uniform probability distribution over the interval and yields an average value of just M.[163] Nonetheless, in unusual situations for which neither the midpoint of the interval nor any other value represents the best point assessment of the target probability, because any value within this interval is epistemically acceptable, yet no comparative epistemic weighting of values within that interval is possible, then some nonepistemic criterion of decision may be inevitable. A maximin strategy is one such criterion, but it is certainly not the only one possible.[164] Of course, no extant jury instruction or legal rule prescribes such an approach, but neither does such a rule proscribe it.

This maximin procedure is different from and more claim-favorable than a rule that would simply prescribe a decision based on $M - \Delta$ as the most conservative estimate of $P(C|E)$. (Notice that criterion (2.3′) also can be

---

[162] To illustrate the impact of these adjustments, reconsider the example used in regard to criminal cases in § 2.2.1, starting with the Blackstone ratio and adjusting for incarceration costs: assume that $U_{(+)} = 2$, $U_{(-)} = 2$, $D_{(+)} = 12$, and $D_{(-)} = 1$. Then $P^* = 0.82$. Now suppose that the fact-finder is able only to affirm that the probability is within an interval of width 0.2, that is, that $P(C|E)$ lies somewhere in the interval $(M - 0.1, M + 0.1)$ for some value M and that this interval includes P^*. Then criterion (2.3′) prescribes a verdict for the prosecution just when $M > 0.88$. Put differently, it prescribes such a verdict just when the minimum plausible probability is greater than 0.78.

[163] Whether the principle of indifference can be extended to continuous distributions is, however, a quite controversial topic. See Gillies (2000) at 37–49 and Franklin (2001).

[164] See, e.g., Troffaes (2007) (reviewing a range of methods for decision making under uncertainty using imprecise probabilities).

stated as $M - \Delta R > P^*$ and that $|R| \leq 1$, so using $M - \Delta$ as one's estimate of $P(C|E)$ and comparing that to P^* is equivalent to using the maximin procedure only when R is at its maximum value of 1; for any other value of R, the maximin test will be less demanding on the claimant because $M - \Delta < M - \Delta R$.) The latter approach, which relies on what is often described in the literature as "lower probabilities,"[165] might seem appropriate in that the fact-finder would have confidence that $P(C|E)$ is at least as high as $M - \Delta$. The problem with such a procedure in the adjudicative context is that using $M - \Delta$ as one's estimate of $P(C|E)$ is functionally equivalent to using $1 - (M - \Delta)$ as one's estimate of $P(\text{not-}C|E)$, but the corresponding estimate of the latter probability is obtained by using instead $1 - (M + \Delta)$, the complement of the least upper bound on the value of $P(C|E)$, because the fact-finder in this situation can only say that $P(\text{not-}C|E)$ is at least as large as the complement of $M + \Delta$, that is, $1 - (M + \Delta)$. These two estimates of $P(\text{not-}C|E)$ are not the same: the former estimate is larger than the latter by the width of the interval 2Δ. In other words, one cannot use this method to make *equally* conservative estimates of both $P(C|E)$ and $P(\text{not-}C|E)$ unless one has a distinct decision rule for all those cases in which $P(C|E)$ falls within the interval $(M - \Delta, M + \Delta)$. This, however, would be a plausible place to apply the "equipoise" default rule against the party bearing the burden of persuasion, here the claimant, because in this context (given the precise assumptions), the fact-finder is simply unable to determine whether or not $P(C|E)$ exceeds P^*.

2.3 Competing Theories of Discriminatory Power

The foregoing is enough elaboration of the decision-theoretic model for our purposes. It provides important insights and stimulates important questions about the processes of setting and determining the satisfaction of the burden of persuasion. It leaves open numerous questions, both theoretical and practical. Among scholars who have challenged the decision-theoretic framework, some have chafed at the mathematical formalism of criterion (2.2). Others, not eschewing formal theory as such, have asserted that it is not the *right* formalism. As the saying goes, though, it takes a theory to beat a theory. So it is worthwhile to address at this point two prominent counterproposals of recent years illustrating these reactions. I consider first an illustration of a suggested alternative formal theory.

---

[165] See Shafer (1981) at 8–12, 18–20.

2.3.1 The Standard of Proof and the Regulation of Substantive Conduct

One alternative theory, associated with law and economics, takes the standard of proof as just one tool among many with which to regulate the substantive conduct of potential litigants. Other tools, such as the severity of the potential sanction imposed and the level of investigative oversight (e.g., by police or administrative agencies), clearly can be adjusted to try to generate optimal deterrence of illegal (out-of-court) conduct. These should be supplemented, according this view, by an attention to the *ex ante* incentives that potential litigants face on account of the standard of proof that is set. Prominent among such theories is the work of Louis Kaplow, on which I will focus here.[166] His theory is avowedly prescriptive: he criticizes conventional understandings of the standard of proof – which he characterizes as requirements that $P(C|E)$ exceed some threshold value – as insufficiently focused on social welfare maximization.

Kaplow distinguishes between decision making that is concerned only with the good and bad effects associated with uncertain outcomes, such as decisions about medical treatments, and decision making that is concerned to assist in the regulation of *ex ante* conduct. According to Kaplow, legal adjudication has been categorized by most conventional thinkers as a kind of decision making the optimality of which is determined with little or no direct regard for the effect of the decision on the behavior that gives rise to the necessity of making a decision. To Kaplow, this is a mistake: the proper framework for setting the standard of proof is, instead, the regulation of *ex ante* incentives for conduct. These incentives are a function of how likely it is that someone who acts, whether illegally or legally (Kaplow prefers the terms *harmful* and *benign*), will be subject to sanction.

It would unduly extend the present treatment to try to summarize the components of Kaplow's theory, except to note that he works out the implications, under his stated assumptions, of a contemplated increase or decrease in the standard of proof on the behavior of those who act, whether harmfully or not, in contemplation of the possibility of being subjected to a sanction. His conclusion is that, in terms of the calculus for determining the optimal standard of proof, the factors are many, their magnitudes undoubtedly vary greatly across contexts, and ascertaining the pertinent quantities is likely to be difficult. Nevertheless, he thinks this framework would at least put us on the right path.

---

[166] See Kaplow (2011, 2012, 2014).

As compared with the decision-theoretic account given earlier, Kaplow's theory depends much more specifically and immediately on behavioral reactions of those who act out of court in anticipation of the possibility of adjudication, and accordingly, it involves various assumptions about what motivates and informs such actions.[167] In very general terms, Kaplow assumes the out-of-court actors to be both very narrowly and rationally self-interested and remarkably astute at perceiving what is going on in the world of adjudication. I will take up each in turn and then come back to some deeper problems in his theory.

First, unlike the decision-theoretic analysis presented earlier, Kaplow's theory is based on dubious assumptions about what motivates conduct outside the courtroom. Most significantly, Kaplow's analysis, like much of law and economics, is based on the assumption that people are motivated only by the material costs and benefits of their actions:

> In the absence of legal restraint, it is assumed that individuals will act whenever their private benefit from doing so is positive. With a legal system, they are assumed to act if and only if their private benefit exceeds the expected sanction.[168]

In other words, the law's declaration that "one must not do X" provides no motivation to the actor not to do X, except insofar as the actor can anticipate material sanctions such that the expected sanction exceeds the expected gain from acting, with expected sanctions being the product of the size of the sanction and the probability that the actor will be detected (brought before the tribunal) and a sanctioned will be imposed

---

[167] Kaplow presents an exaggerated contrast between the conventional theory of an odds-threshold (or probability-threshold) decision criterion and the *ex ante* behavior regulation model that he advances. Specifically, what Kaplow calls the conventional approach involves a threshold that is taken as given but *not* as derived from or justified in terms of the decision theory summarized by criterion (2.2). This could make sense if courts and other policy makers favor such threshold standards without endorsing anything essentially like the decision-theoretic analysis. Still, ignoring the well-discussed decision-theoretic justification for odds-threshold standards allows Kaplow to conclude that the conventional view is radically disconnected from considerations of social welfare because the factors reflecting social welfare do not appear *in the decision rule*, rules such as "find for the claimant if $O(C|E) > 1$." See Kaplow (2012) at 772–805. Obviously, this rule does not *advert* to costs or benefits and can be applied by the fact-finder without considering them. Indeed, this is one of its perceived advantages. However, if one takes the threshold as something determined by a public assessment of the utilities expressed in criterion (2.2), then such a conventional rule *does* reflect a calculus of social welfare; it is built into the selection of the threshold value of O^*, even if the calculation involved is not itself communicated to or performed by the fact-finder. It is just not the *same* calculus that Kaplow recommends.
[168] Id. at 752–3.

(a verdict given against the actor). The indicated assumption is the so-called Holmesian "bad man" assumption.[169] It ignores the sage advice that H. L. A. Hart provided half a century ago:

> At any given moment the life of any society which lives by rules, legal or not, is likely to consist in a tension between those who, on the one hand, accept and voluntarily co-operate in maintaining the rules, and so see their own and other persons' behavior in terms of the rules, and those who, on the other hand, reject the rules and attend to them only from the external point of view as a sign of possible punishment. One of the difficulties facing any legal theory anxious to do justice to the complexity of the facts is to remember the presence of both points of view and not to define one of them out of existence.[170]

Undoubtedly, many people operate more toward the polar opposite extreme, what we may call the Hartian "good man," whose actions are guided by social norms the necessity for which arises from the need for authoritative settlement of legitimate differences of opinion about wise policy, about how moral principles apply to concrete situations, and about the resolution of matters as to which a convention is required for successful social life.[171] And this is not to mention the segment of actors who do not make anything resembling a *rational* choice, whether it be of the Holmesian bad man or the Hartian good man type.

This point has significant implications for Kaplow's brand of law and economics.[172] Suppose that we make the contrary assumption that all individuals (or even just those "at the margin" whose conduct might conceivably be affected by a choice of proof standards) are such Hartian good men. In this case, neither the probability of detection nor the probability that a sanction will be imposed will matter, and the effect of setting the standard

---

[169] The reference is to Holmes's famously cynical dictum:

> If you want to know the law and nothing else, you must look at it as a bad man, who cares only for the material consequences which such knowledge enables him to predict, not as a good one, who finds his reasons for conduct, whether inside the law or outside of it, in the vaguer sanctions of conscience.... The prophecies of what the court will do in fact, and nothing more pretentious, are what I mean by the law.

Holmes (1897) at 459, 461.

[170] Hart (1961) at 88.

[171] For a discussion of the centrality of authoritative settlement in the reason for law, as distinct from the control of Holmesian bad men, see Alexander & Sherwin (2001).

[172] Kaplow acknowledges the potential problem of his Holmesian assumption, but he suggests by his passing mention of it that one can relax the assumption "without greatly affecting the analysis." Kaplow (2012) at 753 n. 23. In this, I think, he is mistaken.

on *ex ante* behavior is nil. Of course, neither Kaplow's assumption nor the one just described is realistic, but an argument can be made, based on the nature and functions of law, that a more useful theoretical starting assumption is that all persons are Hartian good men, especially when the theory has a strong normative element, as does Kaplow's.[173] One can relax this assumption for analytical purposes – but this must be done guardedly if the analysis is to serve practical purposes well. After all, aspirations and expectations can change behavior.[174] Legal practices that are based on the optimistic assumption that most people live their lives somewhere toward the Hartian good man end of the behavioral spectrum can help to create a community in which that is the dominant attitude, whereas legal practices based on the opposite, more pessimistic assumption can reinforce and encourage the Holmesian bad man approach among the citizenry. And encouraging people to take the bad man approach to law, decreasing the degree to which people internalize the law's requirements, has seriously negative social welfare implications in the long run. Among other reasons, this is so because law is effective in regulating behavior not so much by virtue of its threats of sanction, but more so by the voluntary cooperation of citizens who take law's substantive norms as authoritative.[175]

It may be possible for Kaplow to complicate his model to account for this issue, but it is not as simple as saying that one need not worry, for purposes of the analysis, about the Hartian good men: some of them will appear as litigants, and they may or may not be individuals against whom a claim is true. Moreover, "bad" and "good" are obviously extremes on a spectrum, with real people falling somewhere in between in terms of their attitudes toward law. The essential point is that the existence in some people to whatever degree of the attitude represented by the Hartian good man dilutes the significance of expected sanctions for those individuals' *ex ante* behavior. If, in fact, at a particular point in time a sufficient proportion of those "at the margin" are far enough toward the Hartian good man end of the spectrum, then the relative importance, from a welfarist perspective, of the effects of proof standards on the often (but not exclusively) *ex post* consequences of decision, as discussed earlier (§ 2.2.1), will dominate that associated with their direct effects on *ex ante* behavior.

---

[173] For a thorough discussion of this point in the context of general legal theory, see Nance (1997).

[174] There is a well-known tendency for people to live up (or down) to the expectations of those in authority. See, e.g., Rosenthal & Jacobson (1968); Livingston (1969); and Miller et al. (1975).

[175] For general discussion, see Nance (2006b).

This possibility is magnified by the problem of informational demands. Kaplow is certainly aware of the complex demands that his theory would place on officials, but he defends the proposition that comparably difficult informational demands exist for the legal system that seeks to identify an optimal threshold odds criterion of decision.[176] Even if this claim were plausible – it is not[177] – there is a difference that Kaplow does not seem to appreciate. His theory also explicitly assumes that adjustments of the standard of proof, indeed, rather marginal ones, can be recognized and acted on by those subject to its norms, the law's audience as it were. The mechanism for this communication between those who set proof standards and potential actors is anything but obvious, and Kaplow provides nothing to support his assumption. Rather, he makes the implicit (apparently simplifying) assumption that the *aggregate percentage* of identified harmful-conduct actors who are sanctioned under the chosen standard of proof is the same as the *ex ante probability*, from the actor's point of view, that such conduct, once detected, will be sanctioned.[178] (An analogous assumption is in play for the actor contemplating benign conduct.) This would be true, for example, if (1) an actor contemplating harmful conduct is so devoid of prescience that he could not in any way anticipate how strong the evidence created by his act would be so that he might have no alternative but to assume that he will be randomly distributed, in terms of the strength of the evidence against him, among the class of individuals whose harmful conduct is detected, and (2) the actor is, at the same time, so perspicacious as to be able to discern fairly accurately the aggregate percentage of that class of individuals that is subject to sanction. But these are quite counterintuitive, even incompatible assumptions.

Perhaps this particular technical problem is fixable; it certainly depends on empirical assumptions that potentially fall within the general framework of Kaplow's theory. In the end, however, if behavioral adjustments are close to being randomly related to policy makers' marginal adjustments in proof standards, then decisions about the latter might as well be made without regard to the effects on *ex ante* behavior. Indeed, the more plausible assumption, given what we know about the behavior of would-be criminals, at least, is that Holmesian bad men ignore the probability of being subject to sanction if identified, assuming that this is more or less a constant, but a largely *unknown* constant, so that what is more pertinent

---

[176] See, e.g., Kaplow (2012) at 786–9.
[177] It is well criticized in Allen & Stein (2013) at 580–4.
[178] Kaplow (2012) at 757–8, 763.

for them is to focus on the probability of being detected, which, after all, is their more immediate concern.[179]

The complex implications of the behavioral realities of a populace that does not consist entirely of Holmesian bad men and the limits of potential actors' ability to register officials' adjustments in the standard of proof, or the effects thereof, on the percentage of similarly situated actors who are sanctioned together suggest that even fairly significant adjustments of the standard of proof might have little impact on *ex ante* behavior. But there is a more fundamental problem. Kaplow's theory incorrectly assumes, as a normative matter, that adjudication ought to be *directly* concerned with such *ex ante* incentives: it is not, or at least it need not be and it ought not be. Kaplow mentions in passing that "rights based" or other "nonwelfarist" theories might view *ex ante* effects on behavior as irrelevant, but he does not develop the idea.[180]

It might seem that the argument presented earlier (§ 2.1) – that adjudication instantiates practical reasoning, with attention paid to the expected costs and benefits of decision – would commit one to a thoroughgoing utilitarian consequentialism in this regard. Not so. The law surely does care about *ex ante* incentives. Its concerns in this regard are quite defensibly manifested by the announcement of a substantive rule, such as a rule stating that "one must not do X." This official announcement is largely effective (mistake and misfortune aside) for regulating the conduct of the Hartian good man. Additional *ex ante* incentives for compliance with substantive norms, speaking to the inevitable presence of persons with at least some element of the Holmesian bad man, are properly provided by rules designating sanctions for the violation of substantive norms, as well as by other governmental actions, such as the selection of a level of oversight by police and administrative agencies, and these levels are properly adjusted with such incentives in mind.[181] When, however, the question is whether a particular individual has committed an act that warrants a sanction under the announced rule, the law's concern shifts to that individual. Why? Because the law's commitment to those it governs is to impose the sanction under

---

[179] There is, of course, an enormous literature about deterrence in criminology, most of which points to the conclusion that the risk of detection matters more to those contemplating criminal acts than the expected punishment if detected. See Nagin (2013). It is doubtful that Kaplow's behavioral assumptions come close to reality except perhaps in the context of sophisticated repeat players in litigation acting with the advice of lawyers who are themselves imbued with the Holmesian philosophy. See Cheng & Pardo (2015) at 200.

[180] Kaplow (2012) at 762 n. 42.

[181] See Nance (1997).

the terms that the substantive law, *ex ante*, has specified.[182] This presupposes that the court can be sufficiently confident that the claim on which the sanction is premised is true.

Kaplow's theory would eliminate this last step in most or all adjudication and use the desired deterrent effect to set directly the level of evidence strength that is required for liability.[183] However, as Kaplow clearly understands and indeed emphasizes, the strength of the evidence is *not* the same as the posterior probability that the claim is true.[184] By (admittedly) divorcing the setting of the standard of proof from consideration of the likelihood that the claim is true, Kaplow's framework takes the focus off the individual litigant. Indeed, one admitted implication of his analysis is that "the optimal evidence threshold could be associated with any *ex post* probability whatsoever."[185] If courts were to follow his model, one could not even have confidence that the probability that liability will be imposed (considered over a set of defendants) is an increasing function of the probability that the claim is true. In particular, Kaplow's model would permit impositions of liability in disregard of an important limitation on standards of proof mentioned earlier: the required minimum proof standard cannot be set less than a (posterior) probability of 0.5, especially for any cause of action premised on the fault of the defendant.[186]

To use a Kantian idiom, focusing proof standards on *ex ante* effects uses the litigant merely as means to the end of controlling the behavior of others. This is quite different from simply acknowledging that social welfare is an unavoidably relevant consideration when, though the claim is probably true, there is still some doubt about the matter, which doubt presents a train of potential *ex post* consequences that must be taken into consideration. Kaplow's normative framework commits him to the familiar utilitarian *reductio ad absurdum*, the idea that even if the tribunal were to know with certainty (or near certainty, anyway) that the defendant did *not*

---

[182] See, e.g., Byrd (1989) (explaining Kant's theory as based on deterrent threats backed by retributivist sanctions). While it is common ground that criminal punishment and punitive damages in tort are used to deter wrongdoing, even here the imposition of the sanction is premised on an appropriate finding of fact; only after that finding has been made may the court consider the level of punishment (e.g., the amount of a punitive damage award) that will achieve the desired deterrent effect.

[183] See Kaplow (2014) at 20–6.

[184] For Kaplow, evidence strength is (appropriately enough) measured by its "likelihood ratio." See id. On the difference between the likelihood ratio and the posterior odds, see infra §§ 2.4 & 2.5.

[185] Kaplow (2012) at 784.

[186] See the discussion at the beginning of § 2.2.1.

commit the act claimed, it still would be appropriate to impose a sanction on him provided that doing so would create optimal incentives for other, out-of-court actors.[187] In particular, if a court were to set a low standard of proof for a claim against a Hartian good man who has the misfortune to end up in litigation in order to create what it takes to be appropriate incentives for Holmesian bad men who are not before the court, then the court is using a person committed to obedience to the rule of law as a tool to create appropriate incentives among (mostly) those who lack that commitment. Such an approach takes welfare maximization beyond appropriate deontological limits.

Indeed, Kaplow's approach would necessitate some rethinking of the rule of law itself. In order to harmonize Kaplow's suggested approach with the law's public pronouncements, we would be required to change substantive remedial laws that now present in the form "If you do X, you will be subject to sanction S." In Kaplow's world, these laws would now have to be announced in something like the following terms: "If it is useful to deter people from doing X, you will be subject to sanction S." Similarly, a more procedurally focused law now stated in the form, "If, based on the evidence in your case, you are found to have done X, you will be subject to sanction S," would become, "If the evidence in your case is strong enough that imposing sanction S on you would be useful in deterring people from doing X, then you will be subject to sanction S."[188] Or, instead

---

[187] See Cheng & Pardo (2015) at 197 (illustrating that Kaplow's analysis could recommend conviction of someone accused of brutal rape and murder based on a very low threshold of proof). Kaplow defends such results by arguing that the same kind of thing can obtain under a rule informed entirely by something like criterion (2.2), as in medical treatment decisions; if adjudication is guided by such a calculus, the utilities and disutilities might be such that a sanction should be imposed based on a very low value of $O(C|E)$. See Kaplow (2012) at 785. The constraints discussed earlier, however, prevent such results, and it is obvious that no such constraints operate in the medical treatment context. Merely deciding to give a medical treatment does not impose the stigma of publicly declaring the patient to have violated a serious social norm, nor is it limited by an *ex ante* commitment that treatment will be given only under stated factual conditions.

[188] Cf. Kaplow (2012) at 809–14 (discussing potential changes to jury instructions that would implement his theory by telling jurors, in a breach of contract case, simply "to come to a reasonable conclusion in light of the risks, on the one hand, that failing to find a breach of contract due to an overly stringent demand for proof might encourage opportunism and discourage contracting and, on the other hand, that finding breach based on flimsy evidence might itself chill contracting and induce excessive caution in contractual performance.") In this light, it is unsurprising that Kaplow uses terms such as *harmful* instead of *illegal* and *benign* instead of *legal*; his proposal actually involves revising the substantive law to conform it to a single principle: using the decisions of courts to *directly*

of reformulating the announced rules in such ways, would Kaplow simply sacrifice the rule-of-law principle and allow a discernible gap between the law as announced and the law as enforced to preserve whatever useful incentive effects and public acceptance follow from the public perception that a citizen is subject to the rules as conventionally announced?

In the end, it is rather misleading for Kaplow to say that "[c]onventional notions that focus on the likelihood that the individual before the tribunal has committed a harmful act turn out to be almost entirely unrelated to welfare-based analysis."[189] One can consistently be committed to the idea that various measures address the *ex ante* incentives of both Hartian good men and Holmesian bad men (and people in between) in the interests of welfare maximization, as well as the idea that the standard of proof in adjudication should be determined, subject to deontological constraints, by the costs and benefits of projected outcomes, all without endorsing the idea that the standard of proof is *immediately* directed toward the creation of desirable *ex ante* incentives for conduct. Kaplow observes that if there are *ex ante* effects in setting the standard of proof, then ignoring those effects can have perverse consequences.[190] This would be true provided that changes in the standard of proof discernibly affect *ex ante* behavior *and* that all else is equal in terms of efforts to control incentives. But ignoring tenuous *ex ante* effects related to the standard of proof does not, of course, entail surrendering the use of other tools (which Kaplow explores) for the social control of Holmesian bad men, including adjustments of the level of sanctions and monitoring efforts, and indeed, these may well be the more efficient means of such control. To be sure, foreclosing the use of any available tool for utility maximization, even under fairly limited circumstances, can (potentially) entail a less "efficient" effectuation of optimal deterrence than would otherwise be possible, but such are the costs of honoring public commitments and respecting individual rights.

All this said, I emphasize that one need not accept the arguments articulated here to appreciate what is to come in later chapters. Even if one accepts Kaplow's theory, or other similar theory that would focus on the effects of the standard of proof on *ex ante* behavior, it is important to emphasize that it is still a threshold theory of decision based on the evidence before the court. Kaplow makes no use of the idea of Keynesian weight, yet changes in

---

affect incentives so as to maximize social welfare. Lawmaking institutions (legislatures as well as courts), as distinct from sanction-imposing institutions, essentially disappear. And with them, the source of guidance for the Hartian good man disappears as well.

[189] Id. at 751.
[190] Id. at 789–96.

Keynesian weight can affect the efficiency of the system by way of its impact on the probative value of the evidence. As we will see, at the margin, augmentations of Keynesian weight offer potential enhancements to expected gains in social utility, which can only arise by way of effects on net probative value. So a theory that can improve practices regarding Keynesian weight also can enhance the effectiveness of theories, such as Kaplow's, that are directed primarily toward regulating *ex ante* behavior.[191]

2.3.2 Relative Plausibility and the Best Explanation

The second counterproposal to be discussed reflects much greater distrust of mathematical formalisms. In a series of articles, Ron Allen has argued that the proper way to construct the burden of persuasion in civil cases is to see it in terms of a comparison between the plausibility of the plaintiff's theory of the case (the specific factual story plaintiff presents to the fact-finder) and the plausibility of the defendant's theory of the case.[192] This is also well within the concept of discriminatory power as I have defined it, although it is not formalized as in criterion (2.2). While Professor Allen tends to regard his theory as descriptive, especially in its later versions, its plausibility in this regard depends to some extent on how viable the theory is prescriptively. As will be seen, Allen offers arguments that his theory is more sensible for practical use than alternatives. For this reason, I consider his theory interpretive.

According to Professor Allen, the relevant comparison is not (and ought not to be) that which is captured by the odds that the facts are so as to instantiate the elements of the plaintiff's claim. This comparison is unworkable, according to Allen, because it entails the assessment of numerous possible factual scenarios that, if true, would warrant plaintiff's recovery but that the plaintiff has not specifically asserted, as well as the assessment of numerous possible factual scenarios that, if true, would warrant a verdict for the defendant but that the defendant has not asserted. For example, the plaintiff might attempt to prove that the defendant was negligent in entering an intersection because the traffic light the defendant faced was red, whereas the defense might assert that the light was green. What, then, of the possibility that the light was yellow? Or of

---

[191] Kaplow cites, but does not incorporate into his theory, some work in the law-and-economics vein that addresses incentives to present evidence. Id. at 742 n. 5. As we shall see, this is where Keynesian weight enters the picture.
[192] See, e.g., Allen (1986) at 426–8; Allen (1991) at 406–13; and Allen & Leiter (2001) at 1527–37.

the possibility that the light was green, but the defendant was negligently speeding anyway? Or the possibility that the light was not functioning properly? Dealing with these unasserted possibilities – even if there is reason in the evidence to think one or more of them obtains – is thought to place too great a cognitive burden on the fact-finder, a burden that can be avoided if fact-finders need only compare the plausibility of the stories actually advanced by the parties (i.e., "red light" or "green light"). And this was Allen's original proposal: each of these stories would be checked by the judge against the substantive law (much as formal pleadings are checked) to determine whether it would, if true, require a verdict for the party offering it. This would avoid the necessity of giving often complex jury instructions on the substantive law because the jury would then properly limit its attention to the comparative evaluation of the plausibility of the parties' factual theories of the case without regard to factual theories not argued by either party or their implications under the applicable substantive law.[193]

To be sure, for Allen, perhaps the principal and motivating advantage of this "relative plausibility" theory has been the avoidance of certain paradoxical results supposedly associated with the probabilistic interpretation inherent in criterion (2.2). Addressing this point requires a brief digression, but it is worthwhile because it considers a recurring issue related to the applicability of probabilities to the interpretation of standards of proof.

The most important argument here concerns the fact that what has been called the claim C in most cases is actually a conjunction of elements constituting the cause of action, such as (A) breach of duty and (B) causation of harm. Denote this $C = A \& B$. (Usually, there will be more than two elements, but the example suffices to illustrate the issue.) The so-called conjunction problem arises out of the question whether the standard of proof applies to the conjunction of the elements $A \& B$ or only to the elements taken serially. For example, the fact-finder might conclude that $P(A|E) > P^*$ and that $P(B|E) > P^*$ and yet that $P(C|E) = P(A \& B|E) < P^*$.[194] In such a

---

[193] See Allen (1986) at 423–34.

[194] Such a set of conclusions does not violate the rules of mathematical probability because, necessarily, $P(A\&B|E) = P(A|E) \times P(B|A\&E)$. For example, if $P^* = 0.5$, one could have $P(A|E) = 0.6, P(B|E) = 0.6$, and $P(B|A\&E) = 0.8$, and then $P(C|E) = P(A|E) \times P(B|A\&E) = (0.6)(0.8) = 0.48$. The problem is obviously more pressing if the elements are stochastically independent so that $P(B|A\&E) = P(B|E)$ because then $P(C|E) = P(A|E) \times P(B|E)$, which in the example gives $P(C|E) = 0.36$. Legal elements rarely present such independence; for example, the probability that the defendant's act caused the plaintiff's harm is not going to be independent of the proposition that the defendant's act was negligent or even the proposition that the defendant intended the harm to plaintiff.

case, is the standard of proof satisfied for the case because it is satisfied as to each element, or does satisfaction of the standard for the case as a whole require additionally that $P(A\&B|E) > P^*$? It is believed by some, including Allen, that extant law has a determinate answer for what is to be done in such a case, namely, that the claimant should win when each element is established by the necessary margin, regardless of what is true about the conjunction. Yet minimizing expected losses would seem to require the result to turn on the probability of the conjunction of elements, that is, the probability that *all* elements of the claim are instantiated. The relative plausibility theory avoids this difficulty because it does not talk in terms of the probability that elements (or their conjunction) are instantiated.[195]

It is doubtful, however, that the law actually has a determinate answer to the hypothetical posed. That is, it is highly unlikely that the expressions of doctrine that often *seem* to say that there is such an answer were formulated with such a conjunction problem in mind, and so it is premature to say that the law faces a paradox. Illustrative is the kind of model jury instruction on which Allen has long relied:

> The burden is on the plaintiff in a civil action, such as this, to prove every essential element of his claim by a preponderance of the evidence. If the proof should fail to establish any essential element of plaintiff's claim by a preponderance of the evidence in the case, the jury should find for the defendant.[196]

Because of ambiguity, the first sentence of this instruction, and many others like it that can be identified, does not unequivocally require that jurors focus only on the elements and not their conjunction. "Every" could connote "each individually," or it could connote "all," or it could connote both. True, the second sentence clearly *does* focus only on individual elements, but what are we to make of that? It is unlikely that the second sentence is simply another way of saying what is said in the first sentence; indeed, that would make the second sentence superfluous. In addition, the second sentence states only *necessary* conditions for a plaintiff to recover; it

---

[195] Most discussions of the conjunction problem, and the presentation in the text, assume that the law's proof standards are not intentionally different for the various elements under consideration. It would be entirely coherent, for example, to have a higher standard for the proof of breach of duty than for the proof of causation. See, e.g., Tuttle v. Raymond, 494 A.2d 1353 (Me. 1985) (announcing a higher standard of proof when punitive damages are claimed, but only for proof of the element that requires a showing of "malice"). For example, one might require clear and convincing evidence of breach of duty but only a proof by a preponderance of the evidence that such breach caused the injury in question.

[196] 2 Devitt & Blackmar (1977) § 71.14.

does not tell the jury what is *sufficient* for such a recovery. Plausibly, the function of the second sentence is to remind jurors that failure to establish any single element by a preponderance of the evidence will be fatal to the plaintiff's claim – a proposition that is consistent with, would give practical guidance regarding, and thus would be an understandable instruction in the context of a rule based on the conjunction of the elements.[197] Continuing the example in the text, if $P^* = 0.5$ and $P(A|E) \leq 0.5$, then necessarily $P(C|E) = P(A|E) \times P(B|A\&E) \leq 0.5$, and the plaintiff should lose. Indeed, this is true regardless of the value of $P(B|A\&E)$, so a determination that $P(A|E) \leq 0.5$ relieves the fact-finder of the need to assess the value of $P(B|A\&E)$. (To illustrate, if a jury finds that it is more likely than not that the defendant was *not* negligent in her driving, then the jury need not expend any further effort to determine whether, assuming that the driver was negligent, that negligence was the proximate cause of the plaintiff's injuries or whether, for example, those injuries were a preexisting condition.) An analogous simplification holds if the fact-finder determines that $P(B|E) \leq 0.5$.

To be sure, some model instructions, on their face, do specify only a serial consideration of the elements.[198] Yet other instructions, on their face, require a consideration of the probability that the conjunction of elements is instantiated.[199] Most instructions, however, miss the issue entirely by speaking only in terms of necessary conditions for a plaintiff victory (e.g., "In order to be entitled to a verdict, the plaintiff must prove ... [each element]") rather than a sufficient condition (e.g., "The plaintiff is entitled to a verdict if the plaintiff proves...").[200] The drafters of

---

[197] See Nance (1986).
[198] 3A Devitt et al. (1987) § 83.02 at 262 (providing a pattern instruction that lists the specific elements for an action for deceit and concludes, "If you find that the plaintiff has established each of these elements by the preponderance of the evidence, then you should return a verdict for the plaintiff.")
[199] See, e.g., Colo. Supreme Ct. Comm'n on Civil Jury Instructions, Colorado Jury Instructions § 9.1 (4th ed. 1999) (requiring proof, by the specified standard, of "all" – not merely "each of" – the elements of a negligence cause of action).
[200] In a later article, Allen and a co-author cite a number of such instructions and insist that they paint a clear picture in favor of the serial consideration of elements and against any consideration of the conjunction. See Allen & Jehl (2003) at 897–904. Indeed, they claim that "we did not come across a single instruction that plausibly could be interpreted to require the finding of the conjunction of the elements rather than each element serially." Id. at 902. Remarkably, one only need look several pages later in their article to find exactly such an instruction. See id. at 927 (quoting Mississippi's medical malpractice instruction, which instructs a verdict for the plaintiff if it is shown by a preponderance of the evidence that "[element 1], and [element 2], and [element 3], and [element 4], and [element 5].")

such instructions seem to be simply unaware of the difference; otherwise, they would realize that they have omitted a crucial part of what the jurors need to know. All this suggests a critical explanatory point: whether the instruction, on its face, calls for a consideration of the conjunction or not, neither norm is likely to have been fully thought through by the drafters. No doubt many people would simply assume that if each element is proved by a preponderance of the evidence, then the conjunction of the elements is so proved. And, indeed, this will be true (albeit contingently) for many cases.[201]

For the same reason, even if the drafters would say – were they to be asked in retrospect – that their intention was to require merely a serial assessment of individual elements, indifferent to an assessment of the conjunction of the elements, this would not mean that the drafters had in mind the kind of problem such an interpretation might present in an appropriate case, like that hypothesized earlier. Typical cases would not place that possibility conspicuously before the legislative mind, and typical cases are the cases with respect to which general instructions are drafted. In the end, when we look at jury instructions related to this issue, we are likely to be seeing a want of logical or probabilistic sophistication or simply of imagination. And when one turns to consider the juror who tries to apply such instructions, a similar naïveté can be expected. In a well-argued case, though, a juror who does recognize the conjunction problem in play likely would feel free, in the face of a great many such jury instructions, to decide based on whether the conjunction is instantiated by the preponderance of the evidence.

Nevertheless, Allen may be correct about the rule that courts would deliberately apply, were they squarely faced with the conjunction problem and fully understood the nature of the issue. If so, then his reform proposal would resolve the problem. However, in that case, so would a proposal that the rule be changed to make the result turn explicitly on the probability of the conjunction of the elements.[202] Consequently, the advantage of Allen's

---

What is more, after stating this *sufficient* condition for a plaintiff verdict, the Mississippi instruction complements the message, exactly as suggested in the text, by stating useful *necessary* conditions for a plaintiff verdict: "However, if you believe the plaintiff has failed to show any one of the above elements by a preponderance of the evidence, then your verdict shall be for the defendant." Id. at 928.

[201] See Allen & Jehl (2003) at 902 n. 36 (commenting on the fact that New Hampshire courts have no preference between, and thus seem unable to tell the difference between, an instruction worded in terms of proving "all" the elements and one worded in terms of proving "each" of the elements).

[202] See Nance (2001) at 1563–75. This point Allen concedes. See Allen (1994) at 607. He argues that such a conjunction-focused rule would, however, generate the paradoxical

"fix" does not consist in its fidelity to extant doctrine, nor in its unique capacity to resolve the conjunction paradox. It must lie instead in its simplification of the task that we ask the fact-finder to perform (or else some unestablished – and indeed unclaimed – improvement in the effectuation of justice).[203] This ends our digression and returns us to the main thread of the discussion.

As originally presented, the effect of Allen's relative plausibility theory, which entails significant modification of extant procedures, is to require the fact-finder to ignore all factual possibilities for which neither party has vouched in their theories of the case (e.g., "yellow light" or "light not working"). None of these possibilities will have been checked against the substantive law by the judge, and the fact-finder has no role in doing so. To be sure, Allen has consistently allowed for the possibility of a party's advancing alternative specific theories of the case, such as, "The light was either yellow or green." But unless an alternative story is advanced by a party (and presumably checked for adequacy against the substantive law by the judge), the fact-finder would not be allowed to take that story into account in its decision.[204] This would very likely simplify the fact-finder's task. It would also, however, present a very serious difficulty: in real cases, fact-finders often – perhaps very often – settle on some compromise version of the facts that is not exactly what either party asserts. And rightly so.[205] The relative plausibility theory, at least in its original form, provides

---

consequence that the burden on the complainant would depend fortuitously on the number of elements into which the cause of action is divided. Id. Without unduly extending this discussion, suffice it to say that this particular red herring has been chased down carefully by Richard Friedman. See Friedman (1997a) at 283.

[203] Laudably, Allen and Leiter place considerable emphasis on the idea that adjudicative procedures should not be designed to require more of human decision makers than they are capable of doing. See Allen & Leiter (2001) at 1499. However, no one can deny that fact-finding is a very difficult and complex enterprise, so merely noting the inferential difficulties associated with a particular theory cannot be enough to refute the theory.

[204] In 1991, Allen was noncommittal on the question of whether the jury should continue to be instructed on the elements of the substantive law, noting that although the practice might be unnecessary and confusing, it would at least have the virtue (to the extent that it is a virtue) that it would allow juries to override the judge's determinations on the application of the law to specified facts. Allen (1991) at 410 n. 118. Also, Allen had come to accept, but still attributed little significance to, the fact that it may be necessary to allow jurors to pick an explanation or story for which neither party has argued. Id.; see also Allen (1994) at 609 n. 21.

[205] See, e.g., Klonoff & Colby (1990) (presenting a book-length treatment of the implications of the proposition that the jury will believe the truth is *no more* favorable, and usually *less* favorable, to a party than what that party asserts).

no acceptable answer as to what is to be done in such cases. It even leads to the most unpalatable conclusion that the fact-finder would be required to ignore what it takes to be the *most* plausible account of what happened when that particular account is not advanced by a party.[206]

In a later article, Allen, joined by Michael Pardo, presents a substantially revised version of the original argument.[207] Drawing on the literature regarding "inference to the best explanation," Pardo and Allen concede that in analyzing a civil case, fact-finders may need to consider (potentially innumerable) versions of the events other than those the parties have specifically advanced; indeed, they will (and presumably should) find and settle on the *most* plausible explanation of the evidence (whether advanced by a party or not), and they must assess what they take to be the most plausible explanation against the substantive elements of the claim – none of which made sense under the earlier version of the theory.[208] This moves the theory decidedly closer to the decision-theoretic model in some respects. Specifically, the decision maker is no longer tied to evaluating only the specific stories endorsed by the parties. However, relative (i.e., comparative) plausibility, as between plaintiff's and defendant's stories, is no longer the key, and in this respect their new theory is a move away from both the decision-theoretic model and the conventional, comparative understanding of discriminatory power. What remains that is most distinctive about their theory is their interpretation (or proposed revision) of the standards of proof themselves. For example, the "preponderance of the evidence" standard would be interpreted (or revised) to require that fact-finders decide the case based *only* on what they take to be the *most plausible* story, regardless of the probabilities associated with less plausible explanations, including (perhaps) those offered by the parties.[209]

---

[206] See Lempert (1986) at 471–7; Leubsdorf (1991) at 458–9; Friedman (1992) at 93 n. 40; and Nance (2001) at 1575–95. Although Allen did not do so, one might try to fix this problem by prescribing a verdict for that party whose story is *most like* the story that the fact-finder believes most plausible. This would present serious problems of specifying what makes one story "like" and "more like" another and in any event would be subject to the objections, noted hereafter in the text, that can be raised against a theory that prescribes the verdict to be based entirely on the most plausible story.

[207] See Pardo & Allen (2008).

[208] Id. at 234–5. Pardo and Allen implicitly acknowledge that the explanatory mode of thinking is, in the first place, merely a "guide to inference," as distinct from structuring the standard of proof itself (see, e.g., id. at 229), an idea that I had suggested in 2001. See Nance (2001) at 1588–95. However, as described in the text, they continue to take the next, dubious step of articulating the standard of proof itself in explanatory terms.

[209] If the fact-finder selects (what it takes to be) the most plausible story, and *if* that story happens to be (essentially) one that a party has advanced, then *a fortiori* the fact-finder will

I had anticipated the difficulties with this theory.[210] Simply put, if S is the most plausible explanation of the evidence E, one that instantiates the plaintiff's claim, it may not be the case that $P(S|E) > P^*$, and deciding a case based *only* on the fact that S is the most plausible explanation may not, therefore, serve to minimize expected error costs, according to the public criterion imbedded in P^*. Continuing the traffic light example, suppose that $P^* = 0.5$ and that the fact-finder assesses the following probabilities for the color of the light: red, 0.4; yellow, 0.3; and green, 0.3. The *most* plausible explanation of the evidence is that the light was red, which implies a verdict for the plaintiff; but it is more likely than not that the light was either green or yellow, and – if the fact-finder concludes that entry into the intersection on a yellow light would not have been negligent – then expected error minimization requires a verdict for the defense. Moreover, if, in order to solve this problem, one allows for the aggregation of various stories favoring each side (disjunctive explanations, such as "the light was either yellow or green") *whether or not* the component stories are all advanced by one party – which Pardo and Allen admit they must[211] – then their theory collapses.

The reason is fairly obvious. If the jury is instructed to fix on the most plausible explanation, and it is unconstrained in terms of the disjunctive explanations that it considers, then the trivially most plausible disjunctive explanation is the disjunction of all possible stories, which has a probability of 1. If, in order to avoid this unhelpful solution, the jury is instead required to identify and compare the disjunction of all nonnegligible stories favoring the claimant (i.e., instantiating all the elements) with the disjunction of all nonnegligible stories favoring the defendant (i.e., not instantiating at least one element), then the theory seems to become the same as the decision-theoretic criterion. The fact-finder must now assess how likely it is, under any nonnegligible disjunctive collection of stories, that the facts instantiate the conjunction of the elements and thus are so as to warrant the claimant's recovery under the asserted cause of action.[212]

---

believe that the story told by that party is more plausible than the story told by his or her opponent. But, as one can readily see, the second "if" is a big one.

[210] See Nance (2001) at 1585–8. For further, related criticism, see Laudan (2007).

[211] Pardo & Allen (2008) at 251–2. See also Pardo (2013) at 597–9.

[212] A "choose the most plausible party-favoring aggregation of stories, even if it is not more likely than not" theory does have an analogue in the repertoire of decision-theory results. As David Kaye has shown, if one moves away from the two-party dispute in which the present discussion has been set and isolates the special case where there are more than two parties, only one of whom is responsible for the plaintiff's loss, and a mistaken attribution of responsibility as to any one of the possibly responsible parties

This collapse of Pardo and Allen's theory can be avoided, but to do so requires some kind of further limitation on the fact-finder's aggregation of stories.[213]

Rather than going down this path, Pardo and Allen give a different kind of answer to the foregoing problem of the "collapse"; they say that there is a difference between probability as used in criterion (2.2) and explanatory "plausibility" so that the probability of a disjunctive story or explanation need not be the same as the plausibility of a disjunctive story or explanation.[214] This is unhelpful for two reasons. First, Pardo and Allen do not articulate or illustrate how the two can be meaningfully different. One can, to be sure, imagine ways in which "plausibility" might differ from "probability," at least by some interpretations of these words. For example, one might assess the "plausibility" of a story in terms of its aesthetic qualities, how good the story is *qua* story. Plaintiff's story might be more plausible in this sense because it has better dramatic appeal; it would make a better novel or movie than defendant's story. But whatever strategic value an advocate may see in trying to provide the "better" story in this sense, this hardly seems like the right standard for adjudication.[215] Second, the

---

is equally unfortunate, then expected losses are minimized by imposing liability on the party whose probability of liability is highest, even if that probability is less than 0.5. Kaye (1982) at 503–8. Imposition of such liability may or may not violate the deontological constraints identified earlier. Without attempting to develop the theory of such constraints in multidefendant contexts, suffice it to say that if the potentially liable defendants can each be shown more likely than not to have breached a duty to the plaintiff by imposing the kind of risk that has eventuated, then attribution of liability to that defendant most likely to be the cause of plaintiff's injury does not offend the constraint. By contrast, if the situation is such that only one of the defendants could have breached a duty of the pertinent kind, then imposition of liability on any defendant requires a probability of breach exceeding 0.5.

[213] Professor Cheng has observed that the indicated collapse can be avoided so that appearances are saved as a descriptive theory if one stipulates that such aggregation may occur but only over stories, such as those in the example in the text, that provide alternative theories of a single element of the cause of action, keeping the theory of other elements fixed for that purpose. See Cheng (2012) at 1263–6. In this case, the theory avoids the conjunction paradox, but it does so at the price of prescriptive arbitrariness: (a) a justification is required as to why only certain categories of stories may be aggregated and not others and (b) that justification must outweigh the loss in expected social utility that results from diverging from criterion (2.2). Id. at 1272–5.

[214] Actually, what Pardo and Allen write, in a brief footnote, is that "nothing about a disjunctive explanation suggests that it necessarily must be Bayesian." Pardo & Allen (2008) at 251 n. 88. But they do not explain further.

[215] Courts do grant wide latitude to parties to try to tell a good story. See, e.g., Old Chief v. United States, 519 U.S. 172, 186–8 (1997) (emphasizing the right of a party to tell a "colorful story with descriptive richness" "not just to prove a fact but to establish its human

criteria Pardo and Allen do offer as useful in assessing the plausibility of an explanation or story – factors such as consistency, simplicity, consilience, and coherence with background beliefs[216] – are natural criteria for the assessment of its epistemic probability.[217] Indeed, they argue that "explanatory considerations help to determine *how likely* one judges particular hypotheses or conclusions to be, and 'it is for this reason that inference can be a good that explanation delivers.'"[218]

Professor Allen and his various collaborators clearly have more work to do to make their theory viable.[219] My example of the red/yellow/green light case suggests what I think may be the right kind of solution: the fact-finder ought to consider the probability that the plaintiff's story (or immaterially diverging variants thereof) is true, the probability that the defendant's story (or immaterially diverging variants thereof) is true, and the probability that the best available third explanatory story is true. In the great

---

significance, and so to implicate the law's moral underpinnings and a juror's obligation to sit in judgment"). The idea is not without its critics:

> This critical dichotomy between teleological rules of drama and interpretation, on the one hand, and the mostly random rules of real life, on the other, has profoundly important implications for our legal system. When we import the narrative form of storytelling into our legal system, we confuse fiction with fact and endanger the truth-finding function of the adjudicative process.

Dershowitz (1996) at 101. In any event, the important point for our purposes is that courts have never taken the step of making aesthetic quality a determinant of the burden of persuasion.

[216] Pardo & Allen (2008) at 230.

[217] See Swinburne (2001) at 74–102 (analyzing the importance of such factors in assessing logical probability).

[218] Pardo & Allen (2008) at 229 (emphasis supplied; quoting Lipton (2001)).

[219] I have emphasized the analysis of the usual "preponderance of the evidence" standard for civil cases, where Allen's theories have their greatest appeal. The problems are considerably worse when one turns to the higher standards, such as the "beyond reasonable doubt" standard for criminal cases. Pardo and Allen offer interpretations of the other standards of proof commonly encountered – see id. at 238–40 – but these do nothing noncircular to give greater clarity of meaning or justification to those standards. See Friedman (2001) at 2047. The basic problem is that once one moves away from qualitative comparisons to a situation in which one side's case must "surpass" the other's by some discernible margin, it becomes very hard to give content to that margin without a ratio, a quantification that Allen's theories do not allow. Indeed, once he turns to the criminal standard, he abandons the comparative emphasis entirely, but without admitting it. Consider the following passage from one of his related papers:

> [I]n criminal cases the decision rule is essentially to determine whether there is a plausible case of guilt, in which case one convicts unless there is a plausible case of innocence (*even if less plausible than that of guilt*).... The question of proof at trial is always how has something been proven compared to the alternatives.

mass of cases, an appropriate combination of these probabilities may be unlikely to diverge significantly from the target probability $P(C|E)$. That is, fourth stories (fifth stories, and so on) are likely to be sufficiently improbable as to be practically negligible, at least as long as they are substantially different from the preceding ones. To be sure, I do not have the empirical basis to substantiate such an intuition, but I suspect that it is the direction in which Allen and Pardo must go if they are to complete their theory in a way that is both descriptively plausible and normatively appealing.[220]

In any event, this quick review of the relative plausibility theory serves to emphasize that an explanatory focus is a critical analytical tool that fact-finders will and should use in assessing the discriminatory power of the evidence.[221] The importance of this tool was made salient for adjudication by empirical work supporting the so-called story model, which posits that fact-finders attempt to construct stories that explain the evidence.[222] But it is still only a tool. Critically important is to differentiate between such methods for analyzing evidence and the standard that they are used to inform: it is the attempt to construe the latter in terms only of the former that creates the problems.[223] Admirably, some scholars who emphasize the analytical value of inference to the best explanation in the adjudication context have found it necessary, nonetheless, to state explicitly that even after the best explanation has been determined, it cannot be endorsed by the fact-finder unless it *also* satisfies the standard of proof, which then must be given some independent meaning.[224] This meaning, moreover, will need to come to grips with the significance of second-best stories, third-best stories, and so forth. With this distinction in mind, we can consider the contrast between explanatory approaches and "Bayesian" approaches to inference. The task of the next section is to distinguish the decision-theoretic model presented earlier from Bayesian analysis of

---

Allen (2006) at 5 (emphasis added). The second statement in this passage is true but (jarringly) inconsistent with the emphasized portion of the first statement. His suggested test for criminal cases is simply not comparative in any meaningful sense.

[220] Later work by others sharing an interest in developing inference to the best explanation into a decision criterion has so far failed to come to grips with the problem of aggregating the significance of third (fourth, etc.) stories. See, e.g., Bex & Walton (2010).

[221] See generally Haack (1993) chap. 4 and Lipton (2001) chaps. 8 & 9.

[222] See Pennington & Hastie (1991, 1993).

[223] See Nance (2001) at 1588–95.

[224] See, e.g., Amaya (2009) at 142–4. Nancy Pennington and Reid Hastie, who pioneered the story model of jury inference, note that selection of the best explanatory story is one stage of the process, whereas another is assessing that story against the standard of proof, which, accordingly, must have separate content. Pennington & Hastie (1993) at 201.

evidence and to relate the latter to the explanatory focus described here. This will serve to place the entire discussion of discriminatory power in clearer context when the questions of Keynesian weight and tenacity of belief are taken up in later chapters.

2.4 Free Evaluation versus Structured Analysis of Evidence

One of the motivating concerns of those who press the explanatory approach (see § 2.3.2) is that an articulation of the standards of proof like criterion (2.2) is focused on the end product of deliberation rather than the process of arriving there, giving no direction to jurors as to how to go about assessing the evidence in the case.[225] One can, of course, imagine giving fact-finders instructions that they should examine the various possible hypotheses to see how they fare as explanations of the evidence presented. How significant this would be as guidance in analyzing the evidence in a case is questionable; fact-finders are likely to do this anyway as a matter of common sense. Any more detailed specification poses a potential challenge to what was described earlier as the principle of free evaluation of evidence (§ 2.2.2). The law generally eschews providing anything approaching a recipe for decision – and for good reason.[226] This is not to say that advocates may not *suggest* such structures for the analysis of evidence. It is only to say that fact-finders are free to adopt or reject such suggestions.

Of course, the same objection can be raised against any attempt by law to require fact-finders to engage in a specific form of mathematical reasoning about probabilities. It is certainly true that the prevailing inferential antinomianism means that fact-finders need not process the evidence in overtly mathematical ways. And while the impact of the evidence in a case can be decomposed along Bayesian lines, as sketched later, and it may in particular contexts be useful for theorists, advocates, or even fact-finders

---

[225] See, e.g., Pardo (2009) at 1092–3. In a later article, Professor Pardo notes

> Like the probabilistic conception, the explanatory conception is also ultimately concerned with the likelihood or probability of contested propositions at trials. The primary difference, however, is that the explanatory conception posits explanatory rather than explicitly probabilistic criteria to guide inferences and to arrive at judgments about these propositions.

Pardo (2013) at 597 n. 212.

[226] "There is no precise algorithm available to explain to jurors, or for that matter to historians, anthropologists, or astrophysicists, how to connect evidence to organizing theories." Allen (1991) at 412–13.

to do so explicitly, there is nothing about the canonical standards of proof, even as interpreted using criterion (2.2), that presupposes or requires this.

One can, for example, decompose the "posterior odds" on the left side of the inequality in criterion (2.2) using the following mathematical tautology, a version of "Bayes' rule":

$$O(C|E) = O(C) \times L_C(E) \qquad (2.4)$$

The first term on the right-hand side of equation (2.4), $O(C)$, is called the "prior odds" and indicates the odds that the fact-finder would place on the claim being true before (or, more precisely, without) taking into account the (admitted) evidence E. This strikes some commentators as problematic, at least at the start of a trial, because they believe that jurors should not have any such odds before taking evidence into account. More about this later (§ 2.5). For now, consider the remaining term on the right-hand side of the equation. This is called the "likelihood ratio" for the evidence (relative to the hypotheses C and not-C) and is just the ratio $P(E|C)/P(E|\text{not-}C)$. It represents the degree to which the appearance before the court of evidence E would be more (or less) likely on the assumption that C is true than on the assumption that it is false.[227] Such a decomposition can be used to think about the evidence as a whole or to isolate a particular item of evidence for analysis. To do the latter, all one must do is think of $O(C)$ as the odds in favor of the claim based on all the other evidence in the case besides the particular evidence E in which one is interested.[228]

To grasp the usefulness of the likelihood ratio intuitively, consider the analysis of a single item of evidence or, more precisely, evidence of the following proposition of fact: that a compound in the blood of the defendant matches a compound found in the blood from the perpetrator left at the scene of a crime. How probative is this evidence in a case where the defendant does not deny the crime occurred but denies that he perpetrated it or was ever anywhere near the crime scene? The answer, according to equation (2.4), depends on the comparative effectiveness of the two hypotheses ("defendant is perpetrator" and "defendant is not perpetrator") in explaining the evidence of the match. Putting aside certain subtleties, if the defendant is the perpetrator, then it is almost certain that one would get evidence of a match, and $P(E|C) \doteq 1$. If the defendant is not the perpetrator, then someone else is, and the chance of getting a match with

---

[227] See Nance (2001) at 1595–6.
[228] For extended treatments of the usefulness of such Bayesian decomposition of the posterior odds in litigated cases, see Robertson & Vignaux (1995) and Aitken & Taroni (2004).

the defendant depends on how common the compound is in the blood of innocent persons. If, for example, the compound is present in everyone's blood, then again $P(E|\text{not-}C) \doteq 1$, and the likelihood ratio for that evidence is approximately 1, which means that it does not significantly change the odds of guilt that one would have without regard to the evidence of a match, as one would expect. If, however, the compound in question is present in the blood of only 20 percent of the relevant suspect population, then $P(E|\text{not-}C) \doteq 0.2$; that is, the chance that the defendant's blood would match the perpetrator's blood in this respect by coincidence is only about 0.2.[229] In the latter case, a likelihood ratio of about $(1.0/0.2) = 5$ means that the odds of guilt should increase roughly fivefold based on the evidence of the match.[230]

Focusing on the likelihood ratio reveals a connection to the idea that juridical inference is "explanatory" in character. The likelihood ratio directs our attention to (or, if you prefer, confirms that it is appropriate for us to direct our attention to) the comparative plausibility of the competing claims C and not-C in explaining the evidence E.[231] Further, the likelihood ratio, indeed all of equation (2.4), can be reformulated in terms of the comparison of only two specific hypotheses – the claimant's theory of the case and the opponent's theory of the case. To do this, simply rewrite equation (2.4) in terms of probabilities, rather than odds, and then replace C with claimant's theory of the case and not-C with the defendant's theory of the case; the equation remains valid. If the claimant's theory of

---

[229] To speak of the "relevant suspect" population raises the problem of the selection of appropriate "reference classes" from which to calculate frequencies. In the example, are we to use the class of all humans, all male humans, all male humans residing "near" the scene of the crime (whatever "near" means), all adult male humans of a certain race, or some other identifiable group? See Gillies (2000) at 119–23 (analyzing the general philosophical problem and describing a pragmatic approach to its solution). In the legal context, this problem has seemed overwhelming to some but not to others. Compare Allen & Pardo (2007) (arguing that the reference-class problem is so severe as to preclude the effective use of mathematical models, except for very limited purposes) with Lempert (1993a) (discussing some important considerations in the selection of a practical reference class in the context of DNA identification evidence); Nance (2007a) (arguing that the reference-class problem is ubiquitous, that people routinely manage to solve it pragmatically, and that the law may do so as well, even in the absence of a theoretical solution); and Cheng (2009) (suggesting a solution to the reference-class problem derived from statistical theory).

[230] See Finkelstein & Fairley (1970). For simplicity, the illustration in the text has ignored a variety of important subtleties concerning potential false reports of a match, such as processing errors and intentional falsifications by police or forensic scientists. These subtleties must be addressed in any attempt to model, prescriptively or descriptively, practical decision making. See Nance & Morris (2002, 2005).

[231] See Swinburne (2001) at 102–7 and Lipton (2004) chap. 7.

the case is several times more plausible as an account of the evidence as a whole than the opponent's, then equation (2.4) suggests that the evidence strongly favors the claimant (depending, of course, on how the fact-finder assesses possible "third stories").[232] Importantly, the Bayesian framework, as an elaboration of the decision-theoretic model, provides normative appeal that supports the usefulness of explanatory accounts even if the latter are taken as primarily descriptive.[233] Moreover, the decision-theoretic framework, to which Bayesian analysis is a potential supplement, admits of other forms of probabilistic analysis when useful in a particular context.

However, an explanatory focus has one decided advantage over Bayesian analysis. The latter takes hypotheses as given and provides an illuminating structure that incorporates comparative explanatory analysis. *But it does not provide the hypotheses to be considered.* This weakness of the Bayesian formalism has often been noted. Samir Okasha puts the matter succinctly, albeit in the context of the philosophy of science:

> Explanatory considerations invariably guide the construction of new theories: indeed, often the *point* of inventing a new theory is to explain an anomalous phenomenon.... In those cases where agents respond to new

---

[232] How specific the opponent must be in presenting a theory of the case is an interesting procedural question, but even if specificity is required from both parties, the two hypotheses offered should not be considered exclusive from the point of view of the fact-finder, which should remain free to adopt some third theory of the case. See supra § 2.3.

[233] Those who support explanatory interpretations of the standards of proof (see § 2.3.2) have been ambivalent in their recognition of this compatibility. For example, Professor Pardo has stated:

> Under probability approaches, decision-makers infer conclusions based on how likely a proposition appears, given what is known about the evidence. The explanatory approach reverses the inferential process. Under this approach, decision-makers infer conclusions based on how well each proposition, if true, would explain the evidence.

Pardo (2009) at 1102. In light of equation (2.4), this is a curious remark. Pardo's assertion that probabilistic approaches look to "how likely a proposition appears, given what is known about the evidence" is, of course, a reference to important terms such as $P(C|E)$, the probability that the claim is true, given the evidence. But his argument ignores the potential use of Bayes's rule, which translates terms such as $P(C|E)$ into something using terms such as $P(E|C)$, the probability that the evidence would be explained by the hypothetically assumed truth of the claim. "Reversing" the inferential focus in the manner described by Pardo is exactly what Bayes's rule is used to accomplish. In other work, however, Pardo and Ron Allen were more qualified in their rejection of the Bayesian framework in favor of an explanatory one; indeed, they conceded that the two are compatible. See Pardo & Allen (2008) at 251–3. And in more recent work, Professor Pardo recognizes the "reversal" inherent in Bayes's rule but argues (creatively) that the Bayesian "reversal" nonetheless does not yield the *same* results in every case as an explanatory approach and that the results of the explanatory approach make it a more accurate descriptive theory of juridical inference. See Pardo (2013).

evidence by inventing new hypotheses, the Bayesian model is silent. But [inference to the best explanation] provides a useful, if schematic account of what is going on: the agents are trying to explain the new evidence. They think that the best, or perhaps the only, explanation of the evidence lies outside the space of the possibilities they have previously considered, so rather than conditionalizing, they invent a new hypothesis.[234]

This observation applies as well in the context of adjudication. Of course, the logic of adjudication itself provides contending hypotheses, C and not-C in our recurring representation. But these are hypotheses at a relatively high level of abstraction. As explained previously, C represents the set of stories, a group of theories of the case, each of which instantiates all the elements that the claimant must prove, whereas not-C represents the set of all other stories, all other possible theories of the case. At this level of abstraction, it is often (though not always) difficult to make much headway in attempting to formulate epistemic probabilities. The claimant typically provides a theory of the case instantiating the elements of the cause of action, while the defendant offers a theory of the case that does not. The fact-finder considers these and other possible theories that account for the evidence. In this latter activity, as already noted, the fact-finder may need to generate its own hypotheses. The explanatory focus provides a way of searching over the set that C represents (or that not-C represents) to find plausible theories of the case.[235]

With hypotheses in hand, Bayesian logic can be a useful way to structure thinking, as illustrated by the example of forensic "match" evidence. As a theoretical matter, one can expand the Bayesian decomposition by iterating as to each item of evidence considered. This produces a relationship in which each additional piece of evidence changes the odds by a multiplicative factor corresponding to its likelihood ratio. To represent this, suppose that the aggregate evidence E in equation (2.4) is decomposed into a conjunction of n distinct evidentiary items $E = E_1 \& E_2 \& \ldots \& E_n$. Then the likelihood ratio can be expanded as follows:

$$L_C(E) = L_C(E_1) \times L_C(E_2|E_1) \times L_C(E_3|E_1 \& E_2) \times \cdots \\ \times L_C(E_n|E_1 \& E_2 \& \cdots \& E_{n-1}) \tag{2.5}$$

where $L_C(E_i|E_j)$ is the likelihood ratio for evidence E_i (relative to the hypotheses C and not-C) given E_j – that is, the ratio of $P(E_i|C \& E_j)$ to

---

[234] See, e.g., Okasha (2000) at 707.
[235] For further discussion of the relationship between this "abduction" to new hypotheses and Keynesian weight, see infra § 3.4.

$P(E_i|\text{not-}C \ \&E_j)$.[236] (One need not think of such decompositions only in terms of the temporal sequence in which items of evidence are presented to the fact-finder: although it may not be obvious, the order of the decomposition does not affect the final result and so can be selected for computational or expository convenience.) By taking the natural logarithm of each side of this equation, one obtains an additive measure in which each positive natural log (corresponding to a likelihood ratio larger than 1) counts in favor of the claim and each negative natural log (corresponding to a likelihood ratio smaller than 1) counts against the claim:

$$\ln\left[L_C(E)\right] = \ln\left[L_C(E_1)\right] + \cdots + \ln\left[L_C\left(E_n \mid E_1 \& E_2 \& \cdots \& E_{n-1}\right)\right] \quad (2.6)$$

This produces a metric that corresponds roughly to the intuition of the scales of weight described in the Chapter 1. Positive-valued log-likelihood ratios on the right-hand side of the equation will move the odds in favor of C, whereas negative-valued log-likelihood ratios will move the odds against C. If one adds up the positively signed log-likelihood ratios and compares that to the sum of the negatively signed log-likelihood ratios, one can determine the net effect of the evidence. It is interesting, and perhaps intellectually comforting, to know that the intuitive "adding" of evidence favorable to each side has some theoretical analogue.[237]

To be sure, it would be impractical in the ordinary case to ask that fact-finders explicitly go through such a computation, whether of the multiplicative or additive kind, for an entire case composed of a mass of diverse evidence.[238] But this does not mean that such Bayesian decomposition cannot be a useful model for various narrower purposes, as illustrated earlier in regard the forensic science of identification.[239] Moreover, debates about quantification often assume, incorrectly, that meaningful quantification of odds or probabilities, as called for by criterion (2.2), is

---

[236] See Nance (2001) at 1596–8. For the special (if unusual) case in which the items of evidence are "stochastically independent" of one another, i.e., $P(E_i|C\&E_j) = P(E_i|C)$, the formula simplifies to $L_C(E) = L_C(E_1) \times L_C(E_2) \times L_C(E_3) \times \cdots \times L_C(E_n)$. See, e.g., Aitken & Taroni (2004) at 248.

[237] Accordingly, some theorists have called the log-likelihood ratio of the evidence the "weight" of the evidence. See Aitken & Taroni (2004) at 99–100. The insight is not entirely theoretical: experimental evidence indicates that cognitive errors associated with probabilistic inference (e.g., neglect of base rates and overestimation of the probability of conjoint events) can be reduced by logarithmic presentation formats. See Juslin et al. (2011).

[238] The point is readily conceded even by those who advocate the usefulness of Bayesian models of juridical inference. See, e.g., Friedman (1997a) at 286–7 and Lempert (1997) at 317.

[239] See Koehler & Shaviro (1990) at 275–7.

necessarily tied to a fully Bayesian account of how fact-finders assess the evidence, as if the very limited quantification inherent in criterion (2.2) necessarily means that fact-finders must do the computation involved in equation (2.5). The critique of "Bayesianism" then makes the quite plausible point that a fully Bayesian analysis of the evidence in an even modestly complex litigated case would entail hideously difficult computational problems beyond the capacities of ordinary fact-finders.[240] But this is less consequential than those who emphasize it seem to believe. No doubt actual decision processes involve the use of a variety of psychological tools that simplify the inferential tasks and that may or may not be particularly well suited to the litigation context.[241] In the end, however, the questions of whether and how fact-finders arrive (or should arrive) at a probability or odds with regard to the claim are quite distinct from the questions of whether and how they use (or should use) that assessment of probability or odds to decide the case pursuant to the standard of proof.[242]

Nevertheless, it remains possible that fact-finders use methods of inference that, for practical purposes, approximate the process idealized in equation (2.5) or equation (2.6). Even if all that fact-finders do is to isolate some individual items of evidence from the rest and think of each of these in terms of its likelihood ratio before arriving at their own holistic assessment of the odds required to apply criterion (2.2), such piecemeal assessments may well contribute to the accuracy of the holistic assessment. In this regard, it should be noted that Alvin Goldman and his colleagues have proved interesting theorems related to Bayesian revisions of odds, theorems that complement what I have described (in § 2.2) as the law's aspiration to objectivity.[243] Specifically, Goldman notes that if fact-finders use their *subjective* likelihoods (the numerator and denominator of the likelihood ratio) to revise their prior odds, there is no assurance that their revision will approach the truth.[244] If one adds the assumption that

---

[240] The observation is, of course, a much broader one, not limited to the litigation context. See Harman (1986) at 25–7.

[241] See generally Nance (2001) at 1598–1607 (rejecting a variety of arguments appearing in the literature against Bayesian modeling of adjudicative inference).

[242] See Tillers & Gottfried (2006) at 142–3 (noting that jurors might apply a probabilistic standard of proof without necessarily using an explicitly Bayesian or otherwise quantitative method of analyzing the evidence) and Clermont (2009) at 470, 482–5 (2009) (making a similar point).

[243] See, e.g., Goldman (2002).

[244] There is a considerable literature about the phenomenon of "convergence," according to which it is thought that individuals who repeatedly revise their odds in accordance with Bayes' rule will gradually converge on the same probability, even if they begin from

the fact-finders' likelihoods are not too far off the objectively correct likelihoods, though, then fact-finders' odds revision can be expected to approach the truth, regardless of their prior odds.[245] To make good such a theory, Goldman must try to give meaning to the idea of objectively correct likelihood ratios, a task that he endeavors to do.[246] The details need not concern us here. The point of importance is that a number of rules structuring the trial, such as those that structure jury deliberations, seek to facilitate the effort of fact-finders to arrive at accurate likelihood ratios. Put in explanatory terms, rules structuring jury deliberations attempt to assist jurors in arriving at more accurate assessments of the comparative capacity of competing hypotheses in explaining the evidence before the court than they would otherwise achieve. The Bayesian decomposition of the likelihood ratio in equation (2.5) can serve as a framework with which to model and critique such inferential processes.

Such ideas still speak more to potentialities than to extant, useful inferential tools, and it will be readily acknowledged that the Bayesian decomposition shown earlier is not as overtly useful in the typical case as a graphical analysis of the inferential connections among items of evidence and between them and the material issues to be proved. The idea of creating "charts" that visually display such inferential connections is one way of marshaling the evidence.[247] For a simple example, consider a criminal case of alleged burglary by the accused B in which the only evidence is prosecution testimony PT_1 identifying the accused as someone seen running from the crime scene R, prosecution testimony from a second witness PT_2 that the accused appeared the day after the burglary with an amount of cash that he (the accused) had claimed not to have the day before the burglary C, and defense testimony by another witness DT_3 offered by the accused

---

different "priors." Goldman maintains that such eventual convergence, "in the limit" as revisions become infinite in number, is of little practical use. Id. at 240 n. 10.

[245] Id. at 241–5 (indicating that this result holds as long as the fact-finder's prior probability is neither 0 nor 1, the fact-finders likelihood ratio is not 1, and the observed evidence E is true).

[246] See id. at 245–51 (sketching a theory of objective likelihoods using the counterfactual nature of likelihoods in the adjudicative context). Compare Fallis (2002) at 228–31 (arguing that objective likelihoods are rarely determinable in the kinds of cases involved in adjudication but implicitly assuming that objective probabilities can only be – in terms of the classification scheme discussed in § 2.2.2 – empirical).

[247] The construction of such structures was advocated and illustrated long ago by Wigmore in his brilliant but less well-known treatise, *The Principles of Judicial Proof*. Wigmore (1913). By its third edition, Wigmore had changed the name, calling it *The Science of Judicial Proof*. See Wigmore (1937). This tradition is carried on today in the work of others. See, e.g., Anderson et al. (2005).

```
PT₁ ─────────► R
              ▲  ╲
              │   ╲
DT₃ ────► E        ► B
                  ╱
                 ╱
PT₂ ─────────► C
```

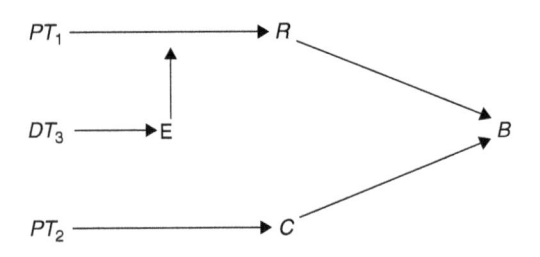

Figure 2. Illustrative evidence marshaling chart.

that the first witness has poor eyesight E. For this case, such a chart might look like that in Figure 2.

Such charts can be created by counsel for litigants, of course, in their preparation of the case, and they could be created (or at least used) by a judge or jury if there is the time to do so. The charts can become more complicated by adding symbols and notations concerning the source of evidence and the type or strength of the inference that is thought to be involved or by specifying the generalizations about the way the world works that support the inferences from one node in the chart to another.[248] For example, the inference from R, the proposition that the defendant was seen running from the scene of the crime, to B, the proposition that the defendant committed the burglary, is plausibly (though not conclusively) supported by the generalization that "a guilty person is more likely to run from the scene of a crime than an innocent person" or, perhaps, a stronger generalization, such as, "someone who runs from the scene of a crime is likely to be guilty."[249] A review of the more detailed chart methods offered by various theorists reinforces the conclusion that these devices can be of considerable assistance in marshaling evidence and exploring inferential connections. They decompose a mass of evidence into analyzable chunks and serve to highlight the importance of such background assumptions about the way the world works generally. But they hardly attempt to eliminate the exercise of

---

[248] Wigmore provides a detailed system with a variety of features. See Wigmore (1937) at 858–81. Anderson and his colleagues provide a system that uses a set of notations similar but not identical to that used by Wigmore. See Anderson et al. (2005) at 123–44. For an interesting discussion relating Wigmore's charts to modern trends in informal reasoning, see Goodwin (2000).

[249] On the important difference between these two types of generalization, see Nance (2007c). As with all inferences, the strength of the inference can be affected by other evidenced facts that affect the probability embedded in the supporting generalization. See, e.g., United States v. Myers, 550 F.2d 1036 (5th Cir. 1977) (discussing facts that can qualify the strength of the inference from flight), cert. denied, 439 U.S. 847 (1978).

judgment, whether in the assessment of probative value of individual items or in the overall assessment of discriminatory power of the evidence. In any case, their use by a fact-finder is, and is likely to remain, entirely optional, if only because of the difficulty of compiling a uniquely correct chart for any case with any degree of complexity. As with other structured approaches, they are valuable aids for thought, not recipes for decision.

This discussion easily blends into a consideration of more purely descriptive questions concerning the complicated process of human inference, and it might be misleading if I did not give some further indication of what I believe to be the proper eclecticism on that score. This topic, once again, is not my direct concern here. The purposes of attempting to develop an accurate descriptive theory of inference at trial include understanding the ways in which fact-finder inferences can go wrong and how they can be improved by particular rules that regulate the trial process. Burdens of proof, broadly construed, may have such regulative functions, but the standards of proof, and the assessment of discriminatory power that they prescribe, are thoroughly normative and address the rational, epistemic assessments of the fact-finder. A theory of the standards of proof, a theory that attempts to give greater content, meaning, and precision to the standards of proof, will share this prescriptive emphasis. It will not purport to describe how the members of the tribunal make decisions. And the rationalist models that have been much discussed to a considerable extent have this normative point: they are concerned with what fact-finders should do and with what advocates should be allowed and encouraged to ask fact-finders to do in the performance of their epistemic task.

Debate continues concerning the usefulness of formal probability, including Bayesian analysis, as a tool in developing a descriptive model of human inference.[250] For some time, critics of Bayesian styles of analysis have drawn on the psychological literature that reveals particular difficulties that ordinary people have with rules of formal probability. The most prominent competitor offered in the legal context is the "story model" mentioned earlier (at the end of § 2.3.2), according to which fact-finders (with or without the help of the parties) attempt to construct stories to explain the evidence, generally gravitating to the one that appears most plausible. The attractiveness of the story model – its resonance with what lawyers have learned to do to convince decision makers and its congruence

---

[250] Compare Oaksford & Chater (2007) (arguing that everyday rationality is best understood as probabilistic) with Gigerenzer (2008) (arguing that rationality is best understood in terms of the degree of success achieved by the heuristics used in decision making as affected by the particular environment in which the decision must be made).

with how jurors make and report their decisions – is often taken as evidence against the descriptive accuracy of Bayesian inference models. It is safe to say that if one had to choose between the story model and a model based on the use of equation (2.5) or equation (2.6), the story model would be the better description.[251]

The matter has become more complicated, however, by the introduction of new "dual process" models of information processing.[252] According to these models, people actually use two modes of analysis: "system 1" processing, in which there is rapid, relatively effortless, and intuitive incorporation of new information based on learned associations and "system 2" processing, experienced as slow, effortful, and conscious reasoning pursuant to semantic rules. Each, in turn, has its place and its advantages and disadvantages, with system 2 processing (sometimes) capable of overriding system 1 processing.

In applying this dual-processing idea, it is natural to identify the use of stories with system 1 processing and to identify the use of formal deductive and inductive logic, including that exemplified by Bayesian probabilistic analysis, with system 2 processing.[253] After all, one intuitively associates the patterns of evidence with stories drawn from one's past experience. Using any kind of formal analysis is more conscious and effortful. But this may not be the best way to apply the dual-processing idea. Recognizing the conscious effort involved in "constructing" stories and checking them against the evidence, a case can be made for identifying story construction with system 2 processing, at least in large part. System 1 processing then would be identified with an even more automatic, more associative form of inference. This can be found in the idea of "coherence networks," loosely modeled on the neural networks of the brain.[254] From this perspective, the

---

[251] See, e.g., Pennington & Hastie (1992) (reporting results of empirical studies suggesting that individuals incorporate new information in a manner more consistent with the "story model" than with sequential Bayesian revision).

[252] See Kahneman (2011).

[253] Essentially this identification takes place in Griffin (2013) at 298–301.

[254] Essentially this identification takes place in Spottswood (2013). The evidence marshaling charts previously illustrated in the text are closely related to and can be developed into so-called Bayesian networks that articulate the various intermediate propositions of fact involved in inference and their inferential connections. Schum (1994) at 156–94. An analogy between such networks and the neural networks of the brain can be exploited, conceiving the incorporation of new evidence within such networks as the reaching of a reflective equilibrium in the pertinent "Bayes' net" or as using some other information-processing algorithm or heuristic adapted to particular decision environments that approximates the results generated by Bayesian models within applicable time and calculation-resource constraints. See generally Rao et al. (2002).

construction of stories, on the one hand, and the use of formal (deductive or inductive) logic, including probability theorems, on the other, would constitute two different, perhaps complementary forms of system 2 processing.[255]

Some such complex integrative theory is probably necessary for a reasonably adequate descriptive theory of factual inference. But one factor remains constant in these various descriptive formulations: application of the standard of proof is a distinctive component of system 2 processing, one that can function to override the conclusions that a juror might reach without such a standard.[256] And the important point for our present purposes is that no such descriptive theory poses a threat to the idea that, at the end of the day, the decision maker can assess, in an approximate way, the comparative probabilities (the odds) of a claim being true as opposed to being false. And while the fact-finder's odds may, of course, be tainted by bias or other forms of irrationality, against which we should be on the alert, the ability of fact-finders to assess the comparative probability of the competing claims is sufficient to invoke the decision-theoretic criterion.

2.5 The Importance and Sources of Background Information

As explained in the preceding section, the fact-finder's assessment of the odds on a claim can be analyzed with reference to Bayes's rule:

$$O(C|E) = O(C) \times L_C(E) \tag{2.4}$$

Once again, to invoke such a probability rule does not necessarily mean that the fact-finder determines $O(C|E)$ by determining the numbers on the right-hand side of this equation and performing the indicated multiplication. It does mean, however, that the fact-finder's prior and posterior odds ought to be related as indicated by the equation. Consequently, this decomposition of $O(C|E)$ facilitates an important observation about what I have called "discriminatory power": it does *not* depend solely on the admitted evidence E; it also depends on the prior odds $O(C)$. This dependence occasions a number of questions and controversies.

First, it might be thought that $O(C|E)$ is not, therefore, an appropriately "pure" measure of the strength of the admitted evidence E. Indeed, arguably, the likelihood ratio is the better measure for this very reason. The

---

[255] Cf. Stanovich (2011) at 25–6 (subdividing system 2 processing into "algorithmic" and "reflective" processes).
[256] See Griffin (2013) at 298–9 and Spottswood (2013) at 191–2.

latter does not depend on the prior odds, but only on the evidence and the hypothesis (and, of course, uncontested background information).[257] Consequently, I have not offered $O(C|E)$ as a quantification of the "probative value" of the evidence. I have used the distinct term *discriminatory power* and identified this with the posterior odds $O(C|E)$ to emphasize that it represents the net impact of the evidence, taking into account prior odds as well as the probative value of the evidence, for this is what must be compared to an appropriate standard of proof to determine whether the claim has been adequately proved.[258]

Of course, if one takes the prior odds as even, 1:1, certainly plausible on average for civil cases that reach trial without settlement,[259] then there is no difference between discriminatory power, as I have quantified it, and probative value, as quantified by the likelihood ratio. This could easily lead one to conclude that an explanatory focus, captured in the likelihood ratio, is all that matters. This is explicit in the theory advanced by Ed Cheng. He argues that the standard of proof should be understood as a requirement that the likelihood ratio attain a certain value: in the usual civil case, that it exceed 1; in criminal cases, that it exceed the value necessary to reduce the probability of false-positive verdicts to a fixed acceptable level.[260] To be clear, Cheng's assertions are intended as descriptive, not prescriptive: his view is that one can explain features of the law – whether they be desirable or not – by understanding standards in this way. In the course of his argument, he hypothesizes that the law's normative requirement is that the prior odds be taken as 1:1, at least in civil cases. While commenting that such a norm is "arguable," albeit "potentially controversial," he provides very little evidence that such a legal norm actually exists.[261] This is rather

---

[257] For a thorough examination of various possible measures of probative value, see Schum (1994) at 200–69.

[258] As stated in regard to the "preponderance of the evidence" standard for civil cases:

> Compelling a decision in favor of a party who has introduced evidence that is simply better than that of his adversary would not be objectionable if we hypothesize jurors who bring none of their experience to the trial and who thus view the evidence in a vacuum. Of course, no such case could exist. We expect and encourage jurors to use their own experience to help them reach a decision, particularly in judging the credibility of witnesses.

2 McCormick (2013) § 339 at 660.

[259] A well-known principle of settlement theory is that strong cases for either plaintiff or defendant will tend to settle, leaving mostly close cases to be tried; under certain assumptions, this leads to an anticipated win rate for plaintiffs of 50 percent. See Priest & Klein (1984).

[260] Cheng (2012).

[261] Id. at 1267. Cheng's only direct authority for this claim is an assertion to that effect, embracing both civil and criminal cases, made by (Judge) Richard Posner, not writing

striking. One would expect to find authority for such a basic proposition, if indeed it were the case. Moreover, Cheng acknowledges that such a norm, and the resulting decision rule, is suboptimal in that it actually endorses that much discussed error in probabilistic reasoning known as "neglect of base rates" because a fact-finder's prior odds will be affected by base rates for the claim, as perceived by the fact-finder before the introduction of formal evidence. The proposed norm requires that the fact-finder irrationally ignore all such information, at least to the extent that it generates a prior odds diverging from 1:1.[262]

In fact, there are two important categories of such background information. The first category is *non-case-specific* beliefs about how the world works with which a fact-finder approaches the task of adjudication. The law endorses the fact-finder's use of this information under the rubric of "jury notice," so the familiar jury instruction, to the effect that the jury should decide the case only on the basis of the evidence presented in court, cannot be taken literally.[263] No doubt the purpose of such an instruction is to articulate, in a relatively simple way, the idea that the jury should not consider case-specific information that has not been presented in court and that the jury should not undertake, once the jury is empaneled, to develop (by experiment or otherwise) additional general insights on the way the world works that might pertain to the case.[264] None of this means that the fact-finder is expected to leave its background knowledge at the courthouse door. Moreover, such information need not be uncontestable: if a party wishes to contest some general belief that a fact-finder may have about how the world works, the party must do so by expert evidence and argument.[265]

---

in his judicial capacity. Id. at n. 24. (Posner's claim is discussed in the following text.) Otherwise, Cheng's support for the claim is indirect: such an assumption can help to explain (but not to justify) the legal results in so-called naked statistical evidence cases, in which courts (it is claimed) deny recovery when the only evidence favoring the claim is base-rate statistics. Id. at 1269–71. The complex significance of such cases is discussed below in Chapters 3 and 4.

[262] Id. at 1272–5. Cheng's suggestion regarding criminal cases analogizes the decision rule to classical (non-Bayesian) statistical hypothesis testing, which does not directly incorporate information about prior odds or about the utilities of various types of decisions but rather privileges a particular maximum probability of false-positive verdicts. Id. at 1275–8. Cheng makes no attempt to justify the difference in the law's approach; again, his analogy is offered as purely explanatory commentary.

[263] See, e.g., 3 O'Malley et al. (2006) § 101.40 (instructing jurors that they must consider "only the evidence in the case" but then informing the jurors that they may draw such reasonable inferences from the evidence as are justified in light of the jurors' experience).

[264] See Mueller & Kirkpatrick (2012) § 2.4.

[265] Because the matter is not case-specific, lay witnesses will not be competent to testify on the matter. See Fed. R. Evid. 602, 701. Although it is often controversial, it is nonetheless

Such general information is of limited usefulness by itself in a fact-finder's explicit or implicit formation of prior odds. The second category of background information critically complements the first but is perhaps less obvious. In truth, fact-finders are provided substantial *case-specific* information aside from any evidence that is formally introduced. Beyond facts formally admitted in pleadings, stipulated facts, and judicially noticed facts, about which the judge will instruct the jury (when there is one),[266] the parties' opening statements, as well as statements made during *voir dire* of prospective jurors, signal to the fact-finder large amounts of uncontested facts that are the functional equivalent of stipulated facts.[267] Such information inevitably shapes fact-finders' prior odds regarding the case. By placing the particular case within categories of disputes or events more or less familiar to fact-finders, it creates "base rates" for reference classes with respect to which the evidence of contested facts can be assessed.[268]

Even in a criminal case, undisputed background facts shape a fact-finder's prior odds of guilt, the odds the fact-finder tentatively, if implicitly, forms before the formal introduction of evidence. When the fact-finder learns that the prosecution will claim that someone has been robbed at a certain time and place, and the opening statement of the defense simply informs

---

common fare nowadays for courts to admit expert evidence to disabuse jurors of potentially incorrect general assumptions about such matters as the accuracy of eyewitness testimony and the way victims react to crimes. See Mueller & Kirkpatrick (2012) §§ 7.21 & 7.22.

[266] See, e.g., 3 O'Malley et al. (2006) §§ 101.40 & 101.46–101.48 (providing pattern jury instructions for such matters in civil cases).

[267] Saying that uncontested facts are the "functional" equivalent of stipulated facts refers to the role that such facts have in the inferential process used by the fact-finder (whether judge or jury). But it does not represent the formal attitude of the law toward such facts. The law treats stipulated facts as ones that the fact-finder is *supposed* to accept as true. See, e.g., 3 O'Malley et al. (2006) § 101.40, providing model jury instruction that states

> Statements and arguments of the lawyers are not evidence in the case, unless made as an admission or stipulation of fact. A "stipulation" is an agreement between both sides that [*certain facts are true*][*that a person would have given certain testimony*]. When the lawyers on both sides stipulate or agree to the existence of a fact, you must, unless otherwise instructed, accept the stipulation as evidence, and regard that fact as proved.

In contrast, uncontested case-specific facts revealed by the parties' (or their lawyers') statements, but not formally admitted, are ones that the fact-finder almost certainly *will* accept as true, even though they are consistently defined not to be "evidence." See Klonoff & Kolby (1990) at 113–14 (arguing that jurors will accept as true any facts asserted by one party and not contested by an opponent).

[268] Cf. Koehler & Shaviro (1990) at 258–65 (discussing relevance of evidence of base rates and the relationship between base rates and more case-specific evidence but not specifically addressing the issue of base rates derived from fact-finders' background information that are triggered by stipulated or uncontested case-specific facts).

the fact-finder that an alibi will be forthcoming, the fact-finder need not worry much about the question of whether a robbery occurred at the time and place indicated. And if the jury learns, during *voir dire* or opening statements, the uncontested fact (when it is uncontested) that the defendant is holding down a steady job as an accountant, this too will have an impact on the prior odds with which the jury approaches the formal presentation of evidence. None of this violates the so-called presumption of innocence.[269] That principle precludes the fact-finder's reliance, in determining its odds of guilt, on the implicit (or explicitly stated) assessment of the evidence by others – police officers, prosecutors, grand jurors, and so forth – as reflected in the fact of indictment and trial.[270] But even if one removes this specific basis for a fact-finder's initial assessment of odds, there is inevitably much undisputed case-specific information that can and will be used by the fact-finder in deciding the case.

The first category of background information (non-case-specific generalizations about the way the world works) is more troublesome than the second (undisputed case-specific facts) in terms of what I have described as the law's aspiration to objectivity. Information in the latter category is communicated, however informally, in open court and is subject to direct control by the tribunal; the great bulk of information in the former category is not. Still, it would be sticking one's head in the sand to pretend that the former does not enter decision making. Nor could it be otherwise. It is self-defeating to try to articulate norms that make the result of the trial depend solely on the evidence publicly adduced in court. Moreover, the importance of "jury noticed" facts is pervasive throughout the trial, not only at its inception, because each item of case-specific information that is formally adduced will be assessed by reference to background beliefs about the way the world works.

Despite all this, some scholars try to insist on ignoring what jurors almost surely do not. For example, Richard Posner has argued that a fact-finder should be "unbiased" at the beginning of evidence presentation and that the absence of bias means prior odds of 1:1, even in a criminal case.[271] This particular attempt to constrain juridical inference occasioned

---

[269] The specter of "stereotyping" may be raised by the foregoing example. An antidote for this particular intellectual confusion may be found in Schauer (2003) (discussing the inevitability of reasoning by generalizations, often pejoratively characterized as "stereotypes").

[270] See Wigmore (1981) § 2511 at 530 and 2 McCormick (2013) § 342 at 681.

[271] See Posner (1999) at 1514–15. Posner is not entirely clear about the point in time at which he thinks this normative prior is appropriate. As the foregoing discussion demonstrates, it makes a big difference whether one is thinking about the jurors' odds just before the

an insightful response by Richard Friedman, who argued that 1:1 prior odds is arbitrary, irrational, and incompatible with the normative message behind the presumption of innocence.[272] Professor Friedman's arguments stressed, and are most convincing in the context of, identity cases, cases in which the occurrence of a criminal act is not disputed, but the identity of the accused as the perpetrator is. Friedman's plausible suggestion for appropriate prior odds – to ask how likely the allegation would seem if it were made against a random passerby on the street instead of the person sitting in thecourtroom[273] – suggests prior odds much more favorable to the defense than 1:1. To be sure, prior odds of 1:1 are somewhat more plausible in the context of cases in which the accused does not deny her agency but disputes rather her degree of legal responsibility on account of self-defense, provocation, insanity, or some other ground.

Interestingly, there is some empirical evidence about where fact-finders actually start – given that jurors in criminal cases (as in civil cases) are not told what prior odds to assume – evidence that seems to support Judge Posner's assumption. Whereas some subjects appear to use presumed base rates for criminal convictions and other subjects (at least when appropriately prompted) use base rates more in line with Professor Friedman's suggestion, the results of a number of studies suggest that prior odds of guilt for a variety of criminal cases tend to cluster around 1:1.[274] To the extent that, rightly or wrongly, this is the fact-finder's starting point, once again, the discriminatory power of the evidence lies entirely in the likelihood ratio. Still, the studies to date do not fully resolve the matter because they do not account for the wealth of information that jurors receive in addition to the formal evidence in the case. For example, in one of the more interesting of these empirical studies, respondents were presented with a list of crimes by type and a description of the defendant simply as an adult white male. Based only on this very limited information, each respondent assigned prior odds as well as indicated the posterior odds that would be necessary for conviction with respect to each crime.[275] As already

---

formal introduction of testimony (i.e., after opening statements), or their odds at an earlier time, before they hear anything about the case (whatever that could mean), or something between these extremes.

[272] See Friedman (2000).
[273] Id. at 881–2.
[274] See Hastie (1993) at 98–9 (summarizing studies).
[275] Martin & Schum (1987). Although median responses were uniformly 1:1 odds, regardless of the crime, the best measure of central tendency for the prior odds assigned, the geometric mean, varied somewhat with the crime but remained between 1:2 and 2:1 in favor of guilt, which Martin and Schum described as "excessively high." Id. at 390–3, 402.

suggested, fact-finders invariably have considerable information about the case at the beginning of the formal introduction of evidence, certainly more than assumed by such a design. As a consequence, one can expect a great deal more variation in the prior odds in real cases.

2.6 Concluding Remarks

Inevitably, there is extensive debate about the usefulness of any decision-theoretic model such as the one described in § 2.2. Its seeming quantitative nature is anathema to many lawyers. Again, I have emphasized it for three reasons. First, because it is analytically precise, it provides a context in which to distinguish clearly the nature and function of Keynesian weight, which is the subject of Chapter 3. Second, as an appropriately rough and approximate guide, it has been powerfully endorsed as part of what the law is in fact doing by the Supreme Court's employment of it in its due process jurisprudence. Third, so far nothing more helpful has been as fully or successfully articulated and developed. If its ambitions are modestly understood, the decision-theoretic model is capable of embracing a diverse set of insights and inferential tools.

Still, I have not here attempted to address all the various arguments that this debate has spawned, for my concern is different. Many of those who are suspicious of quantification of odds or utilities nonetheless would give meaning to the standards of proof in terms of an assessment of what I have called "discriminatory power," even if it is not taken as determined by the specific odds ratio in criterion (2.2).[276] Even those who would use litigants merely as means to the end of creating appropriate incentives for substantive behavior employ a threshold decision criterion that is based on a comparison of how the evidence that the fact-finder has before it relates to the competing hypotheses. This core understanding of the burden of persuasion is what has been challenged by the arguments on which I shall focus attention in the following chapters.

We can now address what is, for the present work, the most important question: putting aside special proof devices, such as presumptions, does the assessment of the discriminatory power, whether quantified or not, coupled with a comparison of that result to the applicable standard of proof, whether quantified or not, exhaust the considerations that must be taken into account in deciding whether the burden of proof has been met? As stated in Chapter 1, those who give a negative answer to this

---

[276] See, e.g., Walker (1996) at 1095 n. 45, 1116–20.

question generally raise two related arguments. One is based on the idea of Keynesian weight, and the other is based on the idea of tenacity of belief.

In discussing these ideas, it is useful to have some working model of discriminatory power, and for this purpose, I will use the decision-theoretic model in its odds-form criterion (2.2) or its equivalent probability-form criterion (2.2'). I will sometimes refer to such a theory of discriminatory power as an "odds threshold" or "probability threshold" theory, for it posits that the essential judgment that must be made in determining whether the burden of persuasion has been satisfied is whether the odds or probability that the asserted cause of action has been instantiated exceeds a predetermined threshold. Again, such a model is subject to the possibility that the law permits some degree of ad hoc tailoring of that threshold by the fact-finder in the context of the particular case as well as the presumably more unusual possibility that the fact-finder will step out of its conventional role, as when the jury engages in nullification by giving a verdict contrary to its own assessment of the ultimate facts.

To reiterate, however, the bulk of the following discussion does not depend on the usefulness or appropriateness of the decision-theoretic model. One can easily imagine a theory of adjudication that proceeds by rejecting some of the assumptions on which the foregoing presentation has been based, such as the assumption that the fact-finder acts within the constraints of given rules of substantive law. Thus one might imagine that all the talk of such rules, both before and after the trial, is mere lawyers' talk and that what "really" happens is that fact-finders are attracted to a verdict for the party they believe to be morally more deserving, regardless of the legal rules. But this moral assessment surely would be affected by the fact-finders' beliefs about what happened between the parties. And those beliefs can be better or worse informed. This fact alone opens the door to the discussion of Keynesian weight.

3

Keynesian Weight and Decision Making
Being Prepared to Decide

He that judges without informing himself to the utmost that he is capable, cannot acquit himself of judging amiss.
— John Locke (c. 1690)[1]

One of the criticisms directed at the decision-theoretic model discussed in Chapter 2 (§ 2.2) is that the probability (or odds) that the claim is true cannot capture all of a decision maker's epistemic concerns. The question persists as to whether some additional epistemic concept or factor needs to be put into the mix of decision making. A similar concern presents itself for criteria of discriminatory power that are focused not on posterior odds assessments but rather solely on assessments of the strength of the publicly produced evidence (§ 2.3.1) or that are theory focused in that they require the fact-finder to compare the probability (or "plausibility") attaching to the claimant's theory of the case with that attaching to the defendant's theory of the case or to select the most plausible explanatory theory (§ 2.3.2). It is this quite general concern that gives rise to the question of Keynesian weight.

I begin by motivating this concern through a look at the problem of "naked statistical evidence" (§ 3.1). I then examine the nature and importance of Keynesian weight (§ 3.2), and identify a crucial but underappreciated dimension of Keynesian weight, its excusable preference structure (§ 3.3). In the rest of the chapter, I relate the understanding thereby developed to modern theorizing about informal reasoning (§ 3.4), comment on the possibility of quantifying Keynesian weight (§ 3.5), illustrate how the misunderstanding of the role of Keynesian weight is sometimes attributable to the erroneous assumption that it must figure as merely one ingredient in a holistic judgment of epistemic warrant (§ 3.6), relate it to decision making with belief functions that do not conform with the axioms of probability (§ 3.7), and conclude by relating the solution of the problem of Keynesian weight to the goals of adjudication (§ 3.8).

[1] Locke (1690) at 278.

While I draw on Keynes's insights, this is not a work in intellectual history, and I do not purport to follow Keynes in any detail.[2] Indeed, Keynes did not develop his idea of weight at any great length. I also draw on a number of secondary contributions, works developing aspects of Keynes's insight. These writers proceed from varying assumptions about the nature of probability, and their treatments of Keynesian weight are not identical.[3] I shall exploit common features where there is agreement about the nature of Keynesian weight, but I will also make clear where I disagree with each of these theorists and how I would develop the idea of evidential weight discussed by Keynes.

Throughout this discussion, I emphasize application of the ideas to adjudication. But one important conceptual point should be noted: in this chapter, references to a "decision maker," even when applied in the legal context, should be understood in a "corporate" sense unless the context clearly indicates otherwise. That is, the decision maker is the tribunal as a whole, including judge and jury, as well as all officers of the court, even the parties insofar as they are prescribed roles to play in litigation. Some readers, especially lawyers I fear, will have difficulty maintaining this decontextualized focus, wanting urgently to get to the practical bite of the argument as it affects the participants. To be sure, this assumption of a corporate decision maker will be relaxed when it becomes necessary to differentiate among the roles of the various juridical actors. That will occur in Chapter 4. At this point, however, it is important not to get caught up too deeply in controversial questions about juridical roles and legal rules lest one lose sight of the philosophical forest that subsumes these doctrinal trees.

3.1 Motivation: Paradoxical Cases of "Naked Statistical Evidence"

In the legal context, the argument from Keynesian weight arose out of attempts to solve certain puzzles associated with a probabilistic interpretation of the standards of proof, such as that provided by criterion (2.2). Typical is the "gatecrasher" scenario, a potential civil dispute posed

---

[2] I should mention, in particular, that Keynes was skeptical about the usefulness of the standard probability calculus for representing the epistemic probabilities involved in much practical decision making. See Keynes (1921) at 20–40; see also Runde (1994). On this issue, see supra § 2.2.2.

[3] Important secondary discussions of the Keynesian sense of weight appear in the following articles: Cohen, J. (1985); Davidson & Pargetter (1986); and Runde (1990). Extensive discussion of Keynesian weight can be found in the monograph, Cohen, J. (1989).

by Jonathan Cohen in which it is assumed that if such a criterion were applied, the critical probability P^* would be 0.5:

> Consider, for example, a case in which it is common ground that 499 people paid for admission to a rodeo, and that 1,000 are counted on the seats, of whom A is one. Suppose no tickets were issued and there can be no testimony as to whether A paid for admission or climbed over the fence. So by any possible criterion of mathematical probability there is a .501 probability, on the admitted facts, that he did not pay. The mathematicist theory would apparently imply that in such circumstances the rodeo organizers are entitled to judgment against A for the admission-money, since the balance of probability ... would lie in their favor. But it seems manifestly unjust that A should lose his case when there is an agreed mathematical probability of as high as .499 that he in fact paid for admission.... [T]here is something wrong somewhere. But where?[4]

The extensive discussion of this and similar hypothetical cases in the academic literature has tended to focus around two broad themes.[5] On the one hand, there are those who have argued that whatever the probabilities may show, a decision based only on probabilities is inconsistent with doing justice, perhaps because it is thought to treat the individual merely as a member of a statistical aggregate or because it would have undesirable behavioral consequences, such as creating perverse incentives for the behavior of the litigants or those similarly situated. On the other hand, there have been various arguments focused more on epistemic considerations, emphasizing the deficiency in the evidentiary grounds for concluding that the burden of proof has been satisfied. My interest lies in the latter kind of argument, although the policy of containing costs of decision is so ubiquitous that it cannot be shunted aside even in the epistemic realm.[6]

---

[4] Cohen, J. (1977) at 75. Cohen's assumption that the normative P^* that derives from a "mathematicist" interpretation is 0.5 is itself problematic; P^* is, arguably, somewhat higher than 0.5, at least for the kind of case posited. See the discussion of civil cases, especially in regard to the principle of civility, in § 2.2.1. Although for purposes of his example, he is entitled to assume that P^* is set at 0.5, this discrepancy may contribute to one's intuitive sense that allowing a verdict for the plaintiff would be problematic.

[5] See Koehler & Shaviro (1990) at 248 (in debates about the relevance of statistical base rates, "commentators have not always distinguished clearly between verdict accuracy and what we will term 'policy concerns' (*i.e.*, policies distinct from verdict accuracy that are implicated by trials)") and Redmayne (2008a) (distinguishing moral from inferential accounts of the denial of liability).

[6] To the extent that a clearly nonepistemological consideration is involved – as when the argument is that liability in one case would have to be generalized so that *every* attendee at the rodeo would be liable and the rodeo owner would be overcompensated – the argument usually amounts to the suggestion that the substantive law needs to be refined, modified from

In thinking about the epistemic issues raised by the hypothetical gatecrasher case, it is helpful to be clearer than Cohen was about the evidence involved in the case. There are at least four distinguishable pieces of evidence in the hypothetical, only the first of which is overtly statistical. First, there is evidence about the number of attendees who paid and the number who did not. Second, there is the evidence that A was an attendee. Third, although this is only implicit, there is evidence that A has been chosen as a defendant without any other reason besides the aforementioned statistical information for assigning him to the class of attendees who paid or the class of attendees who did not. And fourth, there is reason (of some kind, we are not told what) to believe (conclusively) that there can be no testimony regarding whether or not A paid.[7] (Presumably, this last means that A was not available either to testify at trial or to be deposed before trial in a manner that would make the deposition admissible at trial.) In his statement of the hypothetical problem, Cohen did not explicitly foreclose the possibility of testimony about whether *other* specific attendees paid or not, which testimony would, of course, potentially change the probability that A paid, but this appears simply to have been an oversight. That is, it appears that Cohen intended to hypothesize that no further evidence could be obtained from *any* source to help place A in one class or the other. The second and third (and possibly the fourth) items of evidence amount to saying that A was randomly selected from among those who attended.[8] Aside from A being a random attendee, all the discriminatory power of the evidence, therefore, resides in the first piece of evidence, which, of course, is the point of Cohen's hypothetical.

Even with all these assumptions, there is an inferential "gap" between the statistical data, the ratio of assumed gatecrashers to total attendees, and the epistemic probability of interest, the probability that A was a gatecrasher given the information posited. Some attempts to explain "what's

---

its conventional form, perhaps by creating some form of proportionate liability or improving (if necessary) rights of contribution among defendants as a class or imposing rules that would obviate the need for courts to confront such cases. See, e.g., Orloff & Stedinger (1983) (discussing an "expected value" liability rule, by which the plaintiff is awarded $P(C|E) \times D$, where D is the amount of the award if C were known to be true; noting that such awards avoid bias in the distribution of errors among plaintiffs as a class and defendants as a class) and Levmore (1990) at 694–6 (discussing rules that would create incentives for parties to avoid placing courts in the position of having to decide some kinds of cases).

[7] In a later article, Cohen clarified, only somewhat, by supposing that "perhaps the defendant was prevented by death from giving evidence on his own behalf and the relentless management pursued the case against his estate." Cohen, J. (1981) at 627 n. 2.

[8] Id. at 627 (clarifying that the plaintiff chose A "at random off the seats").

wrong" in the hypothetical have argued that the latter probability is not equal to 0.501, as Cohen assumes, but rather some figure less than 0.501 and that this explains why it would be improper to give a verdict for the plaintiff. Most prominently, David Kaye at one point argued that the failure of the plaintiff to present further evidence, evidence that is probably readily available to the plaintiff, itself warrants a reduction in the epistemic probability from the ratio of 0.501 to some lower figure.[9] There are two reasons to reject this argument. First, it violates Cohen's implicit assumption that no further evidence was available to be had, although admittedly Cohen was not entirely clear about this in his statement of the hypothetical.[10] Second, even if we take the hypothetical at face value – allowing for the possibility of additional evidence about whether other specific attendees paid or not – again, there is no reason, from the problem as posited, not to do the same thing with regard to the fact that the defense has presented no further evidence. Without more information, the argument seems entirely symmetrical, which leaves the epistemic probability at 0.501.[11] In any event, Cohen is entitled to assume such symmetry for purposes of his hypothetical.

Starting with Cohen, several scholars have then argued that what is "wrong" in such "naked statistical evidence" cases – that is, what should, and perhaps would, prevent a verdict in favor of the plaintiff – is a deficiency in what Keynes called the "weight" of the evidence: the evidence, though favoring the plaintiff in terms of a comparative assessment, is simply too thin, too weak, to support a verdict for the plaintiff.[12] Evidence, or

---

[9] Kaye (1979a) at 106–8; Kaye (1981) at 637–45.

[10] I agree with Ron Allen about how one should read Cohen's hypothetical: "The only sensible way to understand the hypothetical is that it presents the question of what should be done when this is all the evidence there is." Allen (1986) at 412.

[11] Again, this was Professor Allen's position. Id. at 412. Richard Lempert disagreed with Allen on the ground that it is not necessarily the case that the defendant would have access to the same evidence as the plaintiff. Lempert (1986) at 457 n. 46. But no facts in the hypothetical provide any basis for believing this to be true, or to be known by the tribunal to be true, so Allen was adding a plausible (and probably intended) assumption to the hypothetical, whereas Lempert defends Kaye's argument by challenging the hypothetical, suggesting new unknown facts that, if known, would affect one's reaction to the situation. To be clear, I think there is much truth in the arguments made by Kaye and Lempert. It is possible, for example, that missing evidence that might warrant modifying the probability of the claim is peculiarly available to only one side of the dispute, which would eliminate the symmetry in the hypothetical, provided that some evidence of that fact is known to the decision maker. But such a possibility also would not necessarily warrant a verdict (directed or otherwise) *for the defense* because the missing evidence might be peculiarly available to the defense. See infra § 4.3.

[12] Davidson & Pargetter (1987) at 183–5; Friedman (1996) at 1819; Stein (2005) at 64–106; and Ho (2008) at 166–8.

at least evidence of the right kind, is simply missing, or so it is claimed.[13] For present purposes, the specific "solutions" to hypothetical cases such as the gatecrasher scenario are less important than the general lessons to be learned from these exchanges about the idea of Keynesian weight.

The epistemic issues of interest here are also distinct from questions of purely descriptive psychology that are raised by such cases. As to the latter, the apparent reluctance to award verdicts for plaintiffs in such "naked statistical evidence" cases, which has been confirmed experimentally, is likely attributable to multiple factors, factors that apply even in some cases not traditionally conceived as nakedly statistical. In a series of experiments, Gary Wells provided important evidence regarding the psychological propensities involved.[14] Wells's paper reported the results of experiments that are incompatible with each of the following purported explanations of the indicated reluctance: (1) that it is the result of the decision makers having a subjective probability smaller than the objective chance reflected in the evidence (e.g., as a result of a missing evidence inference against the plaintiff because of evidence the plaintiff may have withheld), (2) that it is the result of decision makers having the wrong probability criterion, (3) that it is the result of discrimination by decision makers in favor of evidence that has causal relevance to the litigated event, (4) that it is the result of the decision makers' perception of the excessive liability that would be imposed2 on defendants in a long run of cases, and (5) that it is the result of decision makers' concerns about sample sizes or time-frame limitations on the evidence presented. To be sure, Wells's results do not mean that any of these factors is without some impact; rather, his results indicate that none of these factors is adequate to account for *all* the observed divergences (rational or irrational) between what one might expect from an unadorned probability-threshold decision criterion such as criterion (2.2′) and the actual decisions of test subjects.

---

[13] It is often claimed or assumed, as part of such arguments, that courts would not in fact allow a judgment for the plaintiff under the assumed facts. Insofar as such claims are considered descriptions of what courts in fact do or predictions of what courts will do, they are not supported by substantial authority in the case law. See, e.g., Brook (1985) (noting that the usually cited authorities typically do not involve such naked statistical evidence and that when courts are actually presented with what seems to be naked statistical evidence, such as the market-share evidence used to identify which manufacturer of a defective drug sold the drug to the plaintiff many years ago, the courts are not nearly so unreceptive to such evidence as has been supposed). See also Koehler (2002) (assessing the conditions under which courts treat background "base rate" probabilities as relevant).

[14] See Wells (1992).

By contrast, Wells found consistent support in his results for the hypothesis that in order for evidence to affect a decision maker's choice of verdict, *"the evidence must be presented in a form that makes that evidence believable or not believable depending on what one assumes about the ultimate fact."*[15] To a certain extent, that is support for an explanatory descriptive theory of how fact-finders assess evidence. But a careful reading reveals that it is a very specific kind of explanatory emphasis. Thus the testimony of a witness who, on the basis solely of information showing that an ultimate fact is 80 percent probable, asserts (unequivocally) that the ultimate fact is true is more likely to affect the verdict positively than the testimony of a witness who asserts that based on the available information, the ultimate fact is 80 percent probable, and this is so even if the decision maker attributes the same probability, here 80 percent, to the truth of the ultimate fact at issue in each case.[16] As applied to this comparison, what Wells means by the italicized hypothesis is that one cannot, with logical consistency, reject the ultimate fact in the first case without rejecting the witness's testimonial assertion, but one can, with logical consistency, reject the ultimate fact in the second case without rejecting the testimonial assertion.

There are at least two ways to interpret this phenomenon. It may mean that decision makers are loathe to render a verdict that requires them to declare that a witness is lying or mistaken, as would be true of a verdict against the ultimate fact in the face of the first witness's testimony but would not be true of a verdict against the ultimate fact in the face of the second witness's testimony. This would seem to be another application of a very broad principle of civility: one ought not to assert that a witness, sworn to tell the truth, is lying or mistaken unless some good reason is presented to believe that this is so. It would cohere with the idea that fact-finders seek to find an explanation of the evidence that allows them to believe the testimony of all witnesses.[17] Alternatively, it may mean that decision makers are inclined to rely on an assertion by a witness that relieves them of having to make the (inevitably) probabilistic ultimate determination, one that seems to allow the decision maker to say, if the decision turns out to be wrong, that the responsibility for the error lies with the witness rather than the decision maker.[18] The first possibility, while perhaps involving an

---

[15] Id. at 746 (emphasis in original).
[16] Id. at 749 ("It seems that reliance on probabilistic information is qualitatively distinct from reliance on someone else's belief or opinion, even if that person's belief or opinion is itself based merely on the probabilistic information.")
[17] Cf. id. at 750.
[18] Id.

ethically admirable trait, will be of no avail to fact-finders in cases where there is direct conflict in testimony so that the testimony of (at least) one side's witness inevitably must be rejected. The second possibility does not suffer from this problem. It involves fact-finders attempting to ensure for themselves a personal excuse in the event of error. Obviously, however, it suggests a phenomenon that should not be encouraged: a failure to accept the responsibility of decision. Indeed, it is essentially for this reason that the rules restricting testimony would ordinarily preclude a witness, at least a lay witness, from testifying as indicated by the first hypothesized witness: such unequivocal testimony would either fail to report that of which the witness has personal knowledge,[19] or it would be the statement of an opinion that is not sufficiently helpful when compared to a report of the underlying statistical information alone.[20]

Later research confirmed the "Wells effect" but suggested yet another explanation of it. These researchers found evidence supporting the idea that the variation in willingness to award a verdict, even when the subjects report the same probability of the claim being true, arises from the ease with which subjects can imagine a story consistent with nonliability.[21] This explanation generally reinforces the story model of jury inference, although it implies that jurors do not ignore alternative stories once they have settled on what they take to be the "best" one.[22]

In any event, the present inquiry is not directed at giving a complete psychological explanation of such inclinations. I have discussed some of the empirics on this matter in part to illustrate its complexity and in part to help distinguish the present line of inquiry. The present inquiry is, once more, directed at learning what can be gleaned from the discussion of such cases for a general theory of proof burdens and how Keynesian weight figures into such a theory. Even if it is the case that concerns about the inadequacies in Keynesian weight cannot explain some of the examples that instantiate the psychological reluctance first identified in connection with naked statistical evidence cases,[23] we may still come to appreciate the role of Keynesian weight by examining the arguments on the point. And it will

---

[19] See, e.g., Fed. R. Evid. 602.
[20] See, e.g., Fed. R. Evid. 701(b).
[21] See Niedermeier et al. (1999).
[22] Id. at 542.
[23] Concerns about deficiencies in Keynesian weight do not seem to be consistent with the difference in results between two experimental conditions tested by Wells, the "tire tracks" version of his experiment and the "tire tracks–belief" version. See Wells (1992) at 747. The explanation of this difference must be sought elsewhere.

be made plain in what follows that concerns about Keynesian weight are legitimate in such contexts.

But not *only* in such contexts. The paradoxical element of such cases inures in all fact-finding by virtue of unavoidable features of factual inference. Fact-finders rely on generalizations about the way the world works in drawing inferences from case-specific pieces of evidence (e.g., that a witness testified) and from evidenced, case-specific propositions of fact (e.g., what the witness asserted to be true). These generalizations are inherently statistical, although they are usually evaluated only intuitively, without any explicit calculation.[24] As a result, as Alex Stein has argued, the epistemological problem presented with regard to the ultimate facts by naked statistical evidence cases is actually presented with regard to factual inferences in *every* litigated case, although the problem is usually not so conspicuous.[25] As we will see, the insights associated with Keynesian weight are therefore also ubiquitous, and many examples offered in what follows will have nothing to do with the special problems usually associated with naked statistical evidence.

3.2 The Nature and Importance of Keynesian Weight: A First Look

A good place to start is to review what Keynes said regarding "weight" of the evidence:

> As the relevant evidence at our disposal increases, the magnitude of the probability of the argument may decrease or increase, according as the new knowledge strengthens the unfavourable or the favourable evidence; but something seems to have increased in either case – we have a more substantial basis upon which to rest our conclusion. I express this by saying that an accession of new evidence increases the weight of an argument. New evidence will sometimes decrease the probability of an argument, but it will always increase its "weight." ... [W]eight, to speak metaphorically, measures the sum of the favourable and unfavourable evidence, probability measures the difference.[26]

---

[24] See supra § 2.4, text accompanying Figure 2.
[25] Stein (2005) at 64–106 (discussing the "Gatecrasher" case, the "Blue Bus" case, the "Prisoners in the Yard" case, and the "Two Witness" case and relating them to the philosophical puzzles called the "Lottery Paradox" and the "Preface Paradox"). I do not subscribe to Professor Stein's resolution of these paradoxes, but it seems clear that whatever analysis is needed to resolve them is also needed to confront the ubiquitous use of generalizations in the process of inference.
[26] Keynes (1921) at 71, 77.

This is a simple yet insightful point. If one flips a small, round, flat object (not a real coin, for that would introduce a variety of *ex ante* expectations) and one obtains 8 "heads" out of 10 flips, one would plausibly estimate the odds on getting heads on any given flip as 8:2, or the probability of getting heads as 0.8. And if, instead, one estimated after 800 heads were obtained in 1,000 flips, one would still estimate the probability at 0.8. But one would have a firmer basis for doing so. Alternatively, to take into account the *ex ante* principle of indifference, as between heads and tails, one might use Laplace's rule of succession. By this rule, one starts with the fraction 0.5 as the probability of a heads – reflecting the contingent fact that, as between heads and tails, one has no reason to favor one result over the other before conducting the test – and then one revises the probability estimate by adding the number of heads m obtained to the numerator and the number of trials n to the denominator, for an estimate of $(m + 1)/(n + 2)$.[27] With 8 heads out of 10 experimental tosses, one would then estimate the probability as $(1 + 8)/(2 + 10) = 0.75$. The same basic point applies because one might compare this estimate to an estimate based on 751 heads out of 1,000 flips, for which Laplace's rule would yield an estimate of the probability of heads as $(1 + 751)/(2 + 1{,}000) = 0.75$. Again, the estimate is the same, but the basis for it is firmer.[28] This "firmer basis" reflects an increase in Keynesian weight.

The example highlights an aspect of Keynesian weight that is not often identified. In referring to increasing weight by adding relevant evidence in the form of additional flips, it is understood that the flips are designed to be representative of the flip the probability of which is being assessed. The greater the representativeness, the better the evidence that results. For example, if the probability to be assessed is that of an ordinary person's flip of the object, it would not do to substitute a mechanical flipping device that is so precise that exactly the same conditions of flipping are reproduced each time. Indeed, if the conditions are controlled precisely enough, the object will land the same way, either heads every time or tails every time (quantum mechanics adjustments being negligible). That is, what makes the human flipping of the object a nondeterministic experiment (aside from unpredictable wind variation and such) is that flipping by a

---

[27] See Cohen, J. (1989) at 97 (discussing strengths and weaknesses of Laplace's rule) and Gillies (2000) at 69–72 (showing how Laplace's rule can be derived from the theory of subjective probability using a version of the principle of indifference).

[28] Of course, such examples suggest a relationship between weight and confidence intervals; when confidence intervals for probability estimates are possible, then increases in weight will sometimes narrow the confidence interval. But the relationship here is complex. I return to it later (§ 5.1).

human hand introduces a variety of random factors into the initiation of the flip itself. This means that there is a distinct idea of the improvement in the *quality* of the evidence used. That is, improvement of Keynesian weight can result from the acquisition of *more* relevant evidence (100 flips instead of 10) – a "quantitative" improvement – or it can result simply from an improvement in the *quality* of the evidence that is obtained (10 highly representative flips instead of 10 poorly representative flips). Although this qualitative aspect is important, it is often suppressed in discussions of Keynesian weight, with no serious theoretical loss.[29]

That said, Keynes's point readily generalizes to any theory about the discriminatory power of evidence as between contending hypotheses, whether or not articulated in terms of probabilities and, if so, whether or not based on the particular "logical" theory of probability that Keynes endorsed.[30] As explained in Chapter 2, the discriminatory power of the evidence is the degree to which a rational decision maker is convinced of the truth of a proposition *as compared with* some competing hypothesis (which can be simply that the former proposition is false). It is a function (in part) of the extent to which the proposition provides a better explanatory account of the evidence than does the competing hypothesis (§§ 2.3, 2.4, and 2.5). But this comparative measure can be based on relatively "thin" evidence (i.e., evidence of small quantity or poor quality) or on relatively "rich" evidence (i.e., evidence of large quantity and high quality), the difference between which concerns weight in the Keynesian sense. Keynesian weight can be said to refer to the relative "completeness" of evidence, the extent to which the evidence as a whole addresses the important inferential questions that are raised by the competing hypotheses, including questions of the reliability of the items of evidence considered.[31] Again, an increase in Keynesian weight can increase, decrease, or leave unchanged the degree to which the evidence favors one side or the other.

---

[29] An improvement in quality is a "substitution" that can be decomposed into two steps: the addition of one item of evidence and the elimination of another. If the item eliminated is itself relevant (albeit inferior to the added item), one does not need the second step. That is, an improvement in quality can be understood as an increase in quantity. The second, eliminative step arises only from the importance of economy in decision making when the original evidence has, in the context of the added evidence, only marginal probative value. This "substitution" effect is a common feature of many common-law admissibility rules designed to improve the quality of evidence received at trial. See § 4.1.3.

[30] Keynes (1921) at 77 (making a similar observation).

[31] Stein (2005) at 91–106. Although there is little harm in speaking this way, it does pose problems of giving concrete meaning to the idea of "complete" evidence. On this, see §§ 3.3 & 3.5.

Of course, estimating the "bias" of a coinlike object is not much like deciding the facts that are typically disputed. A somewhat different example will add precision while couching the issue in terms of competing adjudicative hypotheses and also distancing the discussion from overtly statistical forms of evidence. From a baseline of given evidence with regard to a proposition and a competing hypothesis, consider the effect of conducting a test for which a positive result supports the proposition and a negative result supports the competing hypothesis. (In the adjudication context, this might be, for example, a DNA test comparing two biological specimens, or more simply but more abstractly, it could be the "test" of calling a witness to the stand who is expected to be able to support or refute the claim.) The quantitative aspect of Keynesian weight is reflected simply in conducting the test. The qualitative aspect is reflected in the quality of the procedures used in performing the test. Properly conducting the test and obtaining a result therefrom (regardless of whether the result is positive or negative) are what increase weight in the Keynesian sense, but (in itself) they have an indeterminate effect on the degree to which the evidence favors the proposition or the competing hypothesis. Conversely, *which* value is obtained from the test (positive or negative) is what affects the discriminatory power of the evidence as a whole, but it has no effect on Keynesian weight.[32] Strictly speaking, it makes no sense to think in terms of the degree to which the Keynesian weight of the evidence as a whole "favors" a hypothesis over its competitor. But one can speak of the degree to which, for a given level of Keynesian weight, the discriminatory power of the evidence favors the hypothesis, and one can speak of a change in Keynesian weight resulting in a change in the discriminatory power of the evidence.

Of what significance, then, is Keynesian weight to the decision maker? Keynes himself expressed doubt about the utility of the separate concept of evidential weight:

> For in deciding on a course of action, it seems plausible to suppose that we ought to take account of the weight as well as the probability of different expectations. But it is difficult to think of any clear example of this, and

---

[32] And what about the possibility of an "indeterminate" result from the test? If the test is conducted but yields nothing in favor of the hypothesis or against it, does that nonetheless involve an increase in Keynesian weight? Not according to Keynes, although he does not speak specifically to this point, for the evidence of the test result in that case would be irrelevant, and for Keynes it seems that evidence is relevant if and only if taking it into account would increase Keynesian weight. Keynes (1921) at 72. Addressing this issue would require a deeper excursion into the matter of the criterion of relevance than is here needed. The matter is taken up further, infra § 4.1.1.

> I do not feel sure that the theory of "evidential weight" has much practical significance.[33]

But he then continued, in the very next paragraph, to develop the core of that practical significance:

> Bernoulli's second maxim, that we must take into account all the information we have, amounts to an injunction that we should be guided by the probability of that argument, amongst those of which we know the premises, of which the evidential weight is the greatest. But should not this be re-enforced by a further maxim, that we ought to make the weight of our arguments as great as possible by getting all the information we can?[34]

That is, Bernoulli advised that one take all known (relevant) evidence into consideration, and Keynes added that one should expand the package of relevant evidence as much as feasible. Intuition certainly supports the ideas that one should use all the relevant information one has and that one should be open to, and indeed seek, additional evidence in many contexts. But can it be demonstrated why and to what extent this is so? Keynes was not optimistic.[35]

In the decades since Keynes wrote about evidential weight, scholars have wrestled with questions of both the meaning and the usefulness of the concept. As we shall see, a significant portion of this debate has not emphasized the importance of a key distinction that separates discriminatory power from Keynesian weight. Specifically, Keynesian weight is subject to the decision maker's control in a sense that discriminatory power is not. Within practical limits, Keynesian weight can be (and is) *chosen*, for example, by choosing to conduct some test the result of which is expected

---

[33] Keynes (1921) at 76.
[34] Id.
[35] Keynes thought that managing these kinds of questions is a very difficult task, at least conceptually:

> It is difficult to see, however, to what point the strengthening of an argument's weight by increasing the evidence ought to be pushed. We may agree that, when our knowledge is slight but capable of increase, the course of action, which will, relative to such knowledge, probably produce the greatest amount of good, will often consist in the acquisition of more knowledge. But there clearly comes a point when it is no longer worthwhile to spend trouble, before acting, in the acquisition of further information, and there is no evident principle by which to determine how far we carry our maxim of strengthening the weight of our argument. A little reflection will probably convince the reader that this is a very confusing problem.

Id. at 76–7.

to favor one hypothesis over the other. By contrast, for a given level of Keynesian weight, discriminatory power can only be *assessed*, by observing the result of the test and placing that result in the context of other evidence relating to the hypothesis. In saying this, I do not need to deny that there are creative, perhaps even ethical components to the assessment of discriminatory power.[36] Nor do I mean to deny that assessments of utility (costs of various sorts) normatively constrain the selection of Keynesian weight. I mean only to say that in the typical decision problem there is a distinctively different and greater freedom in the selection of Keynesian weight than in the assessment of discriminatory power.[37]

To the extent that the level of Keynesian weight can be selected, it thus poses a separate and distinct kind of decision problem: to make the first-order decision or to postpone that decision while seeking (or otherwise taking into account) additional information. In the 1960s, I. J. Good proved that the intuitions of people like Bernoulli and Keynes were correct; Good showed that when using the decision-theoretic approach from which criterion (2.2) is derived, "in expectation, it pays to take into account further evidence, provided that the cost of collecting and using this evidence, although positive, can be ignored."[38] More recently, without

---

[36] Cf. Shafer (1986) (emphasizing the "constructive" character of probability judgments).

[37] Cf. Swinburne (2001) at 3 (distinguishing *synchronic* justification of beliefs – justification at a given time and with given evidence – from *diachronic* justification of beliefs – synchronic justification that results from, and is conditioned on, adequate investigation). Swinburne argues that one's beliefs at a given time and on given evidence cannot be chosen, whereas the extent of the investigation that informs one's beliefs can be. Id. at 23–4.

[38] Good (1966). To be clear, Good did not purport to show that the utility of decision always increases with accretions of relevant information; he showed only that the *expected* utility of such a utility-maximizing decision criterion would not decrease with such accretion, and it increases if there is any positive probability that the new information can affect the contemplated choice of action. One who uses such a criterion will, in the long run of decisions, have net utility gains from taking additional costless relevant evidence into account. Here is a nice summary sketch of the proof:

> [Let G stand for "Go" and W stand for "Wait-and-see" whether some additional, probabilistically relevant proposition, C, is true. Now suppose] the simple case of two alternative actions A_1 and A_2 (accept or reject some bet, say). If you take option G, then you will now choose one of these – A_1, say. Let $EU(A_1|C)$ be the expected utility of this action assuming C. Then we can decompose the expected gain of taking option G and so choosing A_1 as
>
> (I) $EU(G) = EU(A_1|C)\Pr(C) + EU(A_1|\text{not-}C)\Pr(\text{not-}C)$
>
> Now, suppose you take option W instead and find out whether C. The discovery that C might make you choose A_2 rather than A_1. Alternatively, the discovery that not-C might make you do this. (Both discoveries cannot make you switch; otherwise, you would not have preferred A_1 to start with.)

explicitly discussing Keynesian weight, Bryan Skyrms has both identified the limitations of Good's result and extended it in important ways.[39] But again, Skyrms's extensions assume that information acquisition is costless. When those costs cannot be ignored – and, of course, in practical decision making they rarely can be – then there is necessarily a tradeoff between the anticipated information acquisition (and use) costs and the increase in the expected maximum utility to be obtained from the decision.[40]

As suggested in Chapter 1, the Keynesian weight with respect to a hypothesis is always at the same level as the Keynesian weight with respect to its competitor because both are being assessed relative to the same total mass of evidence.[41] For example, if one starts with the probability of hypothesis H_1 considered relative to evidence E_1 and the probability of H_2 relative to E_2, one would not determine (or act on) the relative odds of H_1 and H_2 without considering, as to each, the combined evidence E_1 and E_2. This follows from the Good/Skyrms results. Consequently, Keynesian weight is a function of the evidence considered with respect to designated competing hypotheses. For simplicity, I sometimes refer to the weight of evidence relative to a hypothesis, but that should always be understood as shorthand for the weight of the evidence relative to a set of competing hypotheses. Often the competing hypothesis is the negation of the hypothesis, as in criterion (2.2). Unfortunately, certain confusions related to this point persist, in part because of the way Keynes expressed his views. In particular, Keynes did not explicitly think of weight as a function of *competing* hypotheses (and the evidence therefor) but only as a function of a single hypothesis (and the evidence therefor). He did, however, readily

> Suppose, without loss of generality, that discovering C makes you switch to A_2. Then
>
> (II) $EU(W) = EU(A_2|C)\Pr(C) + EU(A_2|\text{not-}C)\Pr(\text{not-}C)$
>
> But this must be larger than $EU(G)$, because if $EU(A_2|C)$ was not bigger than $EU(A_1|C)$, you would not have chosen A_2 when you discovered C.

Beebee & Papineau (1997) at 239–40.

[39] See Skyrms (1990) at 87–106. One can broaden the insight expressed in the Good/Skyrms results, removing it from the decision-theoretic context, by formulating a relationship between augmentations of relevant evidence and "expected probability error" or "expected certainty" (i.e., using probabilities but without involving utilities). This is discussed later in connection with the idea of resiliency of probabilities. See § 5.1.
[40] Id. at 101–4.
[41] See Cohen, J. (1985) at 268–70. Cohen advances the idea that Keynesian weight addresses the problem of "how to grade our entitlement to detach an unconditional probability from a conditional one." Id. at 267. I do not pursue this idea here. See also Cohen, J. (1989) at 103–4.

acknowledge that the weight of a hypothesis (relative to given evidence) must be the same as the weight of the evidence with respect to the negation of that hypothesis (relative to the same evidence).[42] And the point readily generalizes to the analogous proposition for any competing hypotheses.

This observation defuses an argument presented by Alex Stein, a scholar clearly sensitive to concerns about Keynesian weight. He suggests a dilemma faced by anyone endorsing the applicability of mathematical probability in modeling practical decision making based on uncertainty about a specific event:

> Consider a reasoner who faces a high but not weighty probability, on the one hand, and a weighty but low probability, on the other hand. Which of the two probabilities is more dependable than the other? This question does not have a readily available answer. There is simply no metric by which to compare the two sets of probabilities.[43]

What exactly is Stein comparing in this passage? One possibility, in line with what has been argued earlier (and suggested by the phrase "two sets of probabilities"), is that Stein contemplates two evidentiary states with different weights in which the same set of target probabilities (the probability that the claim is true as opposed to the probability that it is false) is at issue. For this situation, as we have seen, one must choose how much Keynesian weight is appropriate, and higher weight is chosen because of the increase in the expected gain in utility of decision. (There are no costs of obtaining the higher weight, for Stein's hypothesis contemplates that the evidence of higher weight is already available to the decision maker.) In choosing to go with higher weight, a comparison of the probabilities of the competing hypotheses is unimportant, and Stein's dilemma disappears. One only compares probabilities after choosing the evidence of higher weight.

Another interpretation, however, seems closer to Stein's intended argument: perhaps Stein contemplates being required to decide between two stories, say, the story of the claimant and the story of the defendant, in a situation where the probabilities favor the claimant, but the weights favor the defendant. For example, the probability that the claimant's story is true is 0.6, but the weight of that probability is very low, whereas the probability that the defendant's story is true is only 0.4, but the weight of that probability is very high. Stated this way, the matter does indeed seem problematic. But if this is what Stein means, the answer is that the dilemma posed is based on a false premise. The weight of the evidence for those competing

---

[42] Keynes (1921) at 73.
[43] Stein (2011) at 223 n. 69.

hypotheses is always the same; weight does not "favor" one hypothesis over another.

One might try to suggest that weight can be attributed to the evidence associated with a particular hypothesis *by itself*, which inevitably is to say, *as compared with its negation*, and then argue that two mutually exclusive but not complementary hypotheses can be compared in terms of both probability and weight.[44] For example, if S_π is the plaintiff's story and S_Δ is the defendant's story ($S_\Delta \subsetneq \text{not-}S_\pi$), E is the evidence being taken into account, and, say, $P(S_\pi|E) = 0.4$ and $P(S_\Delta|E) = 0.3$, then it would seem to make sense to speak of the weight of the evidence E being different in regard to the two probabilities. This is true, however, only because the two hypotheses are not being considered in relation to each other. Symbolically, we might express this by using $W_E(X, Y)$ to denote weight of the evidence E with respect to competing hypotheses X and Y and writing this inequality as $W_E(S_\pi, \text{not-}S_\pi) \neq W_E(S_\Delta, \text{not-}S_\Delta)$. But even if there is some quantitative or qualitative measure of weight that would allow this comparison, as indeed Keynes imagined there might be, it would be pointless, at least in the adjudicative context.[45] When the sets of competing hypotheses are different, the weights involved are, strictly speaking, noncomparable. On this interpretation of Stein's argument, the seeming paradox arises precisely because he is *purporting* to compare the probabilities and weights of the evidence relative to the competing hypotheses S_π and S_Δ, not either one of these as compared with its negation. But as to these hypotheses, when competing with each other, there is only one pertinent weight, what would by this notation be called $W_E(S_\pi, S_\Delta)$, and the decision resolves to the comparison of probabilities.[46]

Taking stock, I have argued that these two dimensions of evidence, discriminatory power and Keynesian weight, are fundamental to decision making under conditions of uncertainty. Someone contemplating action faces *two decisions* that correspond to these two senses of evidential weight. When, for example, a certain action is desirable if and only if some proposition is true, then one's choice depends on the discriminatory

---

[44] Stein's arguments elsewhere seem to confirm this way of interpreting his dilemma. See id. at 241–2 (arguing as if the claimant's hypothesis can be supported by a different Keynesian weight than that which supports the defendant's hypothesis).

[45] For discussion of the quantification of Keynesian weight, see infra § 3.5.

[46] I have simplified in the text by assuming that no other "stories" are under consideration, as under the relative plausibility theory of discriminatory power. As discussed in § 2.3.2, the decisionally pertinent comparison is between C and not-C, where S_π instantiates C and S_Δ instantiates not-C, and as to which the pertinent weight is $W_E(C, \text{not-}C)$.

power of the evidence regarding its truth. (The truth or falsity of the proposition might affect the expected total utility of the action, as illustrated by criterion (2.2).) But that decision can be *displaced* by a second: the decision whether to decide about the contemplated proposition (and consequent act) based on the available information or, in the alternative, to postpone that "primary" decision to collect additional information relevant to it. Keynesian weight relates to this "decision about deciding" because this second-order decision depends on whether Keynesian weight is adequate to warrant making the primary decision.[47] A rational choice requires two determinations, however implicit, corresponding to these two dimensions of the evidence.[48]

Some discussions of Keynesian weight, whether or not by that name, that appear in the philosophical literature also tend to be framed in ways that can obscure application of the idea to the context of adjudication. Take, for example, Hans Reichenbach's discussion of "higher-order probabilities" in his 1949 treatise on probability.[49] He argues that if "before a horse race, a well-versed expert of the sport tells us that the winning chances of the favorite amount to 80 percent, and another racing fan, more enthusiastic than expert, claims the same probability for the victory of the favorite, we shall evaluate the two identical statements differently: we place more trust in the statement of the expert."[50] The analogy to adjudication is fairly straightforward, as we might imagine two witnesses testifying in the same case, one with what is clearly assumed to be a greater degree of reliability. If the two witnesses testify in a corroborating fashion, as in Reichenbach's example, then the greater part of the effect on the discriminatory power

---

[47] A decision-theoretic "monist" might argue, in reply, that one need not conceive of decision making in this two-step fashion. In principle, one can imagine the decision maker making *one* decision among *three* options: (1) accept the hypothesis or claim, (2) reject the hypothesis or claim, or (3) postpone the decision. This way of putting things, however, hides the fact that if the last option is chosen, the process is not ended, at least not the same way it is ended if either of the first two is chosen. It thus obscures the fact that the third option is quite different in nature. Most important for our purposes, it misses something that will be developed extensively in Chapter 4: the task of choosing between option (1) and option (2) – that is, accepting or rejecting the claim – can be, and often is, assigned to a different institutional actor within an adjudicative system (namely, the fact-finder) than the actor who is assigned the task of choosing between option (3) and going forth with a choice between options (1) and (2) (namely, the judge).

[48] The question naturally arises whether a decision about whether to acquire additional evidence can itself be modeled using an expected utility criterion analogous to criterion (2.2). See, e.g., Rescher (1989) at 124–6 (providing a rudimentary model along these lines) and Swinburne (2001) at 166–82 (giving richer details of such a decision criterion).

[49] Reichenbach (1949).

[50] Id. at 324.

of the evidence will come from that of the expert, whereas if, contrary to the hypothetical, the two opinions were in opposition, we would naturally tend to favor that of the expert, *ceteris paribus*. But then Reichenbach continues, "This means that his [the expert's] statement has a higher probability of the second level. It is obvious, however, that the higher probability of the second level is not expressible by a change in the probability of the first level: we must not assume the probability of the victory of the favorite as smaller or greater *if our only basis is the information given by the inexperienced fan*. If we have no better information, we should rather refrain from betting than bet on the basis of a value other than 80 percent."[51]

In Reichenbach's revised hypothetical, as indicated by the emphasized passage, it is clear (albeit implicit) that he contemplates not one, but two races. As to one, the only evidence is that of the expert; as to the other, the only evidence is that of the enthusiastic fan. Otherwise, the two races are assumed to be indistinguishable. Reichenbach then tells us that it might not be irrational to place a bet on the favorite in the one race, when supported by the opinion of the expert, even if one would rationally refuse to do so in the other race, when supported by the opinion of the enthusiastic fan. Now, one cannot say (at least, not from what has been developed so far) that the Keynesian weight of the evidence in the first case is greater (or less) than the Keynesian weight in the second case, but one might well say that the Keynesian weight in the second case is "insufficient" in some sense. (The precise sense is the subject of the next section.) Reichenbach's prescription is important: if the evidence is insufficiently trustworthy, as in the latter race, then "refrain from betting." Here, of course, is where the analogy to adjudication becomes complicated.

As explained in Chapter 2, the option of "not betting" is not available to the fact-finder. Because of the principle of finality of adjudication, the fact-finder's "not betting" must be treated by the law as a verdict for either the claimant or the defendant, which is to say that it is the functional equivalent of betting all the same. The key to completing the analogy is Reichenbach's phrase, "if we have no better information," for even if "not betting" is not ultimately an option, it might be one in a temporary sense. In the adjudicative context, "not betting" at the moment can be an opportunity to obtain additional information *before* the verdict is required. There are various procedural steps prior to the determination of a verdict that might make this possible, though these are generally not in the purview of the fact-finder as such. Importantly, Reichenbach stops

---

[51] Id. (emphasis added).

short of saying what is to be done if there is no further information to be obtained (beyond the opinion of the enthusiastic fan) *and* the option of "not betting" is no longer available. Would he then recommend betting on the basis of the 80 percent probability provided by the enthusiastic fan? This seems to be what he would have us infer. For what else is there to do? One would hardly invoke a "default rule" to bet *against* the favorite simply because of the paucity of the evidence relating to the race.[52]

In a more recent discussion of "higher-order beliefs" that connects this idea explicitly to Keynesian weight, Nils-Eric Sahlin uses legal adjudication as an explicit illustration.[53] Sahlin invites us to compare two criminal cases in which (apparently) the defendant denies that she had anything to do with the crime. In one case, clear eyewitness testimony placing the defendant at the scene of the crime combines with forensic science evidence (i.e., hair fiber and shoe prints) to produce a combined "evidentiary value" that warrants a high "level of conviction" that the defendant is guilty. (Sahlin describes this level as between "confirmation" that the defendant is guilty and "obviousness" that the defendant is guilty, and he offers the suggestion that this might translate to a probability of guilt between 0.8 and 0.9.) In the second case, the evidence is more ambiguous, involving "a number of rather weak pieces of forensic evidences" and a complicated chain of "circumstantial evidence which appears to link the defendant to the crime." However, "despite the fact that each piece of evidence viewed independently is very weak, most of the evidentiary facts concur and since there are so many of them, it is argued that the combined evidentiary value is high enough to convict the defendant," yielding a "completely reasonable and rational assessment" that it is "confirmed" or "obvious" that the defendant is guilty, "given that we are asked to give as precise an evaluation as possible."[54]

Two points are important here. First, Sahlin hypothesizes that the most precise evaluation possible in the two cases yields approximately the same level of conviction about the guilt of the defendant, the same degree of probability that the defendant is guilty. For this reason, he concludes that "in both these criminal cases there will be a verdict of guilty."[55] (From context, it is clear that Sahlin is not really attempting, as this language

---

[52] I am assuming away, of course, the possibility that one has additional evidence, not mentioned by Reichenbach, that would, for example, make the enthusiastic fan a "negative barometer," one whose predictions are more likely to be wrong than right, as well as suspicions about the fan's nefarious motives in making his or her assessment.
[53] Sahlin (1993).
[54] Id. at 18–20.
[55] Id. at 20.

suggests, to make a *prediction* of how a court would decide the two cases; rather, he is making the evaluative judgment that if the two cases were allowed to go to verdict, the court would be as warranted in convicting the defendant in the second case as in the first.) The second point is that this remains true even though, in the second case, "one is somewhat worried about what one does not know. Crucial pieces of evidence or information may be missing and have thus not been presented at trial."[56] In other words, in the second case, but not the first, one is concerned about a deficiency in the Keynesian weight of the evidence presented.

Sahlin uses the term *epistemic risk* to describe the difference between his two hypothetical cases, and he poses a critical question. Despite his endorsement of a rational and reasonable verdict against the defendant in both cases, the two cases involve different epistemic risk. So we should ask, says Sahlin: "What is an acceptable level of epistemic risk? Is a verdict of guilty reasonable if the combined evidentiary value meets our evidentiary requirements but at the same time results in a high degree of epistemic risk-taking?" Sahlin comments that "this type of *epistemic risk-taking* often [is not] thought of as genuine risk-taking and its importance for rational decision-making is thus often forgotten. This fact may of course have more or less serious consequences depending on how our legal system is constructed."[57] But, if a guilty verdict by the fact-finder is rational and reasonable in both cases, when and how should the legal system take into account this problem of epistemic risk? More generally, when and how should the legal system take into account deficiencies in Keynesian weight? These questions are still to be addressed.

What we may conclude already, however, is that one must be careful in thinking about the idea of "risk aversion" in this context. A person who is risk averse is someone who prefers a certain gain to an uncertain gain the expected value of which is the same.[58] Such a person is willing to take a lower expected gain to achieve less potential variance in the return on investment.[59] Accordingly, one might explain a preference of a bettor to bet on a race that is supported only by Reichenbach's expert witness over a bet on a race that is supported only by Reichenbach's enthusiastic fan

---

[56] Id. at 19.
[57] Id. at 20.
[58] For example, if given a choice between (a) an investment with a certain return of 10 and (b) an investment with a 50 percent chance of return of 20 and a 50 percent chance of a return of 0, and thus an expected return of $(0.5)(20) + (0.5)(0) = 10$, the risk-averse investor will choose (a).
[59] See Polinsky (1989) at 53–5.

(*ceteris paribus*, of course) on the grounds that the bettor is risk averse and there is more risk in the latter case. Similarly, one might explain a tribunal's preference to "bet" on Sahlin's first case rather than on his second case (again, *ceteris paribus*) on the grounds that the tribunal is risk averse. But this last comparison makes clear how the analogy to decision making in adjudication must be understood: ordinarily, the tribunal does not get to choose which *case* to decide, which case to favor with a "bet"; it must decide all cases that properly come before it for a final decision.[60] One can, of course, say that the tribunal chooses which *side* to bet on, but this cannot be based on risk avoidance: the two sides of the dispute are "flip sides" of the same decision problem, with a given – that is, the same – degree of epistemic risk. Most important, in finally deciding a given case, one cannot *avoid* the uncertainty associated with one's estimates of $P(C|E)$ by applying a default rule in favor of one party or the other.[61] If the law is to avoid, or at least reduce, what Sahlin calls epistemic risk, it must do so by choosing to decide what might be considered a "different" case, namely, the same controversy but with the a different package of evidence.

3.3 Adequacy of Keynesian Weight as a "Preferential" Requirement

The discussion of the preceding section allows us to address paradoxical cases like the gatecrasher case posed at the beginning of this chapter. Nonlawyer theorists such as Reichenbach and Sahlin have identified the inferential dilemmas presented by deficiencies in Keynesian weight. Meanwhile, some of those legal scholars whose intuition is that "something is wrong" in allowing the claimant to recover in such cases have in mind the idea that the level of Keynesian weight is somehow inadequate. In this section, I merge these two lines of thought to explore more deeply the nature of Keynesian weight and its pragmatic role in decision making.

---

[60] Some theorists have toyed with the idea of developing a mechanism by which to limit which cases are considered by the court in light of the quality of the evidence that will eventually be developed and adduced. See, e.g., Sanchirico (1997). If such a mechanism were practicable, then courts could limit the use of adjudicative mechanisms to cases of relatively high posterior probabilities or relatively high Keynesian weight, either of which would be useful in allocating limited governmental resources for adjudication to those cases in which the largest utility gains could be expected.

[61] As already discussed (§ 2.2.3), severe uncertainty about $P(C|E)$ might necessitate an appeal to a more complex decision criterion, such as a maximin rule. For discussion of related ideas, see infra § 5.1 (discussing the significance of resiliency in the estimation of probabilities).

One instructive early example is an argument by Barbara Davidson and Robert Pargetter, which is set in the criminal-law context:

> Suppose we have ten defendants and absolutely reliable evidence that of the group, nine are guilty and one is innocent.... There is a high probability for any of the defendants that he or she is guilty. Yet surely we must say that there is no guilt established beyond reasonable doubt for that defendant. And making the probability even higher is no help: the same point applies if there were ninety-nine known to be guilty among one hundred defendants.[62]

Implicit in their argument is that the defendant whose guilt is at issue in the example is selected at random from the group of ten, or what amounts to the same thing from the court's viewpoint, that there is no evidence before the court that can serve to identify the one of the group who is innocent. And the intuition that guilt beyond reasonable doubt has not been established rests on the importance of acquiring such individuating evidence. Davidson and Pargetter then provide a solution to their version of the paradox in terms of Keynesian weight: they argue that an explicit weight requirement must be *coupled with* a requirement of sufficiently high probability of guilt.[63]

This is certainly a move in the right direction, but it is just here that one must be careful. There are (at least) two ways to understand this distinct idea of a separate requirement of Keynesian weight. By one account, the deficiency in Keynesian weight in this example is akin to a failure of the odds on guilt to reach the level required by criterion (2.2). It is something that the decision maker assesses, not chooses. It supposes that there is some level of Keynesian weight – some minimum that does not depend on the costs of acquiring evidence – that must be achieved for a positive verdict to be rendered. In default of achieving this level, a negative verdict is proper. Davidson and Pargetter suggest as much by saying that the evidence in their example does not satisfy the beyond reasonable doubt standard appropriate for criminal cases. This is the framework that most legal scholars have used when importing the concept of Keynesian weight into the analysis of adjudication.

By the other account, which I defend here, the extent of the deficiency in Keynesian weight is a product of the choice of the decision maker. To say that Keynesian weight ought to be greater is to say that the decision maker ought to choose a greater Keynesian weight.[64] One cannot infer anything

---

[62] Davidson & Pargetter (1987) at 183.
[63] Id. at 183–6.
[64] There is an obvious sense in which "ought to be greater" does not *entail* "ought to be increased." By "ought to be greater," one might mean simply that "a verdict ought not to be

about discriminatory power from such a conclusion, and to argue that Keynesian weight *ought* to be increased is to presuppose that Keynesian weight *can* be increased or, at least, that it ought to *have been* increased.[65] At one point in their paper, Davidson and Pargetter seem to accept this construction of the requirement. In discussing the foregoing example, they comment: "A piece of evidence could radically change the probability that [the selected defendant] was guilty, and *we know some such evidence is available for one of the defendants*."[66] They do not elaborate on how they know that "some such evidence is available." Presumably, they refer to the fact that the one innocent defendant could testify to facts showing his innocence. Of course, this ignores the possibility that the guilty defendants also could testify to (what they claim to be) facts showing their innocence and do so in such a way that the fact-finder would not be able to discern which defendant is telling the truth. It also ignores the possibility that all defendants would insist on their right not to testify.[67] But we cannot know any of this until such testimony is obtained or all reasonable attempts to obtain it are exhausted. It is *this* fact that warrants the conclusion that a verdict, whether positive or negative, is not appropriately entered on the merits on the given state of the evidence in the hypothetical.

---

rendered if the Keynesian weight is not greater than it is." The question then is how to make this idea practically meaningful.

[65] On the principle that "*ought* implies *can*," see, e.g., Henderson (1971); Sinnott-Armstrong (1984); and Howard-Snyder (2006). It may be linguistically permissible to assert that something ought to be done when it cannot be done. Putting aside metaphorical and purely aspirational claims (e.g., when "one ought to do X" means only that "it would be good for one to do X if that were only possible"), we can be more precise: it is coherent to say that something ought to have been done even though it no longer can be. Compare Henderson (1971) at 105–7 ("The force of my example, then, is that 'ought' does not imply 'can' when used in reference to a situation in which [the person acting] can fairly be said to have rendered [himself or herself] unable to carry out [his or her] duty.") with Howard-Snyder (2006) at 235 (expressing the principle in a time-dependent manner: "If S ought ... to do A at T', then there is a time T^* such that S can at T^* do A at T'." Thus, if it would *have been* better for the decision maker to have obtained additional information before rendering a verdict, but the decision maker has by unreasonable action made that impossible, one might rightly say that the decision maker "ought to have more information," even though the present reality is that he or she cannot. See Swinburne (2001) at 178–82. What pragmatic significance does such an expression carry? It imports a moral criticism of the decision maker's unreasonable action, with the possible implication that some consequence might rightly attach thereto, if only a criticism for having decidedly badly, if not erroneously.

[66] Davidson & Pargetter (1987) at 184 (emphasis added).

[67] Why might the *innocent* defendant refuse to testify? Many explanations are possible: perhaps he has serious prior convictions that, under existing rules, would become admissible against him if he testifies. See, e.g., Fed. R. Evid. 404(a), 609.

A homey example illustrates the point more generally. Victor is trying to decide between purchasing car *A* and purchasing car *B*. Victor must pick a car; he cannot decide not to buy either of them. (As we have seen, this assumption is crucial to maintain an analogy to adjudication.) Victor has accumulated information on several points of comparison, including purchase price, safety, and size. At this point in his deliberations, car *A* is the clear favorite over car *B*. That is, the discriminatory power of the evidence favors the truth of the proposition that car *A* is better for Victor than car *B*. However, as yet, Victor has no information about the comparative measures of fuel economy for the two cars. Jessica reminds Victor of the absence of information about fuel economy and argues that he ought not to accept the indicated proposition. Jessica's argument, of course, concerns the question of whether the Keynesian weight of the evidence is adequate for Victor to make his choice. Ought Victor to accept her argument? That will depend on answers to two further questions. First, how important is fuel economy to Victor's choice of car? And second, how costly would it be for Victor to obtain the necessary information with regard to fuel economy? If the importance is high relative to the information acquisition cost, then Victor should accept Jessica's argument and take steps to obtain the necessary information. If, however, the importance is low relative to the information acquisition cost, then Victor should reject Jessica's argument. In particular, if comparative data on fuel economy are not available to be obtained, regardless of how important they may be to Victor if they were available, then it makes no sense for Victor not to act on the existing evidence favoring car *A*.

The example of Victor's decision is chosen to highlight very general features of decision making, and for this very reason it might be challenged as a poor analogy to adjudication. Obviously, one might quibble with the example because Victor's choice does not involve a purely factual question, but this is unimportant to the point being made. In any event, the example can easily be constructed to make Victor's choice depend on whether the fuel economy of car *B* exceeds that of car *A* by a certain amount or percentage. Then the question for Victor is straightforwardly factual, and he faces the same dilemma: to try to acquire comparative fuel economy data or to make his choice between the cars without such information. Similarly, one might quibble with the fact that Victor's choice does not directly impinge on the interests of others, but again, this does not affect the point being made. In his study of ignorance, Nicholas Rescher observes:

> Vincible ignorance is that which an individual can overcome with a reasonable amount of effort.... If something significant is at stake – either

prudentially in affecting a person's well-being or *morally* in affecting the well-being of others – we would expect people to devote duly proportionate efforts to remove vincible ignorance and would fault them (prudentially or morally) for not doing so.[68]

Elsewhere, Rescher crisply states: "Culpable ignorance obtains when the requisite information is available, but insufficient, incompetent, or inadequate efforts are made to obtain it."[69]

Returning to the hypothetical by Davidson and Pargetter (i.e., one innocent man among nine guilty), once one posits what those writers clearly assumed – namely, that further individuating evidence, though not now before the court, is (or was) available to be brought before it – then the argument from a want of Keynesian weight can get off the ground.[70] If, for example, we are told that the police are aware of, have ready access to, but have not presented an alibi witness for one of the 10 persons in the example, then we may rightly conclude that conviction of any one of the 10 should not rest on the evidence currently before the court. Just how and by whom this conclusion should be enforced are other matters: to answer these questions, one must distinguish among the roles of the juridical actors, a matter to which I turn in Chapter 4. In any event, it is true, as Davidson and Pargetter commented, that this conclusion does not depend on whether the innocent person is one among 10, or one among 100, or one among 1,000.[71] Conversely, if we are convinced that no such further evidence can be acquired, then the force of the epistemic intuition that conviction is impermissible dissolves, at least as long as the probability of guilt is high enough to satisfy the applicable standard for discriminatory power.

This latter conclusion remains controversial, as we shall see, and it is not entirely clear how Davidson and Pargetter come out on the matter. On the one hand, they insist that the nature of the determination that must be coupled with an assessment of the probability of the claim being true is

---

[68] Rescher (2009) at 12.
[69] Id. at 11.
[70] Cf. Koehler & Shaviro (1990) at 259 ("Only when differentiating evidence becomes available does it make sense to regard an individual member's probability as anything other than the base rate frequency for the general reference class to which he belongs.")
[71] This conclusion assumes that obtaining the additional evidence remains cost justified in each of the contemplated contexts, as suggested by the language used by Davidson and Pargetter and by the example provided in the text. Once one relaxes that assumption, then it may matter how many guilty persons are among the group, but only because it matters whether the cost of the additional evidence is worth the expected impact on the case. I return to this point at the end of this section.

one that looks to the *resilience* of that probability.[72] This resilience depends, in turn, on the likelihood that some fact may be true that would, if true, change $P(C|E)$. It also depends on *how much* it would change $P(C|E)$ if that fact were true. And they are clear that when a decision maker thinks about this, it does not matter how likely it is that such a possible fact could be evidenced by testimony that could be "discovered or presented."[73] So their coupled requirement would seem to be indifferent to considerations of the availability of further evidence. However, they are noncommittal when it comes to the question of how high the level of resilience must be to support a verdict,[74] which means that, at least in principle, they leave open the possibility that the required level could be, in part, a function of what evidence is available.[75] Moreover, in a separate article that is not focused on adjudication, they emphasize that Keynesian weight is just one factor in the rationality of decision making, and they acknowledge specifically that "[i]f the stakes are minor or if the cost of raising a probability of low weight to one of high weight is too high, it may be perfectly rational to act on a probability of low weight."[76]

Perhaps surprisingly, many influential academicians have rejected this conclusion, at least in the context of adjudication. Jonathan Cohen did so in his seminal work,[77] and both Alex Stein and Hoc Lai Ho have done so (albeit somewhat more ambiguously) in more recent work.[78] Although

---

[72] Davidson & Pargetter (1987) at 184. The idea of resilience is considered more fully in Chapter 5, where I explain why we should reject these theorists' suggestion that Keynesian weight be identified with resilience of probability assessments (§ 5.1) and why a separate adjudicative requirement of sufficient resilience is undesirable (§ 5.2).

[73] Id. at 185.

[74] Id. at 186.

[75] Interpreting their argument is difficult because their presentation is marred by an equivocation about the meaning of "evidence." Sometimes they write in terms of evidence being something that might or might not be "available" (e.g., testimony about a factual proposition), whereas at other times they write in terms of evidence being something that can "obtain" or not, be true or false, be more or less probable, such as the factual proposition that is asserted by testimony. In thinking about evidence, it is critical to keep these two ideas distinct. See Schum (1994) at 16–19.

[76] Davidson & Pargetter (1986) at 228. They are not alone in being ambiguous on this critical issue. See, e.g., Hart & McNauton (1958) at 45–6 (accepting the possibility of a judgment against a defendant implicated only by statistical evidence when the defendant *unjustifiably* refuses to cooperate in the search for additional evidence).

[77] See Cohen, J. (1977) at 247–52, 272–7.

[78] See Stein (1996) at 316; (2005) at 82, 100–3, 122–4. The ambiguity of Stein's more recent statements on the matter is analyzed elsewhere. See Nance (2007) at 144–54. Professor Ho clearly, albeit tangentially, rejects the availability of potential evidence as central to the question. See Ho (2008) at 136 n. 190.

their views are otherwise quite different, these scholars proceed from something like the following premise:

> [E]vidential support for factual propositions is determined comparatively. Decision-makers determine its relative strength – or informativeness – by measuring the gap between the existing composition of evidence and its *ideal composition*.[79]

From this premise, for example, both Cohen and Stein reach the conclusion that, at least in a criminal case, *no such gap* is to be permitted in cases that go to conviction. Thus, according to Cohen, under the "beyond reasonable doubt" standard a criminal prosecution must fail for want of "maximal" weight if a "vital" eyewitness dies (without the fault of either party) before testifying, that is, even if the testimony of the witness is *not* available to the tribunal and that unavailability is not the fault of either party.[80] For Cohen, such maximal weight is achieved only when one takes into account "the totality of relevant evidence" and *not* simply "the totality of discoverable relevant evidence."[81]

One might be inclined to think that Cohen's specification of the witness as "vital" means simply that without that witness, the aggregate evidence does not reach an appropriate probabilistic threshold, such as that stated in criterion (2.2). But Cohen is explicit in rejecting anything like criterion (2.2) as an interpretation of the standard of proof. Cohen's claim is that the loss of this "vital" witness must sink the prosecution even if criterion (2.2), or anything much like it, is satisfied. It is a deficiency in Keynesian weight that is the source of the trouble for Cohen, not any deficiency in the assessed probability of the defendant's guilt.[82] Cohen's claim, however, must be rejected. Either his use of the word "vital" here creates an unexplained and unhelpful tautology (i.e., implicitly equating "vital" with "necessary" without providing any noncircular criterion for what makes the witness "necessary"), or else the conclusion reached is both normatively implausible and strikingly inaccurate as a description of prevailing practice.

---

[79] Stein (2005) at 43 (emphasis added) (discussing Cohen's theory of "Baconian" probability, itself based on the idea of Keynesian weight).
[80] Cohen, J. (1986) at 642.
[81] Id. This implies that Cohen believes that a conviction would properly be denied if an eyewitness is known to exist but cannot be "discovered," which from the context could only mean "brought before the court, perhaps by admissible deposition." Thus death of such a witness is not the only contingency that will preclude conviction in Cohen's view.
[82] He developed this claim more extensively in his earlier monograph. Cohen, J. (1977). Cohen's affirmative theory is addressed infra, § 3.4.

I will spend little time documenting the inaccuracy of Cohen's position as a description of prevailing legal practice. Anyone familiar with criminal practice knows that many cases go to conviction despite the death, disappearance, or other unavailability of important witnesses who have not given pretrial statements admissible at trial. The most obvious example is that homicide cases routinely go to conviction despite the absence of perhaps the most important witness, the victim. And there are countless other examples that do not involve any potential claim of "waiver" or "forfeiture" of rights by the defendant.[83] For example, convictions have been affirmed even though potentially critical witnesses, other than the alleged victim, have died or become physically unable to testify,[84] disappeared,[85] or simply exercised a privilege not to testify.[86] Even the rule that on its face seems most favorable to Cohen's position, a Michigan rule that once required the prosecution to call all eyewitnesses to crimes (called "*res gestae* witnesses") in fact ran directly contrary to his position because the rule provided for an exception whenever the witness was unavailable to testify despite reasonable efforts by the state to obtain the witness's presence at trial.[87]

At least as important for our purposes, the normative implausibility of Cohen's conclusion is readily discerned by comparing the situation described – the death of an important eyewitness, presumably before

---

[83] Cf. Giles v. California, 554 U.S. 353 (2008) (holding that the accused may forfeit the right to confront a hearsay declarant by taking action that purposefully prevents the declarant from testifying).

[84] See, e.g., United States v. Lang, 904 F.2d 618 (11th Cir. 1990) (affirming conviction despite the unavailability of an important witness because of illness and the inadmissibility at trial of said witness's grand jury testimony) and Commonwealth v. Meech, 403 N.E.2d 1174, 1178 (Mass. 1980) (affirming a first-degree murder conviction despite the death of a witness whose testimony at grand jury was inadmissible at trial on behalf of the defense).

[85] See, e.g., United States v. Carson, 455 F.3d 336, 376–8 (D.C. Cir. 2006) (affirming a conviction despite the disappearance of two witnesses whose grand jury testimonies were held inadmissible on behalf of the defense) and United States v. Pena, 527 F.2d 1356 (5th Cir. 1976) (affirming a conviction despite the disappearance of a government informant before trial and despite the inadmissibility of testimony, offered by the accused, reporting what the informant had said about the event being litigated).

[86] See, e.g., United States v. DiNapoli, 8 F.3d 909 (2d Cir. 1993) (conviction affirmed despite the inability of the defense to either call witnesses, who exercised Fifth Amendment privilege not to testify, or to present their grand jury testimony) and United States v. Watson, 525 F.3d 583 (7th Cir. 2008) (affirming conviction even if hearsay of nontestifying codefendant were considered inadmissible).

[87] See People v. Serra, 3 N.W.2d 35 (Mich. 1942) (affirming conviction despite failure of the prosecution to present an eyewitness to the crime when the prosecution made efforts to obtain his presence at trial). Even this qualified rule requiring the prosecution to present all *res gestae* witnesses was weakened by legislation in 1986. See People v. Koonce, 648 N.W.2d 153 (Mich. 2002) (discussing the change).

her testimony could be recorded in some fashion that could be used at trial – with a different situation, one in which an important potential eyewitness did not arrive at the scene in time to see what happened. On what ground might one conclude that evidence of "ideal composition" requires the consideration of testimony of an actual eyewitness who in fact dies before trial? Whatever that ground might be, it then also requires, in the second case, consideration of the potential testimony of the might-have-been eyewitness, that is, the testimony that the person would have been able to give had she arrived in time to observe the event in question. From the point of view of a tribunal called on to render judgment, there is no significant epistemic difference between, on the one hand, a witness who once existed but no longer does (owing to no fault of either party) so that whatever information that witness had has been lost to the tribunal and, on the other hand, a witness who never existed so that there was no information to lose.[88] Both situations involve a counterfactual assumption that, if somehow realized, could yield important evidence. What would make the existence or identification of one counterfactual problematic but not the other? And if both possibilities violate the indicated criterion of maximizing weight, then no case will ever satisfy it because one can always hypothesize counterfactual situations that would, if actualized, yield additional relevant evidence that would, if taken into account, increase Keynesian weight and, indeed, reduce our uncertainty about the case.[89]

The central conceptual dilemma here is whether or not the proper articulation of the weight requirement is *preferential* in character. That is, in considering whether the absence of some potential item of case-specific evidence is fatal to the claim, are we to take into account the availability of that evidence and excuse its absence if it is unavailable to the court, thus allowing the claim to go forward to a verdict that is otherwise considered warranted? Or is the weight requirement *strict* in the sense that the want of certain evidence precludes a verdict because it produces a fatal inferential weakness the importance of which does not depend on whether that weakness can be practicably eliminated?

---

[88] A potential difference between the two scenarios is pragmatic rather than epistemic: in the first context, a rule precluding a positive verdict might have the desirable effect of causing juridical actors, such as the police, to take actions before the witness might die to preserve her testimony in some way that would be admissible at trial, whereas no such option is available in the latter context. I will return to this kind of consideration in Chapter 4.

[89] Professor Stein draws conclusions similar to Cohen's. Stein (2005) at 178–83, 199–200. And they are subject to a similar critique. See Nance (2007b) at 144–54.

Our example of Victor's automobile purchase decision clearly points to a preferential weight requirement, and considerable philosophical work, from a variety of starting points, supports this conclusion. For example, Gilbert Harman proposed a principle of reasoning that "tells one not to accept a conclusion unless one is justified in accepting the proposition that there is no *obtainable* undermining evidence against that conclusion."[90] Nicholas Rescher argued that in putting knowledge to practical use, "we have to settle for the best we can obtain at the time."[91] And Richard Swinburne has emphasized that costs of various sorts constrain the appropriate extent of inquiry: "[t]he more trouble and expense required to obtain new evidence, the less investigation is required."[92] Even Jonathan Cohen, when not addressing legal adjudication, seemed to be quite aware of the importance of the availability of potential evidence to an argument that Keynesian weight is inadequate for practical judgment:

> What is important, in practice, therefore, is for such a probability to have as much weight as is permitted by the methodology of estimation, by pertinent economic constraints, by the current state of scientific knowledge, by the nature of the subject-matter and by any other limits to enquiry.[93]

Yet every scholar (at least every one of which I am aware) who has endorsed a distinct Keynesian weight requirement for adjudication (whether or not by that or similar name) has treated it as strict in the foregoing sense.[94] Perhaps they do so because they merge Keynesian weight with discriminatory power into one overall determination and then apply the strict rule that does rightly pertain to discriminatory power. After all, as a general proposition, the party bearing the burden of persuasion is not

---

[90] See, e.g., Harman (1980) at 166 (emphasis added).
[91] Rescher (1989) at 10. Rescher continues

> Rationality consists in the use of reason to resolve choices in the best feasible way.... Rationality requires doing the best one can with the means at one's disposal, striving for the best results that one can expect to achieve within the range of one's resources.... Rational inquiry is a matter of epistemic optimization, of achieving the best overall balance of cognitive benefits relative to cognitive costs.

Id. at 11–13.
[92] Swinburne (2001) at 177.
[93] Cohen, J. (1985) at 265. But see id. at 273 (oddly reiterating the peculiar legal application discussed in the text – the unfortunately missing witness situation).
[94] Simon Blackburn, in reviewing Cohen's work, rightly articulated a preferential structure with regard to Keynesian weight, but he did not translate this into an explicit legal requirement, except to say that a court may be considered "negligent" if it fails to exhaust all practically available leads for additional relevant evidence. Blackburn (1980) at 154–6.

excused from satisfying this assigned burden simply because that party cannot obtain and present evidence that will satisfy it.[95] To be sure, the law sometimes – rightly or wrongly – reacts to anticipated deficiencies in the evidence by which a party may achieve the requisite discriminatory power by weakening otherwise applicable restrictions on the admissibility of evidence.[96] This does not – or, at least, it is not supposed to – lighten the burden of persuasion; it is supposed to increase the admitted evidence with which the burdened party can meet the standard of proof.[97] Officially, at least, the burden of persuasion is not to be reduced just so that the burdened party can satisfy it. Nor should it be. But transferring this mode of thinking from discriminatory power to Keynesian weight is a mistake, one that has helped to prevent scholars from perceiving the proper role of Keynesian weight in legal decision making.

The root of the problem is that when Keynesian weight is the matter at hand, no notion of "ideal" evidence (or, for that matter, "maximal" or even "adequate" evidence) can be articulated that is (1) distinct from the idea of the evidence that is reasonably available to the tribunal and (2) does not lead to unacceptable consequences such as the one illustrated earlier.[98] For stochastic phenomena, such as our object-flipping hypothetical, the only meaningfully "ideal" evidence set, other than the largest cost-justified sample, is an infinite sample – for instance, an experiment involving an infinite number of flips of the object that (somehow) do not alter the object being flipped. For nonrandom phenomena, deterministic within the limits of free will and quantum theory, such as whether or not the defendant shot the deceased, the only similarly ideal evidence set would be one that entails practical certainty about the event in question – such as the fact-finder's direct observation of the alleged crime and all pertinent events and mental states leading up to it under perfect conditions of observation. Short of these unrealistic extremes, one has only pragmatic

[95] Formally distinguishable – although equally mistaken – is using the difficulty of proof as a reason to choose a lower standard of discriminatory power for all cases of a certain type, that is, not as an ad hoc reaction to the difficulties experienced by a particular litigant in a particular case. See, e.g., Addington v. Texas, 441 U.S. 418 (1979) (citing difficulties of proof as one reason not to impose, as a matter of constitutional law, the "beyond reasonable doubt" standard in involuntary commitment proceedings).
[96] See, e.g., Fed. R. Evid. 413–15 (creating an exception to the rule banning the use of prior bad acts to show a propensity to commit such acts when the prior bad act and the alleged bad act both involve sexual assault or child molestation).
[97] See Karp (1994).
[98] This critique was anticipated, albeit in a somewhat different context, by A. J. Ayer. See Ayer (1957) at 14–17.

compromises between the anticipated usefulness of potential evidence and the costs of acquiring and using it. Consequently, all one can expect, as a condition on the choice among competing hypotheses, is that Keynesian weight of the evidence with respect thereto be *practically optimized*. Once this is done, decision should proceed based on the discriminatory power of the evidence on hand.[99]

The term *practical optimization* is used here to differentiate these decisions from decisions that are indifferent to, or at least not determined by, anticipated costs and benefits of various kinds, such as decisions controlled entirely by deontological norms that are considered practically immune from mundane cost considerations.[100] The term is *not* meant to suggest that an accurate psychological description of the decision process for any given actor involves what decision theorists refer to as "unbounded rationality" (involving perfect information and infinite calculation resources) or even "optimization under constraints" (which accepts some constraints on the information or the resources available to the decision maker), though they may for various purposes be usefully modeled as if they do. Whatever epistemic devices may be used in the evidence search process and at whatever level of Keynesian weight one arrives before making a decision, what matters is that such tools contribute to achieving a body of evidence that is not discernibly worse than can be obtained under any practically identifiable and available alternative, within any deontological constraints that may apply.[101]

How much investment in additional evidence is warranted depends not only on the costs of obtaining various additions to the stock of evidence but also on the stakes involved in the decision. If Victor's purchase of a car is only for casual use, the acquisition of additional information

---

[99] See Runde (2000) at 230:

> On Keynes's theory, uncertainty arises out of the incompleteness of the body of evidence bearing on an hypothesis (if the evidence were complete, it would have the capacity to provide certain knowledge of the truth or falsity of that hypothesis). As we often cannot wait on certainty before acting, Keynes takes it for granted that it is rational to be guided by the evidence that we do have at our disposal at the time of decision.

[100] In a particular context, of course, deontological norms may determine whether additional evidence is practically available. Norms foreclosing the use of torture, for example, may limit the practical availability of additional evidence. See, e.g., United Nations Convention Against Torture Art. 15.

[101] Cf. Gigerenzer et al. (2008) at 3–9. Thus I do not limit myself to a technical use of the word "optimization" that entails a "mathematical process – computing the maximum or minimum of a function." Id. at 84.

regarding fuel economy is not so urgent as it would be if he planned to use the car extensively. Similarly, a litigated case in which the stakes are very high, such as a capital criminal case, warrants more extensive investigative expenditures than would a minor traffic offense. Of course, one might argue that the standard of discriminatory power is also different for these two criminal cases, so let me make the contrast more stark by considering a pair of civil cases for which the standard of discriminatory power is identical, but the standard for Keynesian weight is not. In case 1, a probate proceeding, it is uncontested that the will of testator 1 directs that A shall receive a bequest of $5,000 if and only if the average life span of a certain type of fish exceeds six months; otherwise, the $5,000 goes to B. In case 2, another probate proceeding, it is uncontested that the will of testator 2 directs that C shall receive a bequest of $5 billion if and only if the average life span of that certain type of fish exceeds six months; otherwise, the $5 billion goes to D. In both these cases, there is no reason to take O^* to be anything other than 1:1, or so I shall assume. Even if so, however, the stakes involved warrant a higher expenditure of resources to determine the factual condition in case 2 than is true in case 1. (Consider, for example, the different answers appropriate in the two cases to the question of whether a highly reliable expert on fish of this type ought to be brought before the tribunal to testify, at a cost of $20,000.) It is intelligible, therefore, to speak of a "higher burden of proof" in case 2, but one must be careful in using any such language. In particular, nothing has been said at this point about how this requirement is practically implemented (e.g., on whom this burden falls or how it is to be enforced), and there is no reason to assume that it is implemented the same way that requirements on discriminatory power are implemented. The matter is addressed in Chapter 4.

In terms of the decision-theoretic model presented in § 2.2, what is "at stake" in a case is some increasing function of each of the social utilities and disutilities that may result from the decision, that is, $U_{(+)}$, $U_{(-)}$, $D_{(-)}$, and $D_{(+)}$. If one holds any three of these numbers constant and increases the remaining one, what is at stake increases, plausibly, by the same amount. The simplest measure of what is at stake, therefore, would be the sum of these four magnitudes. In any event, what is most important is that the stakes are a function of the *choice* between C and not-C; the stakes do not change depending on whether the decision is in favor of C or in favor of not-C. In this sense, the stakes involved in deciding whether to accept C (as opposed to the alternative hypothesis, not-C) are the same as the stakes involved in deciding whether to accept not-C (as opposed to the alternative hypothesis, C).

Finally, a practical limit on the decision maker's acquisition of evidence arises from the expected impact that contemplated evidence will have on the decision. In the context of Victor's choice of a car, for example, if it were the case that fuel economy does not vary much from one kind of car to another, and if the balance of other factors dramatically favors car *A*, then Victor might conclude that even relatively inexpensive (but not costless) information regarding comparative fuel economy is not worth obtaining because it is unlikely to affect the balance of discriminatory power. Thus a decision maker's assessment of whether an increase in Keynesian weight is cost justified can depend on a tentative assessment of the discriminatory power of the evidence already available. More precisely, it can depend on the extent to which discriminatory power exceeds the critical threshold required for a verdict.[102]

3.4 Keynesian Weight and the Importance of Informal Reasoning

Preceding discussion (§ 2.4) addressed the relationship between the structural analysis of inference and the application of a standard of discriminatory power. That discussion emphasized the importance of an eclectic open-mindedness when it comes to the description of actual inference practices and the compatibility of such eclecticism with a prescriptive decision standard informed by criterion (2.2). As we have seen, however, some theorists believe that the analysis of inference, in a largely descriptive modality, has rather stronger implications for how one conceives the standards of decision. Now that we have a working conception of Keynesian weight, this section returns to the topic of inference analysis and its relationship to Keynesian weight.

One of the principal advocates of the importance of Keynesian weight to problems of adjudication was Jonathan Cohen. He argued that the decision criteria for adjudication should be understood in terms of the satisfaction of requirements built on Keynesian weight together with principles of eliminative induction championed by Bacon and Mills.[103]

---

[102] See Swinburne (2001) at 168–74.
[103] Cohen, J. (1977). Part of the appeal of Cohen's approach, to those who found it appealing, is that it offered solutions to various supposed "paradoxes" associated with applying "Pascalian probability" (i.e., some theory of quantifiable probability conforming with the Kolmogorov axioms) to the probabilistic requirements of proof. I discussed one such paradox, the paradox of conjunction, in § 2.3. Another, the paradox of negation, is just the problem involved in the gatecrasher case. Cohen originally pointed to at least four others, supposedly distinct. In the years since he wrote, however, much critical commentary has largely defanged these alleged paradoxes. See, e.g., Schoeman (1987) at 76–91 and Logue (1995) at 150–4.

Cohen's development of this idea is complex, but it rests on the idea that Keynesian weight can be ranked on the basis of how many tests of a hypothesis have been conducted. For each adjudication, there will be a maximal number of such tests, and the tests can be ordered in terms of importance, or so Cohen claimed. The larger the number of tests to which a hypothesis is subjected, starting with the most important, the greater is the Keynesian weight of the evidence. Because Keynesian weight does not differentiate between the hypothesis and its negation (or a competing hypothesis), this ranking of the number of tests conducted is supplemented by a determination of the number of such tests passed by each hypothesis. This means counting the number of the (ordered) tests passed by the claims of the opposing parties. In criminal cases, Cohen argued, for proof to be "beyond reasonable doubt," all tests must be conducted, thus producing maximal Keynesian weight, and the test results must be uniformly favorable to the prosecution. For civil cases, the preponderance of the evidence favors a party if that party's hypothesis survives a larger number of the tests than the opponent's hypothesis survives. Here not all tests must be conducted.

Cohen's theory was both insightful and provocative. But it suffers from several critical difficulties. Aside from his unworkable idea of "maximal weight" (see § 3.3), he assumes that each test can be resolved unequivocally in favor of one party or the other and that which side it favors is all one needs to take from the results of conducting the test. Cohen is not clear as to what constitutes such a test in the adjudicative context, but it is difficult to construct any meaningful formulation that will have the needed property. If a test is simply the taking of the testimony of a percipient witness, for example, what if the result of the witness's testimony is partly favorable to one side and partly favorable to the other? Assuming that the testimony unequivocally favors one side rather than the other, at least on balance, how is one to take account of the *degree* to which the testimony favors one side? For example, if a civil plaintiff's hypothesis barely satisfies each of ten tests, is it clear that the plaintiff should prevail over a defendant whose hypothesis overwhelmingly passes the first nine tests but barely fails the tenth?

The same problems are presented by more complicated conceptions of a "test" that Cohen suggests. In a surprisingly brief treatment, he models fact-finding, in both civil and criminal cases, as a form of presumptive reasoning.[104] Evidence invoking a generalization favoring one side is tentatively defeated by the other side's evidencing an exception to that

---

[104] Cohen, J. (1977) at 247–56.

generalization, to which the first party responds by presenting evidence that defeats the exception raised, and so forth. Thus a "test" seems to be construed here as a whole body of evidence: the combination of an argument by one side and the evidence that is used to support it, a defeating argument by the other side and the evidence that is used to support it, and possibly a defeating reply by the other. The test result is then simply a matter of which party is left standing (in some sense) after this dialectical to and fro. But even with this more complex idea of a test, or set of tests, again there is a problem of *synthesis*. Once one acknowledges, as one must, that the result of a given test of this sort will very often be a matter of degree, it is plain that such tests do not yield a series of binary results that can simply be *tallied*, as Cohen would have us do, but rather a series of judgments about matters of degree that need to be synthesized by resort to a probabilistic appraisal or some other measure of discriminatory power.[105]

While Cohen's theory articulates important aspects of the methodology of inductive logic, to *equate* the results of this method of presumptive reasoning with the assessment of discriminatory power is to make the mistake of conflating a method of evidential analysis with the standard that the method is used to inform. This is evident in Cohen's arguments against the articulation of standards for discriminatory power in terms of subjective probabilities. Cohen is among those who insist that the latter fails because such an articulation does not "elucidate the reasonings appropriate to jurors and advocates," providing the means by which judges can give "guidance" to jurors about how to assess a case.[106] Providing such guidance, however, threatens to run afoul of the principle of free evaluation of evidence and presupposes that the instruction will be more helpful than confusing (see § 2.4). Yet Cohen's ideas are ultimately too subtle and complex to be useful in this way. Moreover, if such instruction of the fact-finder is meant to stand on its own, allowing the courts to forgo criterion (2.2) or some comparable (if nonquantified) standard, then the instruction must provide something in the nature of a "recipe" for fact-finding. For want of a method of synthesis Cohen's explanation falls short of this as well. If, however, the contemplated "guidance" is to operate only in conjunction with a distinct standard for discriminatory power, then the latter must be doing work for which Cohen's theory does not allow.

Even if these serious problems could be solved, the question would remain whether a decision procedure such as that which Cohen puts

---

[105] See the helpful discussion in Schum (1994) at 243–61, 342–4.
[106] Cohen, J. (1986) at 646, 648.

forth would be desirable. Without fuller development of his theory, this is difficult to discern, and in the years since Cohen wrote, there has not been a groundswell of support for such development. In part, this must be because Cohen never answered this pressing question: if (as Cohen himself believed) such a developed system would produce results substantially different from the prescriptions of criterion (2.2) – recall the discussion of his "vital witness" claims in § 3.3 – then what reason can be given for deciding cases in ways that we expect will *not* maximize welfare (subject, of course, to appropriate deontological constraints)? Cohen provided no such reason.[107] Instead, he relied on the normative power of the actual: it must be good because this is (supposedly) the way we do things. Yet the difficulties suggested earlier make it very hard to imagine that this really is the way we do things; at least, it seems to be a seriously incomplete characterization.

Cohen's theory nonetheless illustrates important general features of the inference process that people typically employ. Part of what motivated Cohen's theory was his concern that the analysis of legal standards of proof cohere well with the inferential methods the fact-finder is likely to use – ordinary commonsense reasoning. And his method of "presumptive" reasoning draws on an important heritage of theory concerning informal reasoning, a tradition including the work of such people as Wigmore,[108] Toulmin,[109] Rescher,[110] and Walton.[111] In this body of work, one finds a rich inventory of argument forms applicable to adjudication, including inference to the best explanation, argument from a position to know, and argument from commitment. These argument forms often involve much the same dialectical structure used by Cohen: evidence and argument making a certain inference "plausible" are offered by one party, and evidence and argument are offered in response by the opponent, attempting to challenge the conditions that warrant the plausible inference or to trigger a defeasing condition that undermines the validity of the initial plausible inference, and so on.

Such argument forms serve important functions relative to both the assessment of discriminatory power and the choice of Keynesian weight. As already discussed in connection with explanatory theories of discriminatory power (§ 2.4), plausible reasoning serves as a tool for the

[107] See Stein (2005) at 105–6, 144–5.
[108] Wigmore (1937).
[109] Toulmin (1958).
[110] Rescher (1976).
[111] Walton (2002).

analysis of evidence in commonsense terms. Even as litigation comes with ready-made contending hypotheses (*C* and not-*C*), those general claims typically will be refined at trial to specific theories of the case, one or more for the claimant instantiating *C* and one or more for the defendant instantiating not-*C*. In deliberation, though, the fact-finder will often find it necessary to consider other alternatives. And as Peirce noted, abduction (or inference to the most plausible explanation) becomes a critical tool by which commonsense reasoning develops such additional hypotheses.[112] An assessment of Keynesian weight must be made relative to the contending hypotheses, and as these hypotheses change, some modification of the practical optimization of Keynesian weight may become necessary.

To illustrate the role of abduction most abstractly, I draw on the work of John Josephson. Importantly, Josephson provides an analysis of abduction that incorporates considerations of evidential completeness. He articulates the pattern of reasoning as follows:

D is a collection of data (facts, observations, givens).
[Hypothesis] *H* explains *D* (would, if true, explain *D*).
No other hypothesis explains *D* as well as *H*.

Therefore, *H* is probably correct.[113]

Josephson then identifies five considerations that, in some collective manner, determine the warrant for this inference. Significantly, he separates the five considerations into two groups. Collectively, the first three considerations determine the strength of the conclusion, the "force of the *probably* in the conclusion statement":

(1) How decisively the leading hypothesis surpasses the alternatives;
(2) How well the hypothesis stands by itself, independently of the alternatives;
(3) How thorough the search was for alternative explanations.[114]

The other two he calls "pragmatic considerations" that affect one's "willingness to accept the inference":

(4) How strong the need is to come to a conclusion at all, especially considering the possibility of gathering further evidence before deciding; and
(5) The costs of being wrong and the rewards of being right.[115]

---

[112] See Peirce (1955) at 150–6.
[113] See Josephson (2001) at 1622.
[114] Id. at 1626.
[115] Id.

It is easy to trace some of the connections between his formulation and the theory that is advanced here. His first consideration, which addresses the degrees of plausibility among the contending hypotheses, is obviously related to the odds on a claim as stated in criterion (2.2). While Josephson refers to a multitude of potential alternative hypotheses, we have seen that criterion (2.2) is compatible with the consideration of multiple alternative hypotheses (or stories) constituting the claim C and multiple alternative hypotheses constituting its negation not-C. His second pragmatic consideration, number (5) in the list, is another way of articulating the ratio of utilities and disutilities expressed by criterion (2.2), except, of course, that Josephson is providing an account of inference by the unitary decision maker, an account that does not require the separation of the roles of fact-finder from policy makers in the manner that was articulated in Chapter 2. Most important for our immediate purposes, his first pragmatic consideration, number (4) in the list, addresses the adequacy of the evidence-search process in light of what is at stake. It carries its distinctiveness on its sleeve by its reference to the possibility of gathering further evidence "before deciding." It refers, that is, to a different decision, the decision about whether to proceed with the primary decision, the choice among competing hypotheses.[116]

But does consideration number (4) exhaust the matter of Keynesian weight? What about Josephson's second-listed consideration, pertinent to the strength of the "probably" in the inference, namely, "how well the hypothesis stands by itself, independently of the alternatives." Is the analysis here affected by the absence of evidence, regardless of its practical accessibility, in the manner of a "strict" Keynesian weight requirement (see § 3.3)? Because this consideration is explicitly distinct from the comparative assessment prescribed by his first consideration, one might be tempted to think that it might be. A careful examination of how Josephson understands the role of consideration (2), however, dispels this idea. Indeed, it reveals no essential role for Keynesian weight. Instead,

---

[116] Josephson elaborates elsewhere in a passage that dramatizes the difference between trials and many other inquiries involving an abductive component:

> Often abductive processes are not immediately concluded, but are suspended to wait for answers from information-seeking processes. Such suspensions of processing can last a very long time. Years later, someone may say, "So that's why she never told me. I was always puzzled about that." Centuries later we may say, "So that's the secret of inheritance. It's based on making copies of long molecules that encode hereditary information."

Josephson & Josephson (1994) at 14.

First Abduction Problem		Second Abduction Problem	
D_1	Explained by H and by H_a	D_1	Explained by H and by H_a
D_2	Explained by H but not by H_a	D_2	Explained by H but not by H_a
D_3	Explained by H but not by H_a	D_3	Explained by H but not by H_a
D_4	Inconsistent with H and H_a	D_4	Inconsistent with H and H_a
		D_5	Inconsistent with H and H_a
		D_6	Inconsistent with H and H_a

Figure 3. Two abductive-inference problems.

consideration (2) relates to, and must be taken together with, the question of whether additional explanatory *hypotheses* should be sought, rather than additional *evidence*. It is thus tied closely to his consideration (3).[117] In particular, it seems directed at the concern that a hypothesis may be the "best of a bad lot," where neither that hypothesis nor the alternatives being considered are tolerably good explanations. In such a context, inference to the best explanation is not a useful tool.

It is instructive to consider how the analysis can be affected by what Josephson calls "noise" in the data.[118] Consider two different abductive-inference problems. In the first, the data to be explained are four, D_1 through D_4. The second problem is identical, except that it has two additional data points, D_5 and D_6. In both problems, assume that hypothesis H explains only the first three data points and is inconsistent with the others, whereas the only alternative hypothesis considered, H_a, explains only D_1, is consistent with but does not explain D_2 and D_3, and is inconsistent with the others. This situation is illustrated in Figure 3.

In both problems, H explains more than H_a; indeed, if one further assumes, for simplicity, that none of the data points is more important than the others, one might plausibly say that H explains three times as much as H_a in both problems. This provides information pertinent to Josephson's first comparative consideration. And from that perspective, it might appear that the inference to H is well founded, equally so in the two problems. In both problems, however, H cannot be correct if it is inconsistent with what we know to be true. Neither can H_a. How, then, is a decision

---
[117] Josephson (2001) at 1627–9.
[118] Id. at 1628.

maker to respond? The obvious option is to consider additional hypotheses. Here is where the inference processes in the two problems diverge. In the first problem, one might be willing to select H as the best explanation by attributing D_4 to what Josephson calls the "noise" hypothesis; that is, one might be willing to question whether D_4 is an accurate datum that really must be explained. However, if one goes down this road in the second problem, there are three data points, D_4 through D_6, that would all have to be ignored as noise in order to settle on H. In other words, in the second problem, more so than in the first, one is inclined to stress the need to expand the set of hypotheses under consideration so as to be able to explain more data. Again, the reason to test even the best of the available hypotheses, in this case H, against data (or predictions) in the non-comparative way specified in consideration (2) is to assay the importance of putting more energy into the development of additional hypotheses as opposed to accepting some degree of noise.

Of course, the consideration of an additional hypothesis may be limited to assessing its explanatory power relative to the existing stock of evidence, but it also may suggest the possibility of gathering additional evidence that will help to discriminate among the expanded set of hypotheses. This implicates Josephson's consideration (4), which is where Keynesian weight enters the picture. The important point is still that Keynesian weight retains its distinctiveness, its connection with an information seeking process that is analytically separate from the assessment of the likelihood of the contending hypotheses.[119]

Returning to the more "retail" analysis suggested by Cohen, a number of presumptive argument forms employed in the analysis of evidence have

---

[119] The artificial intelligence enterprise in which Josephson is engaged focuses on "qualitative knowledge and problem solving structures." Josephson & Josephson (1994) at 43. His models generally work with qualitative expressions of confidence stated in terms of degrees of "plausibility," such as "very implausible" and "highly plausible." Id. at 266–7. One may wonder, therefore, whether the "probably" in the conclusion of the abductive inference pattern articulated in the text is compatible with a decision-theoretic criterion such as my (2.2). Josephson states his general view of the relationship between "plausibilities" and "probabilities" as follows:

> Just now it seems most likely that plausibilities may consistently be interpreted as mathematical probabilities, but that there is no significant computational payoff from making this interpretation, and it appears to oversimplify a multi-dimensional phenomenon into a single dimension.

Id. at 269. The most conspicuous oversimplification is, of course, to ignore the distinction between the primary decision and the decision about whether to conduct additional inquiry. See infra § 3.6.

been usefully articulated by Douglas Walton. An illustration is "argument from expert opinion":[120]

MAJOR PREMISE: Source E is an expert in subject domain S containing proposition A.
MINOR PREMISE: E asserts that proposition A is true (false).
CONCLUSION: A is true (false).

This argument is not deductively valid: the conclusion can be false even when both premises are true. Yet, as Walton argues, the argument seems valid in a pragmatic sense, namely, that if the premises are true, some presumption (logical or rhetorical, not necessarily legal) arises that the conclusion is true. What also arises from this invocation of expertise is the creation of a series of questions, each of which can be used as leads in the search for additional important information (the practical optimization of Keynesian weight) and the answers to which can affect the assessment of discriminatory power. Walton describes these questions as follows[121]:

1. *Expertise Question*: How credible is E as an expert source?
2. *Field Question*: Is E an expert in the field that A is in?
3. *Opinion Question*: What did E assert that implies A?
4. *Trustworthiness Question*: Is E personally reliable as a source?
5. *Consistency Question*: Is A consistent with what other experts assert?
6. *Backup Evidence Question*: Is E's assertion based on evidence?

These are all good questions to ask. It need only be emphasized that having asked these questions of a given expert and having obtained the answers to them (thus augmenting Keynesian weight), it will often, perhaps usually (but not always), be the case that the answers, by themselves, do not leave one wholly convinced that the asserted proposition A is true or false or that the expert's opinion can be completely ignored as unhelpful. For example, the answer to the first question, the question of expertise, is going to be – and by the phrasing of the question, is expected to be – gradational: the decision maker will not likely consider E wholly noncredible or wholly credible; rather, the expert will be more or less credible. The same is true, if less obviously so, of most of the other questions. What one will have, after assessing these issues, is some degree of persuasion about A, which must be combined with other evidence on the matter, including contrary expert testimony offered by an opponent, if any.[122]

---

[120] See Walton (2002) at 49.
[121] Id. at 50.
[122] Walton's discussion is ambiguous when it comes to the question of how the important tool box of argument structures he explores is to be integrated into the determination of

146   THE BURDENS OF PROOF

To summarize, developments in the theory of informal reasoning, as well as its near cousin, ordinary-language epistemology,[123] may yet produce convincing reasons to think that the analysis of evidence by adjudicators is fundamentally incompatible with any criterion of discriminatory power in probabilistic terms, such as the decision-theoretic one stated in criterion (2.2). So far, though, it does not seem to be the case that there is any necessary inconsistency between these two lines of thought. While these disciplines may employ a different vocabulary and a different way of structuring analysis, there is no conceptual impediment to the use of

> whether the standard of proof has been met. On the one hand, there are several passages in which he denies the pertinence of "probabilities in the statistical sense" (id. at 17, 218), and this might seem to place him inevitably at odds with any mathematical standard like criterion (2.2). But a close reading reveals that Walton is not really opposed to thinking of legal proof in terms of epistemic probabilities. Rather, he appears to reject modeling the legal inference process in terms of probabilities understood in a certain way, that is, pursuant to theories that define probability in terms of the result of a *counting* exercise. For example, Walton differentiates an older sense of the word "probability" (which he thinks is better characterized today as "plausibility") from the "modern sense of statistical inference, where exact numbers can be calculated to measure a weight of acceptance" (id. at 15). As to the latter, he seems here to have in mind one of several specific theories of probability that necessarily permit the calculation of such "exact" numbers. He might be thinking in terms of the so-called classical theory of probability, first used to understand games of chance, which defines the probability of an event (say, getting a spade in a random draw from a standard deck of cards) as the number of possible ways that such an event can occur (13 spades) divided by the total number of equally probable elementary outcomes (52 cards). See Gillies (2000) at 14–22. Or – if one does not place too much emphasis on his word "exact" – he might be thinking in terms of more sophisticated theories that either define probability in terms of long-run frequency of occurrence (frequency theories) or inevitably use such frequencies to measure probabilities of chance events (propensity theories). Not surprisingly, if one thinks of probability in such terms, then probability will not be suitable for modeling standards of legal proof. But few, if any, of those who endorse something like criterion (2.2) in the adjudicative context think in these terms, at least not with regard to the ultimate probabilities that appear in that criterion. (See supra § 2.2.2.) It is not surprising, then, that Walton's ultimate expression of opinion on the matter is to allow for the possibility that informal reasoning is compatible with "some form of inductive (probability-based) reasoning." Walton (2002) at 111. In later, more tentative work, Walton (joined by Floris Bex) attempts to model standards of proof explicitly. Bex & Walton (2010). Ironically, their theory involves comparing hypotheses in terms of *counting* the number of supporting (and contradicting) arguments. Id. at 39, 42. Whatever the descriptive accuracy of such modeling, it does not account for the prescriptive need to be able to give different strengths to different arguments and to combine them in some way more subtle than merely counting. To be sure, the authors do close with a suggestion for extending the theory to accommodate that need. Id. at 46. Somewhere in this process of elaboration, epistemic probabilities will emerge.

[123] See, e.g., Smith (2010) (presenting a "normic support" theory of epistemic justification).

informal reasoning tools to inform a holistic assessment of odds.[124] As illustrated by the argument from expert opinion, one of the most important contributions of such informal reasoning tools is that they rely on recurring features of the environment to identify promising and efficient lines of inquiry, the development of which may involve augmentations of the Keynesian weight of the evidence on which the adjudicator relies. Once again, however, the analytical tool must not be confused with the standard it is used to assess. In the adjudicative context at least, any informal reasoning that relies entirely on answers to binary "yes/no" questions to component inquiries bearing on the ultimate factual issues inevitably must be supplemented by a synthesis that translates those answers into a gradational measure of epistemic warrant.

3.5 The Quantification of Keynesian Weight

I have argued that decision making must be content with the practical optimization of Keynesian weight and that the demand for Keynesian weight rightly exhibits an excusable preference structure. I have so far largely avoided the theoretical question of whether Keynesian weight is (at least in theory) quantifiable, representable as some real-valued number, however precise, assigned as a function of any given collection of evidence relative to a fixed set of competing hypotheses. In this section, I will explain the extent to which I think that this can be done. In the process, I will address the related issue of whether evidential completeness can be quantified. The reader uninterested in such theoretical issues may pass on to the next section. The question of quantification of weight will take us well beyond anything Keynes had to say on the matter. Indeed, Keynes was skeptical of the universal quantifiability of either probability or weight. For simplicity, and to reflect the divergence from Keynes's particular discussion, in this section only, I will drop the adjective *Keynesian* and refer simply to weight.

---

[124] As Walton puts the matter:

> What is needed is not a numerical approach of calculating the chances that each individual proposition is true or false. What is needed is a holistic approach of judging the weight of each inference within the whole body of relevant evidence in the case, where the inferences are chained together in a network of argumentation. This argumentation on both sides is then evaluated holistically to judge whether the burden of proof appropriate for the case has been met by one side or the other.

Walton (2002) at 218. For further discussion of the "holism" of inference, see infra § 3.6.

Keynes argued, and it is generally agreed, that the weight of two different evidentiary states, relative to a given hypothesis, sometimes can be *rank ordered*. In particular, the principle already employed in the text is that with respect to competing hypotheses (which may, in a given context, be a hypothesis and its negation), any mass of evidence E_2 will have greater weight than mass E_1 if E_2 contains all the evidence in E_1 that is relevant to the competing hypotheses plus some additional evidence relevant thereto.[125] But Keynes seems to have believed, and Jonathan Cohen argued, that there is no broadly applicable metric for the "amount" of one's evidence or knowledge with respect to a hypothesis.[126] Without a metric for measuring it, weight may not be a *linear ordering*, even as to a particular hypothesis; that is, it may not be the case that for every two sets of evidence regarding the same hypothesis, either one has greater weight than the other or their weights are the same.[127] If presented with two sets of evidence, one will be able to discern which has greater weight only under limited conditions, such as when one evidence set is a proper subset of the (relevant portion of the) other. Even then, one cannot, generally speaking, say *by how much* the weight of one evidence set exceeds the weight of the other.

Other scholars, however, have argued, or at least assumed, otherwise. Charles Peirce, for example, opined that "to express the proper state of belief, not one number but two are requisite, the first depending on the inferred probability, the second on the amount of knowledge on which the probability is based."[128] Relying on articulations of weight sometimes used by Keynes, Jochen Runde has made this somewhat more concrete by arguing that it is more accurate to describe weight as "the balance of the absolute amounts of relevant knowledge and relevant ignorance" or, equivalently, "the degree of completeness of the information on which a probability is based."[129] Such language contemplates the possibility of creating a ratio between "relevant knowledge" and "relevant ignorance," and Runde does just that. If we let $K_{(C,E)}$ represent the appropriate measure of relevant knowledge with respect to the claim C based on evidence E and $I_{(C,E)}$ be the appropriate measure of relevant ignorance, then Runde proposes the following quantitative definition of weight:

$$V(C,E) =_{\text{def}} K_{(C,E)} / I_{(C,E)} \tag{3.1}$$

[125] See Keynes (1921) at 71–2.
[126] Cohen, J. (1985).
[127] See Enderton (1977) at 170.
[128] Peirce (1932) at 421.
[129] See Runde (1990) at 280–3.

with values that range potentially from zero to infinity as $K_{(C,E)}$ increases and $I_{(C,E)}$ decreases. Runde also discusses the possibility of defining weight in terms of the degree of completeness of evidence, defined by the ratio $K_{(C,E)}/(K_{(C,E)} + I_{(C,E)})$.[130] Completeness would vary from 0 to 1 as knowledge increases and ignorance decreases. He takes the two articulations to be "equivalent" because (like probabilities and odds) if one knows the value one of these measures, then one can compute the value of the other. The latter formulation suggests – though it does not entail – the possibility of attaining "complete" information, in the sense that no further evidence can possibly be obtained.

Taking the latter point first, generally speaking, this will not be the case in legal adjudication or in other contexts of practical decision making. Complete information in this sense will almost always remain an unattainable goal: for any conceivable state of evidence, further information generally will be obtainable if sufficient resources are devoted to it, but at some point the expected informational yield will not be worth the effort.[131] Indeed, Runde himself is careful to reject the idea that there is a theoretical ideal of total knowledge of the evidence relevant to a proposition. Moreover, he correctly observes that relevant knowledge and relevant ignorance are not necessarily in a zero-sum relationship: it is possible that an increase in the amount of evidence can cause *both* one's knowledge and one's ignorance to increase.[132] Nevertheless, he clearly posits that a meaningful ratio of knowledge to ignorance is possible for any given state of the evidence.

Now, there are contexts, albeit abstract ones, that can be modeled in the way this language of "completeness" seems to suggest, and this may have led some jurists to assume the broader applicability of such a model. For example, if one is trying to estimate the percentage of defective widgets in a delivery of 1,000 widgets, one could base that estimate on an examination of a small random sample of 20 widgets or a larger random sample of 75 widgets, and the weight of the larger-sample estimate would exceed that of the smaller-sample estimate. Moreover, ratios could be created, for either estimate, between the number of widgets tested and the number not tested. And one could have "complete" evidence in this context: one

---

[130] Id. at 281.
[131] It may or may not be the case in any particular context that the marginal cost of obtaining and using further information rises steadily, and the expected informational yield declines steadily, as the amount of evidence is increased. Compare Posner (1999) at 1481–3 with Lempert (2001) at 1641–3.
[132] Runde (1990) at 281–2.

could examine all 1,000 widgets. Then one would know exactly how many were defective (assuming that one's "examinations" were themselves error free). But then one would also not be *estimating*, which is the point of the exercise – to avoid examining them all, presumably because of cost constraints. It is the assumption that not all will be examined that creates a problem of induction, and it is just this step that is necessary to make this example a pertinent analogy to factual adjudication. In the unusual case where the parties are disputing how many of the widgets were defective, all 1,000 of them are still available for what the parties acknowledge to be error-free testing, and cost considerations do not require an estimating procedure that does not test all the widgets, it might seem that one could speak of "complete evidence." In this case, however, the phrase is also something of an oxymoron. Given the assumptions, once the tests were conducted, there would be no reasonable dispute over the number of defective widgets, and a trial would not occur, at least not on this issue. In any event, absent unusual circumstances such as these, completeness of the evidence is inherently a cost-limited concept: a *reasonable degree* of completeness of the evidence is all that can be demanded (§ 3.3).

Suppose, however, that we characterize the upper limit on weight as that which is reasonably obtainable. It would then seem possible to compute the necessary ratio not only in cases of estimation – such as the defective-widgets problem when constrained by cost limitations – but also in a broader category of cases that would include binary determinations of liability. Our problem is to discern what such a quantitative articulation of weight should look like.

The simplest function that would satisfy the ordering property of weight would look something like that presented in Jonathan Cohen's theory, examined in the preceding section: assign a unit increment for each additional item of relevant evidence considered. With n items of relevant evidence before the tribunal, the weight would be just n. If the practical optimization of weight requires N pieces of evidence, the degree of completeness would be n/N. For convenience, let us call this the "sparse measure" of weight – sparse because it strips each item of evidence of that which differentiates it from other items of evidence, not only its "directionality" (which side it favors) but also its "strength" (how much it favors that side).

Aside from the difficulty of individuating items of evidence out of a complex mass (to which we must return later), an obvious objection to such an articulation is that the weight of each individuated item of relevant evidence is the same. While the directionality of the evidence cannot matter to weight, its strength is something worth retaining in one's definition. In thinking about whether a given accretion of evidence is cost justified, one must have some sense of the epistemic value that the evidence will contribute to the adjudication, which means some sense of how it will affect discriminatory power. (This is inherent in Cohen's notion that different tests of hypotheses can be ordered in terms of their importance.) Which side will be favored by the new evidence is generally unknowable before the evidence is obtained, and in any event, it is unimportant for this purpose, but how large the effect may be is often something that can be at least roughly anticipated. For example, in considering whether it is worthwhile to augment the existing evidence package by adding the testimony of someone believed to have been a witness to the litigated event, one may not know whether the witness will testify for or against the claim, but one might well know, and would want to consider, whether the witness was 10 feet from some critical event, such as a conversation, or 100 feet from that event. Depending on the event at issue, the potential testimony could have very great or only slight bearing on the case, and this difference would affect one's decision about whether to obtain the witness's testimony. Such considerations will be especially important in prioritizing the acquisition of evidence; if one must choose between the acquisition of potential evidence F_1 and the acquisition of potential evidence F_2, one would want to have a criterion of weight that would reflect the difference between what F_1 would be expected to contribute and what F_2 would be expected to contribute. There also could be synergies between items of evidence that would need to be taken into account.

Thus another distinctive feature of the idealized widget example illustrates a serious obstacle in cases of more heterogeneous evidence. Implicit in the widget example is that the only way in which weight can be augmented is by increasing the size of the sample of widgets. This is a measurable difference; indeed, it is a countable difference, nicely captured by the indicated sparse measure of weight. But it is quite different from the situation in more general contexts, including almost all litigated cases. One can plausibly say that the weight of a sample of 10 widgets is larger than that of a sample of 5 widgets.[133] One also can plausibly say that if the practically optimal sample size for the defective-widgets case is 15, then the increase in sample size from 5 to 10 increases Runde's ratio $V(C|E)$, from 1:2 to 2:1 (or, equivalently, increases the "completeness of the evidence" ratio from 1:3 to 2:3). But how much "larger" is an evidence package

---

[133] This follows from the simple principle of strict set inclusion expressed earlier, provided that the sample of 10 includes the sample of 5. If it does not, then the rank ordering expressed in the text may be a rational extension of that principle to situations of random sampling. This illustrates that set inclusion is not the *only* rational basis for making ordinal comparisons of Keynesian weight.

that is augmented with the testimony of an additional person? Even if we begin with an assumption that there are 15 witnesses to be heard from, an increase from 5 to 10 in the number of witnesses actually heard cannot be put into such a ratio; to do so would assume that the weight of each potential witness is the same. Only in special situations would such an assumption be plausible. Our sparse measure is conspicuously unhelpful in this regard.

Ideally, an articulation of weight should retain all the features of one's measure of probative value except directionality. A theoretical solution thus presents itself in terms of likelihood ratios. Recall equation (2.4):

$$O(C|E) = O(C) \times L_C(E) \tag{2.4}$$

where $L_C(E)$, the likelihood ratio for evidence E relative to claim C, is just $P(E|C)/P(E|\text{not-}C)$. This ratio contains two distinct pieces of information, the amount by which the prior odds should be adjusted and the directionality (increase or decrease in the odds) of that change. For example, if $O(C|E)$ is three times greater than $O(C)$, this means that the prior odds are adjusted by a factor of 3 *and* that the factor of 3 *increases* the prior odds (multiplying by 3). Conversely, if $O(C|E)$ is only one-third of $O(C)$, then the prior odds are adjusted by a factor of 3, but that factor *decreases* the prior odds (dividing by 3). This presents the possibility of operationalizing the weight of an item of evidence E with regard to the claim C as follows:

$$W_C(E) = L_C(E) \quad \text{if} \quad L_C(E) \geq 1$$
$$= [L_C(E)]^{-1} \quad \text{if} \quad L_C(E) < 1$$

The effect is to strip the likelihood ratio of its directionality: evidence making the odds on the claim three times greater than it would be without that evidence has the same weight as evidence making the odds of the claim one-third what they would be without that evidence.

Although essentially equivalent, the effect may be more transparent – and more in keeping with Keynes's additive language – if one reformulates in terms of logarithms. Because of the properties of the natural log function, when the likelihood ratio is greater than or equal to 1, the natural log of the likelihood ratio will be greater than or equal to 0, and when the likelihood ratio is less than 1, the natural log of the likelihood ratio will be less than 0. An alternative operationalization of weight would set it equal to the magnitude of the natural log

$$W_C(E) = |\ln L_C(E)| \tag{3.2}$$

This version also strips the evidence of its directionality by treating all natural log likelihoods for evidence as positively signed. And because $\ln(1/x) = -\ln(x)$, two items of equivalent weight according to the preceding criterion will retain that equivalence under the present criterion. (In terms of the preceding example, $|\ln(1/3)| = |\ln(3)| = 1.61$.) One can easily imagine using such a measure of weight to create the ratios suggested by Runde, using the weight of the evidence on hand as the numerator of equation (3.1) and the weight of the evidence yet to be obtained as the denominator.[134]

Of course, the likelihood ratio of evidence not yet acquired will be only very roughly estimable. But there is a more important difficulty from a theoretical perspective. The weight of any mass of evidence will not be invariant under decomposition. That is, if one tries to compute the weight of a mass of evidence by decomposing it into smaller pieces and adding up the weights of the pieces, the resulting sum will depend on how the decomposition is performed, and the sum of the weights of the pieces will, in general, not equal the weight of the total mass.[135] This is somewhat disconcerting, but much more problematic is the consequence that the accretion of relevant evidence does not necessarily result in an increase in weight, an essential feature of the notion of weight developed here.[136]

The latter difficulty (but not the former) can be corrected by incorporating another critical (and deliberate) component of Cohen's theory: operationalizing weight as a real-valued function of an *ordered sequence* of items of evidence. If $\{E_1, ..., E_n\}$ is an ordered sequence of evidence items with respect to the claim C, then its weight $W_C(E_1, ..., E_n)$ would be defined as follows:

$$W_C(E_1,...,E_n) =_{def} \left|\ln\left[L_C(E_1)\right]\right| + \left|\ln\left[L_C(E_2|E_1)\right]\right| + \cdots \\ + \left|\ln\left[L_C(E_n|E_1 \& E_2 \& \cdots \& E_{n-1})\right]\right| \quad (3.3)$$

---

[134] Using the likelihood ratio to operationalize the concept of probative value is a familiar strategy, as is use of the log-likelihood ratio to make probative value additive. See Schum (1994) at 218–20. There is much to say for a concept of weight defined in terms of the logarithm of the likelihood ratio. See Good (1968). This, however, will not work for the concept employed here, for reasons explained in the text.

[135] It is easy to see that the additive property of equation (2.6) is not preserved. For example, suppose a mass of evidence consisting of only two items, E_1 and E_2, and suppose that $L_C(E_1) = 2.0$, $L_C(E_2) = 0.1$, while $L_C(E_2|E_1) = 0.5$. By the suggested measure of weight and using equation (2.5), $W_C(E) = W_C(E_1 \text{ and } E_2) = |\ln[L_C(E_1 \& E_2)]| = |\ln[L_C(E_1) \times L_C(E_2|E_1)]| = |\ln[(2)(0.5)]| = 0$. But $W_C(E_1) + W_C(E_2|E_1) = |\ln[L_C(E_1)]| + |\ln[L_C(E_2|E_1)]| = |\ln(2.0)| + |\ln(0.5)| = 0.69 + 0.69 = 1.38$, so $W_C(E_1 \& E_2) \neq W_C(E_1) + W_C(E_2|E_1)$.

[136] Notice, in the example in the preceding note, that $W_C(E_1) = 0.69 > W_C(E_1 \& E_2) = 0$. See Cohen, J. (1985) at 272 (criticizing Good's definition of weight on this ground).

The right-hand side of this equation is similar to that of equation (2.6) except that all negatively signed natural logs have been replaced with their magnitudes: directionality of each E_i is thereby eliminated, but (marginal) strength of each E_i is retained. Moreover, the value of the function increases (additively) with each additional item of relevant evidence, in accordance with Keynes's intuition. I shall refer to the quantification of weight specified by equation (3.3) as a *rich* measure of weight because it incorporates the information about the strength of each item of evidence.[137] (Criterion (3.3) includes criterion (3.2) as a special case for a single item of evidence.)

What, then, are the problems inherent in such measures of weight? One problem is shared by both the sparse measure and the rich measure of weight: as noted earlier, the weight of a mass of evidence depends on whether and how it is decomposed into a sequence of components. There is little reason to think that there is a unique decomposition, for example, a "finest" possible decomposition, for every composite group of evidence, such that one might simply define the weight of the composite in terms of the sum of the weights of the individual components of that unique decomposition. More plausible, but still problematic, is the possibility that there is a way to decompose a given mass of evidence so as to *maximize* its weight as computed with equation (3.3).[138] A still more promising possibility is to define the ordered sequence by the very process of the accumulation of evidence, which produces a unique sequence *historically*. A decision maker generally does acquire items of evidence, or at least packets of evidence, in a particular order. Alternatively, following Cohen again, one could define the unique ordered sequence in terms of a normative criterion that determines in which order potential items of evidence ought to be sought. Finally, one could combine these last two suggestions, using the historical sequence to determine the weight of the evidence on hand (what Runde would call the "relevant knowledge") and a prescribed (anticipated)

---

[137] This definition of weight need not be restricted to competing claims that are complementary, such as C and not-C, although this will be most pertinent to the final verdict in adjudication. A more general formula can be stated for the weight regarding any two competing stories – say, S_π for the complainant and S_Δ for the defendant – by substituting, in definition (3.3), S_π for C and S_Δ for not-C.

[138] Interestingly, in an adversarial presentation of evidence, the effect of the choice of advocates will be to decompose the mass of admitted evidence in a manner that tends to increase, if not maximize, weight: if composite evidence E consists of two distinguishable parts E_a and E_b such that E_a favors the claimant and E_b favors the defense, then one can rely on the incentives of the parties to separate these components for presentation by the claimant and defendant, respectively. This can happen even when the composite evidence E is essentially neutral because E_a and E_b offset each other. See infra § 4.1.1.

sequence to determine the weight of evidence yet to be acquired (what Runde would call the "relevant ignorance").

Perhaps one of these is the best that can be expected in terms of a theoretical quantification of weight. Fortunately, it is not clear why, as a practical matter, one needs to worry about a ratio such as that suggested by Runde once one has at one's disposal the guiding principle for practical choice about evidence development. After all, the question of weight comes up only in connection with the issue of whether and how, at the margin, to augment the evidence on hand. Consequently, it is not important how one determines the unique sequence that decomposes the evidence that one already has. With respect to *potential* evidence, one also does not need to decompose any contemplated item of evidence into smaller "chunks" at the acquisition stage. The circumstances of its acquisition will determine the items of evidence acquired. Thus one only needs to compare at the margin what various items of evidence might contribute.

For example, one can articulate a rational preference for the acquisition of potential evidence F_1 over potential evidence F_2. If the cost of acquisition were the same, a decision maker ought to be more interested in acquiring F_1 than F_2 when $W_C(F_1) > W_C(F_2)$; conversely, if they have equal weight, one ought to choose first the one that costs the least.[139] More generally, for a set of m distinct potential items of evidence $\{F_i, i = 1, \ldots, m\}$, in principle, one could arrange them in decreasing order of ratios of weight to acquisition cost using (3.2) as the measure of weight

$$W_C(F_1)/K_1 \geq W_C(F_2)/K_2 \geq \cdots \geq W_C(F_m)/K_m$$

where K_i is the cost of acquisition associated with evidence item F_i. This creates a prioritization for the acquisition of additional evidence as long as the ratio remains above some point of insufficient return on investigative cost.[140] What is at stake in the decision helps to determine a minimum ratio below which it is not rational to obtain the evidence. As explained in § 3.3, the stakes

---

[139] Of course, I am not suggesting that juridical actors will actually compute such measures, although this would be possible in certain special cases. I assert only that the intuitive judgments that tribunals make about augmentation of weight can be understood and guided in these general terms.

[140] The acquisition of one item of evidence may change how the rest are evaluated. I do not mean to suggest that the prioritization is static. Moreover, this can lead to path dependency: there may be more than one practical optimization of Keynesian weight. This is not problematic, however, because path dependency is perfectly understandable in the investigation of claims. Once five neutral witnesses have given testimony on a particular point, especially if they are consistent, it may well be cost ineffective to obtain the sixth, and which one is "the sixth" may depend on how the first five are acquired.

of the decision are plausibly measured as proportional to the sum of the four magnitudes $U_{(+)}$, $U_{(-)}$, $D_{(+)}$, and $D_{(-)}$.[141]

This relatively practical solution will not help, however, if one is trying to make a meaningful comparison of the weight of the evidence already on hand with that for the evidence that one might be able to obtain, as is suggested by Runde's formulation in equation (3.1). Insofar as one has an interest in such a ratio, one would need a criterion for determining how to decompose uniquely both the evidence already at hand and all the evidence to be acquired. The latter, moreover, is never fully defined. The task is complicated by the difficulty of assessing, however approximately, the weight of evidence that has not yet been obtained and so the content of which can only be roughly anticipated. These difficulties are daunting when one attempts to quantify the degree of completeness of the evidence, even as a theoretical matter.

Despite these difficulties, I do not claim that a generally valid theoretical formalization of evidential weight or completeness is impossible. Fortunately, no such claim is necessary for my purposes. Certainly, some theorists, Runde for example, assume that it is meaningful to quantify weight. But even those who believe it can be quantified are not thereby committed to the proposition that a valid general formula exists by which one can compute a meaningful measure of weight from other relevant variables. And even if such a general formula exists, or can be determined for limited classes of cases, that would do nothing to establish a maximal or sufficient weight that is distinguishable from the weight that results from practical optimization. Put otherwise, the decision whether Keynesian weight is adequate to proceed to the determination about the underlying hypothesis or claim does not depend on any such quantitative measure of either the weight of the evidence on hand or its degree of completeness. It depends, instead, on what further weight can be obtained and at what costs.

3.6 Keynesian Weight and "Holistic" Accounts of Epistemic Warrant

What emerges from the foregoing is a structure of practical decision making in which considerations of both Keynesian weight and discriminatory

---

[141] My search model differs from that of Richard Posner in that Posner supposes that the decision maker has epistemic access to a special quality of an item of evidence – the probability that if the potential evidence is considered by the fact-finder, the case will be decided *correctly*. Posner (1999) at 1481. While the potential weight of the evidence will often be only dimly estimable, it will almost always be known better than the probability of which Posner writes.

power are necessary. On this point, several commentators have concurred, though not necessarily using my terminology.[142] But what often has been misunderstood is that the consideration of Keynesian weight is "orthogonal" to, or independent of, the consideration of discriminatory power.[143] The pragmatic implication of this independence is that a decision maker – legal or otherwise – should practically optimize Keynesian weight as a *condition on* making a judgment of discriminatory power between contending hypotheses, not as *part of* that judgment. Once Keynesian weight is thus optimized, it no longer plays a role in the decision. Conversely, when Keynesian weight is not optimized, within practical limits, the priority for the decision maker is to eliminate the deficiency. There is no "tradeoff" between the two orthogonal considerations: a higher Keynesian weight does not warrant a lower critical probability P^* for one's decision, nor can one justify relying on a low Keynesian weight by reference to a particularly high probability $P(C|E)$. With minor exceptions, the two decisions do not interact in this way.[144]

The relationship between these considerations and assessments is nicely illustrated by the law of damages. Once liability is established in a civil case, damages often must be awarded, and the determination of a monetary *amount* of damages is less like the binary (liable or not liable) decision modeled by the test of criterion (2.2) and more like the estimation of the bias of a flat coinlike object or the estimation of the number of defective widgets in a shipment. In the latter context, threshold probability tests are less helpful. Not surprisingly, in proving damages, the legal test explicitly endorses the preferential structure endorsed here. That is, the law drops the usual test for discriminatory power, leaving only the requirement of as much precision in the proof of damages as it is reasonable to expect under the circumstances, a proof standard of an entirely different kind.[145]

---

[142] See Brilmayer (1986) at 681–5; Davidson & Pargetter (1987) at 183–6; Friedman (1996) at 1819; Nance (1998) at 625; and Stein (2005) at 120.

[143] "Keynesian weight is logically independent of Pascalian probability." Cohen, J. (1989) at 104.

[144] One such exception was mentioned at the end of § 3.3: a tentative assessment of discriminatory power may lead to the conclusion that an increase in Keynesian weight is not likely to affect the discriminatory power enough to change the decision. Here what matters is not specifically a high value for discriminatory power but rather a relatively large difference between its assessed value and the critical minimum, e.g., between $P(C|E)$ and P^*. A different kind of interaction can occur between discriminatory power and Keynesian weight when the *explanation* of the fact that Keynesian weight has not been practically optimized itself has probative value. See § 4.2.

[145] See Bigelow v. RKO Radio Pictures, 327 U.S. 251 (1946) and Boyce v. Soundview Tech. Group., Inc., 464 F.3d 376, 391 (2d Cir. 2006).

All that matters is whether Keynesian weight has been practically optimized on the issue of damages so as to permit the best practical estimate.[146] This does not mean, however, that in proof of liability, the *only* demand is proof by the appropriate threshold-probability standard of discriminatory power. In this context, both ideas are in play. What should be required to warrant liability is that weight be practically optimized *and* that the claimant's case be established by a margin of the odds appropriate to such a civil case.[147] Exactly how the law tries to practically optimize weight is the subject of Chapter 4. Here I address a central problem introduced by the failure to distinguish these two components of decision making. It concerns the idea of "holistic" decision making.

There are several accounts of decision making that conjoin or mix the two considerations – discriminatory power and Keynesian weight – without grasping their distinctiveness or the implications thereof. Such accounts are "holistic," but the idea goes decidedly beyond the kind of holism that I accepted earlier (§ 3.4) as an inevitable part of most determinations of discriminatory power. This more expansive holism comes in a variety of forms, but only two will be identified here. Some such accounts are "synthetic," by which I mean that they combine discriminatory power and Keynesian weight into a single measure of epistemic warrant that can be tested against a standard of proof. Others are "gestalt," by which I mean that the factors determining discriminatory power and those determining Keynesian weight are taken to be so related that no single variable capturing the force of the evidence can be compared with any particular numerical standard, probabilistic or otherwise, yet the various factors are somehow combined in an act of epistemic judgment. I reject both these expanded forms of holism. In the rest of this section, I will discuss two noteworthy examples to be found in the literature. (Additional examples will be discussed in Chapter 5.)

---

[146] Of course, the best practical estimate may be so uncertain as to be essentially a shot in the dark, and the law may in this context plausibly remit successful plaintiffs to "nominal" damages (e.g., $1). This phenomenon was one of the reasons that led Keynes to doubt that many epistemic probabilities that arise in the law can be quantified. See Keynes (1921) at 24–8.

[147] It is somewhat misleading, therefore, to describe the special proof-of-damages rule as a "lowered" standard of proof, as if the standard involved a unitary measure that is adjusted. See, e.g., Brickmann (2004) at 883. More precise would be to say that the proof standard for damages is simply different because one part of the usual two-part requirement is dropped as inapt. Still, a one-part test is, in a sense, "less demanding" than a two-part test. Cf. Friedman (1997b) at 1974–5.

Synthetic in the sense just described is the admittedly brief suggestion made by Richard Friedman that one might adjust the threshold probability required by the standard of proof so as to reflect the degree of evidential completeness.[148] Specifically, Friedman suggested replacing criterion (2.2′) with the following: decide for the claimant just when

$$P(C|E) > P^*/Q \qquad (3.4)$$

where P^* is the familiar ratio of utilities already defined in criterion (2.2′), and Q is a measure of the completeness of the evidence. Although Friedman did not elaborate, presumably he intended that Q be set equal to 1 when the evidence is complete (though he does not elucidate what that would entail) so that the decision criterion reduces to criterion (2.2′) and that Q should trend toward 0 when the evidence is increasingly incomplete, thus increasing the probability required for a positive verdict to some figure higher than P^*. There is then a tradeoff between probability and completeness: the less complete the evidence, the higher is the probability required to warrant a positive verdict.

As we have seen, however (§ 3.5), a quantitative measure of Q is elusive. Without a practical, even if approximate, quantitative measure of completeness, the formula provides no meaningful guidance. And if Q is not even theoretically well defined in quantitative terms, the modification of the decision criterion is meaningless. These, however, are not the only problems with Friedman's suggestion. Observe that if Q were smaller than P^*, then a verdict for claimant would be precluded, no matter how high the value of $P(C|E)$. This generates the interesting feature that the minimal degree of completeness consistent with a positive verdict increases as P^* increases. Now this would seem to correspond to our intuition that, for example, criminal cases ought to be more thoroughly investigated than civil cases. But this does not work: the factor influencing the optimal amount of investigation is the importance of the controversy, plausibly measured by the stakes, not the utility ratio that determines P^*. For example, we have seen that one can easily imagine extremely important civil cases for which the minimal degree of permissible evidential completeness is very high even though P^* is as low as 0.5. These difficulties arise because Friedman's suggestion synthesizes into one holistic judgment assessments that I have described as orthogonal, related to two, largely independent decisions.

---

[148] Friedman (1997a) at 279.

Friedman does not offer a satisfactory justification to motivate the further development of his speculation. What he does say is that it responds to our intuitions, arising especially from cases of naked statistical evidence, about the need for evidential completeness:

> [M]ost people have a much less satisfied feeling granting relief in a case in which the evidence is very incomplete, even if justifiably so, so that it is difficult to fill in a detailed picture of what happened. So we might say that the less complete the evidence the greater the probability must be to warrant relief for the plaintiff.[149]

The first assertion may well be true, but the second does not follow. Granted that some decisions are more difficult, more disconcerting, or less satisfying for the decision maker than others, it does not follow that the decision criterion should vary as a consequence. Take, for example, any game in which an issue arises over a score or an infraction of the rules. Some decisions about such issues are more difficult, more disconcerting than others just because they are "close calls," but this does not mean that the criterion of choice changes. One needs a reason to change the criterion. Whatever it is in the legal context, it must speak to the following puzzle: one can easily imagine two cases of *equal* degree of evidential completeness (assuming *arguendo* that such a thing can be measured), where the ratio of utilities represented by P^* is the same in each case, and the assessed probability of the claim is the same as well, and yet one of them is still more difficult to assess, more disconcerting, and thus less satisfying for the decision maker. Friedman's criterion (3.4) provides no means of varying the threshold probability to reflect *that* epistemic angst. Why the difference?

At one point Friedman suggests "a feeling of inertia, that because of an 'above all do no harm' orientation we should hesitate to grant relief to the plaintiff unless we have a relatively filled-in picture of what happened."[150] This interesting suggestion, however, does not take us to something like criterion (3.4). It is certainly plausible that there is a disutility associated with positive verdicts that is not associated with negative verdicts – positive verdicts often impute wrongdoing that negative verdicts do not, and they may set in motion the costly legal machinery of enforcement. As discussed in Chapter 2, however, these factors are readily taken into account in either the allocation of the burden of persuasion or the determination of P^* via the utilities associated with positive and negative verdicts. With these adjustments made, what is a "harm" to be avoided under this

[149] Id.
[150] Id.

principle? Friedman's suggestion seems to endorse what has been called "omission bias."[151] Yet he provides nothing to explain why omission bias is *more* justifiable, or justifiably more intense, when evidence is *less* complete. Without such an explanation, whatever omission bias is justifiable is incorporated into P^* without the need of the adjustment provided by Friedman's Q factor.

Although Friedman suggested an adjustment of the critical probability, the standard of proof, there is another way to state his idea. Friedman's proposal is functionally equivalent to a rule that would discount the probability by a measure of completeness and then compare that discounted probability to the usual standard of proof, deciding for the claimant just when

$$P(C|E) \times Q > P^*$$

Stated this way, it is clear that the proposal fails to incorporate the point made by various scholars from Keynes to Reichenbach and Sahlin (§ 3.2): the relative incompleteness of the evidence, without more, does not warrant a discounting of the assessed probability any more than it warrants an increase in that probability.[152] In the end, because Friedman's proposed modification necessarily moves decisions away from the expected utility-maximizing decisions, one needs more justification for doing so than simply the feeling of dissatisfaction of the decision maker in the face of the unavoidable difficulties of judgment. The decision maker may well feel that "it would be better" if there were fuller information, but this counterfactual complaint is of no moment when fuller information is simply not to be had. And when it can be had, this kind of adjustment is not the right response to the situation.

Less easily interpreted in this regard is the extensive treatment of warranted inference by Susan Haack, whose theory I will use as my example of "gestalt" holism. In articulating the justificatory elements of warranted, nondeductive inference – whether scientific, adjudicative, or otherwise – Haack identifies three critical factors: (1) "supportiveness," that is, how strong the connection is between the evidence and

---

[151] See the discussion in § 2.2.1.

[152] I am here (like Friedman) putting aside any inference from spoliation. The matter is different if one attends not to the inadequacy of Keynesian weight per se but rather to the explanations of such a deficiency. If this explanation can be attributed to some strategic withholding or destruction of evidence by a party, then that fact, if known to the fact-finder, can warrant an adjustment to the probability $P(C|E)$ or even to the threshold value P^*. See Friedman (1997b). The advisability of permitting this sort of adjustment is taken up further in § 4.2.

the hypothesis (the stronger the connection, the more it is supportive of the hypothesis); (2) "independent security," that is, how solid the evidence itself is, independent of the hypothesis; and (3) "comprehensiveness," that is, how much of the relevant evidence the evidence considered includes.[153] The first two factors provide a useful way to break down, analytically, the determination of discriminatory power of the evidence as to the hypothesis and its negation. The distinction between them is certainly familiar to lawyers, intelligence analysts, and others who work with probability assessments.[154] But Haack is quick to insist that the third factor, comprehensiveness, works in a special way: for one thing, it is *not* true that the more comprehensive the evidence, the stronger is the warrant for the hypothesis. Whether the increased comprehensiveness increases support for the hypothesis depends on the *content* of the additional evidence; "if making the evidence more comprehensive also makes it less positive, the increase in comprehensiveness lowers the degree of warrant of the conclusion."[155] This seems to be just the distinction that, following Keynes, I have drawn between the augmentation of evidence and the effect thereof on discriminatory power (§ 3.2).

Obviously missing from Haack's list, however, is an explicit factor analogous to the utilities involved in criterion (2.2). Haack's more thorough philosophical presentations, although frequently involving adjudicative examples, do not address specifically the question of the warrant requirements in legal standards of proof or for any other practical decision. No doubt this is in part because her project there is broader. She addresses warranted inference in theoretical as well as practical contexts. But close inspection reveals the same "what's at stake" idea at work when she does pause to address practical decision making. For example, in explaining what it means to say, in ordinary talk, that a person A is "completely justified" in believing a proposition p, she argues that such an assertion is "highly context-dependent":

> [I]t means something like: "in the circumstances – including such matters as how important it is to be right about whether p, whether it is A's particular business to know whether p, etc., etc. – A's evidence is good enough (supportive enough, comprehensive enough, secure enough) that he doesn't count as having been epistemically negligent, or as epistemically blameworthy, in believing that p."[156]

[153] Haack (1993) at 81–9; Haack (2008) at 264.
[154] See, e.g., Schum (1994) at 93–109.
[155] Haack (2008) at 264.
[156] Haack (1993) at 88 (emphasis added).

While the parsing is difficult, many of the familiar components of both decision theory and the practical optimization of Keynesian weight are present in Haack's account.[157]

Nevertheless, her account is holistic in that she describes comprehensiveness as an integral component of a single judgment of the warrant in believing an hypothesis. Its "gestalt" quality appears when she argues that because comprehensiveness of the evidence is one of three different components of epistemic warrant, "there may be no linear ordering of degrees of warrant."[158] She offers this as one reason to believe that degrees of epistemic warrant cannot be mathematical probabilities, that is, cannot be required to conform to the axioms of mathematical probability or (presumably) usefully modeled as if they do. Once one recognizes the orthogonality of evidential completeness, however, one can acknowledge an inability to combine Keynesian weight and discriminatory power into one quantitative measure without any resulting threat to understanding the degrees of epistemic warrant that determine discriminatory power as mathematical probabilities. Because Keynesian weight does not figure in the determination of discriminatory power, it poses no obstacle to understanding the latter in terms of such probabilities.[159]

---

[157] Interestingly, the passage quoted in the text then shifts back to the theoretical and continues

> [b]ut philosophical talk of "complete justification" is best construed in a more demanding, context-neutralized fashion. [It] would require A's C-evidence to be conclusive and maximally comprehensive, and his C-reasons to be maximally independently secure.

Id. at 88–9. As indicated in my previous discussion (§ 3.3), I think that it will be very difficult to give coherent meaning to such a formulation because the qualifying word "maximally" has no theoretical limit. But because Haack is dealing at this point with purely theoretical discourse, I need not claim that it is impossible, only that it is irrelevant to law's pragmatic goals.

[158] Haack (2012) at 217–18.

[159] As summarized in a later work that explicitly addresses legal standards, Haack offers two additional reasons for her opposition to "legal probabilism." Haack (2014) at 61–2. One of these will be addressed later in this section. The last reason she states as follows:

> The mathematical probability of ($p\&q$) is the product of the probability of p and the probability of q – which, unless both have a probability of 1, is always less than either; but combined evidence may warrant a claim to a higher degree than any of its components alone would do.

Id. at 62 (reason (c)). To sort this out, one must first make a minor correction. Haack errs in asserting that $P(p\&q) = P(p) \times P(q)$. This is true only if p and q are stochastically independent, and she provided no such assumption or reason to make such an assumption. Her argument, however, can easily be generalized because it is true under all conditions to which the mathematical axioms of probability apply that $P(p\&q) = P(p) \times P(q|p) \leq P(p)$. Similarly, $P(p\&q) = P(q) \times P(p|q) \leq P(q)$. Thus it is true that for a mathematical probability function

More can be said. Haack *seems* to argue that if an increase in comprehensiveness of the evidence renders the evidence neither more positive nor more negative with regard to the hypothesis (in my terms, has no effect on discriminatory power), then the hypothesis is not warranted to a greater (or lesser) degree by virtue of the increase in comprehensiveness.[160] This claim, whether or not it is proper to attribute it to Haack, is partly right and partly wrong. Once one distinguishes the warrant respecting one's epistemic judgment for or against the hypothesis from the warrant for *making that judgment* – or, in the alternative, seeking or taking into account additional evidence on the matter – then the case posited presents an increased warrant of the latter kind. As Haack states, it is not in itself an increased warrant for the hypothesis or an increased warrant against it, but it is an increased warrant for making the choice. The warrant is increased by adding (and taking into account) an additional item of potentially relevant evidence E_{n+1} even if, as it turns out, this does not affect discriminatory power, a fact illustrated by the observation that one cannot then be faulted for choosing to accept or reject the hypothesis at issue on the ground that one has not yet obtained (or taken into account) E_{n+1}.[161]

$P(\cdot)$, $P(p\&q)$ is less than or equal to $P(p)$ and to $P(q)$, for all propositions p and q. With that correction, one can confront her claim that "combined evidence may warrant a claim to a higher degree than any of its components alone would do." Unfortunately, the passage taken as a whole conflates two different problems: on the one hand, those associated with determining the probability of conjoint propositions, and on the other hand, those associated with determining the probability of claims for which conjoint propositions are evidence. In a following paragraph of her book, Haack applies her argument to a problem that actually concerns the proof of a claim that is itself a composite of elements, regardless of how one conceives of the evidence for that claim. Id. at 63. This distinct conjunction problem is well discussed in the literature; it is addressed in some detail elsewhere (see § 2.3.2). But the probability of interest, in her observation about combining evidence, is instead the probability of a claim *conditioned on* the conjunction $p\&q$, and it is not the case that $P(C|p\&q)$ is necessarily less than or equal to $P(C|p)$ and to $P(C|q)$. Suppose, for example, that C is the claim that a card randomly drawn from a standard deck of cards was or will be the king of hearts; suppose that p is the evidential proposition that the card drawn is red, and suppose that q is the evidential proposition that the card drawn is a face card. Then $P(C|p\&q) = 1/6$, which is both *greater* than $P(C|p) = 1/26$ and *greater* than $P(C|q) = 1/12$. In fact, mathematical probabilities are no obstacle to the reinforcing relationship among pieces of evidence that Haack describes. For a sophisticated analysis, see Schum (1994) at 282–4, 390–409.

[160] Haack (2008) at 264–5.
[161] See Haack (1993) at 87 (noting difficulty in explaining the "comprehensiveness" factor and commenting that "the role of the comprehensiveness clause is most apparent negatively, when one judges someone unjustified or little justified in a belief because of their failure to take account of some relevant evidence"). Such fault finding assumes, of course, that there was reason to believe that the content of E_{n+1} *might* have affected discriminatory power, even though in the event it did not; it also presupposes that it was practicable to take E_{n+1} into account (see § 3.3).

Indeed, in this sense, the warrant for making the judgment is increased regardless of the content of E_{n+1}, provided only that E_{n+1} was potentially relevant to one's assessment of discriminatory power. But whether and how the addition of E_{n+1} affects discriminatory power, and thus the rationality of choosing to accept or to reject the conclusion at issue when such a choice must finally be made, is entirely mediated by the first two of Haack's factors. In particular, these factors allow fully for the operation of the idea that supportiveness is higher when favorable evidence appears from a greater variety of complementary directions.[162] Put differently, the degree of comprehensiveness *vel non* of the evidence (an aspect of Keynesian weight) should be distinguished from *diversity of support* in the evidence for (or against) a conclusion (an aspect of discriminatory power). It seems that Haack generally has the latter idea in mind when she emphasizes the role of "comprehensiveness" of evidence. Even if we draw this distinction, though, and assume that Haack's references are in fact references to diversity of support, and even if Haack is correct that diversity of support is an aspect of warrant that is distinct from supportiveness and independent security, and even if Haack is correct that the multiplicity of factors entering into epistemic warrant (i.e., degree of supportiveness, degree of independent security, and degree of diversity of support) means that such warrant is not linearly ordered – a conclusion about which I remain skeptical[163] – this still does not prevent us from separating out comprehensiveness of evidence *vel non* as informing a different kind of decision than that which is informed by the other aspects of epistemic warrant.

To summarize, properly understood, Keynesian weight is pertinent to that part of decision making that can be called the "evidence-search problem," whereas discriminatory power is pertinent to what may be called the "final-decision problem." In the search context, one obtains evidence until the cost of acquisition exceeds the anticipated benefits of the search effort. One increases Keynesian weight, when this is practically feasible, as a condition precedent to, but not part of, making the decision on the underlying merits. In the final-decision context, one chooses according to the discriminatory power of the evidence so as best to deal with the

---

[162] Haack illustrates the implications of this point in criticizing the "atomistic" epistemology that seems to be latent in the "reliability" requirement for expert testimony derived from the *Daubert* case. Haack (2008). In this critique, I concur. See Nance (2003).

[163] See supra § 2.2.2. For a Bayesian account of the importance of diversity of support, see Horwich (1982) at 118–22.

remaining uncertainty.[164] By the decision-theoretic approach, the latter task entails maximizing the expected gains (minimizing the expected losses) of the decision, given that remaining uncertainty. (All of this must, again, be understood as potentially subject to deontological constraints.) Existing legal scholarship tends (in varying degrees) to miss this point by treating the two requirements as interdependent component parts of the *same* judgment.[165] In part, this may be because, in ordinary inference tasks, the two may not be consciously differentiated, and indeed, they may operate in tandem, with iterations between evidence search and tentative decision making before the final decision is made. In such contexts, it is plausible to describe the decision maker's warrant in believing a hypothesis as embracing both these components. Even then, however, they remain analytically distinct. To avoid being misunderstood, I should emphasize that I would not deny that each of these two distinct components of rational decision making typically must, in practical matters, proceed in a largely qualitative, even "holistic" fashion (though this does not necessarily preclude some degree of quantification of the results). But it is both unnecessary and confusing to think of them as component parts of the *same* holistic judgment.

Importantly, this perspective blunts the force of an argument that has been used by various scholars (including Jonathan Cohen, Alex Stein, and Susan Haack) to reject the idea that the strength of the epistemic warrant in support of a hypothesis can be expressed in terms of probabilities conforming to the usual mathematical axioms.[166] The argument starts from the observation that a low mathematical probability for hypothesis H entails a high probability for not-H because the axioms of mathematical probability require that $P(H) + P(\text{not-}H) = 1$. In contrast, so the argument goes, both one's epistemic warrant for H and one's epistemic warrant for not-H may be low. Thus epistemic warrant does not obey the complementation principle required of mathematical probabilities. When this argument is made, it is invariably supported by the observation that such a situation of

---

[164] See Nance (2010) at 1103.
[165] In addition to the scholars already discussed in the text, see Cohen, N. (1985) (merging issues of evidentiary completeness with the test for adequacy of discriminatory power to be applied by the fact-finder); Franklin (2006) at 162 (recognizing the separation in the civil adjudication context but falling back on a commingling of the issues in the criminal context); and Ho (2008) at 165–70 (treating Keynesian weight as one factor among several relevant to determining the plausibility of the affirmative hypothesis to be proved).
[166] See, e.g., Cohen, J. (1989) at 17–18; Stein (2011) at 241–2; and Haack (2014) at 62 [reason (c)].

noncomplementation can occur when there is (as yet) too little evidence to accept or endorse either *H* or not-*H*.[167]

The argument seems appealing. After all, with little information on the basis of which to discriminate between the two hypotheses, it seems hard to endorse either one. But the argument equivocates about what it means to accept or endorse *H*. This meaning depends on the alternatives being considered. It may be true that there is too little evidence to warrant accepting or endorsing the truth of *H when the alternative is postponing choice* until additional evidence has been obtained – that is, a situation of inadequate Keynesian weight. In this sense, it is also correct to say that one has too little evidence to accept or endorse not-*H*. It would be more precise to say that there is too little evidence to accept the propriety of *making the choice* between *H* and not-*H*. But that is entirely distinct from the question of one's warrant for accepting or endorsing *H* in a context, such as rendering a verdict in legal adjudication, where the option of seeking additional evidence has been taken off the table. Admittedly, when one is forced to choose based on very little information, one may feel discomfort, and one may have relatively little confidence in the choice that is made, but this does not mean that one cannot make a rational choice by attributing odds on *H* as compared with not-*H*. Moreover, if one makes such an attribution, then it is reasonable to maintain that the probabilities involved in such odds should conform to the axioms of mathematical probability.

3.7 Decision Making with Non-Bayesian Belief Functions

In this section, I take up a fairly technical theory of belief functions developed by Glen Shafer. His is a theory of how to combine degrees of belief derived from different evidential sources.[168] In his theory, degrees of rational belief do not necessarily obey the standard rules of mathematical probability, in particular, the complementation principle. This section thus extends what was argued earlier to a quantified theory of gradational belief that is more general than probabilities, yet one that is sufficiently developed to allow fairly clear understanding of what the theory entails. The reader uninterested in such a technical theory can safely skip this section without losing the thread of the book's general argument.

---

[167] In one brief passage, Haack also deploys a slightly different example in which the background information is such that the hypothesis is not yet even conceivable. Haack (2003) at 75. In such a case, though, neither $P(H)$ nor $P(\text{not-}H)$ is intelligibly assessed, so the proposition that $P(H) + P(\text{not-}H) = 1$ is not contradicted.

[168] Shafer (1976).

s( )	H	not-H	H or not-H
E_1	0.3	0.2	0.5
E_2	0.6	0.4	0.0

Figure 4. Illustrative Shafer support functions for a binary choice.

Shafer's theory is too complicated to present fully here, but its import for practical decision making can be explained in terms of a specific example chosen to emphasize binary choices such as that encountered in adjudication.[169] So, once again, suppose that one is trying to decide whether to endorse hypothesis H or, rather, to endorse its negation, not-H. Under Shafer's theory, at any given point in one's consideration of evidence relating to such hypotheses, the *support* that the evidence provides may be allocated not just to H or to not-H but also to the set of possible choices, here {H, not-H}.[170] In other words, a portion of the total support provided by the evidence may be "withheld," uncommitted as between the mutually exclusive hypotheses H and not-H. Figure 4 illustrates two different hypothetical allocations of the evidential support under two different hypothetical states of the evidence, E_1 and E_2.

The *support function* for E_1 is written $s_1(\cdot)$; for example, $s_1(H) = 0.3$. Note that under evidence E_1, not all the support is committed to either H or not-H. Significantly, Shafer explains that the amount of support uncommitted or withheld is related to the amount of evidence considered; that is, when there is little evidence regarding the contending hypotheses, uncommitted support will be large, whereas when there is considerable evidence, uncommitted support will be small. He refers to extreme situations in which there is "no evidence," in which case $s(H) = s(\text{not-}H) = 0$ and $s(H \text{ or not-}H) = 1$.[171]

Two observations should be made about this idea of support. First, those who argue that epistemic warrant is noncomplementational may

---

[169] For an accessible treatment of the more general case, see Schum (1994) at 225–43.

[170] In the more general case, allowing for n mutually exclusive hypotheses comprising the set $\Theta = \{H_1, \ldots, H_n\}$, Shafer would allow the support to be allocated among the set of all subsets of Θ, called the "power set" because it contains 2^n elements, subject to the restriction that $s(\emptyset) = 0$ and that the sum of the support values allocated to all the subsets is 1.

[171] See, e.g., Shafer (1976) at 5–6, 38. Another warning about the inconsistency of terminology regarding "weight": Shafer does not explicitly use the idea of Keynesian weight. In fact, his only mentions of Keynes are in connection with ideas other than what Keynes called "weight," contexts in which Shafer *does* use the word "weight." E.g., id. at 88.

have in mind, or be thinking in terms compatible with, the kind of support functions that Shafer employs. Second, the noncomplementational quality of his support functions depends on the ability meaningfully to allocate some part of the support provided by the evidence to some proposition other than the individual hypotheses at issue, even when (as here) they exhaust the possibilities. The uncommitted support value, which is just $s(H$ or not-$H)$ in the (exhaustive) two-hypothesis case, would seem to provide a measure of evidential (in)completeness.[172] When this value is 0, as under evidence E_2, all evidential support must be allocated either to H or to not-H, so it would seem plausible to describe this as a situation of complete evidence, or maximal Keynesian weight, with the extreme opposite, that is, $s(H$ or not-$H) = 1$, representing a total absence of evidence, or minimal Keynesian weight. Similarly, using the ratio of support committed (i.e., allocated to either H or to not-H) to support withheld (i.e., allocated to (H or not-H)) would provide a way to fill out the weight of the evidence as defined by Runde in equation (3.1). Many of Shafer's statements support this interpretation of his theory.[173]

I have already indicated (§ 3.5) some reservations about our ability to provide meaningful quantification of Keynesian weight or evidential completeness in the general case. Indeed, in his primary work on the subject, Shafer provides no insight into the methodology of how one would make the allocation of support between that which is committed and that which is withheld. He simply posits that this can be done. That it makes sense to assume we can do so is to be inferred primarily from the overall usefulness of his theory.[174] Accordingly, I will not pursue here the question of whether

---

[172] In a more general case, when there are three or more (say, n) contending hypotheses that form a partition, support not attributed to the set of *all* contending hypotheses $\{H_1, \ldots, H_n\}$ might nonetheless be attributed to a nonsingleton set such as $\{H_1, H_2\}$. In this case, the condition that $s(H_1$ or $\cdots$ or $H_n) = 0$ would not indicate full evidential completeness; full completeness would require that no support be allocated to any nonsingleton sets, which is the same as saying that $\Sigma_i\, s(H_i) = 1$.

[173] See also Shafer (1976) at 22–5.

[174] He puts the matter this way:

> The theory begins with the familiar idea of using a number between zero and one to indicate the degree of support a body of evidence provides for a proposition – i.e., the degree of belief one should accord the proposition on the basis of the evidence. But unlike past attempts to develop this idea, the theory does not focus on the act of judgment by which such a number is determined. It focuses instead on something more amenable to mathematical analysis: the combination of degrees of belief or support based on one body of evidence with those based on an entirely distinct body of evidence.

Id. at 3.

Bel( )	H	not-H	H or not-H
E_1	0.3	0.2	1.0
E_2	0.6	0.4	1.0

Figure 5. Belief functions for support functions in Figure 4.

Shafer's theory provides the key to a coherent theoretical methodology for the quantification of Keynesian weight.

However that may be, it is from such support functions that Shafer then constructs *belief* functions by equating the rational strength of belief with the support provided by the evidence, subject to the following important aggregation principle: "a portion of belief committed to one proposition is thereby committed to any other proposition it implies."[175] Thus one's belief in A, written Bel(A), includes not only the evidential support specifically for A, if any, but also the support for any other proposition that entails A. Since H entails (H or not-H) and not-H entails (H or not-H), the two hypothetical allocations in Figure 4 produce the belief functions shown in Figure 5.

Thus, for this two-hypothesis context, we have

$$\text{Bel}(H \text{ or not-}H) = s(H) + s(\text{not-}H) + s(H \text{ or not-}H) = 1$$

for any state of the evidence. Notice that a belief function also does not necessarily conform to the complementation principle: for example, $\text{Bel}_1(H) + \text{Bel}_1(\text{not-}H) = 0.5 \neq 1.0$. The belief function will be complementational in this sense only when the evidence is such as to permit no withholding of support; as in the case of evidence E_2, all support is then committed either to H or to not-H. In such a case, Shafer calls the belief function "Bayesian."[176]

We now have enough of Shafer's theory to pose the important question for our present purposes. What is one to do if a decision, either to endorse (and act on) H or to endorse (and act on) not-H, must be made under evidence, such as E_1, in which some of the evidential support is withheld? (There is no new problem in using decision theory for Bayesian belief functions, such as those arising under evidence E_2.) In his original work,

---

[175] Id. at 37.
[176] Id. at 44–5. By "Bayesian," Shafer means simply that the resulting belief functions are probabilities by the standard (Kolmogorov) axioms. Id. at 18–19.

Shafer did not attempt to develop an answer to this kind of question.[177] His theory is a theory of evidence and the adjustment of partial beliefs; it is not a theory of decision making. Utilities of decision make no appearance in the theory. How, then, should one answer the question posed?

If, under evidence E_1, one is to make use of standard decision theory, including the result stated as criterion (2.2), one cannot simply take the belief function values as measures of the epistemic probabilities involved because these belief functions are not always probability measures. Suppose, for example, that one took $P(H|E_1) = \text{Bel}_1(H) = 0.3$. If, by criterion (2.2'), P^* is 0.5, as in some civil cases, this would mean that the claimant should lose. Because remaining uncommitted, as between H and not-H, is no longer an option at the moment of judgment, however, this solution makes sense only if one counts all the uncommitted support as support for not-H. (If not, then $P(\text{not-}H|E_1) = \text{Bel}_1(\text{not-}H) = 0.2$, and the complementation principle with which criterion (2.2') is derived does not apply.) Yet there is no plausible rationale for such an attribution. One cannot treat something as counting against H when the point of its not being committed is that it does *not* discriminate between H and not-H. Significantly, for Shafer one's *doubt* about H is one's belief that not-H: $\text{Dou}(H) =_{\text{def}} \text{Bel}(\text{not-}H)$. Thus $\text{Dou}_1(H) = \text{Bel}_1(\text{not-}H) = 0.2$. One's doubt about H is *not* defined in terms of the total belief attributed to anything other than H, which he calls the *plausibility* of not-H.[178] This appropriately reflects the fact that uncommitted support does not create doubt about H, even though one might – quite distinctly – "doubt" the wisdom of choosing between H and not-H when the evidence is relatively weak and there is a meaningful alternative to making that choice.[179]

---

[177] See, e.g., id. at 84–5.

[178] Shafer (1976) at 43. Shafer uses both the terms *upper probability* of H and *plausibility* of H, denoted $P^*(H)$, so $P^*(\text{not-}H) = 1 - \text{Bel}(H)$. The relationships can be seen in the following graphic, which divides up the unit interval:

Bel(H)	s(H or not-H)	Bel(not-H)

with $P^*(\text{not-}H)$ spanning the middle and right cells, and $P^*(H)$ spanning the left and middle cells.

In dynamic terms, one can visualize that as s(H or not-H) decreases with the accumulation of relevant evidence, the sum of Bel(H) and Bel(not-H) increases, with a maximum sum of 1.

[179] The relevant "doubt" in *this* regard is the value of uncommitted support, i.e., s(H or not-H) in the two-hypothesis context. Under evidence E_1, for example, s_1(H or not-H) = 0.5, a fairly substantial degree of doubt. As we have seen, however, this value, even if it can be

Several suggestions about how to solve this problem appear in the literature. One suggestion (solution 1) would *ignore* the uncommitted support and construct epistemic probabilities using the ratios of belief values for the hypotheses to construct relative odds. Thus, under evidence E_1, the belief in H is stronger than the belief in not-H by a ratio of 3:2, which would be taken as the odds on H versus not-H. Or, converting these odds into a probability, we have $P(H|E_1) = 0.6$. This "simple normalization" of the belief function is mathematically equivalent to, but is not necessarily premised on, the assumption that the uncommitted support should be allocated between the hypotheses in proportion to their existing support values.[180] Such normalization has been suggested in the literature, although it is sometimes explained as being based on the indicated assumption.[181] Of course, it need not be. It can be based simply on the assumption that one cannot rationally make use of information that is nondiscriminating in making one's choice between H and not-H.

Other suggestions are based on the idea that uncommitted support may nonetheless contain *some* information about the hypotheses; they attempt to take advantage of that information in some way. One suggestion (solution 2) is that the entire uncommitted support should be added to the support for each of the hypotheses, and the ratios of the resulting values should be used to determine odds and probabilities. Thus, in the case of E_1, the odds on H would be $(0.3 + 0.5):(0.2 + 0.5) = 8:7$, yielding an epistemic probability $P(H|E_1)$ of 0.53. The intuition behind this suggestion is that the uncommitted support might properly be allocated to either of the contending hypotheses, and giving each hypothesis the full benefit of that uncommitted support does not discriminate between the

---

quantified, does not by itself determine the issue of the ripeness of a decision between H and not-H. One must take into account what may be contributed by identifiable potential additions to the stock of evidence and at what cost (§ 3.5).

[180] In specifying how to combine support functions for different pieces of evidence, Shafer runs into the problem of what to do with support that, by his rule of combination, is allocated to the empty set, which makes no sense. His reasonable answer is to normalize the distribution of support by a proportionate increase in the support allocated to all nonempty sets so that the total support attributed to nonempty sets sums to 1, but their relative values remain the same. Shafer (1976) at 57–73. Analogously, when confronted with an unavoidable choice between H and not-H, if one normalizes by proportionate increases in the support for H and for not-H, thus eliminating uncommitted support, one will obtain the same result specified earlier; proportionate increases in Bel(H) and Bel(not-H) will not affect their ratio. For example, proportionate redistribution of the uncommitted support under evidence E_1 to H and not-H yields the same distribution of support as that for E_2, with the same ratio of Bel(H)/Bel(not-H), namely 3:2.

[181] See, e.g., Strat (1990) at 398 (identifying but not defending this solution).

hypotheses.[182] Another suggestion (solution 3) would divide the uncommitted support equally between the two hypotheses regardless of their respective committed support values. Thus, in the case of E_1, the odds on H would be (0.3 + 0.25):(0.2 + 0.25), and $P(H|E_1)$ would be 0.55. This suggestion also attempts not to discriminate between the hypotheses in the allocation, employing what is thought to be a generalization of the principle of indifference.[183]

All three solutions would permit access to the decision-theoretic criterion when dealing with belief functions that do not conform to the standard axioms for probability, such as the belief functions associated with evidence E_1. They do so by transforming the non-Bayesian belief function into an appropriate probability function that conforms to the standard axioms. Solutions 2 and 3 must fail, however, when action or choice depends on the relative odds of two hypotheses between which the original support was uncommitted. As to these, once again, the uncommitted support tells us nothing that discriminates between those hypotheses.

Solution 1, I conclude, is the only acceptable one. But to make its relevance to legal adjudication clear, it must be suitably generalized to the situation of more than two hypotheses. As discussed in § 2.3, a legal decision maker might entertain more than two theories of the case. Suppose that H_1, H_2, and H_3 are mutually exclusive theories about what happened in a litigated case, the only hypotheses that the fact-finder considers to have any significant degree of acceptability. Suppose further that the truth of H_1 would require a verdict for the claimant, whereas the truth of either H_2 or H_3 would require a verdict for the defense. Under a generalized version of solution 1, one should add any support that is *partially* committed in the sense that it is attributed to $\{H_2, H_3\}$ to the support attributed to H_2 and that attributed to H_3 in determining how much the evidence supports the defense. But one would ignore fully uncommitted or partially committed support that "straddles the fence" between pro-claimant hypotheses and pro-defendant hypotheses, that is, support attributed to $\{H_1, H_2\}$, to $\{H_1, H_3\}$, or to $\{H_1, H_2, H_3\}$. In other words, one should treat the ratio of Bel(H_1) to Bel(H_2 or H_3) as the ratio of odds for purposes of criterion (2.2).[184]

---

[182] To be precise in a way that extends to the case of more than two hypotheses, the odds of any two hypotheses would be determined by the ratio of their "plausibilities." As defined by Shafer, the plausibility of a hypothesis H is equal to 1 − Bel(not-H). Id. at 144. Transforming belief values to probability values using plausibility values is defended in Cobb & Shenoy (2003).
[183] See Smets (2005).
[184] More generally, if the fact-finder takes only n mutually exclusive hypotheses to be seriously plausible, 1 through i of which favor the claimant and $i + 1$ through n of which favor

Support Values Pertaining to Decision about Further Investigation	Support Values Pertaining to Decision on Merits, Assuming It Must Be Made on the Available Evidence	
$s(H_1$ or $H_2)$	$s(H_1)$	(favors claimant)
$s(H_1$ or $H_3)$	$s(H_2)$	(favors defendant)
$s(H_1$ or H_2 or $H_3)$	$s(H_3)$	(favors defendant)
	$s(H_2$ or $H_3)$	(favors defendant)

Figure 6. Functional allocation of Shafer-like support values in three-hypothesis context, where hypothesis H_1 favors the claimant and hypotheses H_2 and H_3 favor the defendant.

By the same token, a measure of evidential completeness in this three-hypothesis case would have to include all support that cannot be taken into account in determining the relevant ratio of belief values, that is, $s(H_1$ or $H_2)$, $s(H_1$ or $H_3)$, and $s(H_1$ or H_2 or $H_3)$. The greater the sum of these three numbers, the greater is the degree of evidential incompleteness. Again, Keynesian weight does not enter into a single, holistic judgment of epistemic warrant for the final decision. Rather, its importance lies in the conditions that the decision maker should satisfy before the final decision is made. These conditions may differ because, in the assumed three-hypothesis case, there are three different support values that might, on further investigation, be reallocated so as to affect the decision. This is summarized in Figure 6.

One might be inclined to think that $s(H_2$ or $H_3)$ is pertinent to decisions about further investigation. After all, such investigation might serve to distinguish between H_2 and H_3. True enough. But this will not contribute practically to the solution of the particular decision problem faced because (by hypothesis) the defendant should win whether H_2 is true or H_3 is true. Consequently, any resources expended on trying to determine how to allocate $s(H_2$ or $H_3)$, as between H_2 and H_3, are likely wasted.[185]

the defendant, then the ratio to use in criterion (2.2) would be $\text{Bel}(H_1$ or $\cdots$ or $H_i)/\text{Bel}(H_{i+1}$ or $\cdots$ or $H_n)$.

[185] I say "likely" wasted for this reason: it remains possible, if I understand Shafer's theory, that one's attempt, by further investigation, to resolve whether $s(H_2$ or $H_3)$ should be allocated to H_2 or to H_3 would result in a realization that the entire scheme of support was in some way in need of adjustment so that support that had been thought appropriately allocated to $\{H_2, H_3\}$ in fact should be allocated to $\{H_1\}$ or to $\{H_1, H_3\}$ and so forth.

In summary, giving the benefit of totally uncommitted or partially committed support that "straddles the fence" entirely to the defendant is not justified by the existence of a default rule for close cases, that is, cases for which the tribunal is unable to say that the required margin of discriminatory power has been attained. Indeed, giving all the benefit of such uncommitted support only to the defendant is no more warranted than giving it to the plaintiff. Either attribution would be arbitrary, and I have found no support for this solution in the technical literature developing Shafer's theory.[186] Among the other, more plausible approaches, if I am correct that solution 1 is correct, then we can restate criterion (2.2) in terms of belief functions: decide for the claimant just when

$$\text{Bel}_E(C)/\text{Bel}_E(\text{not-}C) > O^* \tag{3.5}$$

where

$$O^* =_{\text{def}} \left(U_{(-)} + D_{(+)}\right)/\left(U_{(+)} + D_{(-)}\right)$$

subject to any appropriate deontological constraints that are not contained within the indicated utilities ratio.

Recently, Kevin Clermont has considered Shafer's theory of belief functions and reached similar, but not identical, conclusions. Clermont's theory is too complex to develop here in full.[187] Suffice it to say that when it comes to ordinary civil cases governed by the "preponderance of the evidence" standard, he endorses (though he does not explain) the view that withheld support should be ignored in the fact-finder's decision. He takes the criterion of decision to be whether $\text{Bel}_E(C) > \text{Bel}_E(\text{not-}C)$. This coincides with the criterion endorsed here as long as O^* is equal to 1. Of course, I have argued that O^* need not be taken as equal to 1, or even approximately so, in many ordinary civil cases (§ 2.2.1), but this is a relatively minor point of disagreement. More serious is the fact that Clermont reaches his conclusion while rejecting the idea of interpreting the ratio $\text{Bel}_E(C)/\text{Bel}_E(\text{not-}C)$

---

[186] To be sure, one thing we do find in that literature is the suggestion that the portion of the uncommitted support to be allocated between H and not-H so as to create probabilities should depend on an assessment of the *motives* of some person, if any, who has control of the missing evidence. See Strat (1990). This inventive solution tracks a well-known legal device known as the "adverse inference," discussed infra (§ 4.2), but it can apply only in limited situations – where missing evidence is withheld in bad faith – and such an attribution may not be the best way to deal with such motives when they are identified.
[187] See Clermont (2013) at 201–20. Part of the complexity arises from his invocation of fuzzy set theory, a topic I do not address in this work. See id. at 145–201.

as an odds ratio. His reasons for rejecting this interpretation are unpersuasive.[188] Moreover, this rejection precludes him from giving any quantitative measure, however approximate, to the higher standards of proof. He proposes to interpret the intermediate standard, usually verbalized as "clear and convincing evidence," as a requirement that the burdened party win just when $Bel_E(C) \gg Bel_E(\text{not-}C)$, where he has chosen the double > symbol to indicate that one belief is "substantially greater than" or "much greater than" the other.[189] This may be adequate descriptively, in the sense that courts generally do not quantify the necessary ratio. Clermont insists that his enterprise is descriptive.[190] But he clearly articulates reasons to endorse the conceptions that he purports to describe. As an interpretive matter, such formulations are deficient both theoretically and practically.

[188] He refers to the idea of interpreting the ratio of belief values as the odds on the claim as the "normalization" approach, labeling $b(S)$ and $b(\text{not}S)$ as the "normalized belief functions" for $Bel(S)$ and $Bel(\text{not}S)$, respectively. (As noted in the text, normalizing the non-Bayesian belief functions gives the same probability as does simply ignoring uncommitted support in determining the odds ratio.) He then gives three reasons not to use such an approach:

> First, converting to additive beliefs would reintroduce the probabilistic imaging that originally led us astray into all the problems and paradoxes of the traditional view. Second, I contend that directly comparing $Bel(S)$ to $Bel(\text{not}S)$ actually conforms better to the actual law than the probabilistic view does. Third, normalization requires measurement of $b(S)$ and $b(\text{not}S)$, a complicated step otherwise unnecessary, and a step that is much more difficult for humans than relative judgment.

Id. at 214. Taking the last point first, it is simply not true that one must determine the value of the individual normalized belief functions before looking at their ratio because (using Clermont's symbols) $Bel(S)/Bel(\text{not}S) = b(S)/b(\text{not}S)$. Clermont thinks that the "probabilistic" approach must determine $b(S)$ and place this value on a absolute scale. This would be true under my criterion (2.2'), for example, but articulating the probabilistic approach in terms of odds, as in criterion (2.2) or the belief function version in criterion (3.5), avoids this complication because it also rests on a comparative measure (or "relative judgment"), albeit a quantified one. (His argument cannot be simply that no quantification of that ratio is possible, however approximately, because he elsewhere endorses the idea of the jury's determining the approximate quantitative values for $Bel(S)$ and for $Bel(\text{not}S)$.) This also renders moot his second reason because it is also based on the idea that the law's norms prescribe comparative assessments instead of placing some measure, such as $b(S)$, on an absolute scale. See id. at 214–16. This leaves Clermont's first reason, which is a reference to the paradoxes of the conjunction and aggregation, which he believes can be avoided by the use of fuzzy logic. See id. at 188–201. Although I do not here address fuzzy logic, I have previously addressed the conjunction paradox (see § 2.3.2); aggregation is a variation on that same theme. Finally, and perhaps most importantly, if one does *not* interpret $Bel(S)/Bel(\text{not}S)$ as a ratio of odds, then one cannot use that ratio in the decision-theoretic result of criterion (2.2), in which case the justificatory power of that criterion is not available. Yet Clermont relies on it for justification. See id. at 218 (relying on the minimization of expected error costs).

[189] Id. at 212 n. 586 and accompanying text.

[190] E.g., id. at 152.

As a theoretical matter, by what criterion can it then be said whether or not a belief of strength 0.5 is "substantially greater" or "much greater" than one of 0.3, for example? Clermont identifies no such criterion. As a practical matter, such a formulation says nothing informative to the fact-finder: for one person, 0.5 may be "much greater" than 0.3, but for another person, this may not be so, and if there are many fact-finders (such as a jury), they have nothing from which to reason to agreement about the issue.[191]

However, it is in the context of the criminal law's standard of proof "beyond reasonable doubt" that Clermont runs into the most trouble. Rejecting the extension of his previous idea – that is, rejecting a rule for criminal cases that would require $\text{Bel}_E(C) \ggg \text{Bel}_E(\text{not-}C)$ for a guilty verdict – Clermont asserts that the criminal standard is "different in kind" and that separate requirements must be placed on each of $\text{Bel}_E(C)$ and $\text{Bel}_E(\text{not-}C)$. Giving remarkably little by way of explanation, his twin requirements would be that (1) no reasonable person could hold $\text{Bel}_E(\text{not-}C) > 0$ and (2) the belief in guilt must exceed the plausibility of innocence, which entails that $\text{Bel}_E(C) > 0.5$.[192] This is curious in at least two respects. First, Clermont repeatedly touts the virtues of comparative assessment, only to abandon it here, at least in connection with the first prong of his test, for in this respect he requires the placing of a quantified measure of belief on an absolute scale. He understandably qualifies the meaning of $\text{Bel}_E(\text{not-}C) > 0$ by noting that the beliefs are coarsely graded and that in practice this requirement would mean that there is not more than a "slightest possibility" of innocence. But this remains a thoroughly noncomparative test with a quantified belief value placed on an absolute (albeit coarsely graded) scale.

Second, his requirement on $\text{Bel}_E(C)$ remains comparative, if indeed it does so,[193] only by giving all benefit of the uncommitted support to the defendant. His explanation of this dramatic shift away from his view

[191] This is not to say that jurors could not reach a decision. It is, however, to say that the standard, so expressed, will provide little guidance for, and have little impact on, that decision. Cf. Laudan (2007) at 299–300 (addressing a similar suggestion (by Paul Thagard) for saving inference to the best explanation as a standard for criminal proof: "Does Thagard really believe that jurors, without further ado, could often or easily reach consensus about whether the prosecution's case was 'substantially more plausible' than the defendant's?")
[192] Clermont (2013) at 213.
[193] If one articulates the requirement as $\text{Bel}_E(C) > 0.5$, then it clearly requires a fact-finder to place a quantified measure on an absolute scale. An equivalent articulation is that a conviction is improper unless $\text{Bel}_E(C) >$ (plausibility of not-C). Formally, this requirement looks comparative, but it is not likely that a fact-finder would know how to interpret such a requirement, built as it is on a technically defined concept, Shafer's concept of "plausibility." If stated, instead, in a manner that would compare $\text{Bel}_E(C)$ with $\text{Bel}_E(\text{not-}C)$ – apples to apples, as it were – then it would have to be stated as a

regarding the treatment of uncommitted support in civil cases is the assertion that the "beyond reasonable doubt" requirement should mean "that no great uncommitted belief remains."[194] But what determines how "great" is "too great"? Clermont clearly recognizes, indeed emphasizes, the connection between uncommitted support and the completeness of the evidence developed and presented.[195] And his test for criminal cases is yet another illustration of the tendency of legal scholars to conflate the adequacy of investigation with the adequacy of discriminatory power. Suffice it here to reiterate that any *unavoidable* incompleteness of the evidence (as distinct from possible strategic explanations of such incompleteness) is useless for purposes of discriminating between hypotheses. Thus an earlier expression of opinion on the matter by Clermont, although no better explained than his later opinion, is the sounder view: "the common-law fact-finder is not supposed to hold an unavoidable paucity of evidence against the burdened party, but is instead in such a situation supposed to decide the likelihood based on the evidence."[196] This proposition holds whether the case is a civil case or a criminal case, and it is not affected by how great the "unavoidable paucity of evidence" may be.

As for *avoidable* incompleteness, another aspect of Clermont's suggestion provides a segue into Chapter 4. At least in criminal cases, he allocates to the fact-finder the task of taking the uncommitted support into account, that is, of *doing something* with it. In this chapter, I have argued that something should be done, provided that the uncommitted support is the result of a failure to practically optimize Keynesian weight. But the fact-finder has very limited options and (as we shall see) not good ones. Thus, if the fact-finder does not have the task of monitoring this, who should take the action to practically optimize Keynesian weight? And how should this be done? Chapter 4 addresses this question in detail.

3.8 Keynesian Weight and the Goals of Adjudication

Two analytically distinct components of decision – (1) doing the best one can to solve the evidence search problem and (2) making the best

---

requirement that $Bel_E(C) > 1 - Bel_E(\text{not-}C)$, a comparison that presupposes computation after placement of *two* variables on an absolute scale – hardly an improvement in practical usefulness.

[194] He allows that he is "open" to similar suggestions for those civil cases for which the intermediate "clear and convincing evidence" standard is employed. Id. at 212.
[195] See id. at 204–8.
[196] See, e.g., Clermont (2009) at 480–1.

possible decision despite the remaining uncertainty – map in complex ways to two related but distinct functions of trial rules: (1) the cost-justified minimization of the aggregate risk of errors and (2) the distribution of the residual risk of error, that is, (aggregate) risk that is not eliminated.[197] Acquiring cost-justified relevant evidence – and thereby increasing Keynesian weight – does not, of course, guarantee a more accurate decision, but it is plausibly *expected* to improve accuracy. It is such an expectation that increases the expected utility of decision and thus justifies the costs of the acquisition and use of such evidence.[198] Thus the evidence-search problem is about minimizing the aggregate risk of error within reasonable cost constraints. The final decision problem must then confront the allocation of the residual risk, that which remains after a reasonably thorough investigation. To be sure, an important insight of decision theory is that this allocation can be and quite plausibly should be done so as to further minimize expected net costs (or maximize expected net utility), even though that may entail an increase in the expected *number* of errors. This is so because employing criterion (2.2) minimizes expected costs regardless of the value of O^*, but it minimizes the expected number of errors only when $O^* = 1$.[199] If O^* is set higher than 1 for a class of cases (e.g., criminal cases), then the increase in the expected number of false negatives (e.g., erroneous acquittals) will be larger than the decrease in the expected number of false positives (e.g., erroneous convictions).

It should be clear that the costs involved in these two steps of a decision process are different in kind. Evidence-search costs are part of litigation costs, whereas the costs that can be minimized by the proper selection of a standard of proof are the costs that follow from mistaken decisions, so-called error costs (though, once again, *errors* are not all that matter). The former "input" costs are sunk costs by the time a verdict is required, whereas the latter "output" costs are affected by the verdict selection. When we think about the question of how much accuracy we can afford

---

[197] See generally Stein (2005) at 11–25 and Pardo (2009) at 1086. Professor Stein refers to "the law's three fact-finding objectives: minimization of fact-finding errors; reduction of the error-avoidance expenses; and, finally, apportionment of the risk of error." Stein (2005) at 11–12. Professor Pardo refers to the "epistemological core of any successful theory of evidence as relating the proof process to the goals of (1) factual accuracy and (2) allocation among parties of the risk of factual errors," leaving "economic" issues aside as part of the "host of other theoretical and practical issues" that evidence law must address. Pardo (2013) at 559–60.
[198] For further discussion of this point, see infra § 5.1.
[199] See Kaye (1999).

from our system of litigation, we are primarily thinking about the input costs. In this context, it makes sense to say that we "purchase" accuracy, or at least its expectation, with expenditure on the collection and analysis of evidence. In contrast, we do not "expend" output costs so much as we unavoidably incur them. We can trade one kind for another (say, greater false-negative costs for lesser false-positive costs), but if so, we do this to minimize their aggregate amount.

Consider, for example, one of the more peculiar statements to be found in Supreme Court jurisprudence on the due process implications for the standard of proof:

> At one end of the spectrum is the typical civil case involving a monetary dispute between private parties. Since society has a minimal concern with the outcome of such private suits, plaintiff's burden of proof is a mere preponderance of the evidence.[200]

In this passage, at least, the Court has conflated the two ideas of weight distinguished here. If society in fact had "minimal concern" with the outcomes of typical civil cases, one would wonder why such cases are not decided by a simple flip of a coin, thereby avoiding most of the costs of litigation.[201] In fact, society tolerates fairly expensive dispute-resolution procedures, even for typical civil cases. The court's statement must be read in the context of its overall endorsement and use of a methodology that, in setting the standard of proof, tries to allocate the risks of error in an appropriate manner.[202] This is very different from the level of society's concern with the outcome: society can be greatly concerned about the result in a dispute for which the risks of error should be distributed equally; conversely, it can have very little concern about the result in a dispute for which the risks should be skewed heavily in favor of one side. Presumably, what the quoted passage is meant to communicate is that society has minimal *differential* in concern, as between the parties, in the outcome of such civil cases.

Some scholars who have correctly recognized the distinct role and importance of Keynesian weight (by whatever name) may have claimed too much for it. It is sometimes suggested that the difference between the civil and criminal standards of proof should be explained entirely in terms of the greater demands on Keynesian weight that legitimately

---

[200] Addington v. Texas, 441 U.S. 418, 423 (1979).
[201] Cf. Kaplow (2012) at 742–3.
[202] Addington, 441 U.S. at 423–33.

condition a decision in criminal cases rather than in terms of differences in the required level of discriminatory power.[203] This is an intriguing suggestion, one that might help to explain why Continental European courts often use burdens of persuasion for civil and criminal cases that are nominally indistinguishable.[204] As explained earlier (§ 3.3), it is certainly plausible that the greater seriousness of the typical criminal case (at least the typical felony) warrants more thorough exploration of the potential evidence than is warranted for the typical civil case. But this does not fully explain the higher proof requirements in Anglo-American criminal cases. After investigation reduces the total risk of error appropriately, there will remain a residual risk of error that must be allocated between the parties. Some criterion, such as criterion (2.2), must be employed to do so, and – if the conventional assessment of the (dis)utilities of outcomes for criminal cases is even substantially correct – the critical odds O^* will be greater for criminal cases, at least for the more serious ones. Even if such criminal cases were extremely thoroughly investigated, every lead followed at an expenditure of resources much greater than is currently encountered, it still would not be appropriate to use critical odds in the range of those appropriate for the decision of ordinary civil cases.

The situation is rather different when thinking about the variation among types of criminal offenses. The problem can be seen by reference to a comment by Davidson and Pargetter on the significance of weight:

> [A]s the seriousness of an offence increases, and thus the negative consequence for the accused if found guilty increases, to maintain the *same* rationality of acting on the probability of guilt would require *both* an increase in the probability of guilt and an increase in the weight of the probability.[205]

There is an obvious problem with this argument. Not mentioned is the fact that what is pertinent to both the required-probability issue and the required-weight issue is the seriousness of the consequences for the accused *and* of those for the public; for example, the importance of errors in favor of the accused (false negatives) also must be considered. An increase in seriousness, which affects the interests of both the state and the accused, pushes in *opposite* directions when it comes to the required probability of guilt because as the seriousness of the crime increases, the costs of false negatives goes up as well as the costs of false

---

[203] See, e.g. Schoeman (1987) at 86.
[204] See Clermont & Sherwin (2002).
[205] Davidson & Pargetter (1987) at 187.

positives. (An analogous conflicting pressure occurs with respect to the positive utilities associated with correct verdicts.) In the aggregate, these may or may not be entirely offsetting (see § 2.2.1). When it comes to the question of the necessary Keynesian weight, though, these increased costs (and benefits) associated with more serious cases all push in the *same* direction – in favor of more thorough investigation to reduce the chances of either kind of error.

It should be added that none of this means that the decision maker approaches the final decision problem without error minimization in mind. Even after the evidence-search problem has been solved and even in the context of a specific rule allocating the risk of residual error – that is, a rule specifying the burden of persuasion – there is the distinct matter of the care and attention that the decision maker gives to the assessment and analysis of the evidence that is on hand.[206] This assessment can be done well or badly, thoroughly or off-handedly, and how carefully the decision maker performs this task will naturally affect the likelihood of error. Given the level of performance that takes places in regard to this analysis, however, when the final decision problem is faced, the decision maker is, whether directly by his or her own lights or indirectly by applying some rule of decision, allocating the risk of error.

So far we have discussed the optimization of Keynesian weight primarily in the context of decisions made, at the margin, about whether to augment the information before the tribunal. Adding relevant evidence increases Keynesian weight, and we have been considering what is involved in a judgment that it is desirable to do so. But optimization also can necessitate *restricting* the information to be used, reducing the Keynesian weight of the evidence available to the fact-finder. There is little recognition of this in the philosophical literature; it is generally taken to be almost axiomatic that one ought to make use of all relevant information at one's disposal. Thus one finds many references to the principle of total or complete evidence – that inductive inference ought to proceed on the basis of all logically relevant evidence – without much attention to the problems inherent in giving meaning to "total" or "complete" evidence.[207] Indeed, so strong is this inclination that philosophers who turn their attention to

---

[206] See Ho (2008) at 186–7 (distinguishing "care" in the assessment of evidence from "caution" in making a decision). See also Swinburne (2001) at 166–7 (distinguishing the inquiry into justification of belief that is associated with checking the correctness of one's beliefs from the inquiry into justification associated with the acquisition of additional evidence with respect thereto).

[207] See, e.g., Carnap (1950) at 211; Salmon (1973) at 91; and Skyrms (2000) at 31.

law often show little tolerance for rules and procedures that would limit a fact-finder's access to relevant evidence.[208]

To be sure, some philosophers have taken seriously concerns about the costs of acquiring information as well as the capacity of decision makers to deal with large amounts of information and the costs of doing so,[209] and this has become a common subject in the literature of the economics and psychology of decision making.[210] The problem cannot be avoided: just as a decision about whether to augment the evidence to be used is affected by cost considerations, so is a decision about whether to try to take into account relevant information already available. The law, in its practical concern over the costs of litigation, does not ignore these matters. The costs involved, moreover, may be the obvious – time and money – but they also may be "inferential costs," that is, potential adverse effects on the accuracy of adjudication that can result from the attempt to use information that is available for use. The most obvious source of concern here is that the fact-finder may be overwhelmed trying to deal with information of only very limited probative value. But other kinds of inferential costs are also possible.[211]

Moreover, practically optimizing evidence and maximizing the expected utility of the decision itself are not the only goals of a system of adjudication. Sometimes competing goals, such as providing a forum for the nonviolent settlement of disputes and reinforcing the legitimacy of the law, are parts of what is usually involved in constructing systems of procedure.[212] Furthermore, there are side constraints on our pursuit of truth, such as the protections of privileged information. Working out the details of the accommodations that must be made between such conflicting values understandably occupies a great deal of lawyers' time. But such preoccupations should not blind us to the central truth that trials, as a distinct element of procedure, are properly designed with epistemic considerations at their core. Trials, and the rules that structure and govern them, are shaped by what the Supreme Court has called "the normally predominant principle of utilizing all rational means for ascertaining truth."[213]

---

[208] The *locus classicus* for this view is, of course, Bentham (1827). For its modern expression, see Laudan (2006).
[209] See, e.g., Rescher (1989).
[210] See, e.g., Gigerenzer et al. (1999).
[211] See infra § 4.1.3.
[212] See, e.g., Summers (1974).
[213] Trammel v. United States, 445 U.S. 40, 50 (1974).

4

Keynesian Weight in Adjudication

The Allocation of Juridical Roles

> *The first therefore, and most signal Rule, in relation to Evidence, is this, That a Man must have the utmost Evidence, the Nature of the Fact is capable of; ... less Evidence doth create but Opinion and Surmise, ..., for if it be plainly seen in the Nature of the Transaction, that there is some more Evidence that doth not appear, the very not producing it is a Presumption, that it would have detected something more than appears already, and therefore the Mind does not acquiesce in any thing lower than the utmost Evidence the Fact is capable of.*
> – Chief Baron Geoffrey Gilbert (c. 1726)[1]

In Chapter 3, the decision maker was treated as unitary: the same individual, or undifferentiated group of individuals, was treated as responsible for all the actions necessary to decision making. In particular, this decision maker had responsibility for making both the principal decision – to accept the claim or to reject it – and the preemptive decision – to postpone (or not to postpone) the principal decision to allow for the augmentation of Keynesian weight, as well as the responsibility for conducting the investigations that would effectuate such augmentation. In this chapter, this assumption is relaxed. I differentiate between the roles of the various persons and subsidiary groups of persons (such as juries), who participate in decision making in the adjudicative context. This allows me to work out some of the implications of the foregoing analysis for practical adjudication.

Of course, the devil is in such details, and because the roles of adjudicative participants are complex and not so clearly delineated as one might expect, there is more here with which the legal practitioner or academic lawyer may want to disagree. Still, the framework developed in the preceding two chapters will motivate insights that otherwise are not available, and the result is a coherent theory of adjudicative proof burdens and their management. I do not, of course, claim that the resulting theory captures every nuance of our adjudicative systems. As emphasized at the end of

[1] Gilbert (1754) at 3–4.

Chapter 3, there are a number of goals and concerns that can compete with the essentially epistemic focus presented in this book. Still, it is striking just how much of our extant practices are illuminated by the present analysis.

As a starting point, one consequence of the analysis in Chapter 3 is that a demand for more Keynesian weight makes sense only when one can identify available information that can be (or could have been) obtained at reasonable cost. Suppose, then, a situation in which Keynesian weight *can* be increased at reasonable cost? Does any particular actor in adjudication really need to worry about this? The analysis in Chapter 3 suggests a positive answer: ordinary decision makers routinely consider the adequacy of their evidence relative to the decision they must make before making the decision, and decision theory supports such behavior. But if this is so in the legal context as well, the question is presented: *Which* actor or actors in the adjudicative system do or should have responsibility for addressing Keynesian weight?

Almost all extant analyses (other than my previous work) that have emphasized the role of Keynesian weight in adjudication have assumed or concluded, often based on examples such as the gatecrasher hypothetical, that the fact-finder has primary responsibility to enforce a standard for such weight.[2] This conclusion rests on the premise that the assessment of the weight of evidence is part of the role of the fact-finder in applying the standard of proof. Even those who do not speak explicitly in terms of Keynesian weight but recognize the importance of evidential incompleteness and the need to solve the evidence-search problem seem to place considerable emphasis on the fact-finder in this regard.[3]

---

[2] See, e.g., Cohen, J. (1977, 1986); Davidson & Pargetter (1987); Cohen, N. (1985); Friedman (1997a) at 279; Franklin (2006) at 162; and Ho (2008) at 166. A possible exception is Alex Stein. See Stein (2005) at 11–16, 80–91 and Nance (2007b) at 161–2 (discussing Stein). See also the brief suggestion in Kaye (1986) at 664 n. 17. David Hamer is an important exception. He concludes that "there is no need for the juridical standard of proof to incorporate a weight requirement." Hamer (2012b) at 136. It is not, however, entirely clear whether by this he means only that the burden of persuasion applied by the fact-finder need not incorporate a weight requirement (a proposition with which I largely agree) or he also means that there is no need for a distinct weight requirement (a proposition with which I would not agree).

[3] For example, Vern Walker has articulated a "theory of uncertainty" in which the problem of evidential completeness and the evidence-search issue are integral components. Walker (2001) at 1528–32. He argues that his theory of uncertainty "can help a factfinder to analyze which kinds of uncertainty are present in which degree, to perform a cost/benefit analysis for action to reduce those uncertainties, and to decide which uncertainties are tolerable under the circumstances." Id. at 1555. It is unclear what "action" Walker contemplates (besides thinking harder about the problem), but a natural reading of his paper does suggest

This focus on the fact-finder is understandable, but mistaken. It seems to follow from the judicial comment, often made in response to what a common-law court considers an unwarranted objection to admissibility, "Questions of weight are for the jury."[4] It would seem, therefore, that the jury should be the agent, or at least the primary agent (subject only to review for reasonableness by the court), for consideration of questions related to the adequacy of evidential weight. As already observed, however, there is weight and then there is weight. Insofar as one is referring to discriminatory power, the foregoing reasoning is correct. Insofar as one is referring to Keynesian weight, it is not. There is no established principle of common law to the effect that consideration of the adequacy of Keynesian weight (by whatever name) is exclusively, or even primarily, a jury function. Nor could there be under prevailing practice. In both common-law and civil-law adjudication, the judiciary (and often the legislature) is heavily involved in the practical optimization of Keynesian weight, and for good reason. This chapter explores that involvement and its implications.

4.1 The Law's Management of Keynesian Weight

All modern legal systems employ rules of adjudication that attempt to improve Keynesian weight as compared with what it would be without such rules. The most obvious are the rules, which take various shapes and are subject to various exceptions on grounds of "privilege," that require witnesses to attend court and respond to questions. Both direct and cross-examinations, whether conducted by parties or by judges, expand the scope of information available to the tribunal. This "quantitative" improvement in Keynesian weight is further augmented by an effort at "qualitative" improvement in the form of rules that place the witness under the potential threat of a perjury indictment.[5] Beyond such features common to all adjudicative systems, there are rules peculiar to certain systems that serve similar purposes.

In relatively "inquisitorial" systems of adjudication, such as the civil-law systems employed in countries of western Continental Europe, judicial involvement in practical optimization of Keynesian weight is direct and

---

that, in a jury trial, he contemplates the jury doing a cost/benefit analysis of the adequacy of the evidence and, based thereon, potentially taking (unspecified) actions to require further investigation by the parties.

[4] See Wigmore (1983) § 29.
[5] On the distinction between quantitative and qualitative improvements in Keynesian weight, see supra § 3.2.

obvious. Judicial officers act as investigators of the disputed incidents, at least in principle. Based on witness lists and documents provided by the parties, such a magistrate pursues lines of inquiry until satisfied that enough evidence has been acquired to decide the case. Thus the judiciary's management of the question of Keynesian weight is conspicuous, as is the distinct role judges have, once Keynesian weight is practically optimized, in deciding the case based on discriminatory power.[6]

For this reason, it has been claimed that civil-law adjudication does not recognize the distinction between the burden of production and the burden of persuasion – only the latter matters to Continental jurists.[7] This is true, of course, in the sense that there is no burden of production *on the parties*, and thus "there is no procedural motion available to test whether sufficient evidence has been introduced on a point to permit the court to decide on that matter."[8] However, the court's failure to investigate adequately can be the basis for a review of the judgment on appeal. Appellate courts in civil-law jurisdictions, at least those at the first level of appeal, sometimes return such cases to the original trial court for the consideration of additional evidence, but more often they simply take the additional evidence and render a new judgment.[9] Thus it would be more accurate to say that *the parties* bear no burden of production of evidence in such civil-law jurisdictions, not that no such burden exists. Rather, to the extent that a civil-law court retains an inquisitorial character, that burden rests on the judiciary itself, beginning with the original investigating magistrate, and its satisfaction is tested not by motion imposing a sanction on an opponent at trial but rather by appeal.

In common-law adversarial adjudication, judicial involvement in the investigation of cases and the selection of evidence for consideration is radically curtailed; overwhelmingly, parties are assigned these tasks. The common law's preference for a passive judiciary is often explained, or rationalized, in terms of a concern that an actively investigating magistrate will be inclined to prejudge the case, searching then only (or primarily) for

---

[6] See, e.g., Langbein (1985) (summarizing German civil practice and comparing it with Anglo-American "adversarial" practice). This, at least, is how the system is supposed to work. In reality, supposedly "investigating" magistrates may do little of it, as appears to be the case in French civil practice. See, e.g., Beardsley (1986). When combined with an absence of party-initiated discovery, this produces "an approach to fact-finding which appears to have the main aim of resolving factual issues by means other than the arduous sifting of evidence." Id. at 473.

[7] Taruffo (2003) at 672.

[8] Riddell & Plant (2009) at 82.

[9] See, e.g., Murray & Stürner (2004) at 373–86 and Herzog (1967) at 397–408.

evidence that will confirm the magistrate's initial hypothesis.[10] However the difference is explained, there is no question that the judiciary in an adversary system ordinarily has very little role in selecting the witnesses or documents to be considered or in questioning the witnesses who do testify. As a consequence, management of Keynesian weight is much more indirect. But it is no less real. In the following sections, I examine this phenomenon.[11]

4.1.1 *Discovery and Relevance: Adversarial Duty and Privilege*

At the initiation of a lawsuit, some part of the evidence in the possession of the claimant likely will be favorable to the defense, whereas some part of the evidence in the possession of the defense likely will be favorable to the claimant. In the absence of some mechanism for requiring the sharing of information, one can safely predict that these portions of the potential evidence will not see the light of day in the courtroom. "Discovery" refers to a set of rules and procedures by which a party can, with the support of the power of the court, obtain access to information initially in the possession of an opponent. The adversary system relies on discovery to ensure the opportunity – and on the predictable incentives of the parties to provide the motivation – for parties to present to the tribunal evidence of significant probative value to the case. Discovery ensures that a great deal of the pertinent information will be presented and so predictably augments the Keynesian weight of the evidence as a whole.

This adversarial presentation of evidence allows courts to get by with a relatively simple criterion of relevance, when this is understood as a requirement on the admissibility of evidence at trial. By this criterion, evidence is relevant if and only if taking that evidence into account changes the probability of some material fact.[12] This plausible-sounding criterion,

---

[10] See, e.g., Fuller (1971) at 43–4.
[11] Because this chapter gets more deeply into the details of adjudicative rules, when discussing adversarial systems, I tend to focus my discussion on American law, with which I am most familiar. Also, I make no attempt to address the question of what kind of adjudicative system – pure inquisitorial, pure adversarial, or some mix of the two – does or would do best in terms of the practical optimization of Keynesian weight or it terms of broader tradeoffs between accuracy and costs. There is an interesting law and economics literature addressing such issues. For a good introduction, see Parisi (2002).
[12] "Evidence is relevant if: (a) it has any tendency to make a fact more or less probable than it would be without the evidence; and (b) the fact is of consequence in determining the action." Fed. R. Evid. 401. (Unlike this version of the rule, which became effective at the end of 2011, the previous version of Rule 401 clearly made the conditions both necessary

however, is theoretically underinclusive. If E_1 is evidence that increases the probability that the claim C is instantiated, and if E_2 is evidence that decreases the probability that C is instantiated, then it is certainly possible for the effect of E_2 to offset exactly E_1, that is, $P(C|E_1\&E_2) = P(C)$. This means that, by the standard criterion, the conjoint evidence $E_1\&E_2$ is irrelevant, even though each of its two components would be relevant if taken alone and even though one can make a very good case for the epistemic importance of considering both E_1 and E_2 – which constitutes an accretion of Keynesian weight, as compared with considering neither.[13] Theorists have wrestled with how to complicate the criterion of relevance to handle this problem. Keynes himself argued that E should be considered relevant to the claim C if and only if E entails a proposition F such that $P(C|F) \neq P(C)$. Thus, for the preceding example, if E is the conjoint evidence $E_1\&E_2$, then E entails E_1 and E entails E_2; for both reasons, E is relevant under Keynes's criterion.[14] Other theorists have found Keynes's solution to be inadequate and have offered refinements.[15]

Fortunately, however, the law need not be very concerned that this difficulty will result in the exclusion of such offsetting evidentiary items because the conjoint evidence $E_1\&E_2$ typically will be divided among the litigants, the claimant presenting E_1 and the defendant separately presenting E_2.[16]

---

and sufficient for the evidence to be relevant. It read: "'Relevant evidence' means evidence having any tendency to make the existence of any fact that is of consequence to the determination of the action more probable or less probable than it would be without the evidence." The stylistic change was not intended to make a substantive difference.)

[13] See Popper (1959) at 407. Flipping a coinlike object is the example used by Popper. Suppose that the object appears symmetrical and balanced so that one's *a priori* estimate gives a probability of 0.5 of getting heads. On a propensity theory of objective probability, the propensity of the object to come up heads can best be measured by a large sequence of flips. In a sequence of 100 flips, take E_1 to be the set of all flips that result in heads, and take E_2 to be the set of all flips that result in tails. If the test yields 50 heads and 50 tails, then E_2 offsets E_1 in the way described in the text. The estimate of the probability that derives from conducting these 100 flips, though it be the same number (0.5) as the *a priori* estimate based on the principle of indifference, is in some sense better than the *a priori* estimate; it has greater Keynesian weight. As we imagine our example extending to a very large number of flips – again assuming with equal numbers of heads and tails resulting – the hypothetical test approaches "ideal evidence" of the flipping propensity of the object, yet the entire mass of evidence, $E_1\&E_2$, remains irrelevant by the conventional criterion. Popper called this the "paradox of ideal evidence."

[14] See Keynes (1921) at 71–2.

[15] See, e.g., Cohen, J. (1985) at 267–8; Schlesinger (1991) at 163–71; O'Donnell (1992); Gärdenfors (1993) at 35–53; and Gemes (2007).

[16] An exception is when the doctrine of "verbal completeness" can be invoked to require the proponent to present evidence of the entirety of an out-of-court verbal utterance. See, e.g., Fed. R. Evid. 106. As far as the relevance issue is concerned, however, this will rightly be understood in terms of the separate relevance of each part of the whole statement. See generally Nance (1995a).

When E_1 is presented, it will be rightly taken as relevant, and when E_2 is presented, it will also be rightly taken as relevant. The fact-finder may, of course, put E_1 and E_2 together and treat them as offsetting. Thus a credible eyewitness for C may just offset a credible eyewitness against C, with the result that the fact-finder ends up looking to other evidence to discriminate between C and not-C.[17] In so doing, though, the fact-finder also would know that it had the opportunity to learn what the two eyewitnesses had to say and to decide, for example, whether one of the two was more credible than the other. Thus there is value in having received both eyewitness testimonies, even if the court is inclined to believe that they do exactly offset each other. For the practical purposes of adjudication, then, the official criterion of relevance is generally quite workable as long as one is focused on the question of whether a given item of evidence is helpful to the fact-finder in assessing discriminatory power.[18]

In some respects, the use of the adversary process is an attempt to optimize Keynesian weight by the litigational equivalent of the "invisible hand" of economic competition. As in market economics, when competition works, it does so without the actors necessarily desiring, or even contemplating, the end they are serving. And like the invisible hand of economic theory, perhaps even more so, the system of discovery and party incentives is not always successful in serving the desired end. There are gaps in the tools of discovery in civil cases so that some evidence cannot be obtained by an adversary.[19] Further, discovery mechanisms are discernibly less expansive in criminal cases so that, in such cases, there is a more significant element of trial by surprise.[20] In both contexts, placing primary control of evidence presentation in the hands of litigants increases the opportunities for parties to destroy or withhold evidence and thereby prevent discovery.[21] And, of course, lawyers (let alone parties acting without the benefit of counsel) are not always efficient in anticipating what needs to be discovered, even if the legal tools are available to them.[22]

---

[17] Indeed, such bundling of evidence into offsetting groups that can then be effectively ignored may be a very useful device for handling large amounts of information.

[18] Important exceptions are discussed later. They relate to the problems of (a) evidence that is irrelevant but uncontested (see § 4.1.4) and (b) evidence that is sought because it might be relevant but turns out to be irrelevant (see § 4.2).

[19] See, e.g., Cleary & Strong (1966) at 837–44 (noting the problem of documents located outside the court's jurisdiction and the problem of documents subject to a claim of privilege that the holder might waive only at trial).

[20] Id. at 844–5; Whitebread & Slobogin (2008) at 671–9.

[21] See, e.g., Nesson (1991).

[22] Cleary & Strong (1966) at 839, 842.

Even if relevant evidence comes to the attention of both parties, it may not be viewed as sufficiently helpful by either to be offered in court, even though the fact-finder might find it quite useful.[23] Relatedly, there may be the opportunity to obtain what might be highly probative evidence, yet neither party may want to seek it because of doubts about what they will find. This situation puts Keynesian weight in the sharpest relief because one can be fairly confident that developing a certain line of evidence will be probative without having any confidence about which side it will favor.

It may help to drop into this otherwise abstract discussion an illustration of the kind of thing that can go wrong in the development of evidence for trial. My anecdote will concern the last-mentioned situation and is drawn from the third trial arising from the brutal 1954 murder of Marilyn Sheppard in a suburb of Cleveland. Her husband, Dr. Sam Sheppard, was convicted of the murder despite his claim that his wife had been killed in their home by an intruder. After several years in prison, his conviction was overturned on due process grounds in an important opinion by the United States Supreme Court.[24] On retrial, he was acquitted. Many years after his death, evidence (including a noncustodial confession by the Sheppard's one-time window washer) came to light and motivated his son (through his father's estate) to sue under Ohio's wrongful conviction statute, a civil action in which factual innocence must first be determined, by a preponderance of the evidence, before compensation can be awarded for the incarceration. During jury selection for the civil trial in 2000, a reporter who was working on a book about the famous case noticed that fingernail scrapings from the victim, which had been preserved, had not been tested for DNA that might serve to identify her attacker, it being likely that she fought hard for her life. When approached about the matter, neither the attorney for the plaintiff's estate nor the prosecutors who defended the state in the civil suit had any interest in doing the tests, even though they had gone to great efforts to prepare the case in other respects, including the commissioning of other DNA work. Apparently, each side was concerned that the results might disturb the strategy on which they

---

[23] The polarization inherent in adversarial litigation causes underutilization of evidence possessing weak or ambiguous but not insignificant probative value. See Damaška (1997) at 98–100. Indeed, experienced litigators who advise practitioners about winning strategies emphasize the importance of sticking to the evidence that strongly supports one's case, leaving aside neutral or even weakly favorable evidence. See, e.g., Klonoff & Colby (1990) at 63–85.

[24] Sheppard v. Maxwell, 384 U.S. 333 (1966). Much of the opinion relates to the total lack of effort by the trial court to control prejudicial pretrial publicity.

had settled for the upcoming trial; each side, confident in its case, was uncomfortable with what the result of the suggested tests might reveal.[25]

Now, none of this means that the common law is content to leave Keynesian weight in a suboptimal state if available discovery requests and party incentives are incompletely effective. In fact, the law employs numerous supplemental tools to achieve retail augmentations of Keynesian weight. The following subsections assay these tools. The law uses these tools to improve the state of the evidence on which the fact-finder decides the case, much as the government might intervene in the free-market system for production of goods and services to offset market defects, not with the goal of undermining or displacing the market itself but rather with the goal of improving its operation.[26]

This is a good place to reiterate certain points about the relationship between adjudicative and economic theory.[27] By employing an analogy to the "invisible hand" of economic theory, I do not mean to suggest that the law does or should assume that its citizens in general, or litigants in particular, necessarily take the extreme "external point of view" associated with the Holmesian bad man, who responds only to material incentives.[28] Nor are the aforementioned tools needed only with respect to litigants and trial lawyers who take this external point of view.[29] The law's responses to defects in the discovery system and the incentives of the adversary system function as much to remind "good" litigants of their duties to the court as to force "bad" litigants unwillingly to comply with those duties.[30] Because the law has seen fit to place in the hands of litigants the control of evidence development and presentation, the litigants collectively have a responsive duty to practically optimize Keynesian weight. The law presupposes that this will generally be the result of the operation of adversarial incentives but insists that, when it does not, the parties' duties can be reasserted.[31]

[25] Neff (2001) at 345–6.
[26] As will be noted later, the law also takes steps to prevent the presentation of evidence requiring excessive cost, but the law's norms tolerate a considerable degree of flexibility here owing in part to the fact that some litigants, especially those who are "repeat players" in litigation, may find that the expenditure of seemingly disproportionate resources to litigate a single case is justified by the possible gain relating to other potential cases as to which the instant case may serve as precedent.
[27] This discussion repeats themes articulated earlier (in § 2.3.1).
[28] Compare Holmes (1897) at 459–61 (describing the "bad man" from whose viewpoint one must understand the law) with Hart (1961) at 88 (arguing that taking only this extreme "external point of view" obscures important features of law).
[29] Compare Stein (2005) at 154–5.
[30] On the importance of this distinction in understanding the basic structures of law generally, see Nance (1997, 2006b).
[31] See generally Nance (1988).

These duties are qualified by their position within an adversary system. That is, a party's duty to present evidence that the litigant would otherwise not choose to present, thus augmenting Keynesian weight, is subject to an adversarial privilege, whereby the putative holder of such a duty may excuse compliance with that duty or deflect its assertion, by convincing the court that the opponent has an adequate, meaningful opportunity to present the evidence in question. When this is shown, the court can encounter a difficult question about how to proceed. For example, in the Sam Sheppard civil case mentioned earlier, the adversarial privilege is available to both parties as to the undeveloped DNA evidence from the victim's fingernail scrapings. In such cases, if the court is aware of the potential evidence, the court must choose from among three possible courses of action. First, it can decide that the Keynesian weight of the case is practically optimized without the additional evidence, thus leaving the matter unexplored, which can be appropriate if the costs involved in obtaining such evidence are high relative to its expected usefulness and the stakes involved in the case. If, however, the evidence needs to be presented to the tribunal, then the court has two further options. It can depart from the essentially adversarial mode of presentation by calling witnesses *sua sponte*, for which there is adequate authority in Anglo-American law.[32] Or it can choose to remain largely within the adversarial framework by recognizing and imposing on one of the parties a fresh obligation to present the missing evidence, pursuant to doctrines discussed in the following sections of this chapter.

With these general comments in place, we may now examine some of the tools that courts use to facilitate the practical optimization of Keynesian weight when this does not automatically occur by virtue of the effects of adversarial incentives within our imperfect system of discovery.

4.1.2 *Discovery Sanctions and Related Preemptive Rulings*

When a party fails to honor its obligations under the rules of discovery, sanctions may be used to make the system work. Most of these sanctions do their work before trial, facilitating the exchange of information that leads to the competitive presentation of proofs described earlier (§ 4.1.1). But some violations of duties of disclosure cannot be rectified this way. And, in fact, there is a diverse body of doctrines (under rubrics such as

---

[32] See, e.g., Fed. R. Evid. 614 (recognizing the authority of the court to call and interrogate witnesses, whether lay or expert) and Fed. R. Evid. 706 (recognizing the authority of the court to appoint expert witnesses).

discovery sanctions or due process rulings) by which judges nonsuit parties or preemptively foreclose certain factual issues on account of suppression of or failure to present evidence, even though a reasonable fact-finder might conclude that the standard of proof has been met (and thus the requisite discriminatory power achieved) without the specific evidence in question.[33]

To illustrate, under the discovery rules for civil cases, a court can issue an order to the effect that a product be taken not to have been defective where the plaintiff destroys the alleged instrumentality of the injury before the defense can examine it.[34] It does not matter that the fact-finder could reasonably believe the plaintiff's claims notwithstanding the destruction of evidence; the plaintiff's conduct means that there was an inexcusable deficiency in the evidence or, to be more precise, in the Keynesian weight of that evidence. Obviously, such sanctions are not imposed uniquely on plaintiffs. Thus a court can impose a default judgment against a defendant who destroys critical documents and thus makes it impossible for the jury to be presented with a case with practically optimized Keynesian weight.[35] And this is true even if it might be possible, after taking the destruction of evidence into account, for the jury reasonably to find, by the necessary margin of discriminatory power, in favor of the spoliating defendant.

In criminal cases, too, obstructing the development of evidence, and thus interfering with practical optimization of Keynesian weight, can result in preemptive sanctions. For example, under federal law, when the government's claim of confidentiality for an informant is rejected, the prosecution must choose between disclosing the informant's identity and dismissing the prosecution.[36] Similarly, when the prosecution has destroyed material evidence in violation of federal or state constitutional requirements, the courts may impose dismissal even if the remaining evidence would be sufficient to satisfy the government's burden of persuasion.[37]

---

[33] See Nance (1991) at 845–50, 853–6; Nance (1998) at 630 n. 25; and Nance (2010) at 1099 n. 39, 1110–15, 1134 n. 157.

[34] See, e.g., Fed. R. Civ. Pr. 37(b)(2)(A)(i) and Silvestri v. General Motors Corp., 271 F.3d 583, 594–5 (4th Cir. 2001).

[35] See, e.g., Fed. R. Civ. Pr. 37(b)(2)(A)(vi) and Telectron, Inc. v. Overhead Door Corp. 116 F.R.D. 107 (S.D. Fla. 1987).

[36] See Roviaro v. United States, 353 U.S. 53, 60–1 (1957); see also California v. Trombetta, 467 U.S. 479, 486–7 (1984).

[37] See, e.g., United States v. Ramirez, 174 F.3d 584, 589 (5th Cir. 1999) and United States v. Cooper, 983 F.2d 928, 931–2 (9th Cir. 1993).

4.1.3 Admissibility Rules

The preceding discussion of the relevance requirement (§ 4.1.1) highlights a fact that is obvious enough, on reflection, but is worth identifying explicitly: very often, rules of admissibility are rules about the practical optimization of Keynesian weight.[38] At first, this seems counterintuitive. In most fields of inquiry, the problem is generally the need to acquire additional evidence, and the notion that one would *exclude* evidence, especially relevant evidence, seems oddly misplaced. Of course, fields of inquiry other than law generally get by with little attention to the idea of admissibility or the need to exclude evidence, other than the obvious concern to *ignore* (which is not the same thing as *exclude*) that which is irrelevant. But the law's development of the idea of admissibility is considerably more elaborate.

Practical optimization of Keynesian weight in adversarial trials must and uncontroversially does sometimes involve *restricting* the fact-finder's use of relevant evidence. This is clear enough in rules that exclude undeniably relevant evidence when its probative value is so weak, in context, that its consideration is not worth the tribunal's time and energy and thus not worth the time and energy of a jury to duplicate the judge's determination that it is unhelpful.[39] These concessions to the limited resources, cognitive as well as material, that are available for decision making are indistinguishable, from a policy perspective, from the resource-motivated limits that must inevitably be placed on efforts to augment Keynesian weight.[40] A somewhat different set of limitations on the optimal level of Keynesian weight is presented by admissibility rules that attempt to avoid predictable errors of inference that would be caused by the fact-finder's reliance on the evidence in question or that, at least, attempt to prevent efforts of advocates to invite such errors. Such rules try to optimize Keynesian weight by removing "tainted" evidence from the total evidence package. Paradigmatic in this regard is the general prohibition on the use of unfairly

---

[38] This is least plausible in regard to admissibility rules premised on nonepistemic concerns, i.e., rules designed to serve "extrinsic social policies" such as encouraging safety measures (e.g., Fed. R. Evid. 407) or encouraging socially desirable communications (e.g., privilege rules).

[39] See, e.g., Fed. R. Evid. 403 (permitting the exclusion of relevant evidence when its probative value is "substantially outweighed by a danger of ... confusing the issues, ... undue delay, wasting time, or needlessly presenting cumulative evidence").

[40] See supra § 3.3. The importance of limitations on cognitive resources was a recurring theme in the work of the late Craig Callen. See, e.g., Callen (1994, 2003).

prejudicial or misleading evidence, which embraces a broad spectrum of things such as inflammatory photographs and evidence about a party's wealth,[41] and the more specific prohibition on the use of evidence of a party's bad character, which is thought to be rife with potential for abuse in the hands of juries and perhaps judges as well.[42]

However, this is far from a complete picture. As a direct result of the imperfections of the system of discovery and party incentives discussed in the preceding section, a diverse set of exclusionary rules functions, at least in part, to encourage parties to present better evidence than that which they would otherwise choose to present. These include the rule excluding testimony when an opponent is deprived of an opportunity for cross-examination, the rule that allows courts to exclude relevant evidence as supposedly irrelevant in the absence of further information (the so-called conditional relevance doctrine), the rule requiring authentication of tangible evidence, the rule limiting testimony to that of which the witness has personal knowledge, the hearsay rule, the original document rule, the rules requiring that verbal utterances not be taken out of context (the doctrines of verbal completeness), and the rules limiting a witness's use of opinion testimony. As I argued in a series of articles published mostly in the 1980s and 1990s, these exclusionary rules, when properly understood, function not so much to prevent a fact-finder's overvaluation of relatively unreliable evidence (that which is excluded by the rule) as to encourage parties to present evidence that is more useful to the decision maker, whether judge or jury, than what the parties otherwise would choose to present when acting solely in their self-interest.[43]

This point bears some elaboration because it runs contrary to what is perhaps still the dominant understanding of admissibility rules.[44] The

---

[41] See, e.g., Fed. R. Evid. 403 (permitting the exclusion of relevant evidence when its probative value is "substantially outweighed by a danger of ... unfair prejudice [or] misleading the jury").

[42] See Fed. R. Evid. 404 (prohibiting, subject to various exceptions, the use of evidence of a person's trait of character to infer action by that person in conformity with the character trait).

[43] See Nance (1988, 1990, 1991, 1992, 1995a, 1995b, 1996, 2006a).

[44] For example, one well-known textbook asks and answers

Why do we have or even need rules of evidence? There is no single answer to this question, but certainly a major reason for the rules is to control the information that reaches the lay jury. The received wisdom is that juries must be shielded from evidence that would be inflammatory in order to decrease the likelihood of a verdict prompted by momentary passions or erroneous inferences.

original recording rule is paradigmatic.[45] When secondary evidence (such as testimony) about the contents of a document is excluded under this rule, it is because the law prefers, when feasible, that the proponent present the original document for inspection by the court, not because the secondary evidence is considered intrinsically dangerous. That this is so is shown by the fact that the secondary evidence is readily admitted on the proponent's showing of a recognized excuse for not presenting the original, an excuse such as the fact that the original has been accidentally destroyed.[46] Any misleading potential of the secondary evidence – for example, its potential for overvaluation by the jury – does not disappear just because there has been a finding that the original is not reasonably available to be presented, nor indeed does it disappear if this finding is correct. Such potential is not what the law is worried about. Indeed, if one believed that the reason to exclude the secondary evidence was its inherent tendency to be overvalued or otherwise misused by the jury, then one would be *more* inclined to exclude the secondary evidence when the original has been accidentally destroyed than when the original is in the possession of the proponent. In the latter case, the secondary evidence wears its defects on its sleeve. In other words, the jury is more likely to be suspicious of the secondary evidence in the latter case, once it is apprised of the proponent's possession (as under conventional practice it could be), and that suspicion will serve to prevent any overvaluation. And an even easier case for admission would be the case in which the original was destroyed by the proponent in "bad faith," that is, to prevent its use as evidence. No jury is likely to credit the proponent's secondary evidence when apprised of such a circumstance. Yet, in that case, again, the secondary evidence is excluded.[47] Why? To express and enforce the law's preference for the original. The proponent is told, in effect, that she does not even get the opportunity to try to persuade the jury with the secondary evidence.[48]

Lilly et al. (2012) at 1. These authors continue by noting other occasional purposes of exclusionary rules, including expediting trials, improving the "quality" of the evidence that is introduced at trial, and, of course, protecting certain confidential communications. Id. at 1–2.

[45] See, e.g., Fed. R. Evid. 1002 ("An original writing, recording, or photograph is required in order to prove its content unless these rules or a federal statute provides otherwise.")
[46] See Fed. R. Evid. 1004–6.
[47] See Fed. R. Evid. 1004(a).
[48] Not surprisingly (and perhaps purposely), this will sometimes necessitate summary judgment against the proponent. See, e.g., Seiler v. Lucasfim, 808 F.2d 1316 (9th Cir. 1986), cert. denied, 484 U.S. 826 (1987).

It is easy to see that the entire problem addressed by the original recording rule (and most of the other admissibility rules here under discussion) could be handled differently. When, for example, the original document still exists and is in the possession of the proponent, the paradigmatic application of the rule generally requires the proponent to produce the original. And the question may be posed whether the rule is needed in such cases, in light of the availability of discovery. Why not simply allow the opponent to discover and present evidence of the original if the opponent thinks that is necessary? Is not this the implication of the adversarial privilege noted at the end of the preceding section? Similarly, when the original is no longer available and the circumstances indicate that the proponent may be responsible for causing that unavailability, why not admit the proffered secondary evidence but allow the opponent to invite an adverse inference by the fact-finder against the proponent on account of the proponent's conduct in making the original unavailable? In fact, the law has not made either of these choices. But why? The answers to these questions are complex and imminently pragmatic. As to the first question, the best explanation of the law's current norms is, once again, that there are significant defects in even modern discovery, especially in criminal cases. The original of the document simply may not be practically available to the opponent before trial. And even if it is, having the opponent introduce it at a later point in the trial presents unnecessary complexity for the fact-finder, when its presentation to the tribunal can be demanded up front, thus avoiding the need to deal with secondary evidence that is rendered either redundant or misleading.[49] As to the second question, the best explanation is that the law does not deem the adverse inference as a suitable, or suitably strong, response to the situation. I will expand on the reasons that support this conclusion later (§ 4.2).

Two other potential objections should be addressed. First, with regard to the case of bad faith destruction of the original document by the proponent, it may seem odd to talk in terms of enforcing an obligation to present the original when, by hypothesis, the original cannot be presented. Does this not require something that cannot be done, in violation of the principle that "ought implies can," a principle I have deployed in understanding the debates about Keynesian weight? The answer rehearses a point made earlier (§ 3.3): that the proponent cannot, at the time of proffer, present the original does not mean that he could not have acted previously so as to make it possible to do so, and it is the failure to so act that is legitimately

---

[49] See Nance (1988) at 263–70.

sanctioned. The sanction of exclusion (of evidence that is admittedly relevant and quite possibly the best that is *now* available on the matter) is plausibly appropriate for two reasons. First, a determination by the court (itself made under the "preponderance of the evidence" standard[50]) that the original has been irretrievably lost could be in error (the proponent might be holding it back for strategic reasons), and enforcing the preference hedges that bet. Second, even if the court can be nearly sure that the original is at that point unobtainable, enforcing the obligation to present the original by excluding the secondary evidence in the present case honors the law's commitment to exclude such evidence pursuant to a rule that thereby serves as warning (for future cases) in time for potential proponents to respond.

The second potential objection is that this rule cannot be said to be a rule that augments Keynesian weight because, in a case where the rule has its intended effect, the original has been *substituted* for the originally offered or contemplated secondary evidence. And while the accretion of relevant evidence will increase Keynesian weight, there is no general principle that substituting one item of evidence for another will do so. The answer to this objection is simple but easy to overlook: once the original document is introduced, the conventional rule does not require the exclusion of the secondary evidence; that evidence becomes admissible or not based on other rules. Ordinarily, the secondary evidence will be inadmissible because it is redundant or clearly in error, but that is a separate matter, and in the appropriate case, as when it is claimed that the original has been doctored or cannot be perceived by the fact-finder without assistance, secondary evidence of the original contents still may be useful and admissible.[51]

Using the original recording rule as the paradigm, I have argued that this kind of "best evidence" explanation of our admissibility rules is much more persuasive and broadly applicable than had been thought for most of the twentieth century and that popular explanations based on distrust of the lay jury have been exaggerated. In fact, the best-evidence idea was more commonly endorsed in the late eighteenth and early nineteenth

---

[50] See, e.g., Mueller & Kirkpatrick (2009) at 35–6, 41–2.
[51] See, e.g. United States v. Onori, 535 F.2d 938, 946-9 (5th Cir. 1976) (affirming admission of transcriptions of an admitted tape recording); see generally Wigmore (1972) § 1190. The same structure has been suggested for the hearsay rule [see, e.g., the American Law Institute's Model Code of Evidence § 503(b) (1942)] and is largely, though not completely, accomplished under the present federal rules because of the liberal admissibility of out-of-court statements made by a testifying witness. See Fed. R. Evid. 801(d), 803, 807.

centuries but was eclipsed by a new orthodoxy in the late nineteenth century. At that time, it became common to explain admissibility rules on the now-familiar ground that juries will credulously "overvalue" certain evidence, which on that account should be excluded. To this day, this idea is suggested as the basis for important rules that are better understood as efforts to induce augmentations of Keynesian weight.[52]

Be that as it may, it cannot be denied that some admissibility rules are thought to serve the purpose of preventing jury error because of tainted evidence. And in some contexts this purpose may even be effectively served. Moreover, there is room for debate about which admissibility rules are valuable primarily because of their ability to induce parties to present better evidence, thus augmenting Keynesian weight, and which admissibility rules are valuable primarily because of their role in preventing jurors from relying improperly on the evidence that is excluded.[53] For example, the proper rationale for the important hearsay rule remains controversial, with much continuing allegiance to the idea that the exclusion of hearsay is designed to prevent jury reliance on bad evidence, that is, the hearsay.[54] This is so despite arguments over the years from various scholars that jurors are as capable of handling hearsay as they are of handling other kinds of admissible evidence of questionable reliability (such as eyewitness accounts), so the only viable rationale for the hearsay rule (when applied to hearsay that is not so weakly probative as to be merely a waste of time) is to express the law's preference for, and thus provide an inducement to get parties to present, the testimony of an available declarant.[55] The available empirical evidence about how jurors assess hearsay evidence seems to support the latter view; it indicates that jurors are rather skeptical of

---

[52] Scholars who are sympathetic to my view – see, e.g., Friedman (2003) – follow a tradition that can be traced back at least to the work of Edmund Morgan – see Morgan (1937) – who identified the exaggeration of the role of the jury in the influential work of James Thayer. See Thayer (1898).

[53] See Nance (2001) at 1554–63 (formalizing the difference between an "inducement" theory of exclusion, with its associated "advocate control" principle, and a "taint" theory of exclusion, with its associated "jury control" principle).

[54] See, e.g. Fisher (2008) at 1, 363, 989–90. More nuanced modern views of the hearsay rule still adhere to a discernible element of jury distrust. See, e.g., Mueller (1992). Judge Posner's well-known economic approach to law is unsurprisingly receptive to the importance of understanding the impact of procedural rules (including evidence rules) on the evidence-search problem. Posner (1999) at 1481–7. Yet he seems to adhere to the traditional theory that the hearsay rule is largely attributable to the risk that the fact-finder will overvalue the evidence that is excluded. Id. at 1491, 1530.

[55] See, e.g., James (1940) at 791–7; Nance (1988) at 278–84; Friedman (1992); and Nance (1992). See also Milich (1992).

hearsay anyway, and thus there is little need for protection from inferential error.[56] But this, of course, does not mean that extant doctrine clearly reflects the better view in all its details; it almost certainly does not.[57]

In any event, for present purposes, all that needs to be noted is the role of admissibility rules of various kinds in making marginal or "retail" improvements in Keynesian weight. There are a number of such rules that are valuable at least in part because of their ability to induce parties to present better evidence, and these rules function to augment the Keynesian weight of the evidence package as a whole. Of course, even the admissibility rules that are valuable entirely or primarily because of their ability to prevent jurors from relying improperly on the excluded evidence are quite reasonably understood as restrictions that serve the underlying purpose of optimizing Keynesian weight, namely, facilitating accurate decision making within extant time and resource constraints.

4.1.4 *The Burden of Production*

In adversarial evidence presentations, there are points in the process at which a party can make a motion to terminate the proceedings on the ground that the opponent has not discharged his or her duty to present adequate evidence, his or her "burden of production." This usually occurs at the end of the claimant's presentation of evidence, and it may happen (except in criminal cases) as a motion by the claimant made at the end of the defendant's presentation of evidence. Both parties (excepting, again, the prosecution in a criminal case) usually also may renew such a motion for "nonsuit" or "directed verdict" at the close of the presentation of all the evidence in the case. To protect a criminal defendant's right to a jury trial, the trial court is not permitted to direct a verdict against the accused.[58]

---

[56] See, e.g., Rakos & Landsman (1992); Meine et al. (1992); and Kovera et al. (1992).

[57] See Seigel (1992) (developing detailed suggestions for harmonizing the rule with its "best evidence" rationale). The most significant infelicity of the modern hearsay rule in this regard is its seemingly excessive restrictions on the admissibility of hearsay from an unavailable declarant. Compare Fed. R. Evid. 804 (providing exceptions for limited classes of such hearsay) with Model Code of Evidence Rule 503(a) (1942) (proposing an exception for all such hearsay). The constraint thereby imposed is significantly ameliorated, however, by the large number of hearsay exceptions that apply whether or not the declarant is available (and hence when the declarant is unavailable) – see Fed. R. Evid. 803 – as well as the discretionary "residual" hearsay exception, which now appears as Rule 807, the use of which is facilitated by a showing that the declarant is unavailable to testify. See Nance (2006a).

[58] See, e.g., United States v. Martin Linen Supply, 430 U.S. 564, 572–3 (1977).

Under the usual understanding of this "burden of production" in adversarial trials, the trial judge's role in a jury trial is simply to monitor the plausibility of the jury's possible conclusion that the standard of proof (such as "beyond reasonable doubt") has been met under the evidence adduced at trial.[59] Theoretically, in a bench trial, the judge has the same role *qua* court vis-à-vis his or her own role *qua* fact-finder. Thus, in the usual civil case, on proper motion by the defense, the judge determines only whether a reasonable fact-finder could find the plaintiff's case proved by a preponderance of the evidence. Whether or not we quantify the meaning of "beyond reasonable doubt" or "preponderance of the evidence," these standards are ordinarily understood to refer to what I have called the "discriminatory power of the evidence." Thus the trial judge *seems* to be committed only to monitoring the evidence for plausible adequacy of discriminatory power.

However, the matter is not that simple. Courts have ruled on such motions in a way that takes into account the fact that particular evidence should have been presented but has not been. This can be enough to result in dismissal even when the circumstances, such as mutual access to the missing evidence, are such that nothing can be safely inferred about the content of the missing evidence. Thus a plaintiff's case may be deemed not to have met the burden of production if important evidence is missing, even though the evidence that is presented is sufficient for a reasonable jury to infer that it meets the threshold criterion on discriminatory power.[60] Conversely, a court may notice the fact that certain important but missing evidence is more readily available to the defendant than to the plaintiff and on that ground deny the defendant's motion for a nonsuit, even when no reasonable jury could find that the threshold condition on discriminatory power has been satisfied by plaintiff's evidence.[61] The latter phenomenon is sometimes supported by the invocation of a legal "presumption," which formally shifts the burden of production to the defendant.[62]

---

[59] See McNaughton (1955).
[60] See, e.g., Galbraith v. Busch, 196 N.E. 36, 38–9 (N.Y. 1935) (noting failure to call percipient witnesses readily available to the both parties in holding that plaintiff failed to meet burden of production) and Warren v. Jeffries, 139 S.E.2d 718, 720 (N.C. 1965) (noting failure to inspect condition of car involved in accident, evidence readily available to either party, in ruling evidence of negligence insufficient).
[61] See, e.g., Ybarra v. Spangard, 154 P.2d 687 (Cal. 1944) (permitting the case to go to the jury even when the jury could not plausibly identify, from the plaintiff's evidence, which of several possible tortfeasors were responsible for plaintiff's injuries) and Kolakowski v. Voris, 415 N.E. 2d 397 (Ill. 1980) (following *Ybarra*).
[62] See 2 McCormick (2013) § 343.

The lines between discovery sanctions, admissibility rulings, and rulings on sufficiency that are based on the inadequacy of Keynesian weight are sometimes blurred in judicial opinions. For example, the Illinois Supreme Court has held, in effect, that proof of unlawful possession of cannabis requires the presentation of the results of readily available chemical tests of the possessed substance.[63] This rule appears to obtain no matter how high the probability may be, without such evidence, that the substance is cannabis. Specifically, the court held an admission by the accused that the substance was marijuana to be insufficient, even when coupled with a sheriff's corroborating "look, smell, and feel" testimony identifying the substance. The court's particular path to this entirely reasonable result was to hold that the sheriff's testimony was inadmissible (in light of the availability of the chemical tests) and then to rule that the admission was insufficient by itself.[64] Similarly, the Supreme Court of Florida has held that when a defendant is charged with possession of a controlled substance, that substance, if available, must be introduced into evidence.[65] The rule allows the defendant to insist on presentation of tangible evidence in addition to the testimony of an expert who reports an analysis of the substance in question and, at least in the court's view, facilitates inquiries into the chain of custody of the substance.[66]

The doctrinal confusion that sometimes attends such rulings is attributable to the fact that a Keynesian weight monitoring function is not explicitly built into the conventional standard for sufficiency rulings. This induces courts that are concerned about an unacceptable deficiency in Keynesian weight to explain their decisions in terms of something else. Often this is a not terribly persuasive argument that the evidence fails to satisfy the plausibility standard for discriminatory power.[67] And sometimes, as in the two cases mentioned in the preceding paragraph, this may

---

[63] See, e.g., People v. Park, 380 N.E.2d 795 (Ill. 1978).
[64] Subsequent Illinois case law confirmed that the requirement that the prosecution present the results of such chemical tests does not apply if the substance is not available for testing. See, e.g., People v. Jones, 393 N.E.2d 1132 (Ill. App. 1979).
[65] G.E.G. v. State, 417 So. 2d 975 (Fla. 1982).
[66] This particular ruling is certainly questionable, but what is important for present purposes is to understand the reasoning behind the decision. See Nance (1991) at 853–56.
[67] See, e.g., Galbraith, 196 N.E. at 38–39. This is the best way to understand the decision in the high-profile controversy concerning control of the remains of "Kennewick Man." See Bonnichsen et al. v. United States et al., 217 F. Supp. 2d 1116 (D. Or. 2002), aff'd 357 F.3d 962, as modified on denial of reh'g, 367 F.3d 864 (9th Cir. 2004) (ruling that the claimant Indian tribes had failed to meet the burden of persuasion where the Corps of Engineers, acting in collusion with the claimant tribes, buried the site of the discovery of human remains in order to prevent further investigation of the site by intervening anthropologists).

be made more palatable by excluding crucial evidence that (arguably) ought to have been admissible so that the resulting evidence package more clearly fails the conventionally expressed sufficiency test for discriminatory power. Adding to the confusion is the fact that the criminal law's "beyond reasonable doubt" standard could be understood to point in two directions, one concerning discriminatory power and another concerning Keynesian weight. With regard to the latter, one could say that any degree of doubt, no matter how small, is too large to allow a conviction if it is doubt that results from an inadequate investigation; any such doubt constitutes "reasonable doubt" that precludes a guilty verdict.[68] This tempting verbal way of attaching a distinct Keynesian weight requirement to the canonical expression of the standard of proof is, however, misleading: it has no counterpart in the civil-litigation context, yet a requirement of practical optimization of Keynesian weight makes just as much sense in that context, though it will generally not be as demanding because the stakes are often not as large.[69] And it might be taken to mean that the jury must assess the adequacy of Keynesian weight, a proposition I will challenge in a later section (§ 4.2). Nevertheless, these subtleties do not preclude the possibility that courts interpret the criminal-law standard to impose a Keynesian weight requirement and act accordingly.

In any event, the principle latent in the kinds of decisions just noted is that the burden of production has two distinct components, one of which is not recognized by its conventional formulation. The burden should be understood to consist of the principle that in order to avoid a preemptive termination against the claimant at some point after the end of the claimant's presentation of evidence, (1) the state of the evidence must be such that a reasonable fact-finder could conclude that the applicable standard of persuasion has been satisfied *plus* (2) the claimant must have provided whatever evidence it can rightly be expected to provide to ensure that the evidence is sufficiently complete to allow the fact-finder to make its decision about whether the standard of persuasion has been satisfied. The analogous two-part requirement on the defendant then becomes that in order to avoid a preemptive termination against the defendant at some point after the end of the defendant's presentation of evidence, (1) the state of the evidence must be such that a reasonable fact-finder could conclude that the applicable standard of persuasion has *not* been satisfied *plus* (2) the defendant must have provided whatever evidence he or she can

---

[68] See, e.g., Franklin (2006) at 162.
[69] See Nance (1998) at 627.

rightly be expected to provide to ensure that the evidence is sufficiently complete to allow the fact-finder to make its decision about whether the standard of persuasion has been satisfied.[70] In deciding the second, Keynesian weight portion of each requirement, whether the party whose case is tested is the claimant or the defendant, the court must have in mind whether the particular potential evidence should be required of the claimant or is better required of the defendant. I recognize that this part of each requirement seems insufficiently determinate at this point. The matter of timing – when to test each component – is complicated. I will have more to say about it later (§ 4.3). Assuming that it can be practically worked out, I have argued elsewhere that being explicit in this way would improve the results of decision making by reducing the number of cases that go to final verdict with an inadequate evidentiary base and simplifying the task that the fact-finders must perform in the cases that are submitted to them.[71]

As with admissibility rules that are based on encouraging the presentation of better evidence, these doctrines, through which the judiciary exerts its regulatory influence, tend to have the kind of preferential structure (see § 3.3) appropriate to practical optimization of Keynesian weight. This is fairly clear in cases such as those from the Illinois and Florida Supreme Courts mentioned earlier. It is made even more plain in the Seventh Circuit's opinion in *Howard v. Wal-Mart Stores, Inc.*[72] In what Judge Posner described as a "charming miniature of a case," liability turned on whether the jury believed, by a preponderance of the evidence, that an unknown employee of the defendant company (rather than some unknown customer) was responsible for the soap spill that caused the plaintiff's slip-and-fall injury. The defendant appealed the trial court's refusal to take the case from the jury for failure to satisfy the burden of production. Judge Posner reviewed the very thin evidence presented to the jury, concluding that the jury could plausibly have believed that the "balance of probabilities tipped in favor of the plaintiff."[73] Then, in sustaining the trial court's decision that there was enough evidence to go to a jury, Judge Posner argued as follows:

> Not only is there no reason to suspect that the plaintiff is holding back unfavorable evidence; it would have been unreasonable, given the stakes, to

---

[70] It is easy to see how these two components might be melded together in stating the conventional test as to whether the burdened party has produced evidence sufficient to support a finding under the standard of proof. See, e.g., Park et al. (2011) at 88–91.
[71] See Nance (1998) at 622.
[72] 160 F.3d 358 (7th Cir. 1998).
[73] Id. at 359.

expect her to conduct a more thorough investigation. This is a tiny case; not so tiny that it can be expelled from the federal court system without a decision, but so tiny that it would make no sense to try to coerce the parties to produce more evidence, when, as we have said, no inference can be drawn from the paucity of evidence that the plaintiff was afraid to look harder for fear that she would discover that a customer and not an employee of Wal-Mart had spilled the soap.[74]

Importantly, Judge Posner's stake-sensitive consideration of the availability of additional evidence fills out the duty of the burden of production in a way that clearly goes beyond the question of whether the fact-finder could reasonably find that the balance of probabilities favors the plaintiff. Had the stakes been higher, Judge Posner would have been willing to consider demanding more to avoid the directed verdict. Moreover, by his articulation, what can be reasonably demanded of a party clearly depends on the cost to the party of acquiring additional evidence.

Sometimes this excusable preference structure is not so obvious. The convolutions (and cynicism) of legal reasoning being what they are, in some contexts a doctrine operates strictly, in that no excusing factors are considered, simply because in that context legitimate excusing conditions are sufficiently rare that considering claims of excuse, at least when offered by interested parties, is not worth the effort. Thus a strictly applied rule serves as a proxy for the underlying preferential principle.[75]

This may well be the upshot of one explanation of the law's supposed aversion to naked statistical evidence (§ 3.1). As originally suggested by Lawrence Tribe and later developed by David Kaye, this aversion would make sense as an inducement to present additional evidence "unless there is a satisfactory explanation for the plaintiff's singular failure to do more than present this sort of general statistical evidence."[76] And perhaps it

---

[74] Id. at 360.
[75] This may arise in the admissibility context as well. For example, a hearsay prohibition that does not allow (or does not consistently allow) exceptions for hearsay from declarants unavailable at trial might be justified on the ground that in the great majority of cases, declarants are in fact available, for deposition if not for trial, and it is too costly and error prone for judges to try to determine the validity of all the excuses that will be offered for not producing declarants if a preferential hearsay rule is administered more directly. I do not endorse such a rule but merely note that it is not entirely implausible. Elsewhere I have argued that this may be the underlying intuition behind a strict rule barring "testimonial" hearsay under the Confrontation Clause. See Nance (2004).
[76] Tribe (1971) at 1349. See also Kaye (1979a) at 106 and Kaye (1979b) at 40. Judge Posner distinguished naked statistical evidence cases from the facts of the *Howard* case on just such grounds. See *Howard*, 160 F.3d at 360. See also Baker v. Bridgestone/Firestone Co., 966 F. Supp. 874, 875–6 (W.D. Mo. 1996) (noting that the rule denying recovery in naked

makes little sense *even to entertain* such an explanation. Although there is nothing in the analysis of such scholars as Cohen, Stein, and Ho (see supra § 3.3) to suggest that they endorse such a view, still they and others may be inclined toward conceiving the weight requirement as strict for the following reason: they may think that courts should be unwilling in certain contexts to entertain arguments from claimants to the effect that further, more particularized evidence cannot be presented. In particular, because there is almost never a situation in which *only* such naked statistical evidence is available, we are accordingly suspicious of claims that no case-specific evidence can be found, and we are reluctant to incur the costs of having to adjudicate such claims about the availability of further evidence.[77] In the context of the gatecrasher case, our intuitions thus fight with any hypothetical assumption, such as that seemingly made by Jonathan Cohen, that no additional evidence is available.[78]

While I do not advocate such a strict rule as a proxy for the underlying preferential principle, it is worth acknowledging that there is something to say for it in terms of accuracy enhancement. Granted that an affirmative verdict should not be allowed on the merits, it does not necessarily follow, however, that the party bearing the burden of persuasion must lose the case. I will return to this matter later (§ 4.3). For now, suffice it to say that the burden generally should fall on the claimant not simply because the claimant bears the burden of persuasion but rather because of the need for such a default rule taken in conjunction with the fact, *when it is a fact*, that the balance of reasons does not suggest placing the burden on the defendant.

To be sure, the argument has not gone unchallenged. Lea Brilmayer, for example, argued that such an explanation of the assumed strict rule denying recovery cannot work because no increase in accuracy of decisions would be obtained by such a rule.[79] Such a rule, she argued, will only affect the result (as compared with a regime without such a rule) in cases where additional individuating evidence cannot be produced, and in such cases,

---

statistical evidence cases is relaxed when the plaintiff shows that more particularized proof is unavailable).

[77] See Lempert (1986) at 457 (noting that "in the real world we will never be sure if the conditions of the [gatecrasher] hypothetical are met; much more often than not they won't be met, and more information will be available to the plaintiff"). Cf. Ho (2008) at 119 (noting that in real cases, there will invariably be other evidence besides that which indicates an "objective" probability).

[78] See Lempert (1986) at 454–62. When such an assumption is truly warranted, our intuitions will be less reliable guides about what is to be done.

[79] Brilmayer (1986) at 678–80.

the strict rule actually increases errors. In essence, her argument was that such missing evidence must fall into one of three mutually exclusive categories: evidence that favors the burdened party (the plaintiff), evidence that favors the moving party (the defendant), and evidence that is unobtainable. The first will be presented by the plaintiff even without such a rule, the second will be presented by the defendant even without such a rule, and the third cannot be presented in any case.

This clever argument is nonetheless mistaken because the evidence that is produced by (some) of those on whom the burden is placed would not necessarily favor those burdened parties, contrary to Brilmayer's implicit assumption. That is, Brilmayer implicitly assumes that the discovery system already works with complete efficiency to place all evidence favorable to the nonburdened party in that party's hands. She also assumes that evidence that is favorable to a party in the eyes of the fact-finder will be invariably and accurately perceived as such by that party. These assumptions are incorrect. Consequently, if the burdened party is required to produce evidence that is, or might be viewed as, favorable to an opponent, it will often be the case that presenting such evidence still will be better from that party's point of view than the sure loss associated with failure to meet the burden imposed.

One aspect of Brilmayer's argument does, however, seem to be more on target, even if it is not how she meant it. When she criticized the error-reduction rationale for a strict rule against naked statistical evidence, she did so in part because such a rule would be underinclusive; that is, there will also be cases *not* based on naked statistical evidence that equally demand additional case weight in the interest of enhancing accuracy.[80] But this is in truth an argument against the use of a rule as such because it is in the nature of a rule, in the practical realities of law, that it will be under- or overinclusive, or both, relative to its underlying rationale.[81] Insofar as Brilmayer was arguing against the use of a *rule* of weight (and thus in favor of more ad hoc judgment), arguing that the under- and over-inclusiveness of such a rule is excessive in this context, I am inclined to agree. The appearance before the court of a case based entirely on statistical "base rate" data is simply one of many possible red flags that suggest skepticism about the claim that Keynesian weight has been practically optimized. There are serious limits on our ability to forge rules that would determine in advance the adequacy of evidentiary

---

[80] See id. at 677.
[81] See Schauer (1991).

weight in the enormous diversity of circumstances in which such a question can arise. The assessment of the adequacy of Keynesian weight, no less than the assessment of adequacy of discriminatory power, tends to be case specific and highly contextual.

A closely related hypothetical, even less likely to be instantiated, illustrates a context more appropriately governed by a strict rule. Suppose that the plaintiff in a civil case presents no evidence of liability and rests, and the defendant then moves for a nonsuit based on plaintiff's failure to meet the burden of production. (Or, to eliminate any *ex ante* assumptions about what the defendant might present, one can assume that the defendant also rests and then moves for the directed verdict.) Under the conventional model, whether or not this motion should be granted would depend on whether a reasonable fact-finder could think the plaintiff's allegation is more likely than the defendant's denial without any formal evidence being adduced. This, in turn, will depend on what the reasonable fact-finder would think about typical cases of this type because the fact-finder will have been informed of the nature of the case before any formal evidence is presented (§ 2.5). Given that the case has not settled or been dismissed by the court, a reasonable fact-finder might think that the case is indistinguishably close, but another reasonable fact-finder might think that the plaintiff's allegations are somewhat more likely than the defendant's denial. Or another reasonable fact-finder might think, based on this background information alone, that the case, while close, should just barely go in favor of the defense, especially in light of the failure of the plaintiff to present evidence one might have expected to be forthcoming. In other words, depending on the undisputed background information, this could be a case falling in that middle range of cases that might plausibly go either way – that is, a question for the fact-finder to resolve.[82] Yet a case presented in this fashion would and should result in a directed verdict for the defense based on the failure of the plaintiff to meet his or her burden of production.[83]

The correct solution to this puzzle requires recourse to a Keynesian weight requirement. Simply put, a case in which no evidence is formally introduced is a case for which the evidence is unreasonably incomplete. As a practical matter, there will always be *some* evidence that can be adduced at reasonable cost. Thus our correct expectation, that the plaintiff's case would be dismissed for failure to meet the burden of production, rests

---

[82] See Lilly et al. (2012) § 12.1.
[83] See James & Hazard (1985) § 7.7 at 318.

on the fact that the burden of production does more than monitor the fact-finder's assessments of discriminatory power for reasonableness; it also monitors the parties' presentations for adequacy of Keynesian weight.[84] It is, once again, fair to ask why this burden should fall *on the plaintiff*. Would it not also be the case that there should be some evidence that could be adduced at reasonable cost by the defense? One of the critical points to be made here is that the choice about where to place the burden of increasing Keynesian weight is complex. Suffice it here to say that, in the hypothesized context, it is extremely likely that there exists at least some additional evidence that can be produced by the plaintiff in a way that is at least as cost efficient as having it produced by the defendant.[85]

There are, of course, several counterarguments that might be made in an effort to squeeze this example into the conventional framework. For example, one approach is to say that fact-finders are required to accept 1:1 odds at the beginning of a civil trial regardless of what they actually believe.[86] In such a case, failure to present any evidence results in a directed verdict for the defense under the conventional analysis without regard to Keynesian weight by virtue of the default rule for discriminatory power. But this theory presents serious difficulties: at what point *are* the fact-finders permitted to consider the background information that, had they been free to consider at the beginning of the trial, would lead them (reasonably) to conclude that the odds slightly favor the plaintiff (or the defendant)? The answer cannot be "never," for then fact-finders' belief formation would be so artificially constrained as to be arbitrary. The correct answer to the problem presented will entail satisfying the judge that some form of party obligation regarding Keynesian weight has been discharged. In this case, requiring 1:1 prior odds is a legal fiction that uses a default rule for discriminatory power as an indirect way of allocating the burden to augment Keynesian weight.

Another alternative to preserve the conventional theory would be to insist that fact-finders are not allowed to form *any* opinion about the odds on the claim in the absence of admitted evidence, so the standard of proof cannot be met before the introduction of formal evidence. This, however, is also implausible. Fact-finders must start somewhere; inferences depend on background information, and while we can demarcate the beginning

---

[84] See Nance (1998) at 622–5. See also Franklin (2006) at 161.
[85] Cf. Posner (1999) at 1502–3.
[86] See id. at 1514 ("Ideally we want the trier of fact to work from prior odds of 1 to 1 that the plaintiff or prosecutor has a meritorious case. A substantial departure from this position, in either direction, marks the trier of fact as biased").

of the introduction of formally admitted evidence, we cannot seriously believe that before such evidence is begun, fact-finders have *no* basis for assessing the odds on the claim.[87] Bayesian decomposition, as in equation (2.4), signals this explicitly by emphasizing that the posterior odds of the claim depend not only on the probative value of the evidence formally adduced but also on the prior odds with which the fact-finders approach the formal evidence, odds that are determined by background information. If the suggestion is that fact-finders must ignore what they think, then again the question arises: At what point can they lift this veil of ignorance, and why set the point after the beginning of the formal introduction of evidence? Once more, the suggestion is a legal fiction, concealing (perhaps inadvertently) judicial requirements regarding Keynesian weight.

A revealing glimpse of these matters is provided by an admiralty case of importance in the law regarding historical artifacts.[88] The plaintiff brought an *in rem* action to establish rights as finder and salvor of an abandoned wreck lying at the bottom of the waters of Lake Michigan. He believed the vessel to be the *Seabird*, a passenger ship that sank as a result of an onboard fire in April of 1868. The State of Illinois moved to dismiss the case on the ground that the state owned the wreck and had no responsibility to a salvor. The determinative fact was whether the wreck was "embedded" within the submerged lands of the state; if so, the state had better title than the finder under either the common law of finds or the then newly enacted Abandoned Shipwreck Act of 1987, which (if it applied) also negated salvage claims under federal maritime law.[89] With the benefit of pleadings and motion papers, but without hearing formal evidence related to the motion, the trial judge dismissed, noting that the old wreck was "likely embedded" in submerged lands of the state. The appellate court reversed and remanded for an evidentiary hearing on whether the wreck was

---

[87] See discussion in § 2.5. Cf. Ho (2008) at 93:

> Since the fact-finder is sworn to give a true finding of fact *according to the evidence*, she is obligated to consider the admitted evidence presented before her. It is often added that she must *only* consider such evidence. While there is little harm in saying this, the statement cannot be taken literally. To take it literally would require exclusion even of general background knowledge about the world. Without this knowledge, fact-finding cannot get off the ground.

(Emphasis in original; footnotes omitted.)

[88] Zych v. Unidentified, Wrecked and Abandoned Vessel, 941 F.2d 525 (7th Cir. 1991).

[89] The act confirmed title to such shipwrecks in the relevant state for the purpose of allowing state regulation to protect wrecks of historical significance. Under the act, "the concept of 'embeddedness' serves as a proxy for historic value." Id. at 529.

embedded within the meaning of the act. In doing so, the appellate court did not reject the legitimacy of the trial judge's pre-evidentiary assessment of the odds regarding embeddedness, nor did it instruct the trial judge that she must begin with 1:1 odds before considering formal evidence. Rather, the appellate court simply held that an evidentiary hearing was required, noting that evidence, in the form of the testimony of the plaintiff, was readily available on the matter.[90]

A similar point applies in criminal cases. Undisputed background facts, taken in light of the background beliefs about how the world works, shape a fact-finder's prior odds of guilt, the odds the fact-finder forms, however implicitly, even before the formal introduction of evidence. In an extreme case, something like the hypothetical posed by Davidson and Pargetter (see § 3.3), that uncontested background information might be very thin yet enough that a reasonable fact-finder, without any formal evidence, could find guilt in accordance with the standard of proof governing discriminatory power, that is, beyond reasonable doubt. Once again, it is the almost certain inadequacy of Keynesian weight and the almost certain prosecutorial responsibility for that inadequacy that necessitate a directed verdict in such a case and, indeed, warrants a general rule to that effect.[91]

4.1.5 Recognizing the Forest and Cultivating the Trees

Putting all this together, it is clear that in adversarial adjudication, the responsibility for optimizing Keynesian weight is placed primarily in the hands of the litigants, subject, however, to a plethora of regulatory reinforcements administered by judges in both civil and criminal cases. This allocation of responsibility is not an epistemological necessity. It is, rather, a pragmatic matter of institutional design, whereby certain values, whether accuracy related or otherwise, are advanced by granting substantial control over evidence presentation to the parties, but the goal of practically optimizing Keynesian weight is still pursued.[92] The judiciary retains, even in adversarial systems of adjudication, substantial control that – if suitably

---

[90] Id. at 530. The matter was resolved on remand by the plaintiff's formal admission that the wreck was embedded in the submerged lands of the State of Illinois, which led to a dismissal of his salvage claim. Zych v. Unidentified, Wrecked and Abandoned Vessel, 19 F.3d 1136, cert. denied, 513 U.S. 961 (1994).
[91] Cf. Dunham & Birmingham (1989) at 480–2.
[92] This is one way to understand a recurring theme in the work of Mirjan Damaška, although he does not explicitly use Keynes's concept of weight. See Damaška (1986, 1997).

exercised – permits such practical optimization at both relatively wholesale and relatively retail levels.

Of course, the list of tools discussed earlier is not exhaustive. The multifarious ways in which Keynesian weight is taken into account in the rules that structure trials cannot be easily catalogued.[93] Sometimes the optimization of Keynesian weight can and is pursued only indirectly, promoted for a range of cases rather than assessed (and perhaps marginally adjusted) in a particular case. One of the most important illustrations is the adoption of statutes of limitation and other rules requiring that cases be (reasonably) promptly initiated and (reasonably) promptly tried. Although part of the purpose of these rules is to achieve repose – the ending of controversies (without regard to their merits) so that life outside courtrooms may continue – undoubtedly a significant part of the purpose of such rules is to ensure that cases are tried before critical evidence is lost or deteriorated.[94] Somewhat more specific prophylactic rules preserve critical evidence for possible use at trial in contexts where this seems both possible and worth the effort, such as rules requiring that important transactions be reduced to writing (so-called statutes of frauds)[95] and rules that require the video-recording of police interrogations in contemplation of criminal proceedings.[96]

Although such rules promote the optimization of Keynesian weight in the long run of cases, they rarely pretend to involve a comprehensive assessment of such weight for a particular case. And most admissibility rules, while they will often have the effect of moving a particular case marginally toward the goal of practical optimization, do not pretend to an assessment of the case as a whole. There are good reasons for this. As discussed in the preceding section, in connection with the problem of naked statistical evidence, assessment of the adequacy of Keynesian weight for the entire mass of evidence in a given case, like that of the adequacy of

---

[93] A more extensive catalogue can be found in Nance (1991).
[94] See, e.g., Model Penal Code § 1.06, Comment (1985):

> There are several reasons for the imposition of time limitations. First, and foremost, is the desirability that prosecutions be based upon reasonably fresh evidence. With the passage of time memories fade, witnesses die or leave the area, and physical evidence becomes more difficult to obtain, identify, or preserve.

See generally Corman (1991) at 11–17. See also Hamer (2012a).
[95] Felix & Whitten (2011) at 230 (identifying both the evidentiary and "admonitory" functions of such statutes).
[96] A large number of jurisdictions now have some kind of rule requiring such recording, although the reach of these rules (the suspected crimes to which they apply) and the consequences of failure to record vary considerably. See Gershel (2010).

discriminatory power, tends to be a highly contextual affair, not well suited to abstract rules of wide application. Nonetheless, one can imagine general rules, or at least general standards – other than those discussed earlier – that should apply across many cases and that represent an assessment of the aggregate evidence in those cases. Optimizing Keynesian weight is closely tied to the goal of reducing errors, so the proper rationale of such a rule will be as well, although other considerations, including risk allocation, may become involved. However this may be, one should not simply rule out the possibility that such abstract rules of weight can be useful. Although formal rules about the sufficiency of the evidence as a whole have been in general decline in modern law, there still exist some rules requiring corroboration of certain claims or evidence, especially in criminal cases. The exact relationship between these rules and Keynesian weight is undertheorized.[97]

Consider, for example, the rule requiring corroboration of confessions: a criminal defendant may not be convicted based on his or her confession without some independent evidence that corroborates the commission of the crime.[98] It is now well established that false confessions occur for a variety of reasons, not necessarily associated with explicit coercion.[99] The indicated rule counteracts the natural tendency of police and prosecutors to close cases based only on such flimsy evidence. Yet it poses almost no risk of freeing the guilty because there will be very few crimes for which the *only* available evidence is the perpetrator's confession. The rule, therefore, causes very few erroneous acquittals and quite plausibly prevents a larger number of erroneous convictions.[100] With this reduction in aggregate error, it is unnecessary to justify the rule by reference to some privilege of the accused or in terms of the protection of the innocent despite an increase in aggregate error.[101] And this is a good thing because

---

[97] Some discussion can be found in Stein (2005) at 208, 242–3 and Nance (2007b) at 153–4.
[98] See 1 McCormick (2013) §§ 145–8.
[99] In earlier times, with a paucity of empirical evidence on the matter, much informed opinion held that voluntary false confessions were a rarity. See, e.g., Wigmore (1970) § 820c. More recent data regarding postconviction exonerations show that false confessions, given under a wide range of degrees of volition, are a conspicuous factor leading to false convictions. See, e.g., Garrett (2011) at 14–44, 277–89.
[100] Of course, I do not claim that this or any rule is a panacea. The corroboration rule can be satisfied, and a false conviction result, by the addition of other forms of flawed evidence, such as mistaken identifications. But requiring the addition of other kinds of evidence still must reduce the risk of false conviction without any discernible increase in the risk of false acquittal (or even failure to prosecute).
[101] One must carefully distinguish between corroboration rules that serve to optimize evidential weight from corroboration rules that are intended instead to skew the risk of error

there are reasons to be skeptical of tilting the scales of risk in such ad hoc ways; it invites redundancy, a kind of double counting, when added to the risk allocation inherent in the standard of proof. That is, if the standard of proof is properly set for the class of cases involved, possibly with the help of an ad hoc adjustment by the fact-finder, then any additional skewing of the risk of error in favor of the accused (or any party, for that matter) in the context of rules about particular kinds of evidence is in conflict with the distribution of errors specified by the standard of proof and potentially disturbs the social-optimum decision criterion.[102]

In addition, special metarules – rules about rules – may well be appropriate on Keynesian weight grounds. Because admissibility rules, like most rules, generally involve some degree of over- or underinclusiveness relative to their appropriate goals, it may well be a sound judgment, in a particular case, that the costs of such imprecision exceed the gains, especially in criminal cases. Consider, for example, the leading case of *Chambers v. Mississippi*.[103] Although the holding was expressly narrow, the case has generally been understood as establishing that the federal Constitution guarantees that a criminal defendant has the right to introduce highly reliable evidence that is vital to his or her case notwithstanding the applicability of ordinary statutory or common-law exclusionary rules (at least as long as the proffered evidence is unprivileged).[104] The exclusion (on hearsay grounds) of the corroborated and otherwise apparently reliable

---

in one direction or the other because, for example, a certain kind of claim or defense is "disfavored." See Wigmore (1978) §§ 2036–54.

[102] Larry Laudan develops this argument at some length, although he does so relative to a rather idiosyncratic method of setting the standard of proof. See Laudan (2006). Quite apart from that method, Laudan has been criticized (albeit mildly) on the ground that the standard of proof may not be optimally set by the general formulation and therefore may stand in need of fine-tuning. See Redmayne (2008b) at 182–3 and Pardo (2007) at 372–3. But accepting imperfection in the general standard does not imply that such imperfection can be helpfully addressed by skewing the risk of error pursuant to rules that apply willy-nilly, with no particular relationship to the imperfections encountered. For example, perhaps the standard of proof is set too low for the crime of murder but not for arson. If so, this imperfection is affected only randomly – sometimes helping and sometimes hurting – by a rule that provides special protection for only a limited class of defendants, such as those who confess, whether to the crime of murder or to the crime of arson. If the standard for discriminatory power is set improperly in a particular case, or a particular class of cases, and if attempting to address that defect is worth the effort to do so, then the better approach is some retail adjustment of the standard of proof itself, whether this is done by the judge or by the fact-finder.

[103] 410 U.S. 284 (1975).

[104] The oft-called "*Chambers* doctrine" has created a substantial body of law worthy of an entire treatise. See Imwinkelried & Garland (2004).

out-of-court confession of a third party violated the defendant's right to due process of law. Police and prosecutors knew about the confession well before the trial of the accused, but they did not initiate a prosecution against the confessing person. In reversing the conviction, the Supreme Court emphasized the fact-intensive nature of its holding, and amid the various facts that it thought worthy of note was the fact that when the confessing third party had retracted his confession at a preliminary hearing, "the local authorities undertook no further investigation of his possible involvement,"[105] even though the evidence offered by the defense suggested that considerable information might have been uncovered had such an investigation been pursued. Apparently, the Court was unimpressed by the authorities' investigative efforts, although it is difficult to say just how much this affected the result in the case. In any event, the Court's decision to insist that reliable evidence sometimes be admitted in the face of an otherwise valid hearsay objection has the effect of augmenting Keynesian weight. This is especially warranted when, as the Court emphasized, the hearsay declarant actually testifies.[106] In such a case, excluding the hearsay cannot be useful in expressing a preference for the declarant's live testimony.

The existence and use of the array of legal tools reviewed here show that the law has given a positive, if not always explicit and unambiguous, answer to the question of whether some adjudicative official needs to worry about augmenting Keynesian weight, beyond the regulative impact inherent in permissible discovery and its enforcement.[107]

---

[105] 410 U.S. at 288.
[106] Id. at 301.
[107] Few scholars have suggested that the law can simply ignore the matter. The scholar who perhaps comes closest to doing so is Ron Allen, who has argued that, at least in civil cases, the law should leave the evidence where the parties place it at trial and decide the case without attempting to elicit additional information that the parties, with the benefit of liberal discovery, do not present. See Allen (1986) at 428–31. This bold suggestion entails eliminating, in civil cases, many of those doctrines noted earlier, at least to the extent that they are justified by concerns about Keynesian weight. Conversely, the continued existence of those doctrines testifies to the implicit reluctance of lawmaking institutions to accept Professor Allen's position. Insofar as Allen's conception of the proper trial would tolerate serious inadequacies in Keynesian weight, that conception would seem to be based on the idea that civil adjudication – in contrast to criminal trials – is intended simply to resolve disputes fairly, not necessarily accurately. But, as scholars have long emphasized, fair adjudication presupposes a commitment to accuracy, and accuracy is, indeed, a dominant theme in the long history of writing about common-law trials, both civil and criminal. See, e.g., Summers (1969) at 173–5 and Twining (1984) at 272. This commitment to accuracy of decision is part of what Twining calls the "rationalist tradition." See Twining (1990) at 71–6. Indeed, it is difficult to endorse Allen's position while at the same time endorsing

It would be a mistake, however, to assert that courts consistently and self-consciously invoke the foregoing doctrines whenever there is a need to adjust Keynesian weight. The law is not nearly so tidy as this. Still, to the extent that such doctrines are invoked, and it is not unusual that they are, they are best interpreted as attempts to optimize (or at least marginally improve) Keynesian weight or, in the case of discovery sanctions, to protect the parties' capacity to do so. Once again, this is an interpretive claim: I do not assert that the judges who employ such doctrines are necessarily aware of what they are doing, that they intend to optimize Keynesian weight, or that they even are aware of the idea of Keynesian weight. But they are surely often aware that there is a need to augment (and sometimes to restrict) the information available to the fact-finder so that what is available to the fact-finder is practically optimized in terms of facilitating accurate verdicts.[108]

It is reasonable, therefore, to ask how the system can be improved. Perhaps the most important step is simply recognizing that the doctrines discussed earlier are deployed in service of the goal of practical optimization of Keynesian weight, at least as I have developed that idea. From this starting point, one can work out detailed proposals of interpretation or reform regarding those doctrines. This is the upshot of much of my earlier work, as noted in the preceding two sections. Whether considering admissibility rules – such as the hearsay rule, the original recording rule, the lay opinion rule, the personal knowledge rule, the rule requiring authentication of tangible evidence, or the rule of verbal completeness – or ad hoc rulings on the sufficiency of evidence, in each case, the often-encountered good sense of common-law judges is then revealed as a reflection of the need to make marginal, cost-effective augmentations of Keynesian weight. Of course, the use of any such tool by a court presupposes that the court

---

liberal discovery itself, as Allen certainly does. Allen (1986) at 412 n. 36. Such discovery is justified by its harnessing of private litigants' incentives to find and present all the relevant information the presentation of which is cost justified. See Clermont & Sherwin (2002) at 271 (emphasizing that "the United States has overlaid its adversary procedure with a non-adversarial disclosure and discovery scheme, which signals a special allegiance to truth"). When this goal is incompletely effectuated, the other doctrines discussed earlier step in to fill the gap. But if gap filling is unnecessary, then why is the goal itself worthwhile? And it would be remarkably fortuitous to think that the procedures of discovery necessarily get it just right so that no other tools are needed to practically optimize Keynesian weight.

[108] Of course, the question of whether any or all of these tools are adequate to the task is a different one. For an interesting contribution related to this question, see Leubsdorf (2010) (not explicitly employing the concept of Keynesian weight but nonetheless insightfully discussing how the law's incentives affect it).

perceives the deficiency. Admissibility rules, in particular, have arisen mainly in contexts where the proffered evidence itself exposes the problem, such as when hearsay evidence or secondary evidence of documentary contents is offered. But other deficiencies in Keynesian weight are often readily perceivable as well, such as the obvious percipient witness whose testimony is not presented.

In any event, these localized efforts to interpret particular doctrines do not fully address the question of whether and how to harmonize the use of the various tools for managing Keynesian weight. The task of doing so is complicated by the fact that the various tools are the result of an evolution of legal procedure. For example, admissibility rules developed before the modern expansion of discovery and its associated sanctions. One of the important questions, therefore, is to what extent modern discovery rules render particular admissibility rules unnecessary. By the same token, the availability of options to the use of admissibility rules is affected by the extent to which the courts explicitly acknowledge the component of the burden of production that speaks to the practical optimization of Keynesian weight. No attempt will be made here to provide a complete framework that harmonizes all the tools that have been used to monitor Keynesian weight. What I can offer is a few basic principles that are helpful for any such undertaking that would focus on the use of discovery sanctions, admissibility rules, and sufficiency rules (or ad hoc rulings) at trial.

First, which of these tools is appropriate to use will depend primarily on two factors: (1) whether certain potential evidence is still available and (2) the degree of culpability of the parties in withholding or suppressing the missing evidence. More precisely, it will depend on how confident the trial judge is about the continuing accessibility of the augmenting evidence and how confident the trial judge is that the parties are acting reasonably and in good faith. A third, obvious factor is how central and useful to the dispute the potential evidence might be. Theoretically separate from but pragmatically intertwined with this first set of considerations is the question of which party, if any, should bear responsibility for curing the defect in the evidence or suffering the consequences of not doing so. Inevitably, putting these considerations all together, this must be a highly contextual assessment by the trial judge based, at least in large part, on the information that the parties and their attorneys provide.

At one extreme, when the court is most confident that centrally important evidence has been irretrievably lost and that the loss is the consequence of "bad faith" of a party acting to prevent the use of that evidence at trial, then the case presents the best candidate for the use of a preemptive ruling against that party, whether in the form of a discovery sanction or a sufficiency ruling. Such rulings may extend to all material facts as to which the lost evidence is likely to have been relevant.[109] This kind of sanction makes clear that a party's right to have its disputes fully litigated – at considerable public and private cost – can be forfeited by the party's refusal to play by the rules of litigation.[110] Essentially the same point applies to situations in which the court believes that the missing evidence is still available to be presented though a party has acted to suppress it. But now the remedy of choice is the imposition of a burden of production, with the implied preemptive sanction in the event of noncompliance, a burden that gives the suppressing party the opportunity to reverse course (see Figure 7).

At the other extreme, when the court is most confident that significant missing information can still be made available to the court and the court is most confident that the parties are acting in good faith, little judicial action, beyond the appropriate reminder, may be required. Such a reminder can be provided by the use of an admissibility rule, at least when one can be identified as applicable. A party acting in good faith who offers hearsay, for example, may need only the prodding that comes from a hearsay objection to be reminded that the court prefers to hear the testimony of the declarant.[111] Otherwise, a burden of production may need to be employed. Of course, when evidence, no matter how important, has been irretrievably lost, yet the court is at maximum confidence that the loss occurred without the bad faith (or perhaps negligence[112]) of either party, then the appropriate response is to impose no sanction, at least insofar as such a sanction is concerned with the practical optimization of Keynesian weight.[113]

---

[109] In extreme cases, separate criminal sanctions may be applicable as well. See Gorelick et al. (1989) §§ 5.2–5.10 (discussing federal and state obstruction of justice statutes).

[110] See Nance (2010) at 1096–7.

[111] If no other, more particularized admissibility rule applies, recourse can sometimes be made to the residual discretion of the trial court under Fed. R. Evid. 403, which allows exclusion of evidence the probative value of which is substantially outweighed by the danger of wasting time or attempting to mislead the fact-finder. The rule can be used to express or enforce a trial court's preference for better evidence in light of the fact that in deciding whether given evidence is a waste of time, the court may consider the alternatives available to the proponent. See Fed. R. Evid. 403, Advisory Committee Note. See generally Old Chief v. United States, 519 U.S. 172 (1997).

[112] On the question of responding to negligent destruction of evidence, see Nance (2010) at 1125–9.

[113] Reflecting the twin aspects of the burden of production (§ 4.1.4), in such a case, the mere fact that certain evidence is missing should not be an impediment to placing the case before the fact-finder unless its absence, taking into account any appropriate spoliation inference, renders a verdict for one side implausible under the applicable standard of proof. (On the appropriateness of adverse inferences, see infra § 4.2.)

Principal Factors Affecting Remedy	Evidence available	Evidence possibly available	Evidence irreversibly lost
Both parties acting reasonably	Admissibility ruling		No remedy required
Party acting negligently			
Party acting in bad faith	Burden of production		Preemptive ruling

Figure 7. Matrix of remedial paradigms for missing evidence.

Filling in the details of this set of preferences requires the exercise of considerable practical judgment. (Figure 7 is drawn with wavy lines for the borders to reflect this. The relevant axes are spectra: from evidence that is definitely available to evidence that is irretrievably lost; from parties acting entirely reasonably to at least one party acting in bad faith.) Most important, because the difference in appropriate response, when evidence is certainly lost beyond recovery, is so stark, depending on the good or bad faith (or perhaps negligence) of the party who caused the loss, a court should be reluctant to find bad faith (or negligence); a high standard of confidence is warranted before imposing a preemptive ruling. However, when the court believes that it is just probable (but not highly likely) that important evidence is irretrievably lost and that it is just probable (but not highly likely) that the loss is due to the bad faith (or negligence) of a party, then the court is operating in a context in which admissibility rules (or rulings) have distinct advantages. The court can place pressure to produce the (possibly still extant) missing evidence by excluding other evidence offered on the same point, especially "secondary" evidence that is substituted for the preferred evidence, such as testimony about the contents of a document or the hearsay report of what another person said. In these conditions, using exclusionary rules to regulate Keynesian weight hedges the court's bet in two ways: (1) the court might well be wrong in thinking that the missing evidence has been irretrievably lost, and an exclusionary ruling, dissolved on presentation of the desired evidence, may serve its intended purpose, to encourage the presentation of the desired evidence, and (2) the court might well be wrong about the scienter of a party in the loss of the evidence, and at least then the use of an exclusionary sanction usually (though not always) allows the case to proceed to judgment, albeit with an unavoidable but undeserved handicap placed on one of the parties.

Defects in the discovery process – whereby once extant evidence can be destroyed or withheld – do not, however, explain all appropriate occasions for the application of a remedy to augment Keynesian weight. In some contexts, the augmenting evidence may not yet exist; it may need to be *created* or to *have been* created.[114] To illustrate this point, consider the important "gatekeeping" role imposed by the United States Supreme Court on federal trial courts when dealing with expert testimony. Originating in 1993 with the decision in *Daubert v. Merrell Dow Pharmaceuticals, Inc.*,[115] which concerned scientific evidence, and extended to all other forms of expertise in 1999 with *Kumho Tire Co. v. Carmichael*,[116] the new regime requires that any expert testimony, in order to be admitted in court, must be based on specialized knowledge that is found by the trial court to be "reliable."[117] This is a requirement explicitly more demanding than the independently existing requirement that the testimony be relevant. And it is one about which the trial court is not simply to defer to the consensus among experts themselves (as had sometimes previously been required under the so-called *Frye* test).[118] As articulated, the requirement is quite perplexing. A moment's reflection reveals why.[119]

The explicitly binary concept of reliability employed by the Court – by which expertise is to be judged (using a "preponderance of the evidence" standard) to be either reliable for the particular purpose or not – obscures the obvious fact that reliability is a gradational variable: it comes in degrees.[120] Concluding that expertise is "unreliable" therefore must be

---

[114] This was the problem, for example, with the absence of the fingernail scraping DNA evidence in the Sam Sheppard case. See supra § 4.1.1.
[115] 509 U.S. 579 (1993).
[116] 526 U.S. 137 (1999).
[117] The test was codified in 2000 by amending the rules. See Fed. R. Evid. 702.
[118] In *Daubert*, the Court specifically held that the Federal Rules of Evidence did not endorse the test of "general acceptance in the particular field" that had been propounded in Frye v. United States, 293 F. 1013 (C.A. D.C. 1923).
[119] The following paragraphs summarize and update an argument presented in greater depth in Nance (2003).
[120] The Advisory Committee Note for the 2000 Amendment states: "[w]hen a trial court, applying the amendment, rules that an expert's testimony is reliable, this does not mean

the result of concluding that it is *insufficiently* reliable, and concluding that it is insufficiently reliable presupposes that one knows the competing concern(s) that determines how reliable is reliable enough for admissibility in the particular context. Depending on the nature and strength of the pertinent countervailing concern, expertise of relatively low reliability still might be reliable enough, and, conversely, expertise of high reliability still might be insufficiently reliable.[121]

In this context, there are only a limited number of plausible concerns that might determine how reliable is reliable enough. Most conspicuously, the requirement could be a manifestation of any one, or some combination of, three principal concerns: (1) that lay jurors not be seduced by the aura of expertise or induced by their own lack of understanding to give a verdict on inappropriate grounds (such as sympathy for a suffering plaintiff), (2) that tribunals not waste their time trying to understand the significance of expertise of little or uncertain probative value, or (3) that tribunals not be required to adjudicate on the basis of expertise that is less reliable than it ought to be under the circumstances. Yet, strikingly, the Supreme Court has never told us which of these, if any, it had in mind or which it thought that the drafters of the federal rules or those who approved them had in mind.[122] True, the Supreme Court and inferior courts have identified

---

that contradictory expert testimony is unreliable." No explanation of this puzzling remark was provided. It seems to be simply aspirational: the courts should, indeed must, try to figure out a meaning of "reliable" that does not have the indicated untoward consequence. If one construes "reliable opinion" as "opinion on which one *ought* to rely," then the committee's remark is unintelligible; if, however, one construes "reliable opinion" as "opinion on which one is *permitted* to rely," then the comment makes sense, but the reliability requirement itself then becomes unhelpfully tautological because in all contexts the court ought to admit only that on which the fact-finder is permitted to rely.

[121] As Susan Haack notes:

> [T]he Law Commission for England and Wales proposes requiring that admissible expert evidence be not (as *Daubert* says) "reliable," but "reliable enough" – thus acknowledging, as *Daubert* did not, that reliability comes in degrees: insofar, an advance, but unfortunately, also risking making the reliability requirement essentially vacuous.

Haack (2014) at 25.

[122] The Court's derivation of this requirement was almost entirely formalistic, said to follow from the language chosen by the drafters of the applicable federal rule, which (at the time) simply referred to the admissibility of "scientific, technical, or other specialized knowledge" that would "assist the trier of fact." Several state courts have had no difficulty finding in these words rather different requirements than that found by the United States Supreme Court. See, e.g., Grady v. Frito-Lay, Inc., 839 A.2d 1038 (Pa. 2003); Marron v. Stromstad, 123 P.3d 992 (Alaska 2005); Searles v. Fleetwood Homes of Pennsylvania, Inc., 878 A.2d 509 (Me. 2005); and Higgs v. State, 222 P.3d 648 (Nev. 2010).

various factors to use in deciding whether the expertise is, as applied in the context, reliable, all of which are directed to the assessment of the degree of trustworthiness of the expertise,[123] but this is only part of what one needs to know to apply the test. Consequently, at least as articulated, the requirement was (and continues to be) as unhelpful as the expertise that it was intended to exclude. It is analytically akin to giving trial judges the following instruction: "The court shall exclude relevant evidence if its probative value is substantially outweighed."[124] Even with detailed instruction on how to assess the degree of probative value, such a standard is radically incomplete. It begs the question: "Outweighed by what?" What's more, the Court's multifactored test of reliability is intentionally silent on the question of how one is to combine or prioritize the assessments of the individual factors affecting trustworthiness. At best, the Court's decision simply directed lower courts to "pay attention" to reliability (again, without simply deferring to the opinions of experts in the relevant field).

To the extent that this directive has been an improvement, it is because courts have found helpful ways to "complete" the reliability requirement. To do this, again, one must identify the danger against which it is intended to protect. The first of the plausible motivations noted earlier – what we may call, for brevity, "offsetting jury incompetence" – is often thought to be the engine driving the *Daubert* requirement, and it would at least yield the beginnings of a coherent test for deciding hard cases: expertise would be reliable enough just when it will not be misunderstood or misused by the jury. Some courts seem to treat the matter this way.[125] Certainly, no one doubts that juries make mistakes on issues as to which experts testify. But so do judges, which poses difficult questions of comparative institutional competence. In the end, this way of filling out the reliability requirement faces formidable difficulties, of which the most important are these: (1) the available empirical evidence does not support the idea that juries, any

---

[123] See Fed. R. Evid. 702, Advisory Committee Note for 2000 Amendment (listing factors affecting the reliability of offered expertise).

[124] Cf. Fed. R. Evid. 403 (permitting trial courts to exclude relevant evidence "if its probative value is substantially outweighed by a danger of one or more of the following: unfair prejudice, confusing the issues, misleading the jury, undue delay, wasting time, or needlessly presenting cumulative evidence").

[125] See, e.g., SmithKline Beecham Corp. v. Apotex Corp., 247 F. Supp. 2d 1011, 1042 (N.D. Ill. 2003) ("The primary purpose of the *Daubert* filter is to protect juries from being bamboozled by technical evidence of dubious merit") and Eskin v. Cardin, 842 A.2d 1222, 1226 (Del. 2004) (holding that the trial judge could reasonably have determined the offered expertise to be unreliable and "accordingly" that its relevance was "outweighed by the danger of misleading or confusing the jury").

more than judges, are seduced by the lure of party-sponsored expertise,[126] (2) there is no reason to think, and certainly no data confirming, that judges can effectively anticipate when juries will be misled or befuddled by claimed expertise and intervene in such a way as to improve the accuracy of verdicts,[127] (3) as a doctrinal matter, the Supreme Court's opinions generating the reliability requirement, to the extent that they mention the matter of jury incompetence, actually reject it as an animating concern of that requirement,[128] (4) assuming that judges can accurately make such predictions (or else that they decide on the basis of the proponent's motives rather than the predicted effects), there is ample authority in other rules for the exclusion of any kind of evidence, including expert testimony, that presents this concern, a point also emphasized in *Daubert*,[129] and (5) the reliability requirement applies (inexplicably, on this theory) in bench trials.[130]

---

[126] See Lempert (1993b); Vidmar & Diamond (2001); Nance & Morris (2002, 2005); and Nance (2007d). The following comment is on point:

> It is revealing that not one of the briefs by or supporting Merrell Dow in *Daubert* brought forth any empirical evidence in support of the ubiquitous assertions in ten of the fourteen briefs that jury misunderstanding or overvaluation of expert testimony is a problem in need of a solution. Perhaps this was just good litigation strategy. If a raft of venerable intuitions is on your side, as it is here, and most of the real research is against you, as it is here, then relying on the common intuitions and not even mentioning the word "research" is good litigation strategy. But good litigation strategy does not always produce good law.

Schauer & Spellman (2013) at 26.

[127] See Nance (2003) at 229–31. In this regard, consider Susan Haack's pointed remark:

> [I]f judges need to act as gatekeepers to exclude scientific evidence which doesn't meet minimal standards of warrant because juries may be taken in by flimsy scientific evidence, how realistic is it to expect juries to discriminate the better from the worse among the halfway decent?

Haack (2001) at 233.

[128] See *Daubert*, 509 U.S. at 595–6 (replying to the concern about credulous juries with the comment that it "seems to us to be overly pessimistic about the capabilities of the jury and of the adversary system generally").

[129] See id. 595 (noting that, entirely separate from the reliability requirement of Rule 702, Rule 403 permits the exclusion of expert testimony that poses too great a risk of misleading the jury). Perceptive judges picked up on this point. See, e.g., In re Paoli R.R. Yard PCB Litig., 35 F.3d 717, 746–7 (3d. Cir. 1994) (per Becker, J.) (noting that *Daubert* took the dangers of confusing or overwhelming the jury out of the "reliability" test of Rule 702 and committed it to analysis under Rule 403).

[130] See, e.g., Seaboard Lumber Co. v. United States, 308 F.3d 1283, 1301–2 (Fed. Cir. 2002). Of course, the *process* of implementing the requirement can be different in bench trials, at least when (as is typically the case in federal courts) the gatekeeper and the fact-finder are the same person. For example, in a bench trial, the judge may initially "admit" the challenged expertise and decide later whether to exclude it as unreliable.

The second concern – avoiding the expense of considering minimally useful expertise – is coherent as well, and it represents an appealing ground within the context of often-expressed concerns about the abuse of an expensive litigation system, even in the context of bench trials. But it also presents perplexing puzzles that undermine its plausibility as the pertinent consideration in deciding how reliable is reliable enough. First, if expert testimony, because of weak reliability, is not worth the effort to incorporate it with other evidence in a case, then it can be excluded under other rules as a waste of time, without the need for recourse to a distinct reliability requirement.[131] Second, if the flimsy expertise is not merely a waste of time but is the only evidence on a critical point offered by its proponent, and it is opposed by much stronger evidence, why bother to exclude the evidence before ending the case (some form of summary judgment being appropriate even if the flimsy evidence were admitted)?[132] Finally, in cases where one item of expert testimony has low reliability, but the party offering it has other evidence directed to the same point, whether expert or otherwise, excluding the challenged low-reliability item of expert evidence requires too much of a single piece of evidence and ignores the important point that it might, to a rational fact-finder, be just the additional evidence that tips the balance in favor of that party. Use of an exclusionary rule is then inapt because the right question is the sufficiency of the evidence as a whole.[133] Simply put, ample tools have long been available to deal with very weak expertise; it is just a matter of making sure that the courts use them when appropriate. Still, if judges were sensitive to this point and could avoid a pernicious atomism in the treatment of evidence, a legitimate aspect of the reliability requirement could be to *remind* trial courts of the importance of keeping trials focused on the most useful information, thereby avoiding cognitive and other costs. This is one aspect of optimizing Keynesian weight.

See, e.g., In re Maurice J. Salem, 465 F.3d 767 (7th Cir. 2006). But some courts go further and opine that while the requirement certainly applies in bench trials, it is a more "relaxed" standard. See, e.g., Gibbs v. Gibbs, 210 F.3d 491(5th Cir. 2002).

[131] Again, Rule 403 gives ample authority to exclude evidence that is simply a waste of the tribunal's time. See Fed. R. Evid. 403. Cases that exclude expert testimony as "unreliable" because of conspicuous defects in the expert's logic often could just as easily have excluded that testimony as a waste of time. Any jury would see the defect, especially if the cross-examiner pointed it out, but why put the jury through such a fruitless exercise. See, e.g., Fireman Fund Ins. Co. v. Canon, 394 F.3d 1054 (8th Cir. 2005).

[132] Even in the Bendectin cases that gave rise to the *Daubert* decision, lower courts granted summary decisions for the defense in many cases in which the full panoply of plaintiff's expertise was admitted. See Sanders (1998) at 143–74.

[133] See Haack (2014) at 208–38.

This leaves us with the third concern, namely, that the court should not be forced to decide a dispute on the basis of expertise, no matter how reliable it is, that is not as reliable as the court should reasonably expect expertise on the matter to be. The connection between this idea and the goal of practically optimizing Keynesian weight is obvious. (It involves both quantitative and qualitative augmentations. See § 3.2) And, again, we have a way to save the reliability requirement from the vacuity of its ostensibly binary test: expertise is reliable enough just when it is the most reliable expertise the court should reasonably expect from the proponent. To be sure, the factors now in play (besides the degree of reliability of that which is offered) relate to a variety of conditions about potential alternative presentations, including alternative modes of presentation that do not exceed the legitimate scope of the expertise and potential alternative grounds of presentation, such as the results of potential research and testing. The latter require consideration of the cost conditions associated with obtaining and presenting evidence of superior reliability.[134] But the fundamental objective is to improve on what the court is otherwise going to receive because (and when) the dispute warrants the expenditure of time and money necessary to do so.[135] As Michael Saks nicely put the matter:

> Many fields, perhaps most notably the forensic identification sciences, will do whatever it takes to satisfy the courts and little more. Those fields have little or no existence outside the courts. They have few academic and no commercial counterparts that would carry out testing and development for their own purposes. Some forensic science subfields became interested in conducting research to evaluate themselves only in response to *Daubert*.... If the courts had continued to excuse these fields from testing the validity of their claims, they gladly would have continued to do no research.[136]

---

[134] See Nance (2003) at 240–52.

[135] Once again, the preferential structure of the Keynesian weight requirement argues for a permissive attitude when nothing better can be obtained as a practical matter. For example, the absence of more reliable chemical tests for the presence of an illicit drug may be excusable in favor of less reliable experiential evidence when no sample of the substance is ever available to the prosecution for chemical testing. Compare United States v. Bermudez, 526 F.2d 89 (2d Cir. 1975), cert. denied, 425 U.S. 970 (1976) (conviction sustained on DEA agent's testimony identifying, as cocaine, substance never available for testing) and United States v. Johnson, 575 F.2d 1347 (5th Cir. 1978), cert. denied, 440 U.S. 907 (1979) (affirming admission of testimony of an experienced smoker of marijuana identifying contraband as Columbian in origin when no marijuana was ever seized to be subjected to chemical tests, and there was conflict in testimony regarding the ability of chemical tests to determine source of marijuana) with People v. Park, 380 N.E. 2d 795 (Ill. 1980) (holding sheriff's testimony identifying seized substance as marijuana by "look, smell, and feel" inadmissible in light of readily availability chemical tests of greater reliability).

[136] Saks (2000) at 240–1.

Understanding the reliability requirement in this way would render it intelligible and justifiable, and it would also place it clearly within the set of tools to be used by the courts to make marginal improvements in Keynesian weight. While it might, in principle, be better if incentives for improvement were provided by relevant professional accrediting bodies, in the (frequent) absence of pertinent, empirically assessed professional standards, judicial restrictions may well be unavoidable. And as compared with other tools for the management of Keynesian weight, admissibility rulings have the potential virtue of providing a relatively pointed message, identifying a particular kind or form of expertise as deficient, at least in the context, without precluding a verdict based on other evidence.

In the foregoing discussion I have addressed primarily the fact that various tools can and are used when the situation calls for an augmentation of Keynesian weight, and I have suggested the kinds of considerations that go into the choice of tool. I have not addressed in depth the important question of how the court should allocate the responsibility for increasing Keynesian weight. In some contexts – such as when one party destroys evidence in bad faith – the assignment of responsibility is obvious. In other contexts, though – such as when important evidence has simply not been presented – the assignment is not so obvious. Before considering the question of allocation of responsibility, it is important to consider in some detail the most important confusion that appears in the literature about how the law does and should handle the assessment of Keynesian weight. This confusion concerns the role of the fact-finder.

4.2 The Fact-Finder's Role in Monitoring Keynesian Weight

What can be said about the role of the fact-finder with regard to Keynesian weight? The question is most pressing when, as is certainly true in the adversary system, the role of fact-finder is separated from the other decision-making roles, particularly the roles of the judge as expositor of the law and moderator of the pre-trial and trial processes. What can be said about the petit jury for the most part can be said about the trial judge when acting as fact-finder in a bench trial. So the following discussion focuses on the jury as fact-finder. Thus we ask: In cases where a jury is used as the fact-finder, should the jury monitor the adequacy of Keynesian weight? As already noted, when the question is whether Keynesian weight is deficient, the usual answer given by commentators has been that this is appropriately a matter for the jury, as fact-finder, to consider in applying the burden of persuasion. If so, we are confronted with pressing questions.

Is the jury's role in this regard affected by the showing made earlier that the legal system employs a variety of pretrial and predeliberation tools, administered by the trial judge, in an effort to optimize Keynesian weight? Does the existence of this panoply of tools cast doubt on the supposed role of the jury in monitoring Keynesian weight?

To answer such questions, we should begin by being clear about what it would mean for the jury to monitor the adequacy of Keynesian weight using its application of the burden of persuasion. First, a juror does *not* do this when he or she is allowed, as jurors are in some courts nowadays, to step out of the ordinary role of fact-finder and into the role of investigator by posing questions, usually through the judge, to witnesses.[137] The responses may well augment Keynesian weight, and surely this is the intent of posing the questions, but such innovative devices do not operate through the burden of persuasion; they precede its application. Second, a juror does *not* do so simply by analyzing how reliable or probative the evidence is, for this is inherent in the assessment of discriminatory power. True, a judge (not acting as a fact-finder) who applies one of the tools discussed earlier – whether it is a discovery rule, an admissibility rule, or a rule of evidentiary sufficiency – also may find it necessary to think about the obvious or potential reliability or probative force of evidence that is offered or that might be obtained to be offered. But the judge is thinking about this kind of thing from a different perspective: he or she is answering a question that relates to optimizing Keynesian weight. This question is whether there is reason to suspect that the potential evidence would shed enough light on the disputed facts to warrant its consideration in light of the various costs that are entailed by requiring its presentation. For the jury to be involved in *this* assessment, it must be attaching significance to the absence (or presence) of evidence that goes beyond simply determining the discriminatory power of the evidence that is presented. How and why would the jury do this?

In the context of *restricting* the amount of evidence considered, a limitation on the jury's role is easy to understand. In such a context, the point of restricting the evidence considered – usually saving time and resources – would generally be defeated to a large degree if the jury were charged with monitoring Keynesian weight. But it is not inconceivable that we would allow clearly cumulative and time-wasting evidence to be presented to the jury on the assumption that the jury will not merely ignore the offending material but also discipline the party responsible for

---

[137] See Marder (2005) at 110–14.

presenting it. This could be the foundation for long-run improvements as other litigants react to the message the jury has sent. But the process is rather problematic, for the jury's options are quite limited. Presumably, all the jury could do would be to deny a verdict to the party that would otherwise be entitled to it. This is troublesome in several ways. First, the jury could only effectively use this sanction if the party responsible for wasting the tribunal's time is the party who would otherwise be entitled to a verdict. If that party were going to lose anyway, the jury would be powerless to enforce its monitoring efforts.[138] Second, and more important, any such sanctioning by the jury would be stepping beyond the jury's role as conventionally understood. The jury would say, in effect, "X should win under the applicable standard of proof, but we will give verdict for Y instead because X wasted our time." Juries might, in fact, sometimes do such things, but they are certainly not authorized to do so. There is, in addition, the problem of how the jury is to communicate to the parties the *reason* for the verdict, without which no effective message can be delivered to other potential litigants. Thus, placing on the jury the responsibility for monitoring and enforcing necessary restrictions on Keynesian weight makes little sense, at least when there is available in the courtroom another juridical actor – the judge – much better situated to do so.

The same conclusion emerges with regard to the monitoring of needed *augmentations* of Keynesian weight, although the matter is rather more subtle and complicated. Once again, jurors are deprived of most of the tools that one would expect them to have if they were to exercise effective control over deficiencies in Keynesian weight. They generally cannot question witnesses, subpoena additional lay witnesses, call expert witnesses, or use preferential exclusionary rules that would assist them.[139] These powers are reserved for the parties and the trial judge. And recall the suggestion, made by commentators and courts, that a party may be called on to explain whether it is feasible for him or her to obtain additional

---

[138] If the offending party were the defendant in a civil case for damages and the plaintiff would, in the view of the jury, be entitled to the verdict in any case, then the jury might, conceivably, sanction the defendant's behavior by exaggerating the damages awarded beyond the nominally correct measure. This, of course, would involve the jury's violating its instructions.

[139] Larry Laudan describes these as among "the evidentiary practices [that] hinder the ability of the jury to come to a correct verdict because they block the jury's access to probative evidence." Laudan (2006) at 137. This, of course, assumes that the parties and the judge, collectively, fail to provide the jury with what it needs.

evidence.[140] Assuming that an appropriate demand can be made of a party, how is such a showing to be made? If the party is represented by an attorney, it is almost certainly the attorney who will have the information needed to decide whether the investigation has been adequately pursued. But attorneys typically do not testify, and they are strongly discouraged from doing so.[141] The much more obvious and sensible approach is for the judge to interact with the attorneys to explore the question of the availability of additional evidence, both before the formal trial and at appropriate places during trial. In default of adequate responses from the parties, the judge can invoke the powers at his or her disposal for augmenting Keynesian weight. It is fairly obvious, then, why trial judges have responsibility to monitor the adequacy of Keynesian weight.

Despite all this, when the insufficiency of Keynesian weight is the matter at issue, most scholars so far have tried to place responsibility for its assessment in the hands of the fact-finder, which means the jury in a jury trial, although the literature is not replete with explanations of this preference. The most explicit argument along these lines is Professor Ho's analogy to the criminal investigator. For the investigator, Ho recognizes, there is not only the question of whether the extant evidence warrants prosecution but also the question of whether further evidence should be sought before deciding whether the available evidence warrants prosecution, and Ho clearly attributes this observation to the importance of Keynesian weight, or "comprehensiveness of evidence."[142] Indeed, Ho rightly observes that the detective is blameworthy if, in her haste to close a file, she ignores available leads that might exonerate Y, settles on the belief that Y is the culprit, and acts on this belief by initiating a prosecution.[143] So far, so good.[144]

---

[140] This point was noted in connection with the explanation of a rule against naked statistical evidence and of other rulings relating to the burden of production (§ 4.1.3). See, e.g., Howard v. Wal-Mart Stores, Inc., 160 F.3d 358, 360 (7th Cir. 1998) (noting the implications of the fact, when it is a fact, that a party "does not show that it was infeasible for him to obtain any additional evidence").

[141] See, e.g., ABA Model Rules of Professional Conduct Rule 3.7.

[142] Ho (2008) at 166.

[143] Id. at 166-8.

[144] Ho's moral claim can be correct whether or not policy makers decide that the costs are worth the benefits of attempting to supervise investigating officers in the discharge of their duties. Compare Model Rules of Professional Conduct Rule 3.8(g),(h) (recognizing an affirmative duty to investigate as a matter of professional ethics) with ABA Standards for Criminal Justice: Prosecutorial Investigations § 2.1(a)(2008) (rejecting a duty of professional ethics to investigate unless "required by statute or policy").

But then, in considering the role of the fact-finder, Ho argues (in regard to Cohen's gatecrasher hypothetical) as follows:

> In the gatecrasher ... scenario[], the fact-finder is in a position similar, though not identical, to the detective's. There is at least one major difference. While the detective has the task of conducting physical investigation, the fact-finder in an adversarial setting has neither the power nor the duty to track down evidence. Nevertheless, the general principle with which we are concerned applies equally to the deliberation of both: evidence in support of a hypothesis needs to be sufficiently comprehensive to justify believing it. Much of what was said in the detective example applies to the [gatecrasher] scenario[]. As there are too many important questions yet to be explored, to settle on the belief that [the defendant] did not pay to watch the show ... would be 'jumping to conclusion'. Not only is this belief epistemically unsound, the fact-finder is blameworthy in holding it if she did so out of epistemic laziness or negligence.[145]

Two important observations about this argument are in order. First, by making the analogy to the detective's decision – which is clearly subject to a preferential structure in that the detective's wrongdoing arises only because it is assumed that exonerative leads are *available* to be investigated – Ho seems to concede, at least implicitly, that the fact-finder's reason to reject liability in the gatecrasher case would be based on a similar preferential demand for increased Keynesian weight. As argued in § 3.3, this means that if such evidence is not reasonably available, then this ground for rejecting liability disappears.[146] (Ho does not address the question of how a petit jury is to determine whether such additional evidence is reasonably available or the question of how the jury is to communicate its conclusion on that matter to the parties in such a way that the parties can react thereto prior to verdict. These points are of considerable practical importance.)

Second, Ho makes no case for the proposition that the fact-finder's "epistemic unsoundness" in believing the defendant liable arises from anything other than the "epistemic laziness or negligence" that, analogous to

---

[145] Ho (2008) at 168 (citing the work of Sahlin). Sahlin's views were discussed supra in § 3.2.
[146] In the quoted passage Ho acknowledges that the epistemic unsoundness of the belief arises from the fact that "there are too many important questions yet to be explored," which (given the analogy to the investigator) might contemplate the practicality of obtaining additional evidence for that purpose. Elsewhere, however, he seems clearly to deny that the result in cases such as the gatecrasher problem depends on the availability of additional evidence. See id. at 136 n. 190.

that of the detective, results in the failure to pursue exonerative leads. The detective acts improperly, however, only because she could and should have investigated further but did not. This poses a question: Given that the option of conducting further investigation is not available to the adversarial fact-finder, as Ho concedes, in what way does such a fact-finder – whether a jury or a judge – act out of laziness or negligence in granting a verdict against the defendant on the evidence hypothesized? The only viable answer is that the fact-finder acts wrongfully (i.e., with "epistemic laziness or negligence") if, by entering a verdict against the defendant, she *condones* the behavior of other persons whose responsibility it was to conduct further investigation. This, in turn, assumes that (1) some other actor in the legal system (e.g., Ho's hypothesized detective) should have investigated further but did not (or at least did not make the results of the investigation available to the fact-finder) *and* (2) it is the proper role of the fact-finder to monitor such conduct by the other actor. Admittedly, the adjudicative *system* will have failed if such conduct is accepted or condoned by the granting of a verdict when reasonable investigation has not been pursued or, if pursued by a party, its results are not made known to the jury. It is entirely plausible, however, for the system to be designed such that it is not the role of the fact-finder to monitor such failures. As detailed in the preceding section, this is in fact the norm in adversarial adjudication.[147]

It is not the jury's role, for example, when a party offers secondary evidence of the contents of a document, to assess the adequacy of the excuse offered by that party for not presenting the original.[148] Similarly, it is not the jury's role, when a party offers the hearsay of an allegedly unavailable declarant, to determine whether the proponent has offered a valid excuse for not presenting the testimony of the declarant in court.[149] The judge does

---

[147] Ho's analogy would work quite differently if instead of comparing the detective to the fact-finder – i.e., the petit jury or judge acting as trier of fact at trial – he had compared the detective to a *grand* jury. A grand jury has investigative powers and can follow evidentiary leads itself. See Whitehead & Slobogin (2008) at 633, 647–56. Furthermore, the decision of the grand jury not to indict is not *res judicata*, nor does it trigger constitutional protections against double jeopardy. The government is free to come back to the grand jury after making further investigations, provided that any applicable statute of limitations has not expired. See, e.g., 18 U.S.C. §§ 3288, 3289. Consequently, the grand jury would be within its authority and role to deny an indictment on account of the inadequacy of the investigation that had been conducted without thereby committing itself to a decision on the merits of the claim.

[148] See Fed. R. Evid. 1002, 1004–7.

[149] See Fed. R. Evid. 804.

these things in deciding admissibility.[150] And when, before deliberation, a court directs a verdict against a party on account of missing evidence, the jury, of course, has no opportunity to monitor Keynesian weight.

This suggests a clear delineation of responsibility: judges (not acting as fact-finders on the merits) monitor Keynesian weight, using available tools to ensure a practical optimization of such weight in the evidence presented by the parties, and juries assess discriminatory power, testing the same against appropriate standards. As a first-order approximation, this is accurate as a description of how things work, and how they *ought* to work, in adversarial adjudication. To do otherwise, by assigning the task of assessing the adequacy of Keynesian weight to the jury, unnecessarily puts the jury in a very difficult position.[151] Asserting this entails no criticism or distrust of the jury as a fact-finding institution. (I suspect that there are few who have a greater respect for the work of juries than I do.) It is, instead, a comment intended to forestall a failure by judges and other policy makers to discharge their duties regarding fact investigation, duties owed not only to parties but also to juries and to the public. It is to say that the discharge of this duty should not be ignored or excused by embracing the confused argument that juries are entitled to assess "weight" or the inaccurate argument that juries are better equipped to do so. In this last regard, it is to make a judgment of *comparative* institutional competence that is limited to a context in which the trial judge has pertinent educational, experiential, and case-specific informational advantages and in which the judge's role permits better coordinated, more timely feedback to litigants.

However, there are some complications that must be acknowledged. Some of these derive from the fact that the *explanation* for the deficiency in Keynesian weight – as distinguished from the deficiency itself – sometimes may have probative value on the underlying merits, thus affecting discriminatory power. Usually, this arises in situations where there is a plausible inference as to the motives of a party in not bringing the evidence forward. For example, suppose that a proponent offers secondary

---

[150] See Fed. R. Evid. 104(a), 1008. Strikingly, Professor Ho's inquiry into the rationale of the hearsay rule reveals an entirely appropriate preference for explaining that rule in terms of a concern about Keynesian weight. See Ho (2008) at 264–73. But he leaves unexplored the tension between the fact that lawmakers and judges regulate and monitor Keynesian weight in establishing and applying such admissibility rules and his claim that jurors properly assess the adequacy of the Keynesian weight of admitted evidence.

[151] See Cohen & Bersten (1990) at 237 (arguing that the proposal by Davidson & Pargetter – that juries assess the Keynesian weight of the evidence – requires the jury to speculate about what has not been presented to it, why it has not been presented, and what its impact would be if it were presented).

evidence of the contents of a document, the opponent raises an objection under the original document rule, the proponent asserts that the original was destroyed without bad faith on his part, and the court determines that the original was inadvertently destroyed or was destroyed by a third party, so the secondary evidence is admissible. It is true that, under the conventional understanding, the jury has no role in the ruling on the adequacy of the excuse as a precondition of the admission of the secondary evidence, but the jury still may be given evidence by the opponent in an effort to show that the original was destroyed in bad faith. The applicable federal rule states, with characteristic ambiguity, that the commitment of all admissibility decisions to the trial judge "does not limit a party's right to introduce before the jury evidence that is relevant to the weight or credibility of other evidence."[152] But which sense of "weight" is involved here?

Arguably, such "spoliation" evidence should be admissible to the extent that it rationally affects the discriminatory power of other evidence before the jury, including the secondary evidence of the documentary contents.[153] For the reasons already adumbrated, however, it makes no sense to interpret this provision of the federal rules as conferring authority on jurors to monitor Keynesian weight per se, which itself has no discernible bearing on the degree of discriminatory power. Because the jury's nominal role extends only to assessing discriminatory power, the jury may need to be informed of the limitation.[154] In subsequent paragraphs I will address how problematic such spoliation inferences can be, even when they do not arise in the context of an admissibility rule, and how tempting, even natural, it can be for jurors to want to address the matter of Keynesian weight. Because of this, there is a considerable risk that these distinct ideas will get jumbled up in the jury's consideration, and limiting instructions may not be an adequate solution.[155]

Less problematic, but more subtle, is the significance of evidentiary "gaps." Jurors may rationally and legitimately alter their assessments of discriminatory power as a result of such gaps in the evidence. For

---

[152] Fed. R. Evid. 104(e).
[153] This is the standard result. See, e.g., United States v. Jacobs, 475 F.2d 270, 284–6 (2d Cir. 1973) and United States v. Culberson, 2007 WL 1266131 (E.D. Mich. 2007).
[154] See, e.g., Fed. R. Evid. 105.
[155] I have argued at length that a broad category of evidence – evidence of tampering with evidence – generally should not be admissible because of the risk of confusing the jury as to its role in monitoring Keynesian weight and the risk that the jury will reach an inferior answer that conflicts with that of the trial judge. Instead, stronger judge-administered remedies, including issue preclusion, should be used against those who engage in evidence tampering. See Nance (2010).

example, suppose that a jury would be prepared to make an assessment that $O(C|E) > O^*$ but then learns that the claimant has rested his or her case without presenting a witness on an important matter, one that up to that point the jury expected to be covered by testimony. The jury might then reduce its assessment such that $O(C|E) < O^*$. This does not necessarily entail a judgment that Keynesian weight is inadequate; it might simply reflect a judgment that the absence of certain evidence is, to some degree, incompatible with the truth of the claim so that the gap affects the value of $O(C|E)$. The jury need have made no judgment that some witness *ought to have been presented*; the witness the jury expected may never even have existed. A similar, but even more subtle problem, arises when what is omitted is testimony from a specific witness that the jury would expect to hear if the claim were true but not if the claim were false. The underlying point remains this: even a case that is thoroughly investigated, one in which nothing of significance that is admissible is kept from the jury – that is, a case with practically optimized Keynesian weight – can be a case that has not been proved by the requisite standard for discriminatory power.[156]

An important application of this distinction arises from evidence that is sought by investigators because it might be relevant but that turns out not to be. An earlier illustration is apt. When first explaining the concept of Keynesian weight (§ 3.2), I posed the example of a test (one of forensic science or even one of taking lay testimony) that one conducts to see if it will affect discriminatory power. I noted that a case can arise in which the test result is unhelpful. Thus a forensics test might yield no useful information, or a percipient witness who is deposed might be prepared to testify that he was not looking at the crucial moment and cannot address from personal knowledge the issue of importance in the case. The evidence derived from these tests is arguably irrelevant under the conventional criterion (see § 4.1.1), but conducting these tests was nonetheless useful. The question is posed whether the jury needs to know about such apparently irrelevant results of the inquiry. The argument is that the jury needs to know that such leads have been pursued.[157] As explained earlier, the jury may need to know that the inquiry yielded nothing valuable when, without such information, they might plausibly infer that the absence of such evidence

---

[156] Such considerations can even be encouraged by practices (and instructions) telling the jury to assume that were such evidence reasonably available to be presented, it would have been. That is, in assessing discriminatory power, the jury would be entitled to assume that potential evidence that was not presented was not reasonably available to be presented. See id. at 1118–24.

[157] See generally Saltzburg (1978b).

reflects on discriminatory power. When, however, the absence of such evidence is *neutral* as regards discriminatory power and the only significance of the absence of the evidence is that it indicates a possible deficiency in Keynesian weight, it still may be necessary to inform the jury about the unhelpful results of the inquiry if the jury might otherwise impose a sanction of some kind (e.g., raising or lowering O^*) against a party perceived to be responsible for the failure, the result of the jury's taking on a de facto role in assessing Keynesian weight.

The sometimes subtle nature of the roles of the juridical actors thus tends to obscure the question about how the responsibility for the assessment of Keynesian weight should be assigned. Indeed, a further complexity arises from the fact that, on occasion, the task of monitoring parties in this regard does seem to be assigned – or, more accurately, *shared* – with the jury. This occurs, though not obviously so, when recourse is made to so-called missing-witness or missing-evidence arguments by counsel, often supported by jury instructions authorizing the jury to draw inferences from a party's failure to present evidence. Although details vary, the following jury instruction is representative:

> If a party fails to produce evidence that is under that party's control and reasonably available to that party and not reasonably available to the adverse party, then you may infer that the evidence is unfavorable to the party who could have produced it and did not.[158]

There are many things to say about this sort of device. I have written at length about the matter elsewhere.[159] Suffice it here to make the following observations: first, when jurors take missing evidence into account pursuant to such instructions, ostensibly they are still assessing the discriminatory power of the evidence before them. That evidence permits an inference that certain (other) evidence has been withheld or suppressed under specified conditions. It is *this* inference – as distinguished from the *absence* of the other evidence *vel non* – that they are incorporating into their assessment of discriminatory power.[160] They are not assessing Keynesian weight as a distinct requirement, or rather, they are not *supposed* to be doing so. Moreover, using this inference to assess discriminatory power can be a plausible response to evidence suppression only in certain kinds of cases. For example, if exclusive control of the potential evidence cannot be attributed to just one side of the dispute, then the preceding instruction

---

[158] 3 O'Malley et al. (2006) § 104.26.
[159] See Nance (2010).
[160] See Kaye (1986).

is silent, even though this does not necessarily mean that Keynesian weight has been practically optimized.[161] Thus some kind of legal response may be needed in contexts where the missing-evidence inference, whether or not supported by a jury instruction, is an inapt tool.

Second, even when the conditions are such that the jury reasonably can take the circumstances attending the absence of evidence into account in assessing discriminatory power of the evidence as a whole, doing so is almost always an inferior substitute for augmenting the evidence package. In other words, it is better to get the missing evidence before the court, when this is possible, so that the jury can assess it than for the jury merely to try to draw inferences about the significance of its omission. The latter is inherently more speculative than the former, and while speculative inferences cannot be entirely eliminated from trials, it is certainly a good idea to reduce the degree of speculation to a minimum.[162]

From these two points arises a third. Jurors in many such cases probably do something quite different from what is theoretically prescribed, something that is, in a sense, entirely natural but is nonetheless not role appropriate: rather than confining themselves to assessments of the discriminatory power of the evidence and what the circumstances causing an omission of evidence tell them about that, they are probably penalizing a litigant for what the jury sees as a failure by the litigant to be forthcoming with evidence. Indeed, given the problems noted earlier that are inherent in the jury's use of the absence of evidence to assess discriminatory power, it has been argued cogently that the only truly viable rationale for the continued use of missing-evidence instructions is to encourage parties to present (or punish them for not presenting) the missing evidence.[163] This, when it occurs, is a genuine monitoring of Keynesian weight and, effectively, an after-the-fact imposition, by the jury, of a burden of production.

---

[161] Under modern conditions of litigation, the requirement of differential access stated in the quoted instruction is rarely met because the party requesting the instruction generally has available techniques – the use of discovery, the calling of adverse witnesses subject to impeachment, and so forth – to get the missing evidence before the jury. And some forms of the instruction, which authorize an inference *against the party who would be expected to be favored* by the evidence, if presented, are rendered completely useless: any adverse inference against one side for failure to present evidence is then offset by a comparable adverse inference against the moving party for failure to use these devices to get the evidence before the court. As a result, there is a laudable trend in the case law to eliminate the use of such adverse inferences except perhaps in the rare cases where one side has truly *exclusive* access to the missing evidence. See Nance (2010) at 1094–6.

[162] See Nance (1998) at 634–5.

[163] See Livermore (1984) at 28–9, 40.

Once again, there are cogent reasons to think that this task is not well suited to juries, even if it were a legitimate part of their nominal role.[164] Judges have a distinct comparative advantage in their understanding of the dynamics (the rules, economics, and behavioral norms) of litigation and are therefore in a much better position to assess the arguments that will be made by parties in defense of their choices about evidence preparation and selection. They are also in a better position to give parties reminders of their duties early enough in the process that parties can react. For the most part, juries' responses come in opaque verdicts, after which the parties can do very little. These are undoubtedly important reasons that management of the various rules, mentioned earlier, for the regulation of parties' evidence gathering and presentation is almost exclusively vested in the judiciary, not juries. It may be added here that when a jury does get involved in the regulation of Keynesian weight, there is a risk of wasteful duplication of effort, as well as a risk that the jury will impose an implicit sanction on top of (or in contradiction to) whatever sanction the court has seen fit to impose. Indeed, the jury may do so in substantial ignorance of the efforts the legal system employs to ensure optimization of Keynesian weight. To avoid such redundancy and lack of integration, the jury would have to be educated about the rules and practices of litigation, an education that could be quite difficult to provide and both costly and distracting in the courtroom setting.[165] And even if this education can be suitably provided, there is the risk that the jury will contradict the considered judgment of legal actors, the judiciary, who are better situated to make such judgments.[166]

Judges are not insensitive to this dilemma. Sometimes courts simply choose to avoid the use of missing-evidence instructions by selecting one of the doctrinal tools, discussed in the preceding section, that do not involve the jury. But such jury involvement has a long history, dating

---

[164] Nance (2010) at 1103–9.

[165] In some respects, it would be impossible because trial judges have access to information that would not be admissible before to the jury. See Fed. R. Evid. 104(a) (specifying that in determining preliminary questions, the trial judge is limited only by rules of privilege).

[166] There are many analogous legal and nonlegal problems in which one better-situated person or official is called on to coordinate responses, leading to the foreclosure of responses by others. See, e.g., Crosby v. National Foreign Trade Council, 530 U.S. 363 (2000) (holding that the federal response to abuses in Myanmar must preempt a Massachusetts ban on state entities doing business with companies that do business in Myanmar because of conflicts between the federal and state responses and resulting interference with the ability of the president to coordinate a national message).

from times when there were fewer judicial options, and legal inertia helps to keep them in play. As a result, judges often have sought means for handling the tension while retaining the practice of submitting the issue to the jury for consideration. For example, in some jurisdictions, a party must seek permission from the court before inviting the jury to make an adverse inference from missing evidence, and the court is effectively required to rule on many of the very issues that are to be submitted to the jury before the instruction is allowed.[167] And in most or all jurisdictions, the judiciary has found it necessary to develop a complex body of law on the question of whether to allow a party to invite the inference.[168] This is just what one would expect from the fact that the sanction of giving such an instruction (or simply allowing parties to suggest such an inference by the jury) is being used to set and enforce policy regarding trial preparation. And this is why it is best to describe the jury's involvement in monitoring Keynesian weight by way of such adverse inferences, when it happens, as one that is shared with the judiciary.[169]

Cases involving the apparent destruction of evidence, in situations where the informational content thereof cannot be reconstructed, pose special problems, for then second best may be all that one can get. However, the question remains: what is second best? Ought the law to focus on the fact that such destruction may itself give rise to discriminatory power, an inference from the spoliation conduct? Or ought the law to focus instead on the damage done to the fact-finding process and impose an appropriate, judicially administered sanction? Before the advent of modern discovery rules, traditional practice tended toward the former, whereas now conventional practice represents something of a transition. A court's response depends on certain fortuities, including whether the conduct occurs in a way that brings it within the scope of extant discovery sanctions or admissibility rules that impose exclusion as a sanction for destruction, and appellate courts recognize a substantial degree of trial court discretion, the

---

[167] See, e.g., United States v. Martin, 696 F.2d 49, 52 (6th Cir. 1983) and Simmons v. United States, 444 A.2d 962, 963–4 (D.C. 1982).

[168] See Stier (1985) at 145–51.

[169] One may speculate that judges continue to choose to share the responsibility with juries for much the same reason that, as a historical matter, juries were employed to decide cases at all: to diffuse responsibility away from the judiciary. See Whitman (2008) at 125–57. Whether this is accurate as an explanation of the practice of such sharing is, of course, quite distinct from the question of whether such an explanation provides anything like a justification.

exercise of which is rarely reversed. In this "breathing space," the inertia in the system often continues to embrace the idea of submitting the matter to juries, sometimes with an instruction such as the following:

> If you should find that a party willfully [*suppressed*] [*hid*] [*destroyed*] evidence in order to prevent its being presented in this trial, you may consider such [*suppression*] [*hiding*] [*destruction*] in determining what inferences to draw from the evidence or facts in the case.[170]

While the case is somewhat harder to make in this context, there are still many reasons to think that an argument for an adverse inference by the jury, whether or not supported by such an instruction, is inferior to judicially administered sanctions. Putting aside the possibility of destroying evidence with entirely benign purposes, such as conserving storage space, inferences from intentional suppression of evidence are not as straightforward as one might think. In particular, just because someone is in the right on the merits does not mean that he will perceive that he can win the litigation without cheating. In many, perhaps most such cases, evidence tampering says more about the character of the tamperer than it says about the underlying merits of the dispute.[171] As the revisers of McCormick's treatise put it:

> A question may well be raised whether the relatively modest probative value of this species of evidence is not often outweighed by its prejudicial aspects. The litigant who would not like to have a stronger case must indeed be a rarity. It may well be that the real underpinning of the rule of admissibility is a desire to impose swift punishment, with a certain poetic justice, rather than concern over the niceties of proof.[172]

This involves the jury stepping out of its usual role, perhaps with a wink and a nod from the judge, to impose sanctions for a party's failure to present evidence that would, if presented, help to optimize Keynesian weight. And it involves the jury in the consideration of distracting questions, distinct from the merits, that are often deeply enmeshed in the law and the economics of trial preparation. Some courts today choose, I think wisely,

---

[170] 3 O'Malley et al. (2006) § 104.27.
[171] The potential for prejudicial reaction from the fact-finder may well be greater in the context of evidence tampering than it is in the context of typical "bad acts" evidence governed by the character-evidence prohibition (e.g., Fed. R. Evid. 404). In the usual context of bad acts, the actor's alleged misconduct breaches a duty owed to some private person; evidence tampering involves a breach of duty owed the tribunal, especially the jury, whose task it is to reconstruct past events. One may well expect the jury to react to such an affront.
[172] 2 McCormick (2013) § 265 at 328.

to avoid this by selecting one of the other available doctrinal tools that authorize judicially imposed sanctions.[173]

In the final analysis, while it is not inconceivable to allow the jury to monitor the adequacy of Keynesian weight, doing so involves a significant distortion in the usual understanding of the jury's role. More important, it places on the jury a responsibility for the discharge of which it is poorly equipped, and it requires the development of complex mechanisms for monitoring the monitor. It is, to put it simply, an inferior way to deal with the problem, one that should be avoided whenever possible. However, even if one is not convinced by this last claim, one still should acknowledge that the monitoring and control of Keynesian weight in our adversarial system of adjudication are tasks not generally assigned to the jury. It requires an affirmative argument to explain why in a particular context they should be.

The best candidate for such an argument is the critical role of the jury in criminal cases. We understand that one aspect of the jury's role is to serve as a protective shield between the state and the accused, and it may seem disconcerting to accept the idea that any part of that protection should be ceded entirely to the trial judge, at least when that part concerns the "adequacy" (in a broad sense) of the evidence to support a conviction. The modern judiciary may have many doctrinal tools at its disposal with which to insist on the practical optimization of Keynesian weight, but can we be content to assume that these tools will be used effectively? If not, ought the jury retain some backup role in assessing Keynesian weight?

Two situations must be distinguished here. First, the jury might be allowed to punish the prosecution (or the state more generally) for inadequately performing its duties. To be clear, what is suggested by this argument is that even if the jury accepts that criterion (2.2) – or whatever alternative criterion of discriminatory power is considered appropriate – *has been satisfied*, the jury should retain the option of acquitting the accused precisely because (1) the jury believes that the case has not been adequately investigated (or at least that the results of those investigations have not been communicated to the jury) and (2) the responsibility for this failure lies with the prosecution. It is, in other words, a free-floating authority to sanction the prosecution for poor investigational performance *without regard* to the guilt or innocence of the accused.

---

[173] See, e.g., Telectron, Inc. v. Overhead Door Corp. 116 F.R.D. 107 (S.D. Fla. 1987) (imposing default judgment for defendant's destruction of evidence and discussing and rejecting the alternative of presenting the evidence of destruction to the jury). See generally Nance (2010) at 1099–1115.

The wisdom of according such a role to the jury depends on the degree of one's confidence that the judiciary will perform its role. If the judiciary takes its responsibilities seriously in this regard – and there is no reason to think that it would not do so, especially given proper signals from the lawmaking authority – the need for such a recourse role in the jury diminishes. In previous generations, the jury's role may have been inevitable because the tools available to judges to monitor Keynesian weight were so much less extensive. Discovery was less well developed, as of course were the sanctions that are now used to enforce discovery.[174] The tools are in place today, and it is now largely a matter of judicial will to overcome an inertial reliance on juries to perform some continuing portion of the task of monitoring Keynesian weight that is rightly the judiciary's responsibility. If this will can be mustered as a general proposition, then it should suffice for the jury to retain its power of nullification, with which to handle the occasionally deficient supervisory performance by a trial judge.[175]

The second category of cases assumes that the responsibility is rightly placed on the accused for the want of evidence. Here there may be supervening reasons not to allow the judiciary to enforce any such responsibility. Specifically, to protect the right to jury trial, the court may not direct a verdict for the prosecution as a sanction, and no weaker judge-imposed sanctions may be applicable or effective in the context. This leaves the jury, once again, to impose conviction as a punishment for the failure of the accused to cure defects in Keynesian weight, even though the burden of persuasion *has not been satisfied*. This is an even harder case to make. We are to imagine a jury convicting the accused *not* because it believes the defendant's guilt has been shown beyond reasonable doubt but because the accused has withheld or destroyed evidence that might have generated such proof beyond reasonable doubt. Such a verdict probably would violate existing constitutional requirements that the guilt of accused be proved beyond reasonable doubt. I will return to the solution of this problem in the next section.

We may acknowledge begrudgingly that some divergence from the basic delineation of responsibility is necessary, but this leaves intact an important general principle: ordinarily, it is for judges to monitor Keynesian weight but not discriminatory power, just as, ordinarily, it is for juries to assess discriminatory power but not Keynesian weight. To be

---

[174] See Nance (2010) at 1144–5.
[175] On jury nullification as a recourse role, see Kadish & Kadish (1973) at 37–72. Of course, to perform this role, the jury will somehow have to become aware of the prosecution's default.

sure, the arguments for this delineation are less powerful in the context of a bench trial, with the trial judge wearing both the law-articulating and fact-deciding hats, and in such contexts, it is more understandable that the lines would get blurred. Still, the delineation makes sense even then. After all, an important part of monitoring Keynesian weight is the ability of the monitor to signal to parties the need to augment the evidence package and to do so at a time that makes it possible for parties to react, especially in the context of close calls about the need for the evidence. As is explained more fully in the following section, this also may require a dialogue with the parties regarding the comparative cost conditions associated with producing the missing evidence. It is very difficult for the judge in a bench trial to do this sort of thing if the signal appears *only* as a ruling on the merits for one party or the other, even if the reason for the ruling is explained in the judgment.

4.3 Allocating Responsibility for Curing Deficiencies in Keynesian Weight

To complete the discussion, we must address the question of which juridical actor has responsibility for curing identified deficiencies in Keynesian weight. In the inquisitorial systems of adjudication, responsibility for conducting investigation of the case falls primarily on the investigating magistrate. In adversarial systems, however, this responsibility is obviously placed primarily on the litigants.[176] How this responsibility is allocated among the parties in connection with identifiable doctrinal tools for curing Keynesian weight deficiencies depends on which tool is used. For example, exclusionary rules place the burden on the proponent of evidence that is excluded in preference for other evidence of greater weight (or, at least, greater weight when taken in conjunction with the originally proffered evidence). This simple but important point illustrates something that tends to be obscured by debates about the role of Keynesian weight in the burden of proof. There is no particular reason to take a deficiency in Keynesian weight as always counting against the party bearing the burden of persuasion on the ultimate issue to which the missing evidence likely would relate.

---

[176] See Wigmore (1981) § 2483. Of course, the trial judge in common-law courts has authority to call witnesses, including experts. Id. § 2484. How extensively these powers may be used without undermining the essentially adversarial nature of the proceedings is a matter of debate. See, e.g., Saltzburg (1978a).

Yet this is the unstated assumption of the approach taken by those who think Keynesian weight needs to be assessed by jurors as a routine matter, even if this is subject to a "reasonableness" review by the court. They reason (sometimes implicitly) that when a weight requirement has not been met, the burden of proof has not been met, and because the burden of proof has not been met, the party bearing the burden of proof must lose.[177] Indeed, it seems quite odd to say, in the typical case in which the plaintiff bears the burden of persuasion, that the burden of proof has not been met, but the verdict will be *for the plaintiff*. Once again, though, the matter looks quite different once one separates the two kinds of evidential weight. As to discriminatory power of the evidence, the failure to achieve the proper margin must count against the party with the burden of persuasion. As to Keynesian weight, however, the matter is more complex.

Also informative in this regard is use of the missing-evidence jury instructions. Insofar as such jury instructions are used to monitor Keynesian weight, their use illustrates that a deficiency in Keynesian weight – one that is not handled by an appropriate pretrial measure or exclusionary rule – should count against the party on whom the burden of presenting such additional evidence is properly placed at trial. This choice implicates complex considerations regarding the parties' comparative access to potential evidence. In fact, the rules with regard to the use of adverse inference arguments or instructions generally require that they be imposed on the party with superior or exclusive access to the missing evidence, not necessarily on the party bearing the relevant burden of persuasion.[178]

Whether enforced by missing-evidence instructions or – what I have argued is the generally better approach – by the direct imposition of a burden of production by the court, the exact answer, or rather set of answers, to this allocation question is certainly debatable. I will merely summarize here the results I have articulated in previous work on the question.[179] These results reflect the symmetry of civil parties, each being entitled to equal respect and concern, and the asymmetry of the parties in a criminal case, where there is a special concern to protect the accused from potential oppression by the state, with its comparative abundance of investigational resources. But I also emphasize that the stated results are merely principles or rules of thumb to guide the exercise of judicial decision. Factors not

---

[177] See, e.g., Brilmayer (1986) at 684–5 and Friedman (1996) at 1819.
[178] See supra § 4.2.
[179] See generally Nance (1988, 2010).

considered here might supervene to create a powerful argument inconsistent with the stated results.

Consider first the situation of available evidence that has not been presented but that the court concludes should be presented, and as to which the court determines that it is inappropriate for such evidence to be elicited from witnesses called by the court. In civil cases, the burden ordinarily should be placed on the party for whom the costs of production would be lowest and manageable, given the party's circumstances. This "least-cost provider" principle runs through much of the doctrine regarding missing-evidence instructions and thus reflects judicial intuition. It also reflects that it is reasonable to treat civil parties equally in the sense that each is allowed to avoid the burden if the opponent is better situated to bear it. The status of parties as "repeat players" is not unimportant here because a party who can be expected to be involved in repeated litigation on the same or similar issues can spread some of the costs of evidence production over the long run of cases. In any event, only when the evidence is reasonably accessible to both parties and at roughly equivalent cost, or at least when the court has no grounds to believe otherwise, would the burden be placed on the party bearing the burden of persuasion as a tie-breaking default rule.[180]

---

[180] It has been argued that judges could save on presentation costs by allocating the burden to that party who probably will lose if the evidence is produced. This game-theoretic approach would have the judge attempt to predict who will be favored by the (as yet unpresented) evidence and use this datum to avoid (at least in some cases) the necessity of presentation costs by the court's allocation of the burden. See Hay & Spier (1997) (arguing that courts can and do allocate the burden of production – what they call the "burden of proof" – so as to limit the expected costs of resolving a dispute; modifying the least-cost-provider criterion by incorporating a factor reflecting the judge's assessment of the strength of the evidence already before the court, which the authors implicitly assume will correlate with the probative value of the yet to be produced evidence). The key idea is that if the burdened party knows that presenting evidence will ensure his or her opponent's victory, then the burdened party will simply quit and avoid the presentation costs. See also Hay (1977) (extending the result to contexts in which the parties are uncertain about how favorable the evidence will be). Hay and Spier's theory was constructed to address the question of the initial allocation of the burden of production of the entire mass of (unspecified) evidence related to a cause of action, but it could be applied to the allocation of the burden with respect to a particular item of evidence identified as missing during a trial. In this context, however, it is unlikely often to be the case that either party will refuse, especially midtrial, to present identified evidence and thus incur a certain loss rather than present that evidence (at relatively minor cost), even if it is likely unfavorable, and thereby retain at least the chance of winning. In the unusual case where the cost of presenting a given item of evidence is very large, but not so large as to preclude the court from imposing a burden, it might be possible to improve on the simple least-cost-provider criterion in the manner indicated by their model.

Criminal cases are different in that the burden of producing evidence ought not to be placed on the defense unless the defense has *exclusive* access to the evidence. This is a practical determination, however, one not based only on formalities such as the reach of the subpoena power but also on a consideration of the influence that only the accused can exert to bring evidence to the court. (Think about a case in which the crucial eyewitness is a relative of the accused and has left the country but is known to be in contact with the accused or a case in which the accused refuses to identify the witness or otherwise provide information that would permit the prosecution to obtain the witness's testimony.[181]) Still, in the great bulk of cases, this standard will mean that the burden of curing deficiencies in Keynesian weight will fall on the prosecution, a result that reflects the asymmetry between the parties and their investigative resources.

The second category of cases (civil or criminal) involves irreversible evidence suppression, such as the destruction of an irreplaceable document or the murder of a witness. In such cases, by assumption, the evidence cannot be reasonably obtained for use in the present trial, and the only consideration is how to respond to this fact.[182] Rejecting the use of missing-evidence instructions for the reasons articulated in the preceding section, the better approach is to impose the burden of production on the party responsible for the destruction and on comparative-fault principles if both parties share in the loss. Again, the burden should fall on the party bearing the burden of persuasion as a default rule only when the parties are equally at fault in the loss. Of course, this "burden of production" usually will amount to a partial directed verdict for the nonburdened party, at least if the court is correct in its determination that the evidence is not reasonably available. But it does not necessarily entail such a result, because the burdened party might suddenly "discover" that the evidence can be produced after all, if, for example, the alternative is surely losing the case.

As indicated at the end of the preceding section, criminal cases pose a special problem when the circumstances indicate that the accused is in exclusive control of the missing evidence or when the accused has destroyed evidence the probative value of which cannot be replicated. In such cases, the burden of producing evidence that would otherwise be thought necessary to optimize Keynesian weight, at least in the long run of cases, obviously should not be placed on the prosecution, even with regard

---

[181] Illustrative case law is discussed in Nance (2010) at 1140–1.

[182] We are not here considering the situation in which the act of suppression is itself a crime being prosecuted.

to proof of the prosecution's prima facie case. However, vesting authority in the judiciary to take preemptive action against the accused, if such action rises to the level of granting judgment against the accused, might well be viewed as too great a threat the right of the accused to a jury trial.[183]

In such a context, we are confronted with a difficult choice. We can either create an exception to the otherwise applicable weight-optimizing rules, permitting the case to be decided on what is believed by the court to be less than optimal Keynesian weight, or we can permit the jury to have a role in enforcing a distinct Keynesian weight requirement. The former solution would involve permitting the jury to consider evidence that the accused has suppressed evidence only insofar as that act relates to the likelihood of the guilt of the accused, that is, only insofar as the act of suppression affects the discriminatory power of the evidence as a whole because of inferences as to the motive for the suppression. If no such plausible inference can be drawn because the act of suppression was not an effort to hide evidence, the jury would not be allowed to hear about the missing evidence, however grievous the defendant's conduct in regard to it.[184] The

[183] Affirmative defenses would pose a somewhat different question. Trial judges already make preemptive rulings against the accused on affirmative defenses by way of their decision whether or not the evidence supports giving a jury instruction relating to the purported affirmative defense. The initial burden of production of evidence on such issues constitutionally may be placed on the accused. See, e.g., United States v. Bailey, 444 U.S. 394 (1980). Extending this practice to the monitoring of Keynesian weight – allowing the court to refuse to give such an instruction when important evidence related thereto is in the exclusive control of the defense or has been destroyed in bad faith by the accused – would seem to present no additional difficulties, constitutional or otherwise. It may be better policy, however, to employ such rulings only when the accused controls the evidence and thus can reverse his or her decision to withhold it.

[184] A different question is presented when the issue is whether the prosecution should be allowed to present secondary forms of evidence as to which the evidence rendered unavailable by the accused would ordinarily be preferred. For example, if the defendant has killed a witness, that witness's hearsay statements should be admissible, even if the killing was not done with an intent to suppress evidence, because the preference expressed by the hearsay rule is rendered pointless by the death of the declarant (§ 3.3). To be sure, this does not quite match current law. Unless the hearsay falls within another specific exception, such as that for dying declarations, the death of the declarant at the hands of the accused results in a "forfeiture" of the hearsay objection only under a limiting condition. See Fed. R. Evid. 804(b)(6) (requiring, as a condition on admitting hearsay from a declarant rendered unavailable by the accused, that the accused have killed the witness with the intent to cause the witness's unavailability). See also Giles v. California, 554 U.S. 353 (2008) (unfortunately constitutionalizing this "intent" criterion as part of the Confrontation Clause). However, the suggested rule does obtain in the context of the preference for the original of a document. See Fed. R. Evid. 1004 (requiring, as a condition on admitting secondary evidence of the contents of a document, only that the original was destroyed under circumstances not involving the bad faith of the *proponent*).

latter solution would permit the jury to use evidence of such conduct by the defense not only to adjust its odds of guilt but also (in effect) to adjust the critical value of the odds necessary to warrant a conviction, for example, by way of an ad hoc reduction in the magnitude of disutility attributable to a false positive $D_{(+)}$. Either solution may require some educating of the jury about the means of legal access to missing evidence, but such may be the price of protecting the constitutional rights of the accused. On balance, I think that the former solution is better, even if it is not constitutionally mandated, because it helps to allow the jury to focus on the factual question of the guilt of the accused for the alleged crime. This would leave the state to its independent remedies against the accused, if any, for acts of evidence suppression.

If the law is to be more systematic in its treatment of Keynesian weight, questions will arise about timing. When the tool of choice is an admissibility rule or a discovery sanction, the timing is largely within the control of the parties. When evidence subject to such a admissibility rule is offered, the court responds, at least on objection by an opponent, and when a motion for discovery sanctions is presented, again the court will respond. (In both contexts, the court can postpone a decision at least for a time.) But insofar as the burden of production is used for this purpose, the matter is not quite so obvious. I have advanced the view that the burden of production should be understood to have two components, one testing whether a reasonable jury could conclude in favor of the burdened party with respect to the criterion of the burden of persuasion (e.g., whether $O(C|E) > O^*$), and the other testing whether the Keynesian weight of the evidence has been practically optimized. But there is no necessity that these two tests be conducted at the same time, and there is reason to think they should not be. In the usual case, the first component is tested at the end of the claimant's case on a motion by the defendant and again (at least in civil cases) at the end of the defense case on a motion by the claimant. Because the second component of the burden of production – that which addresses Keynesian weight – often requires an assessment of the total body of evidence the parties would otherwise present, the anticipated contribution and costs of potential evidence, and the differential access of the parties to such evidence, it would make sense to have this component of the burden tested as to both parties simultaneously, either at a pretrial hearing at which the evidence to be presented is assayed or at the close of the trial or both. In particular, if the matter is not resolved pretrial, ordinarily there will be little need to address the question of whether the claimant should be required to present some missing evidence (not addressed by an admissibility rule) until it becomes clear that the defense will not present it during its case. This is not the only conceivable solution, and there may be special situations in which it is clear at other stages of the proceedings that a particular party should be responsible to augment Keynesian weight.

Finally, it should be mentioned that greater tailoring of the production burden can be obtained by separating the matter of investigation and presentation from the question of how the costs thereof are allocated. The usual assumption is that when the burden to present evidence is placed on one party, that party will bear the costs associated with the investigation and presentation of the evidence that is required. This is surely a sound general principle, but it admits of possible modification. The most obvious possibility is the situation in which the evidence that is needed is not peculiarly available to either party. While it may be appropriate to allocate the burden in such cases in accordance with the default rule – placing the burden on the party bearing the burden of persuasion – this does not necessarily mean that the costs should be borne exclusively by that party. One could easily endorse splitting the costs as long as there is no serious risk of creating adverse incentives for the investigating party to escalate such costs. Once recognized, though, there is no reason that such cost splitting must be limited to such cases. It could be applied to any burden imposed by the court with regard to that component of the burden of production that relates to the practical optimization of Keynesian weight, at least for civil cases.[185]

4.4 Final Observations

The practical optimization of Keynesian weight, under a preferential structure that requires only that which can reasonably be presented by the parties, should be, and already is, a principal task of the judiciary, even in adversarial proceedings. To the extent that Keynesian weight is rightly addressed as a component of the burden of proof, it is not as part of the burden of persuasion that is applied by the jury but rather as part of the burden of production that is ordinarily and rightly applied by the court. Sometimes this will be done indirectly, by the application of sanctions or exclusionary rules in particular contexts; sometimes is will be done by the

---

[185] See, e.g., Fed. R. Evid. 706(b) (providing for compensation for court-appointed experts to be paid "from funds which may be provided by law in criminal cases and civil actions and proceedings involving just compensation under the fifth amendment" and, in other civil actions, for such compensation to be "paid by the parties in such proportion and at such time as the court directs, and thereafter charged in like manner as other costs.")

application of a general standard regarding the adequacy of the evidence as a whole to be submitted to the fact-finder for determination under the standard of proof.

One important implication is that the judiciary should be mindful to take steps to prevent the jury from making a distinct, possibly redundant or inconsistent, often poorly informed assessment of Keynesian weight, for the jury will be tempted to do so as part of the natural decision-making process that unitary decision makers would engage. This artificiality is a by-product of separating the roles of fact-finder and trial administrator. But it can be navigated effectively by the use of jury instructions such as the following:

> [Y]ou may take it for granted that all of the available evidence material and favorable to either side has been placed before you by one side or the other, so that you ... are as well informed and in as good a position to decide the case correctly as any jury could be.[186]

Such an instruction makes sense, however, only if its presupposition is true, that is, if the judiciary well implements its duty to ensure that the jury is properly informed. In implementing their regulatory control in this regard, using the panoply of rules discussed earlier, judges should be, and generally are, mindful of the procedures and practical realities of litigation and parties' comparative access to information. These realities are critically important in deciding the question of which party should, at any given point in a trial, bear any requirement that Keynesian weight be augmented.

---

[186] Stocker v. Boston & Me. R.R., 151 A. 457–8 (N.H. 1930).

5

Tenacity of Belief

An Idea in Search of a Use

> [I]n matters of probability, 'tis not in every case we can be sure, that we have all the Particulars before us, that any way concern the Question; and that there is no evidence behind, and yet unseen, which may cast the Probability on the other side, and out-weigh all, that at present seems to preponderate with us.
>
> – John Locke (c. 1690)[1]

I have articulated a two-part theory of the burden of proof, applicable in all conventional forms of trial, whether inquisitorial or adversarial: (1) it is the duty of the court to ensure, through a variety of procedural devices, that the evidence is reasonably complete, that is, that Keynesian weight has been practically optimized, and (2) it is the duty of the fact-finder to determine whether the admissible evidence, assessed in its appropriate context, satisfies a threshold criterion of epistemic warrant, one that is determined by a public assessment of the relative benefits and costs of accurate and inaccurate verdicts. Ordinarily, the fact-finder's determination does *not* involve assessing Keynesian weight or the relative completeness of the evidence. Several scholars have suggested that a third idea is important in knowing whether the burden of proof has been satisfied. This idea is often expressed as "tenacity of belief." There are several versions of this idea; it would be more accurate to say that it is a family of related ideas. In this book, I cannot examine every permutation of the idea that is available, but I will try to identify significant contributions along this line sufficient in number and variety to make clear their relatedness. I will argue that, provided that one takes appropriate account of discriminatory power and Keynesian weight, the idea of tenacity of belief is, in the end, a false lead. Whatever it has to contribute to our understanding of burdens of proof is already embedded in the ideas of discriminatory power and Keynesian weight.

"Tenacity of belief" refers to the degree of resistance a person has to giving up the belief. As with discriminatory power and Keynesian

---

[1] Locke (1690) at 659.

weight, tenacity of belief is a gradational attribute associated with a person's epistemic assessments. It can be applied to beliefs that are conceived as gradational or to beliefs that are conceived as categorical. In the decision-theoretic model presented in Chapter 2, we have a relatively clear and coherent example of how to think about dichotomous legal decisions (liable/not liable) in terms of a requirement that a gradational notion of belief exceed some critical threshold. I have argued that the proper way to think about the decision criterion (2.2′) is to understand that it involves a comparison between epistemic probability (as assessed by the fact-finder) and a critical probability (determined in the first instance by public authority but probably subject to some case-specific tailoring by the fact-finder) and the announcement of the categorical acceptance (or rejection) of a belief in the claim, at least for the purposes of adjudicative finality, based on the result of that comparison (§ 2.2). As stated there, the odds version, criterion (2.2), is more intuitively understandable. But because resilience has been discussed in terms of probabilities rather than odds, in this chapter, I work with the probability version throughout. The question is thus presented: where does tenacity of belief fit within this scheme? Does it fit at all? If not, does it add something of value to the model already presented? To be sure, I have not unequivocally endorsed any particular theory of discriminatory power, and the real issue to be addressed here is the relationship between Keynesian weight and tenacity of belief or, to put the matter differently, the value of tenacity of belief as a desideratum separate from the practical optimization of Keynesian weight.

My conclusion, which will be made clear in what follows, is that tenacity of belief adds very little, if anything, to the foregoing account. As a consequence, the presentation of this chapter is structurally rather different from that of the previous three: here my argument is more thoroughly "parry and thrust," in which I present exemplars of theories that place emphasis on tenacity of belief only to explain why they provide little help. The reader who has followed the arguments so far will probably be able to anticipate some of the counterarguments I present. Nevertheless, I think that this discussion contributes by giving further definition to the theory that has been presented. And I will present, along the way, some additional insights not developed in previous chapters.

To the extent that decision is built on a probability assessment, as is true under the decision-theoretic model that generates criterion (2.2′), the most obvious way to understand the idea of tenacity of belief is to interpret it as referring to the resilience of one's probability assessments.

Several scholars have taken this approach. Hence this chapter begins by considering the relationship between Keynesian weight and the resilience of one's probability assessments (§ 5.1). It then proceeds to examine, more abstractly, the question whether, given a practical optimization of Keynesian weight, a requirement of resiliency serves any useful purpose (§ 5.2). The chapter concludes with an examination of the claim that the law's standards relate to the fact-finder's categorical beliefs rather than partial beliefs, with resilience being the variable that is indexed by the standards of proof (§ 5.3).

5.1 The Relationship between Keynesian Weight and Resilience of Probability

Intuitively, we believe that increasing the relevant evidence we consider increases the accuracy of our judgments. At the same time, as Keynes pointed out, it is possible to increase the relevant evidence considered without even changing the probability assessed; in such a case, the weight of the evidence has changed, but the probability assessment has not.[2] Consequently, if there is something to our intuition, the relationship between Keynesian weight and accuracy is subtle. Echoing the analyses of second-order uncertainty by nonlawyers, it has been argued by some that an increase in (what I have called) the Keynesian weight of the evidence increases fact-finders' degree of confidence in, or the resilience of, their assessment of the pertinent odds or probability, such as $P(C|E)$.[3]

In at least one context, the relationship between Keynesian weight and confidence about probability can be specified with some degree of precision. A familiar result from probability theory concerns estimation of an extant but unknown probability of one of two possible outcomes (a "success") of a repeatable random event in which the outcome of one event is not affected by the outcomes of the other events (a "Bernoulli trial"). The estimate is provided by calculating the proportion k/n of such outcomes in a long series of n repeated trials. The flipping of our coinlike object is paradigmatic. Thus, if $P(\text{success}) = p$, then Bernoulli's theorem states[4]

For any small error ε
and any small difference δ,

---

[2] In terms of Shafer's belief functions (see § 3.7), increasing the stock of evidence can decrease uncommitted support without changing the ratio of Bel(C) to Bel(not-C).
[3] See, e.g., Brilmayer (1986) at 682 n. 14 and Schmalbeck (1986) at 225–8.
[4] See Hacking (2001) at 197–8.

there is a number N
such that for any number of trials $n > N$,
$P[(p - \varepsilon) \leq k/n \leq (p + \varepsilon)] > (1 - \delta)$

By taking a large enough number of trials, one can be assured, at the required level of probability, that the proportion of "successes" k/n is arbitrarily close to (i.e., within ε of) the true probability p.[5] Further conventional probability theory yields the result that the larger the sample size on which the estimate is based, for a fixed value of δ, the narrower is the "confidence interval" of the estimate.[6]

In this context, the connection to resilience is straightforward: the larger the sample size, the more resilient is the estimate k/n to any additional evidence in the form of additional trials. To illustrate, suppose first that the proportion of successes in 100 trials is 0.500. The effect of adding an additional set of 10 trials, itself with 6 successes, is to shift the proportion of successes for 110 trials to 0.509. But if one starts instead with the same proportion, 0.500, based, however, on 1,000 trials and then recomputes the average by adding 10 trials with 6 successes, one gets a new proportion of only 0.501. For the larger initial sample, with a correspondingly smaller confidence interval, there is a smaller change as a result of adding the same new data. This suggests the broader thesis (which, however, I will reject later, at least as a general proposition) that increases in Keynesian weight result in narrower confidence intervals and greater resilience for one's estimate of the epistemic probability underlying criterion (2.2′).

Although he does not write in terms of epistemic probability, Neil Cohen's "confidence interval" approach to standards of proof reflects these ideas. Recognizing that the "true" probability of interest is a value that must be estimated by the fact-finder, Cohen argues that the resilience of the fact-finder's inevitably subjective estimate is affected by the degree of completeness of the evidence presented.[7] Consequently, he argues that the

---

[5] Recalling our earlier discussion of probability ascriptions (§ 2.2.2), the nature of the probability indexed by the function P depends on how Bernoulli's theorem (a mathematical tautology) is applied. For example, if p is interpreted as an objective propensity, then P is an empirical probability, based on that propensity, that the ratio k/n will lie within δ of p. From this empirical probability, given appropriate conditions, one can infer an epistemic probability about the value of p.
[6] The confidence interval for a fixed value of δ is a function of p and n; specifically, it is inversely proportional to $\sqrt{n}$. Id. at 233–4.
[7] Cohen, N. (1985).

burden of persuasion should be understood to require a verdict for the claimant just in case

1. The fact-finder's best point estimate of $P(C|E)$ is greater than P^* (i.e., criterion (2.2')), and
2. The fact-finder has "a certain level of confidence that the true probability, based on all possible evidence," exceeds P^*.[8]

Cohen offers this two-part test as broadening, and thus giving more significant meaning to, the idea of equipoise, in which the fact-finder, unable to say either that $P(C|E) > P^*$ or that $P(C|E) < P^*$, takes refuge in the default rule, the risk of nonpersuasion, to award the verdict to the defendant.[9] Significantly, the first part of Cohen's test reflects an assumption that a best estimate of the probability in question $P(C|E)$ can be stated by the fact-finder. His is not a model of intervals within which no weighting of probabilities is possible (see § 2.2.3), but he argues, nevertheless, that the entire ("one tailed") confidence interval (however its required width is properly set) for the fact-finder's estimate of the true probability must exceed the threshold value P^* for the plaintiff to win the case.[10]

Cohen explores various candidates for an appropriate level of confidence for the second part of his two-part test, tentatively favoring, for civil cases, one that equalizes a certain risk for plaintiff and defendant.[11] Critically, he distinguishes between the risk of "fact error" – that is, giving a verdict for one side when the underlying material facts, were they known, would dictate a verdict for the other side – and the risk of "probability error" – that is, mistakenly assessing which is larger, the "true" value of $P(C|E)$ or P^*. If P^* is set at 0.5 for all or some class of civil cases, then the conventional standard represented by part (1) of his criterion for the burden of persuasion not only speaks to maximizing expected utility of decision

---

[8] Id. at 399.
[9] A more expansive theory of equipoise may be unavoidable from an economic or psychological perspective, but these arguments would not (like Cohen's argument) depend on any necessary connection to the incompleteness of the evidence. See, e.g., Clermont (2013) at 18–23.
[10] Cohen correctly observes that in the adjudicative context, the theoretically appropriate confidence intervals would be "one-tailed" intervals in that we should be concerned only about the possibility that the true probability is *smaller* than the best point estimate. Id. at 402–3. Although it is difficult to imagine that intuitive judgments of fact-finders could distinguish between one- and two-tailed confidence intervals, this is a minor quibble, and my critique of Cohen's theory will address more fundamental issues.
[11] Id. at 409–17.

but also (for marginal cases) equates the risk of fact error for plaintiff and for defendant. Cohen's second requirement would be based on equalizing probability error as well. But adding a requirement that equates probability error – or, indeed, any distinct resiliency requirement – requires, as a consequence, judgments that, at the margin, do not equate the (perceived) risks of *fact* error for plaintiff and for defendant; rather, it skews that risk against the plaintiff. As a result, some cases for which $P(C|E)$, as assessed by the fact-finder, is greater than P^* would have to be decided for the defense, even though doing so involves a greater perceived risk of fact error against the plaintiff than against the defendant.

Now, treating risks associated with civil litigation equally has an obvious attractiveness, but it can mean many things, and it is important to pick the correct sense of "equality" that should govern. Cohen makes a brief but unconvincing attempt to argue that equalizing the risk of improperly estimating the true probability is independently important, even more important than minimizing expected error costs, equalizing the probability of factual error or minimizing the risk of probability error.[12] But most of his presentation is aimed not so much at fixing the right criterion for determining the confidence interval as at demonstrating the relationship between such intervals and the amount (what I have called the Keynesian weight) of the evidence. It is this aspect of his argument that is of greatest interest here.

An initial difficulty in Cohen's argument arises from his assumption that the fact-finder (or anyone else) can meaningfully distinguish between the best point estimate of the probability and the "true" probability of interest. Responding to criticism along this line, Cohen's defense of his approach distinguishes between the actual evidence before the court E and "the totality of all available evidence" T; he argues that the second condition stated earlier, that which requires a certain level of confidence, is necessary just because of the fact that even when $P(C|E)$ is greater than P^*, $P(C|T)$ might be less than P^*.[13] This permits the fact-finder (as well as someone observing the process) to distinguish between the fact-finder's best assessment of the probability of interest and a hypothetical assessment, that which the fact-finder *would* (or should) assess if it had access to the totality of all available evidence T.

This makes the meaning of T quite important. Cohen clarifies that his T does not include evidence properly excluded by the court pursuant to

---

[12] Id. at 417; Cohen, N. (1987) at 93–5.
[13] Cohen, N. (1987) at 85.

admissibility rules.[14] For reasons explained earlier (§ 3.3), one must assume as well that Cohen's notion of "availability" is not some cost-insensitive idea. Thus his "totality of available evidence" must mean "the totality of reasonably available and admissible evidence," which is just evidence of practically optimized Keynesian weight.[15] One can already begin to see the problems for Cohen's theory. Most important, Cohen fails to appreciate the implications of the independence of the Keynesian weight requirement and the probability-threshold requirement (§ 3.6). Instead, he attempts to combine the two quite distinct decisions to which these requirements relate into a single decision directly related to P^*, albeit with two components, a decision made by a single juridical actor, the fact-finder.[16] Previous chapters have clarified how the risk of fact error relates to the decision of the fact-finder whether to declare C or to declare not-C. In the context of *that* decision, the risk of probability error (or what Sahlin called "epistemic risk"; see § 3.2) does not matter. Or, to put it differently, the risk of probability error matters to the fact-finder's decision only insofar as it materializes as fact error, and the risk of *that* happening is, of course, just what is addressed by the conventional probabilistic criterion that is the first part of Cohen's two-part test. To be sure, this does not mean that the risk of probability error has no independent importance, but because of its crucial dependence on the idea of evidential incompleteness, this risk relates to an entirely different decision, the decision of the parties, under the supervision of the court, about whether to submit the case to the fact-finder for

---

[14] Id. at 85 n. 16. As in other helpful analyses of the problem of Keynesian weight, Cohen sets aside the question of spoliation inferences, which unnecessarily cloud the issue. Id. at n. 17.

[15] Unfortunately, Cohen is ambivalent on the point because he also restates in a footnote that his "totality of the evidence" means "all *conceivable* relevant evidence." Id. at n. 18 (emphasis added). Using this last criterion, if we are to take it seriously, he would be deep into the problems encountered by (Jonathan) Cohen, discussed earlier (§ 3.3). In the text, therefore, I stick to the more plausible interpretation of (Neil) Cohen's claims.

[16] Some of Cohen's statements suggest that the first part of his test is actually mute. He states that his model "reformulates the burden of persuasion as that of demonstrating that it can be stated with a particular level of confidence that the probability in question is greater than" the threshold value in question, for civil cases 0.5. Cohen, N. (1985) at 409. And he argues, for example, that "the most that a factfinder can do is state that he or she has a particular level of confidence that the probability exceeds" a given threshold. Id. at 404. And elsewhere, he observes that "[d]escribing the burden of persuasion in terms of confidence intervals or interval estimates is more consistent with the way factfinders and courts intuitively operate." Id. at 406. These statements cast doubt on the idea of a fact-finder making the determination required by the first part of Cohen's test. In any event, his second condition will be more demanding than the first and thus will determine the result, unless the best point estimate chosen is, for some bizarre reason, outside the entire confidence interval.

decision on the current state of the evidence or, in the alternative, to obtain and consider further evidence (subject to potential sanctions in the event of recalcitrance by a burdened party). By merging these risks into a single decision, Cohen is forced to prescribe decisions that vary from that of criterion (2.2′), that is, decisions that do not maximize expected utility. On this basis, he was understandably criticized.[17]

Had Cohen perceived the independence of these decisions and their associated risks, however, he might have seen a different way out of this dilemma. It is based on two critical propositions developed in previous chapters: first, cases need not and ought not be allowed to go to verdict when the evidence is unreasonably incomplete, and second, the imposition of the risk associated with the "probability error" is not necessarily placed on the party bearing the burden of persuasion. On the first point, Cohen assumes that cases will go to verdict with unreasonably incomplete evidence. This may well happen in fact, but it need not be the accepted norm given our expectation that courts appropriately supervise trials. If the evidence is unreasonably incomplete, there are numerous options available to courts to address the deficiency before a verdict is required (§ 4.2). On the second point, Cohen simply states, only in a footnote:

> The risk of nonpersuasion as to probability error falls on the same party bearing the risk of nonpersuasion as to fact error. In our prototypical example, both risks fall on plaintiff; this is appropriate inasmuch as it is plaintiff who is seeking to have the legal system disturb the status quo.[18]

As also shown previously (§ 4.3), this explanation is overly simplified. The foundation of Cohen's risk of probability error is evidential incompleteness. Under established practices, risks associated with the incompleteness of evidence are sometimes placed on the party that does *not* bear the risk of nonpersuasion with regard to fact error, and rightly so. Moreover, in the law's administration of Keynesian weight, distinct from the fact-finder's decision, one can find meaning for the idea of "refusing to decide." Here there are realistic alternatives to putting the case to the fact-finder for a decision. These alternatives include the use of discovery rules, admissibility rules, and sufficiency rules to induce parties to present a more complete evidence package. Indeed, if the job of optimizing Keynesian weight has been properly performed before submitting the case to the fact-finder, then the fact-finder will be deciding on the basis of "the totality of all reasonably available and admissible evidence."

[17] See Kaye (1987).
[18] Cohen, N. (1987) at 86 n. 19.

Now, this job may not be perfectly performed, and in such contexts, it may be suggested that we should interpret the second component of the fact-finder's decision in Cohen's framework as a failsafe, directing the fact-finder to impose a consequence for unreasonable evidential incompleteness that remains when the case is submitted to the fact-finder. The fact-finder then would be using Cohen's criteria for the burden of persuasion as a "backup" to the judicial monitoring of Keynesian weight, imposing a kind of sanction for the parties' failure to make it so that $E = T$. This suggestion, however, faces several difficulties. First, Cohen's proposed test asks the fact-finder to try to determine at what point the risk of probability error is equalized, and it is hard to imagine a fact-finder who would have any idea how to do that.[19] Second, it necessarily makes the burden of the sanction fall on the party bearing the burden of persuasion, which will sometimes not be appropriate if the goal of this requirement is to compensate for an inadequately managed judicial optimization of Keynesian weight (see § 4.3). Third, it presents the possibility of inconsistency between the jury's judgments about confidence intervals (serving as a proxy for assessments of evidential completeness) and the more direct judgments of evidential completeness made by the trial judge, for the judge may have concluded, before submitting the case to the jury, that the evidence is reasonably complete and that no further augmentation of Keynesian weight would be reasonable. Finally, the imposition of a sanction under Cohen's scheme would bear a fortuitous relationship to the incompleteness of the evidence regardless of whether it is the jury or the judge who has responsibility for monitoring such completeness. This last point requires elaboration.

As explained by Cohen, the cause of the imprecision in one's estimate of the probability is the divergence between the evidence actually before the court E and the totality of available evidence T. If these are the same – that is, if the fact-finder is presented with T – we are per force to suppose that there is no problem going with a probability-threshold criterion alone, such as criterion (2.2′); no confidence intervals need be considered. This would seem to accomplish the correct result: refraining from imposing a sanction when the evidence is reasonably complete. A more careful look, however, poses deep problems for such an account. Why, in particular, is it the case that when $E = T$, no confidence intervals need be considered? If

---

[19] Cohen acknowledges that even in highly stylized examples, with statistically normal curves, there is no straightforward way to equalize Type I and Type II probability estimation errors. Cohen, N. (1985) at 411, 417.

we think of Bernoulli trials, this would be true if T were an infinite number of trials, for then the width of the confidence interval would shrink to nil. This seems to have been what Cohen had in mind, if only by analogy.[20] But T is not defined in terms of this kind of theoretical ideal, nor could it be; as already emphasized, it must be defined in practical terms. Even in practical sampling problems, an infinite set of trials is simply not "available" to anyone. And this leads to a puzzle: even with practically optimized evidence T, there typically will be some uncertainty about the target epistemic probability. This uncertainty is the engine of Cohen's theory. Why, then, does *this* uncertainty no longer matter in application of the burden of persuasion, as Cohen seems to say? Why would a confidence-interval approach be obviated when $E = T$?

The answer is that a confidence-interval approach does not matter to the application of the standard of proof when $E = T$ (i.e., when the evidence is practically optimized) *for the same reason* that confidence intervals should not matter to the application of the burden of persuasion when E is a proper subset of T (i.e., when the evidence is incomplete). The uncertainty matters to the imposition of the sanction just when it is associated with an inexcusably incomplete set of evidence *regardless of the confidence intervals involved*. An examination of one of Cohen's illustrations will make this clearer.

Cohen contrasts a number of betting problems, all of which have the same format. They are offered as metaphors for decision making in civil cases for which P^* is taken to be 0.5. It will suffice to focus on just two of his problems, which I do by the ellipses in the following passage:

> An opaque vat contains a large number of balls, each of which is either black or white. The percentages of each color ball in the vat are not known, however. A number of balls is randomly drawn from the vat and shown to the contestant. The contestant is then given the choice of betting, at even odds, on the color of each ball remaining in the vat....
>
> Now if 10,000 balls were drawn from the vat, and 5,500 were white [4,500 being black], ..., on reflection, given the large number of drawn balls, it is unlikely that less than a majority of the balls are white.... Therefore, the contestant will, most likely, bet white....
>
> [By contrast] what if five balls are drawn, three of which are white [and two of which are black]? ... The contestant might still believe that white is the best bet, but it would not surprise him if, in fact, a majority of the balls in the vat were black....
>
> Most contestants would not choose to risk a substantial portion of their life's savings on this last bet. Indeed, if contestants in the game were given three options – (1) bet white, (2) bet black, or (3) don't bet – it is fairly

---

[20] Id. at 404–5, 409.

easy to predict the choice of most contestants in each of the examples described.... In the ... [first] example [5,500 white balls out of 10,000] ..., most contestants would bet white. In the ... [second] example [three white balls out of five], however, most contestants would probably opt for choice number three – don't' bet.[21]

Once again, in the adjudicative context, when the final decision must be made, the fact-finder does not have the option of not betting. Not betting *is* betting, one way or the other.[22] When fact-finders decide for the defendant because they are in equipoise, it is not the case that they are "not betting"; rather, they are betting on the defendant for whatever reasons inform the law's directive to do so when the case is "too close to call." So a genuine "no bet" option makes sense only as a placeholder for options such as collecting further information or imposing sanctions in lieu thereof on parties who have refused to cooperate in the presentation of evidence to the fact-finder, options not normally within the scope of authority of fact-finders. This is how I will here interpret the "no bet" option that Cohen presents – as a decision, made by an appropriate legal actor, to refrain from "betting" until better information is obtained or to impose such a sanction for lack of cooperation.

In any event, the example simplifies the issue of completeness of evidence by relating it only to sample size. Admittedly, in this context, confidence intervals can be created for each of Cohen's examples, and the width of the confidence interval is inversely related to the size of the sample. But what exactly is the relationship between what Cohen calls the totality of evidence T and the size of the samples? His arguments seem to assume that T is the same in the two examples and that a sample size of 10,000 is closer to T than is a sample size of 5. While that might be true in a particular case, it is not a necessary relationship. Specifically, we are not told, in framing his examples, the cost conditions associated with the various samples; all we are told in the preceding excerpt, is

---

[21] Id. at 88–90.
[22] Cohen tries hard to avoid this conclusion: "Under my view of legal decisionmaking, all three choices, including 'don't bet,' are available to the factfinder." Id. Cohen is thereby forced to argue that the consequences of a fact-finder's "refusal to bet" for the claimant or the defendant can only be a loss for the claimant under the default principle of the burden of proof, but he cannot quite bring himself to acknowledge the inevitable consequence of this point: a fact-finder's "not betting" in this way is, for legal purposes, the same as betting on the defendant. Cohen, N. (1987) at 88–91. The closest he comes is at the end of this passage, where he states parenthetically that there is no difference "from the viewpoint of the party bearing the burden of persuasion" between betting against that party and not betting. Id. at 91. But it is not only *this* viewpoint from which there is no difference.

that the stakes could be quite high. We know, once again, that T cannot be the results of an infinite set of trials. But we are not told what, short of that, T might be. One can easily imagine a variation of his first problem in which the sample size of 10,000 is decidedly smaller than the size demanded by T (e.g., T = the results of 15,000 trials), and conversely, one can imagine a variation of his second problem in which the sample size of 5 is exactly that which is demanded for T (i.e., T = the results of 5 trials). In the former case, contrary to Cohen's conclusion, the right choice is option (3) – don't bet until the sample size is increased (a demand that is generally beyond the role of the fact-finder to deliver but that would need to be delivered somehow). In the latter case, again contrary to Cohen's conclusion, the right choice is option (1), bet white, because no further acquisition of evidence is practicable, so "not betting" has no practical meaning that can withstand criticism.

We thus arrive at one important result about the relationship between Keynesian weight and the resilience of probabilities. Insofar as increases in Keynesian weight are reflected in the narrowing of confidence intervals with regard to the target probability, the level of practically optimized Keynesian weight has no necessary relationship to confidence intervals, whether they be 95 percent confidence intervals, 99 percent confidence intervals, or (Cohen's preferred solution for civil cases) confidence intervals determined so as to equalize the risk of probability error in favor of the claimant with the risk of probability error in favor of the defendant. While confidence intervals are related to sample size in such contexts, this relationship does not determine whether the sample size, or the associated confidence interval, has achieved practical optimization. At best, we might conclude that if the practically optimal sample size is N, then evidence consisting of a set of n_2 trials is to be preferred to evidence consisting of n_1 trials whenever $n_1 < n_2 \leq N$. Conversely, at best, we might conclude that evidence consisting of a set of n_1 trials is to be preferred to evidence consisting of n_2 trials whenever $N \leq n_1 < n_2$.[23]

For an example in which explicit confidence intervals cannot be calculated, Cohen uses his model heuristically to explain the refusal to permit a verdict for the complainant in "naked statistical evidence" cases, such as

---

[23] I say "at best" in each case because these conclusions might not hold if the cost conditions are unusually structured. The natural assumption is that the cost of performing trials is proportional to, or at least an increasing function of, the number of trials. But this need not be the case. For example, if $n_1 < n_2 < N$ and the cost of running n_2 trials is, for some reason, much higher than the cost of running either n_1 or N trials, then evidence consisting of n_1 trials might be preferred to evidence consisting of n_2 trials.

the examples discussed in Chapter 3.[24] He argues that in such hypothetical cases, the verdict plausibly should go for the defense, even though the fact-finder's best estimate of $P(C|E)$ exceeds P^*, because the appropriate confidence interval does not lie entirely above P^* (in his examples 0.5).[25] And, he explains, we know this because "a great deal of information" beyond the statistical information is "missing," information about the parties, the testimony of other witnesses, and so forth: "we know that missing information about the defendant and the incident could alter substantially our probability estimate."[26] Cohen does not quite say, however, whether this additional information is taken to be reasonably accessible to the court. If he is assuming that it is, then E is a proper subset of T, and the right question becomes: what should be done about that? "Not deciding" should mean taking the steps necessary to ensure that $E = T$. If, however, he is assuming that all the missing evidence is *not* reasonably available to be presented in court, then $E = T$, and Cohen's confidence interval requirement is muted because $P(C|T)$ *is* the true probability.

One might try to modify Cohen's theory by identifying the "true probability" *not* with $P(C|T)$ but rather with the probability obtained under ideal counterfactual conditions, recognizing that such conditions never obtain and using confidence intervals to address the inevitably remaining uncertainty about the probability of the claim. Even theoretically, defining ideal counterfactual conditions for adjudication gets very tricky, however. For stochastic phenomena such as the sampling problem, T might (for cost considerations) be limited to the result of 100 trials, but the true probability would be identified with the result of an infinite series of trials.[27] For deterministic phenomena – more germane to the typical trial – ideal

---

[24] See supra § 3.1 (Jonathan Cohen's civil case hypothetical) and § 3.3 (Davidson and Pargetter's criminal case hypothetical).

[25] Cohen, N. (1985) at 407.

[26] Id. at 407–8. Cohen is quite aware of the dilemma that Keynes identified: "We realize that there are many more relevant but unknown facts about the incident in question, but we do not know which side they favor – that is, we do not know if they would increase or decrease our probability estimate." Id. at 407.

[27] A better example might be something like trying to determine the probability of radioactive decay for an unidentified isotope, should that ever be litigated. As already noted, truly ideal, and thus unconstrained, counterfactual conditions will often negate the constraining assumptions that define a sampling problem, such as the assumption that one cannot take out all the balls in Cohen's vat and count the number of each kind before being required to bet. To prevent this, one can imagine the counterfactual conditions being ideal in only some respects (an infinite sample) but not in others (no emptying and refilling the vat before placing the bet). Giving a convincing rationale for distinguishing those conditions that cannot be negated by counterfactualizing from those that can is not easy.

evidence can only mean evidence that will produce a probability of either 0 or 1, and T will always be short of such ideal evidence.[28] In either context, it would then be coherent to speak of confidence intervals even when the Keynesian weight has been practically optimized because $E = T$. The advisability of adding the complication of a confidence-interval requirement then depends on making the case that (1) fact-finders are capable, at least pragmatically and roughly, of sensing when the risks of probability error have been equalized or some other such condition has been satisfied (very doubtful), and (2) implementing such a requirement has benefits that are more than worth the costs. It is not clear what the benefits of such a rule would be (see § 5.2), but the costs are fairly obvious. If the parties do not attempt to produce more evidence than is optimal, then such implementation will entail reducing overall expected social utility below the maximum attainable as well as the cost of causing the risk of *factual* error in favor of defendants to exceed the risk of factual error favoring plaintiffs, at least for close cases. And to the extent that plaintiffs, anticipating adverse verdicts, increase the amount of evidence presented beyond what is practically optimal, there is the cost of overtried cases.

The foregoing discussion of Cohen's theory sheds considerable light on the relationship between resilience of probabilities and Keynesian weight. But more can be said. For practical purposes, the important events in most litigation are not random. One might therefore think that the accumulation of Keynesian weight will concentrate our confidence intervals not about some intermediate level of probability but rather about one of the polar extremes of 0 or 1, as suggested earlier. Alex Stein, who also emphasizes the importance of resilience, draws just this implication:

> In the domain of specific occurrences, making the weight standard more exacting excludes from consideration probability estimates far removed from both certainty (indexed as 1) and impossibility (indexed as 0). Only those estimates that come close to certainty (or to impossibility) survive.[29]

This is an intriguing claim. If understood literally, however, it belies experience. First, adding relevant evidence obviously does not always move the probability in the direction of truth, whether that be certainty or impossibility of the claim. The claimant's evidence E_π usually favors the claim so that $P(C|E_\pi) > P(C)$, which would not be possible if the claim were

---

[28] Id. at 397–8 and n. 74.
[29] Stein (2005) at 88.

false and the evidence steadily moved one in the direction of the truth. Conversely, the defendant's evidence E_Δ usually undermines the claim so that $P(C|E_\pi \& E_\Delta) < P(C|E_\pi)$, which would not be possible if the claim were true and the evidence steadily moved the decision maker in the direction of the truth. Further, we know that even in thoroughly investigated cases (i.e., cases in which Keynesian weight has been practically optimized at a very high level, as in very serious criminal cases against well-funded defendants), we may nonetheless find ourselves assessing the probability of guilt at some intermediate level of probability not near to 0 or 1. Certainty or near certainty about the litigated event simply is not available to us in some cases, however deterministic the event in question. Thus, demanding a higher level of weight (as would be proper, for example, in serious criminal cases when compared with minor traffic offences) does not guarantee that a rational fact-finder will assess the critical probability as nearer to 0 or 1.[30]

Still, Stein's claim is suggestive. It requires just one important change to make the argument work. Instead of writing in terms of what *does* happen to probabilities as weight is increased, he should have written in terms of what is *expected* to happen to them. Greater Keynesian weight improves

---

[30] Elsewhere Stein seems to reject his own argument, maintaining that practical optimization of Keynesian weight does not exhaust the importance of evidential incompleteness to the decision maker because

> [t]he Benthamite precept "gather all relevant information that can practicably be obtained" unwarrantedly postulates the existence of a linear progression relationship between the amount of information that fact-finders have and the accuracy of their decision.... [M]y point simply refutes the intuitive (but fallacious) idea that augmentation of information necessarily produces more accuracy in fact-finding.

Stein (2005) at 122–3. This passage is partially correct but still misleading. What Stein presumably means by a "linear progression relationship" is a monotonically (steadily) increasing relationship. So understood, Stein is correct that there is no such relationship between the amount of relevant information and the accuracy of results. But, as we shall see, there *is* such a relationship between the amount of relevant information and important epistemic *expectations* (as well as the expected utility of decision), and this is all that is needed to justify the "Benthamite precept." In fairness to Professor Stein, it should be noted that he seems to proceed on the basis that any accretion of evidence will change the nature of the hypotheses being considered (see, e.g., id. at 88) so that – strictly speaking – it matters not what the effect on the expected certainty of the (thereby displaced) hypothesis might be. I have also emphasized the importance of hypothesis generation (§ 2.4), as well as the role of augmentations of Keynesian weight in that process (§ 3.4), but this does not mean that every accretion of evidence changes the hypotheses being considered, and at the abstract level of "C versus not-C," they rarely change during the course of a trial. When the concrete contending stories being seriously considered do change over the course of a trial, that change means only that there are new opportunities for further epistemic gain by the accretion of evidence.

our epistemic expectations in some sense; otherwise, we would have no interest in acquiring additional evidence. Paul Horwich, writing in the 1980s, proved a theorem supporting such intuition in the context of discussing scientific hypotheses. Horwich defined "expected error in a probability valuation" as the difference between that valuation and the truth value (1 or 0) of the hypothesis in question and proved that expected error so defined necessarily decreases with the accretion of relevant evidence.[31]

Recently, using a different mathematical construct, the same point has been explored in the adjudicative context by David Hamer.[32] He observes that in considering the anticipated impact of fresh evidence, and in the absence of adverse spoliation inferences from the suppression of such evidence, the expected value of the probability of the claim, given the (as-yet unknown) evidence, necessarily equals the probability of the claim without such evidence. That is, $\text{Exp}[P(C|E)] = P(C)$. The fact that the content of the evidence is unknown, combined with the fact that surrounding circumstances (e.g., spoliation efforts by parties) are not available to provide substitute clues as to its content, guarantees that it has no effect on the expected value of the probability of the claim.[33] However, this does not mean that obtaining and considering such evidence will not have an impact. The impact relates to "certainty," which Hamer defines (reasonably) as the larger of the probability or its complement. (Thus, if the probability of the claim is 0.7, its certainty is 0.7; if the probability of the claim is 0.3, its certainty is also 0.7. In words, one is "70 percent certain" about the claim in either case.) Specifically, Hamer shows that although an increase in Keynesian weight has an indeterminate impact on certainty, such an increase in Keynesian weight necessarily produces an increase in *expected* certainty.

---

[31] Horwich (1982) at 127–9.
[32] Hamer (2012b).
[33] Id. at 144–5. The proof is simple and worth stating if only to show that it does not depend, as one might suspect, on the principle of indifference. In its simplest (but easily generalizable form), suppose that new potential evidence E can take only two forms, one supporting the claim E^+ and one undermining the claim E^-. Then the expected probability of the claim, given the new evidence, $\text{Exp}[P(C|E)]$ is just the weighted average of the two possible revised probabilities $P(C|E^+)$ and $P(C|E^-)$. Thus $\text{Exp}[P(C|E)] = [P(C|E^+) \times P(E^+)] + [P(C|E^-) \times P(E^-)] = P(C\&E^+) + P(C\&E^-) = P(C)$. Note that the claim made here is quite different from the (incorrect) assertion that $P(C|E) = P(C)$. Some subtleties aside (see § 4.1.1), the latter assertion entails that E is irrelevant to C, which is no part of the assumptions being made here. What is assumed here is that the probative value of E, or at least its directionality, is as yet unknown. Cf. Stein (2011) at 219–20 (apparently arguing that the principle of indifference – rather indiscriminately applied – commits one employing mathematical probabilities to reach the erroneous conclusion that any unknown evidence is irrelevant).

Whether one describes it as a decrease in expected error in the probability valuation or as an increase in expected certainty, it is this effect that accounts for the fact that increases in Keynesian weight guarantee an increase in the expected utility of the decision.[34] Still, the Horwich/Hamer result is important because it separates the impact of new evidence from the decision-theoretic framework, with its associated utilities, thereby illuminating the purely *epistemic* gain involved.[35] It confirms widely held intuitions about the epistemic gain from evidence acquisition. However, such epistemic gain is not directly commensurable with the costs of evidence acquisition. Granted that a gain in certainty would be an epistemic good, how would one place a value on such a gain? The decision-theoretic result provides one way of making the connection by converting the gain in expected certainty into a gain in expected utility.

But how is this result related to *resilience*? Even if it is true that increasing Keynesian weight does not ensure a probability that approaches 0 or 1, it still could be the case that increasing Keynesian weight leads to more resilient probability assessments, as suggested by confidence intervals for estimating the probability of a Bernoulli trial. Professor Stein endorses this view, arguing that an accretion of Keynesian weight leads to a probability assessment that "is more resilient (more invariant) and, therefore, less likely to be shaken by potential additions to its informational base."[36] But this also turns out not to be true, at least not necessarily. The reason for the difference arises from another crucial difference in the nature of evidence accretion in the context of Bernoulli trials and in the context of typical litigation.

In the context of estimating the probability of a Bernoulli trial, the increase in Keynesian weight is achieved by increasing the size of a sample of similar test runs (flips of the coin, say). This has the effect of subsuming a single flip within a set of "similar" flips, smoothing out variations among particular flips by pooling them among a great many. When increasing the Keynesian weight of evidence in litigation, though, things generally tend to go the other way. One starts with relatively raw data for a large reference class, one that subsumes many individuating differences (e.g., a 30-year-old male accused of robbery), and then refines that class

---

[34] See discussion, supra § 3.2. To similar effect, see also Davidson & Pargetter (1986) at 227–30.
[35] Horwich (1982) at 127; Hamer (2012b) at 145 n. 73.
[36] Stein (2005) at 88. In this passage, Stein actually writes in terms of the *proposition* in question becoming more resilient with the accretion of evidence, but in context it is pretty clear that he meant to refer to the resilience of the *probability* attributed to that proposition.

by adding individuating factors (e.g., evidence of motive or opportunity, evidence of a scar similar to that on the perpetrator, and so forth). As more evidence is taken into consideration, the reference class gets smaller, not larger, because potential comparison cases will be removed.[37] The question, then, is whether in such an increasingly differentiated epistemic environment one obtains an increase in resilience in the assessed probability.

Hamer also provides interesting evidence against such a conclusion. He reports a relatively simple example of multiple evidentiary items, serially taken into account, that shows two things happening at once, as the Keynesian weight increases: (1) expected certainty increases (as it must, by the probability calculus), but (2) the probability of the claim fluctuates more widely – it becomes *less* stable.[38] He emphasizes that this model does not guarantee that resilience will decrease as the weight of evidence increases in practical litigation; he made some contingent assumptions by the nature of the evidence in his model, assumptions that might or might not be representative of real cases.[39] Indeed, one can easily imagine a set of evidence that *would* result in increasing resilience. (Simply think of a case in which each piece of evidence added is uniformly favorable to the claim.[40]) But Hamer's result does show that (1) resilience does not *necessarily* increase with increasing Keynesian weight, and (2) there is reason to believe that in the litigation context, sometimes resilience will not increase as Keynesian weight increases.

Looking at the larger picture, what all this means is that, putting aside the question of the costs of obtaining and presenting new evidence, increasing Keynesian weight is an unequivocal epistemic good in that it increases expected certainty and an unequivocal practical good in that it increases expected utility of decision. These effects, however, are not necessarily connected to increases in resilience of the target probability. It is a mistake, therefore, to *identify* the idea of Keynesian weight with the idea of resilience (or its close cousin, confidence in probability).[41] The two ideas are distinct, and though there are causal connections between them, the

---

[37] Id. at 90.
[38] Hamer (2012b) at 145–50.
[39] Id. at 150–4.
[40] See Stein (2005) at 89–90 (using an example of just this sort to explain his claim that increased weight tends to eliminate intermediate probabilities).
[41] The use of the term *confidence* in regard to decision making is rather more ambiguous than the term *resilience*. By using the former term, one might mean to call attention not to one's degree of confidence in the assessment of $P(C|E)$ but rather to the degree of confidence one has in the appropriateness of choosing between H and not-H on the present state of the evidence. The latter idea is much more closely related to Keynesian weight, as we have seen.

dependence relationships are complex. We should not, therefore, embrace the suggestion by Davidson and Pargetter that Keynesian weight be *identified with* resilience of probability on the (supposed) ground that all that is of value in the former concept is better captured by the latter concept.[42] The contingent relationship between the amount of relevant evidence and resilience of probability assessments requires us to choose to which of these ideas to assign the rubric "weight," and Hamer's result supports sticking with Keynes's original insight, assigning the term *weight* to the former. Resilience, if it is of use at all, deserves to be treated separately.

But of what use is it exactly? Consider the implications of these results for the viability of an approach such as that of Neil Cohen's use of confidence intervals. Think about the plight of a civil plaintiff in a case for which $P^* = 0.5$ and for which (1) the evidence presented by both parties practically optimizes Keynesian weight, in the view of the court in its application of relevant regulatory doctrines, (2) the evidence presented by both parties warrants the fact-finder in assessing that $P(C|E) > 0.5$, but (3) the evidence presented by both parties does not warrant the fact-finder in concluding that the risks of probability error for plaintiff and defendant have been equalized. In response to this situation (which, we may suppose, the plaintiff can anticipate – the situation is even worse if he or she can't), the plaintiff overtries the case by introducing further cost-unjustified evidence in an effort to narrow the fact-finder's confidence interval, only to find that, for the effort, all the plaintiff has done is to widen the fact-finder's confidence interval. Should plaintiffs really be placed in such a "catch-22"? The same dilemma faces any theory of the burden of proof that would require that the probability of interest attain some threshold requirement of resiliency that is defined in a manner that separates that requirement from that of practical optimization of Keynesian weight.

Despite all this, the concept of resilience does have some use. Davidson and Pargetter identified an important connection between resilience and Keynesian weight. Paraphrasing their statement so as to eliminate their identification of "weightier" probabilities with "more resilient" probabilities, the point is this: the harder it is to shift the probability of interest, that is, the more resilient that probability is, the less is the expected gain in utility of determining which of various possible states of an evidenced fact obtains before acting, and so the more rational it is to act on the probability one has at the time. Resilience, therefore, is an ingredient in the rationality of acting on a probability by being an ingredient in deciding

---

[42] Davidson & Pargetter (1986).

whether one should augment Keynesian weight by getting more information before acting on one's assessed probability.[43] This connection places resilience in its proper place; in the legal context, it is a component part of the decision by the court whether the case is ripe for submission of the dispute for decision by the fact-finder.[44] However, as Davidson and Pargetter emphasize, it is only one factor. Other factors include the cost of the acquisition of further information, so it would be incorrect to say that a probability of higher resilience provides less justification for augmenting Keynesian weight than a probability of lower resilience, unless, of course, one adds a *ceteris paribus* assumption to that claim. Other factors, such as the cost of the additional evidence and the extent to which the probability falls below or exceeds some threshold of decision – for example, the difference between $P(C|E)$ and P^* – also will matter.

5.2 The Dubious Value of a Distinct Resiliency Requirement

Suppose, then, that Keynesian weight has been practically optimized by the conjoint operation of discovery, party incentives, rules of admissibility and sufficiency, and so on. That is, the fact-finder has received a case for which Keynesian weight cannot, as a practical matter, be improved. In such a situation, is there any reason for the fact-finder to consider, in addition to the question of whether some threshold criterion of discriminatory power has been satisfied, whether the resilience of the probability or plausibility assessment involved is, by some criterion, "high enough." Although there have been several suggestions that resilience is a separate requirement of legal proof, there have been surprisingly few articulations of reasons supporting such a requirement or of a framework for determining the appropriate criterion of adequate resilience.

For the most part, the suggestions of such a requirement simply have been efforts to explain our intuitions about the right judgment in cases of naked statistical evidence. This is the only normative message to be found, for example, in the papers of Davidson and Pargetter.[45] But the

---

[43] Id. at 228–9.
[44] Unfortunately, Davidson and Pargetter failed to follow through on this insight in their attempt to apply their theory to the adjudication of criminal cases. There they unequivocally place responsibility for assessing resilience on the jury, despite noting that the choice is one "of acting on a probability now, or first determining whether some piece of additional evidence obtains and then acting on the new probability." See Davidson & Pargetter (1987) at 187. They provide no clue as to how, exactly, a jury is supposed to "determine whether some piece of additional evidence obtains" before it renders its verdict.
[45] Davidson & Pargetter (1986, 1987).

previous chapters have explained the core of our epistemic intuitions regarding naked statistical evidence in terms of the practical optimization of Keynesian weight. Because, by the present assumption, Keynesian weight is practically optimized, there is less need for a separate resilience requirement to explain common intuitions. In any event, one needs some kind of theory to support the rationality of those intuitions besides simply a concern about deficiencies in Keynesian weight. Similarly, Brilmayer's arguments against Kaye's "missing evidence" explanation of the result in naked statistical evidence cases lead her to, or derive from, her conclusion that the costs of insisting on additional evidence to optimize (what I have called) Keynesian weight are justified by "collateral values about weight and quality of evidence" and not by improved accuracy.[46] Again, she provides no normative argument in support of such collateral values; she merely observes that an intuitive commitment to something of that sort might explain the law's supposed aversion to naked statistical evidence.[47] But, as shown in earlier chapters (§§ 3.3 and 4.1.4), so might accuracy enhancement, which at least has an obvious normative appeal and which can plausibly be served by a rule prohibiting positive verdicts based on naked statistical evidence. Indeed, the matter is even worse for those who would endorse a separate resiliency requirement. As we saw in connection with Neil Cohen's confidence-interval approach (§ 5.1), such an approach will inevitably cause a divergence between the fact-finder's verdict and the verdict that, relative to the fact-finder's assessment of $P(C|E)$ and policy makers' determination of P^*, will maximize expected social utility. This divergence calls for justification, not simply an appeal to intuitions about the proper results in highly unusual hypothetical cases.[48]

---

[46] Brilmayer (1986) at 685.
[47] See Koehler & Shaviro (1990) at 265–72 (discussing the import of such intuitions).
[48] I should mention here one aspect of Alex Stein's argument, which also plays heavily on our supposed intuitions in the naked statistical evidence cases. As I understand it, his position is that there is no *epistemic* reason for the practical optimization of Keynesian weight, a claim I reject. (See the discussion of Stein in § 5.1.) Yet he also wants to claim that to ignore the level of Keynesian weight would be irrational. See Stein (2005) at 81. As a result, some requirement on Keynesian weight must be selected, but not on epistemic grounds, rather, on grounds of political morality. Given this, Stein argues, the degree of weight required in adjudication, which should be selected by those with political authority, not by fact-finders, can (or must) be chosen with an eye to distributing the risk of error between the parties. As indicated, I do not think that this argument gets off the ground because there are sound epistemic reasons for the practical optimization of Keynesian weight, though, for other reasons, I agree with Stein that setting the level that practically optimizes Keynesian weight is not part of the fact-finder's role. For further discussion of Stein's theory, see Nance (2007b).

272   THE BURDENS OF PROOF

I have identified only one other noteworthy argument for such a separate requirement, an argument that does not depend on trying to explain our (not terribly reliable) intuitions about unrealistic paradoxical cases. To be sure, it is not entirely clear that the author of this argument separates the resiliency requirement from a Keynesian weight requirement; generally speaking, previous discussions in the literature have not clearly distinguished them. Consequently, the author may not have intended his argument to be deployed *in addition to* a Keynesian weight requirement. But one can at least ask whether such an argument can be sustained. In his book on the philosophy of probability, James Logue distinguished between first-order probabilities, such as $P(C|E)$, which he calls p_1, and second-order probabilities, such as the probability that $P(C|E)$ will, if further information were obtained, fall within a certain range, which he calls p_2. The narrower that range, for a given p_2, the greater is the resiliency of the estimate of $P(C|E)$.[49] Logue then argued that resiliency speaks not to the expected utility of the decision but to its *stability*. His argument on the matter is short enough to be quoted in full. He begins by noting the stumbling of English courts toward a two-parameter characterization of the burden of proof and then argues:

> If a justification of that practice is sought, we can find it by noting that the purposes for which trials are held are not satisfied merely by ensuring that more cases are decided correctly than incorrectly (as relying only on p_1 would ensure); stability of decisions, avoidance of revocation of penalties – which are what the high p_2 guard against – are necessary to our confidence in the cathartic as well as fact-finding effectiveness of judicial process, and justifiable on such consequentialist grounds.[50]

Presumably, the idea here is that criterion (2.2′) assumes, implicitly, that once the decision is made, that will be the end of the matter. It thus does not take into account the costs associated with a conclusion, after the judgment, that the decision was in error, resulting in a "revocation of penalties" and the undermining of "our confidence in the cathartic as well as fact-finding effectiveness of judicial process." This is an assumption that may, but need not, be made in articulating criterion (2.2′). For the sake of argument, though, the following discussion will accept it by assuming that criterion (2.2′) does not incorporate these particular consequentialist concerns. In these terms, Logue's argument implies that the law must

---

[49] Logue (1995) at 78–95.
[50] Id. at 154.

separately choose how much it is worth to avoid such problems, which I will refer to simply as after-judgment "embarrassment" costs.[51]

Logue, not being a lawyer, may not have intended his "revocation of penalties" to be confined to criminal cases, as the word "penalties" would suggest to lawyers. Thus we should address the question in a larger framework. Fortunately, it is much easier to assess Logue's suggestion in the civil context. And it is instructive to do so. Aside from a short time period after judgment, during which the judgment can be modified on the basis of newly discovered evidence, the result of a civil judgment is *res judicata* (a "thing decided"); the matter is closed.[52] New evidence does not matter, and because it does not matter, rare is the case in which a party has the incentive to try to undermine the decision by bringing new evidence to light. And suppose that one does make such a challenge, not in the courts but in the press, perhaps merely to "set the public record straight." There could be some embarrassment to the judicial system, but how is such embarrassment to be avoided? And at what cost?

Given the arguments of the previous section, assume that a demand for resilience, as a condition of a positive verdict, does not increase the

---

[51] There is just a hint to this idea in Neil Cohen's defense of his confidence-interval approach. See Cohen, N. (1987) at 86: "Rather, I believe, the factfinder also takes into account its judgment as to how likely the best guess [about $P(C|E)$] is to 'hold up.'"

[52] Summarizing nicely:

> The rules governing the preclusive effect of judgments in the United States are grouped under the label "*res judicata*." The principal purposes of these rules are avoiding the danger of double recovery, promoting the desirability of stable judicial determinations, relieving defendants of the expense and vexation of repeated litigation, and economizing judicial resources. The doctrine of *res judicata* is subdivided into rules of claim preclusion and issue preclusion. The doctrine of claim preclusion seeks to prevent a party from litigating in a subsequent action any matter that was part of the same claim or cause of action adjudicated by a final judgment in a prior action. The doctrine of issue preclusion seeks to prevent relitigation of issues of fact or law that were litigated and determined against a party to a prior action.

Felix & Whitten (2011) at 139. Moreover, the preclusive effect of the judgment extends to challenges mounted in other jurisdictions:

> Mere error in an action leading to a judgment is not a proper ground for refusing effect to the judgment in another state. When a court that has jurisdiction over the parties and subject matter renders an erroneous decision, either on the facts or the law or both, the losing party's relief is by appeal, not by collateral attack on the judgment in a separate proceeding. When the erroneous judgment becomes final, it is as conclusive as any other under the rules of *res judicata* and, therefore, other states must give it effect.

Id. at 146.

amount of evidence presented at trial (Things are even worse if does.). Again, Keynesian weight has been practically optimized; obtaining further evidence is not justifiable, by hypothesis. Thus the import of Logue's argument is that, for the set of cases as to which Keynesian weight has been practically optimized and $P(C|E) > P^*$, the tribunal (whether that be the judge or the fact-finder) would skew decisions in favor of defendants by assigning some of those cases, those with too low of a resilience for $P(C|E)$, to verdicts for the defense. The obvious problem, aside from the decrease in expected utility of the affected decisions, is that the low resilience positive verdicts are not simply eliminated; they are instead moved elsewhere, becoming low resilience negative verdicts, ones with relatively high values for $P(C|E)$ at that. Whatever is gained by way of embarrassment costs in terms of the increased stability of positive verdicts can be expected to be more than offset by increased embarrassment costs associated with decreased stability of the additional negative verdicts, especially when combined with the decreased expected utility of the decision.

Criminal cases, with their obvious asymmetry, might seem to be a somewhat more fertile ground for Logue's argument.[53] In the wake of an erroneous acquittal, *res judicata* and the related constitutional principle prohibiting double jeopardy mean that police and prosecutors have little incentive to bring the error of the acquittal to light, even if they stumble on additional inculpatory evidence. For the most part, erroneous acquittals will appear only indirectly, such as when someone is acquitted and then "reoffends," at which point that person's commission of the prior offense may become evident and public, especially in the context of the trial of the second offense.[54] Another possibility is that the erroneous acquittal may be exposed by a civil suit brought by the victim or his or her family or even by the government in some cases.[55] Success by the plaintiff in such later actions does not necessarily show that the acquittal was erroneous; the second determination, even if it based on a finding of guilt, could be

---

[53] James Franklin makes a brief suggestion along similar lines, specifically limited to criminal cases. See Franklin (2006).

[54] See, e.g., Fed. R. Evid. 404(b)(2), 413, 414, & 608(b) (stating conditions under which prior offenses may be offered as evidence even in the wake of acquittals for those prior offenses).

[55] The doctrine is well established:

> Although an issue is actually litigated and determined by a valid and final judgment, and the determination is essential to the judgment, relitigation of the issue in a subsequent action between the parties is not precluded [if] ... [t]he party against whom preclusion is sought had a significantly heavier burden of persuasion with respect to the issue in the initial action than in the subsequent action.

Restatement (Second) of Judgments § 28 (1982).

in error. Nor does it even show that the two results are technically inconsistent because of the different standards of proof that apply. It may be entirely appropriate, for example, for a perpetrator to be held civilly liable even though he or she is not convicted of the corresponding crime.[56] Still, the inconsistency between the two judgments might seem embarrassing to the legal system, assuming that the public is incapable of understanding such distinctions. But this is a dubious assumption. In fact, such occasional "retrials" may serve instead to vindicate the system, at least to some extent, by providing alternative means of redressing the delict.[57]

With respect to erroneous convictions, while for the most part they are also not subject to outright reversal based solely on new evidence, they are generally subject to some kind of administrative relief from incarceration if innocence can be shown.[58] This is not to suggest that the road to freedom for the erroneously convicted is easy, but it is at least possible.[59] Is this a serious embarrassment to the system, or does it show, again from a broader perspective, that the system works?

Let us assume, for the sake of argument, that there are significant embarrassment costs associated with convictions later shown to be factually erroneous and assume further that the expected embarrassment costs associated with an erroneous conviction are greater than the expected embarrassment costs associated with an acquittal later shown to be factually erroneous. Still, this does not quite make the case for a separate resilience requirement. Because such a requirement would mean that convictions would be allowed only in a subset of cases in which $P(C|E) > P^*$, one would expect an increase in the number of false acquittals above what

---

[56] See, e.g., One Lot Emerald Cut Stone & One Ring v. United States, 409 U.S. 232, 235 (1972) (holding that defendant's acquittal on a smuggling charge did not bar a later civil proceeding to forfeit goods allegedly smuggled because "the difference in the burden of proof in criminal and civil cases precludes application of the doctrine of collateral estoppel.")

[57] Certainly the most prominent example is the criminal acquittal of O. J. Simpson followed by a verdict of civil liability to the family of Nicole Simpson. For interesting insights on the presentation of these trials to the public, see Schuetz & Lilley (1999).

[58] See, e.g., Herrera v. Collins, 506 U.S. 390 (1993). Distinguishable are those contexts in which a conviction is reversed not because new evidence shows the defendant is innocent but because of inadequate investigative work done before trial. See, e.g., Sanders v. Ratelle, 21 F.3d 1446, 1456–60 (9th Cir. 1994) (reversing a conviction because of defense attorney's failure to investigate an obvious lead) and Commonwealth of N. Mariana Islands v. Bowie, 243 F.3d 1109, 1113 (9th Cir. 2001) (reversing a conviction because the prosecutor cannot press ahead while "refusing to search for the truth and remaining willfully ignorant of the facts").

[59] Exonerations based on DNA evidence that was not available at the time of trial are perhaps the most conspicuous examples. See, e.g., Sheck et al. (2003).

would be socially optimal, embarrassment costs aside, subjecting society to increased risks associated with such unapprehended criminals. And even if the expected embarrassment costs per erroneous conviction are greater than the expected embarrassment costs per erroneous acquittal, the increase in the number of acquittals, with lower degrees of resilience for $P(\text{not-}C|E)$, may result in an aggregate increase in embarrassment costs.

Let us further assume, however, again for the sake of argument, that a resiliency requirement imposed on convictions would entail a net decrease in embarrassment costs that offsets any increase in costs of various kinds associated with increased erroneous acquittals. Beyond these considerations, there is an enormously difficult problem associated with answering the question of how the appropriate legal actor, fact-finder or judge, is to determine, and be instructed about determining, the meaning and required level or degree of resilience. The matter would per force be left to the intuitive judgment of the fact-finder, which, especially in the case of a jury, would be remarkably bereft of pertinent information with which to make that judgment. The complexity and arbitrariness of such an enterprise, when combined with the dubious nature of the claim that skewing judgments in favor of either party can reduce aggregate error and embarrassment costs, suggest that the game is not worth the candle. In any event, almost all – if not all – of what is to be gained by a resilience requirement is gained, and in a more sensible fashion, by a properly administered Keynesian weight requirement. Certainly, a case in which very little of the available evidence is before the court is a case with both inexcusably low Keynesian weight and (sometimes, though not inevitably) an inexcusably low degree of resilience in the fact-finder's assessment of discriminatory power. This, no doubt, is the main reason that the two are easily conflated.

The argument presented here obviously depends on certain contingent features of existing legal systems. Adjudicative systems with a much lesser degree of commitment to principles of *res judicata* might find a separate requirement of resilience to be useful in avoiding embarrassment costs. If so, such a system then would face difficult dilemmas in which its courts might want to be *less* thorough in their investigation of certain cases than they might otherwise be in order to improve the stability of the verdict. For example, suppose that some criterion of resilience, however ad hoc, is adopted for a case such that a judgment may not be entered on a probability unless its resilience is greater than k. A court then might find itself in a situation where, with evidence E, it is determined that $P(C|E) > P^*$ and the resilience of this probability is greater than k, so the court accepts that this probability is sufficiently stable to risk embarrassment. But then the court might learn that additional, potentially relevant evidence E_{n+1} can be obtained at a cost that is entirely reasonable given the stakes involved. Having obtained this additional evidence, the court determines that $P(C|E\&E_{n+1}) > P(C|E) > P^*$. This would look like good confirmation, yet it would be entirely possible for the resilience of the new probability $P(C|E\&E_{n+1})$ to be *less* than the resilience of $P(C|E)$ and less by enough to render the new probability too unstable to go forward; that is, the resilience of the new probability of the claim is less than k. If no further identifiable evidence E_{n+2} can be obtained at reasonable cost, the court would seem to be between a rock and a hard place. What is worse, the court would be in no position to know, before E_{n+1} is acquired, that this dilemma awaits.[60]

It is not that resiliency is of no epistemological interest generally. If one leaves the field of decision making entirely, entering a domain in which the issue is whether, in the abstract, to endorse a belief, though no particular decision rides on that endorsement, then practical optimization of Keynesian weight loses the constraints that make it "practical." Without stakes, it becomes difficult to imagine what "practical optimization" can mean. In such a context, which is to say a context of purely theoretical speculation, one's resource constraints will still limit the extent of investigation that can occur at any given point or period of time, but the question will arise whether $P(C|E)$ is high enough to warrant accepting C. Because we are talking about a theoretical question, it would be more appropriate to think of C as a hypothesis rather than a claim, but whatever difference of connotation is involved in such a choice of words, the point remains that for theoretical investigative purposes, one may have to decide whether to treat the hypothesis as true – to take it as part of our corpus of knowledge. Resilience may have a role to play here that is analogous to that served by practical optimization of Keynesian weight. Indeed, it may be an abstract substitute for such practical optimization. Here the question of whether to accept a given proposition, and thus add it to the stock of knowledge on which we base further conjectures, may turn in part on how probable that proposition is and in part on how resilient that probability is to being undermined by new evidence. Without utilities to inform choice, such epistemic commitments may require at

---

[60] Perhaps the situation can be salvaged by a principle that provides that once the necessary resilience is achieved, further evidence will not "count" in terms of the resilience requirement. But I see no plausible basis for such a principle.

least rough or approximate conventions.[61] Compared with practical decision making, such conventions are arbitrary, even if they are necessary. In any event, consideration of these ideas goes beyond the framework of practical decision making in general and adjudication in particular.

5.3 Tenacity of Categorical Belief

Most of the preceding discussion has employed a concept of belief understood in gradational terms: one can believe weakly that a claim is true, strongly that it is true, very strongly that is true, and so forth. And for the most part, I have worked within the tradition that takes these degrees of belief to be expressible as probabilities. Within this framework, the burden of persuasion can be understood as a requirement that, with the assistance of a procedural system designed to help align the fact-finder's subjective probability with an objective epistemic probability of the claim in light of the evidence, the fact-finder's subjective probability must exceed a certain threshold (the standard of proof). This holds whether that threshold is conceived in numerical terms – for example, $P(C|E) > P^*$ – in comparative terms – for example, $P(C|E) > P(\text{not-}C|E)$ – or a combination of the two – for example, $P(C|E) > 5 \times P(\text{not-}C|E)$. When the standard of proof is thus satisfied, the fact-finder declares the claim C to be true, precisely in the sense that it is accepted for adjudication purposes as true whether it is true or not, with all the legal consequences attending such a declaration. Conversely, when the standard of proof is not satisfied, the fact-finder declares the claim C to be false, precisely in the sense that it is accepted for adjudication purposes as false whether it is true or not, with all the legal consequences attending such a declaration.[62]

In contrast, some legal theorists have argued that adjudicative fact-finders are not supposed to think in such terms and that the burden

---

[61] See, e.g., Levi (1980). Robert Nozick offered the following suggestion:

From: $P(E|C) \geq 0.95$
　　　$P(E|\text{not-}C) \leq 0.05$
　　　E
　　　$P(C) > P(E|\text{not-}C)$
infer: C

Nozick (1981) at 257 (notation changed to conform to present text). Utilities play no part here; there are no stakes and no way to assess error costs. In such a context, it might be useful to consider the resilience of $P(C|E)$ as well, provided that this can be assessed.

[62] The significance of the fact that the verdict might be reversed or otherwise modified in subsequent proceedings is discussed in the preceding section.

of persuasion must, accordingly, be framed differently. Specifically, some scholars take adjudicative epistemology to be framed in terms of *categorical* beliefs. Such beliefs are not gradational; they do not come in degrees. Rather, with regard to any proposition *p*:

> [T]hree doxastic positions are available: in addition to believing *p*, one can believe that *p* is false, which is to disbelieve *p*, or suspend judgment about *p*, thus neither believing nor disbelieving *p*.[63]

This is sometimes taken to be a more accurate way to describe the ordinary epistemic assessments of fact-finders, even if it is the case that "[w]hen 'belief' and cognate terms are used in ordinary speech, the reference is usually to the cognitive attitude of partial rather than categorical belief."[64]

There are two very different ways that one can understand this categorical belief idea in its relationship to questions of the burden of proof. On the one hand, it can be understood simply as the use of shorthand expressions in ordinary speech for what might be described more precisely, but at the expense of greater time and effort, in terms of partial beliefs or probabilities. Thus "I believe that *p*" could be merely a shorthand version of "I believe that *p* is more likely than not" or (depending on nuances in the manner of expression) even "I believe that *p* is very likely." Getting into verbal detail about the level of the strength of one's beliefs is, in a great many social contexts, not worth the time and effort. In some contexts, though, especially those in which serious decisions are to be made, this informality could and should be dropped in favor of more qualified or precise expressions of partial beliefs. Litigation being one of these more serious contexts, especially when it comes to decisions about centrally important or ultimate material facts, one then would expect the categorical belief structure to give way.[65] Such an understanding of the role of categorical beliefs poses no serious obstacle to the employment of models of the burden of persuasion that depend on the comparison of degrees of partial belief. Nor do they conflict with the view, articulated here, that optimization of Keynesian weight is conceptually and practically distinct from appropriate decision making under the applicable standard of proof.

---

[63] Ho (2008) at 124 (footnotes omitted).

[64] Id. at 125 ("Ordinarily, one says that one believes that *p* when one merely has a partial belief or suspects that *p*. It is common, when one finds evidence lacking in some respect, to say: 'I don't really *know* that such and such is the case, but I *believe* that it is.'").

[65] Indeed, one can switch from one kind of belief to the other, even if the two kinds of belief are mutually exclusive. Id. at 134.

But there is another way to understand the role of categorical beliefs in adjudication. Perhaps the most fully articulated version of this model in the legal literature is that of Professor Ho. His discussion of the matter is avowedly an eclectic mixture of various nonlegal theories, more in the nature of a quest for a theory, yet he is emphatic that in adjudication, "questions of fact are decided on the basis of categorical beliefs."[66] Ho's reasoning runs essentially like this[67]:

1. A fact-finder's positive verdict about a disputed factual claim *p* entails the assertion that *p*.
2. The assertion that *p* entails a declaration that the fact-finder *knows* that *p*.
3. A declaration of knowledge that *p* not only entails that the fact-finder believes that *p* but also offers an assurance or guarantee by the fact-finder that *p* is true in a way that a declaration of mere partial belief that *p* does not.
4. Thus a verdict that *p* entails an assertion of a belief about *p* that is a categorical belief, not a partial belief.

The same restrictions apply to a fact-finder's verdict affirming that not-*p*.

This approach seems to leave a much larger scope for the application of the default rule against the claimant (again assumed throughout the present discussion to be the party bearing the burden of persuasion). It implies that in all those cases where the fact-finder can say only that it has a partial, not a categorical, belief that the claim *C* is true, no matter how strongly it holds that partial belief, no matter how high it takes $P(C|E)$ to be, the fact-finder must withhold a verdict that *C* is true.[68] Even with a high value for $P(C|E)$ or other conditions that also would preclude a verdict that not-*C* is true, the fact-finder could only place such a case in the third category of doxastic positions, to wit, that the fact-finder must suspend judgment about *C*; it neither (categorically) believes it nor (categorically) disbelieves it, thus triggering the default rule against the claimant.

Moreover, Ho articulates a theory of categorical belief that does not and cannot depend, at least not primarily, on the condition that the fact-finder's partial belief exceed some threshold criterion.[69] He argues that "[t]he

---

[66] Id. at 182.
[67] Id. at 124–35.
[68] Ho typically refers to specific hypotheses favoring the claimant, his proposition *p*, rather than to a range of such hypotheses, such as represented by *C* in much of the previous discussion. But the structure of the argument remains the same if one uses *C* instead of *p*.
[69] Id. at 182 ("A categorical belief cannot be thought of simply as a partial belief that exceeds a certain value of probability").

notion of suspending belief (or more accurately, suspending judgment) applies to a categorical belief but not to a partial belief."[70] In particular, "[o]ne does not lack a belief conceived probabilistically when one sits perfectly on the fence so to speak; rather, one has a partial belief with the exact probability of 0.5."[71] Ho uses this idea to offer a solution to the paradoxical problems of naked statistical evidence (see § 3.1). For Ho, if a fact-finder with an assessed probability greater than P^* (perhaps very much greater than P^*) is nonetheless prepared to say that it must suspend judgment for want of categorical belief, then the verdict must go against the claimant despite the expected loss in utility. Thus Ho uses the unique applicability of the notion of "suspension of belief" to beliefs that are categorical in nature as an argument that our intuitions about naked statistical evidence reveal categorical beliefs at work.[72]

As an initial matter, because his focus is on the fact-finder, Ho's analysis fails to take into account an important way that a tribunal, even one the fact-finder for which employs a partial belief threshold criterion, can "suspend judgment." We examined this thoroughly in Chapter 3. Such a tribunal can conclude that the Keynesian weight of the evidence is not "ripe," not sufficient to permit a verdict for or against the claim. This involves suspending judgment, and it does so for an understandable reason: that the evidence can be and should be improved, in the interest of increasing the expected certainty of $P(C|E)$ and the expected utility of the decision, before the fact-finder commits to a verdict for either side. (It does not, of course, presuppose that the fact-finder at that point estimates $P(C|E)$ as equal to P^*, whether $P^* = 0.5$ or any other value.) Moreover, it provides a different explanation of the problem of naked statistical evidence, one that need not appeal to the idea of categorical belief and one that explains it in terms of reasons for action.

By contrast, it is difficult to see how the absence of a categorical belief that the claim is either true or false provides a *reason* to decide the case in a way that is functionally equivalent to a decision based on the categorical belief that the claim is false, effectively giving preference to the interests of the defendant. At best, Ho seems to assert that a verdict for the claimant based simply on the fact-finder's conclusion that *C* is sufficiently probable (by whatever standard) to warrant a verdict does not involve the fact-finder taking *responsibility* for the truth of *C*. In obvious reply, one can observe that the fact-finder using a partial belief threshold criterion

---

[70] Id. at 132.
[71] Id.
[72] Id. at 135–43.

has taken responsibility for the truth of *C* in exactly the sense required by the law: the fact-finder has declared *C* to be true, for the legal purposes at hand, just because the fact-finder's partial belief, reached in accordance with the law's guidelines, exceeds the appropriate legal standard. This is a serious responsibility, the responsibility "to make an epistemological appraisal,"[73] and Ho does not make the case that the law ought to demand more of the fact-finder.

Ho might try to deflect this criticism by insisting that his theory is descriptive, that, whether justified or not, the law *does* demand more of the fact-finder. To be sure, Ho's categorical belief approach has the advantage, to the extent that it *is* an advantage, that it roughly reproduces the "classical" Continental European view of the burden of proof applicable in all cases:

> [T]he classical view of the burden of proof ... is that the judge may find himself [or herself], after having made the evaluation of evidence, in one of three different situations. About the fact *X* he [or she] may have arrived at the conviction (1) that it does not exist, or (2) that it does exist, or (3) that there is uncertainty about its existence.[74]

The implication of this position is that the judge must decide against the burdened party in both cases (1) and (3). But this view seems to carry an uncomfortable implication: it does not distinguish between types of cases, whether minor civil cases or serious criminal cases, at least in terms of the formal requirement of proof. This, in fact, has been the subject of much critical commentary.[75] It poses the question of how the fact-finder's required categorical belief can be different in different cases or different kinds of cases. Ho's solution to this, allowing it to accommodate common-law variation in the standard of proof, is to acknowledge that "one can believe

---

[73] Here I quote and concur with Susan Haack:

> [W]hat the finder of fact is asked to determine is *not* whether the defendant did it, but *whether the proposition that the defendant did it is established, to the required degree of proof, by the admissible evidence presented*; in other words – subject to the legal constraints signaled by the phrases "to the required degree of proof" and "admissible evidence" – *to make an epistemological appraisal.*

Haack (2012) at 214.

[74] See Bolding (1960) at 18.

[75] See, e.g., id. (arguing for a probabilistic approach to the burden of proof as against this "classical" view) and Clermont & Sherwin (2002) (suggesting that civil-law countries' use of a consistently high standard of proof for all cases may reflect an effort to obtain "the legitimating benefits of the myth that their courts act only on true facts and not on mere probabilities").

categorically that *p* more or less strongly."[76] The strength of categorical belief that is required for a verdict may, therefore, vary as well.

At this point, it is necessary to provide a fuller sketch of Ho's theory of the "standard of proof." Ho distinguishes between two aspects of the standard of proof: the *degree of caution* that must be employed by the fact-finder and the *distribution of caution* that must inform the fact-finder's decision. The latter describes an epistemic attitude that is comparative, in our terms comparing *C* with not-*C*, whereas the former is noncomparative in this sense and speaks to the level of confidence that the fact-finder must have in any proposition that it endorses by its verdict. Ho's account of the *distribution* of caution is fairly conventional: civil cases require an equality of respect and concern for plaintiffs and defendants, whereas criminal cases require an asymmetrical attitude showing greater skepticism toward the prosecution's theory of the case than toward that of the defense.[77] It is in his account of the requisite *degree* of caution that Ho clearly intends to make a contribution. In this regard, he writes:

> The required level of confidence depends on the caution [the fact-finder] must exercise in the context of the case at hand. She must exercise such caution as is commensurate with the seriousness of what is said of, and at stake for, the party who is affected by her finding.[78]

It is not difficult to see the parallel between these two aspects of the burden of proof and the two kinds of "weight" emphasized in the present study. Ho's "degree of caution" is closely related to what I have called "Keynesian weight" and the requirements that are placed on it to warrant a verdict, whereas his "distribution of caution" is closely related to what I have called "discriminatory power" and the requirements that are placed on it by the

---

[76] Ho (2008) at 128.
[77] Id. at 223–8. There are problems here, to be sure. For example, Ho's account makes it difficult to provide any intelligible stopping point in the protection of the accused in criminal cases. If, as he says, the "primary role of the fact-finder" is to "protect the accused against wrongful conviction" (id. at 226), then fact-finders should simply acquit all defendants; there is no basis in that primary purpose for accepting (as Ho does) the "moral judgment" that "it is (*n* times) worse to risk conviction of the innocent than to risk acquittal of the guilty" (id. at 228), whatever the value of *n*. I pass over these issues in order to focus on the matter of resiliency and its connections to Keynesian weight.
[78] Id. at 185–6. This language, and similar locutions that recur throughout his discussion, seem to suggest that only *one* party's interests determine what is at stake, "the" party who is affected by the finding, which contributes rhetorical force to the notion that suspension of judgment should inure to the benefit of that party, presumably the party that does not bear the burden of persuasion. Of course, *both* parties have interests affected by the decision in practically every adjudicated case.

standard of proof. The most important commonality between Ho's theory and mine is that we agree that there are two distinct requirements of proof here, whatever the name we give to them, and the two requirements are described in somewhat similar terms. There are, however, stark differences between our theories.

Consider Ho's explanation of the requisite degree of caution, the analogue of my requirement that Keynesian weight be practically optimized. In Ho's extended discussion of this requirement, applicable in both civil and criminal trials, he elaborates his characterization of the fact-finder's required belief by endorsing the view that such belief, albeit categorical, is nonetheless *context dependent*:

> The meaning of the sentence "S knows that p" is context sensitive.... S counts as knowing p in a particular context only if S's epistemic position with respect to p is good enough to satisfy the standard for knowledge that operates in that context.[79]

Specifically, "[t]he more serious is the allegation or the larger the stake, the greater the caution that must be exercised in deliberation":

> The greater is the stake in being correct on p, the greater the caution that must be exercised in finding that p; the greater the caution that must be exercised, the higher is the epistemic standard that must apply. To insist on the practice of greater caution is to insist on the application of a higher standard of proof. The party against whom an adverse finding is made on evidence that is manifestly inadequate, relative to the standard of caution that is appropriate, is entitled to feel that the court did not value him sufficiently and did not care enough about his interests.[80]

On this basis, Ho defends the idea that the standard of proof is variable, even though it always requires the fact-finder to commit to a knowledge that p in order to warrant a positive finding that p. Moreover, he clearly distinguishes this exercise of caution from carefulness in the consideration of the evidence and arguments that are presented.[81] It is the adequacy of the evidence considered that drives his requirement on the degree of caution.[82]

---

[79] Id. at 202.
[80] Id. at 212.
[81] Id. at 186–7.
[82] At times, it seems as if Ho shifts to considerations that are comparative, such as between the claim, his p, and its negation, his not-p, so that the degree of caution required depends on the relative costs of errors of different kinds. See, e.g., id. at 204 (seemingly approving such analysis in the work of Ralph Wedgwood).

This argument, and the extended passage in which it is found, is partly compatible with the theory of Keynesian weight I have presented. In particular, Ho's argument depends on the intuitively perceived (though not explicitly identified) increase in the expected certainty that, as we have seen (§ 5.1), is the epistemic payoff from increasing Keynesian weight. Ho refers to this variously in terms of the "confidence" or "tenacity" of the fact-finder's categorical belief.[83] As explained in Chapter 3, it is true that the adequacy of Keynesian weight is determined contextually, with an eye to the stakes involved, and that such stakes can vary from case to case. It is possible, for example, that the stakes in serious civil cases will be higher than those in minor criminal cases. In this sense, there is a variable, context-determined requirement of proof, and this matter is distinct from the implications of an appropriate "distribution" of caution (or, as I would put it, distinct from the appropriate requirement on discriminatory power).

There are, however, three clearly discernible points of contrast between Ho's theory and mine, all related to Ho's emphasis on the fact-finder's categorical belief. First, throughout his presentation, Ho places responsibility for use of the requisite "degree of caution" on the fact-finder as such, but the fact-finder does not choose the evidence that is presented for consideration, at least in adversarial trials. Especially in jury trials, the only way for the fact-finder to exercise this sense of caution is by monitoring the adequacy of what the parties have presented. One of my principal arguments is that, for important practical reasons, monitoring of the adequacy of Keynesian weight is properly a judicial function. This practical reality has significant impacts on how we understand the epistemic situation of the fact-finder (see Chapter 4). If I am correct about the respective roles of the fact-finder and the judge (when acting as trial-monitor), then trials, especially trials before juries, require a role separation that may be quite unnatural, viewed from the perspective of ordinary, unitary decision makers reaching categorical judgments, but it is nonetheless very real.[84]

Second, Ho's conception of the adequacy of caution necessary for the fact-finder to decide (or, as I would put it, for a court to authorize a fact-finder to decide) does not embrace the excusable preference structure

---

[83] Id. at 150 ("The notion of tenacity may be said to be related to the notion of confidence thus: the greater the confidence one has in p, the more tenaciously one holds on to the categorical belief that p.").

[84] If this were the only difference between Ho's theory and mine, one might chalk it up to Ho's having an implicit focus on bench trials, where the roles of fact-finder and trial monitor are not clearly separated. However, this focus cannot explain the next two differences.

I have endorsed. While Ho acknowledges that adequacy in the degree of caution is a function of the stakes involved in the litigation, he provides no corresponding acknowledgment that such adequacy is also a function of the cost and availability of additional evidence. Instead, Ho ends up endorsing what I have called a "strict" weight requirement (see § 3.3), without attempting to solve the difficult problems that such a conception forces on us.[85]

The third divergence between Ho's theory and mine is that Ho's discussion of evidential completeness is embedded in an analysis of inference that is holistic in the sense that was criticized earlier (see § 3.6): he takes evidential completeness as simply one of various factors, such as the credibility of witnesses, that determine how strongly an inference is supported.[86] Thus, although Ho discusses "degree of caution" and "distribution of caution" as distinct requirements,[87] and although, for him, a deficiency in Keynesian weight seems to be the driving force behind the conclusion that the decision maker has not exercised an adequate "degree of caution," Ho is unable to maintain the separation. Rather, he merges them by attaching Keynesian weight to the question of whether the fact-finder is sufficiently confident *that the claim is true* rather than to the appropriate question of

---

[85] If Ho does endorse an excusable preference structure, it is very hard to find it in his analysis. Consider this somewhat ambiguous passage, in which Ho addresses the issue of Keynesian weight directly:

> In forming our beliefs, we have to and do take into account the extent of our ignorance... [I]f the trier of fact is aware that the available evidence adduced in support of a hypothesis is significantly incomplete, that too much of relevance is as yet hidden from her, that "there is a significant chance that there is a better explanation" for the event in question, she would not be justified in believing that the hypothesis is true.

Id. at 167 (citation omitted). In the first place, if evidence is adduced in court, then clearly it is "available," and the word seems unnecessary. At the same time, Ho's use of the word "hidden," which ordinarily suggests intentional concealment of information by someone, appears not to have that connotation here. (Ho might be playing on the ambiguity in the latter word. If the missing evidence were intentionally concealed, then there would indeed be a good reason to prevent a finding, but this reason is disciplinary in nature, and one cannot say in whose favor a preemptive sanction should then operate until the party doing the hiding has been identified. See § 4.3.) In context, therefore, the most plausible paraphrasing of the quoted passage is this: when all the evidence available to be presented is presented, a positive verdict may be unjustified simply because the fact-finder perceives that too much evidence remains missing. Elsewhere, Ho more clearly, albeit tangentially, denies that the determination of the adequacy of Keynesian weight is limited by the practical availability of further evidence not presented in court. Id. at 136 n. 190.

[86] Id. at 165–70.

[87] Id. at 185–223.

whether the tribunal is sufficiently confident *about deciding* between the claim and its negation.[88]

These three differences are interconnected. Because Ho is unable to separate the assessment of Keynesian weight from the holistic assessment of the warrant for an inference, and he sees it as the fact-finder's role to determine whether the inference is warranted by the evidence, he has no choice but to assign the assessment of the adequacy of Keynesian weight to the fact-finder. By misplacing responsibility to monitor the adequacy of Keynesian weight, Ho is forced to make decisional "space" for the noncommittal "refusal to decide" in the fact-finder's array of options. Because the fact-finder (at least in an adversarial system) is in no position to conduct further investigation or to insist on such investigation by the parties, Ho has no place to put such noncommittal (refusal to decide) cases but into the default rule favoring the defendant (which is to say, *not* refusing to decide). This, in turn, seems more sensible if one thinks of the refusal to decide as based on a "strict" requirement of weight, indifferent to the costs of information acquisition, that is, one that does not involve an excusable preference structure, because the fact-finder is generally and correctly not called on to enforce such structures. Thus, in his analysis of the requisite degree of caution, Ho has wandered into an analytical trap.

These points are nicely illustrated by an example, called the "airport case," on which Ho relies to illustrate the contextual quality of assertions of knowledge involved in fact-finders' verdicts:

> Mary and John are at the L.A. airport contemplating taking a certain flight to New York. They want to know whether the flight has a layover in Chicago. They overhear someone ask a passenger Smith if he knows whether the flight stops in Chicago. Smith looks at the flight itinerary he got from the travel agent and responds, "Yes I know – it does stop in Chicago." [It matters little to Smith whether this is true or not.] It turns out that Mary and John have an important business contact they have to make at the Chicago airport. Mary says, "How reliable is that itinerary? It

---

[88] For example, Ho argues
  (i) To believe (or more accurately, judge) that *p* is, in the first place, to choose *p* over some other propositions; it is to reject or dismiss the proposition that compete against *p* for truth-regulated acceptance.
  (ii) To believe (or more accurately, judge) that *p* is, in addition to (i), to be sufficiently confident that *p*.
  Id. at 143. It is (ii) that relates to Keynesian weight, of course, and Ho's articulation obscures the point that the uncertainty associated with relative paucity of evidence affects not only *p* but also its competitors.

could contain a misprint. They could have changed the schedule at the last minute." Mary and John agree that Smith doesn't really *know* that the plane will stop in Chicago. They decide to check with the airline agent.[89]

The import of Ho's discussion of this example is that different people (e.g., Smith on the one hand and Mary and John on the other) with the same stock of information may be regarded as having different standards for the assertion of knowledge as to the same proposition (e.g., whether the flight stops in Chicago) because they have different stakes in the results of acting on such knowledge. For Smith, little turns on whether he is right or not; he is taking that flight anyway. For Mary and John, though, it matters considerably whether the itinerary is correct. Thus Smith may "know" that the plane stops in Chicago, and at the same time, Mary and John may be precluded by their context from such knowledge.[90]

Although the subject of contextualism and "pragmatic encroachment" is complex, I am inclined to agree with the basic point of Ho's analysis. There is, however, more here than he considers. The reader may already anticipate the critical observation: there are clearly two decisions in play for Mary and John: (1) whether to take the indicated flight or undertake some other (unspecified) mode of travel (apparently) designed to take them through Chicago and (2) whether to make the foregoing decision based on what they learned from Smith or, instead, to acquire further information (e.g., by checking with the airline agent) before making that decision. Indeed, the omission of the details regarding any alternative itinerary, coupled with the decision that is associated most immediately with their want of knowledge (i.e., whether to check with the agent), shows the primacy of the second decision, at least for Mary and John. The example actually illustrates that if practical interests and consequences do encroach on their knowledge assessment, then both the stakes involved in the former decision and the costs involved in the latter are integral.

Ho recognizes only a partial admixture of pragmatism with categorical belief formation: he accepts it insofar as it arises from the inevitable importance of the stakes of decision to the contextual formation or adoption of categorical beliefs, but he ignores it insofar as it arises from the (equally

---

[89] Id. at 203 (taking the example from Cohen, S. (2005) at 61–62; bracketed material added by Ho).

[90] Ho does not address the possibility that Smith may have reasons to rely on his travel agent that are not available to Mary and John. Nothing in the analysis rests on this possibility.

inevitable) importance of information acquisition costs to such a process. Thus Ho does not pause to consider, for example, the epistemic situation of Mary and John if it were the case that they did not have time or means to make any such additional inquiry. This, in fact, is the critical assumption that makes the example a useful analogy to adjudicative fact-finding. With this new assumption, the stakes for their decision are still different from Smith's. But without any way to augment Keynesian weight, they must choose – to take the flight or not – based on the same information that Smith has. Their inability to augment the Keynesian weight of the evidence either changes their epistemic context with regard to knowledge (as compared with the problem as originally stated), or it does not. That is, one of two things must be true: either (1) whether they rightly can be said to "know" that the flight stops in Chicago depends not only on the stakes involved in choosing which itinerary to follow but also on the costs of additional inquiry before making that choice, or (2) whether they rightly can be said to "know" that the flight stops in Chicago depends on the stakes, but not the inquiry costs. If the former, then the categorical judgment that Ho contemplates must involve Mary and John in the practical optimization of Keynesian weight, as in fact occurs in their example but contrary to what the law generally prescribes for fact-finders, and Ho's theory faces a serious problem as an analogy to adjudication. If the latter, then Mary and John are put in a position where they cannot "know" either that the flight does stop in Chicago or that it does not, but they must nonetheless make a decision about whether to take the flight or not, which means that their categorical belief will not determine their decision; that is, they will be forced to decide on some other basis, such as probabilities and the management of the risk of error.[91]

The set of issues concerning inquiry costs, to the extent that they are mentioned in Ho's account, are set aside as matters concerning the "rationality of inquiry" as opposed to the "rationality of belief."[92] Ho ostensibly

---

[91] Ho's theory at places seems to depend on the idea of knowledge, and I have said little about the philosophical debates concerning knowledge claims. My view commits me to the proposition that having practical knowledge entails that one's degree of partial belief is strong enough that one is willing to act on it. The converse may not be true, however, because knowledge may entail more than that. See, e.g., Pardo (2010). To the extent that it does, however, requiring a fact-finder in the adjudicative context to have knowledge would be counterproductive. See, e.g., Enoch et al. (2012) at 211–14 (arguing that accuracy has at least lexical superiority over knowledge as goals in the adjudicative context).

[92] See Ho (2008) at 189–90.

limits his interest to the latter. But this is quite strange. One could just as easily set aside consideration of the stakes as itself related to the "rationality of decision" rather than the "rationality of belief."[93] This is what Ho tries to do by his initial insistence that fact-finding is a theoretical undertaking, but he is forced to qualify this with regard to consideration of the stakes of decision (see § 2.1). Yet he would not qualify this by a consideration of the costs of additional inquiry. As his example nicely illustrates, this will not work: once one takes either of these steps – separating out the rationality of decision or the rationality of inquiry from the rationality of belief – the epistemic landscape changes. The tools with which the epistemic agent forms ordinary categorical belief, the tools with which one transforms partial belief into categorical belief, are seriously compromised.

We thus arrive at the central point of this section: in any context where a decision must be made, the rationality of categorical belief cannot be separated from either the rationality of the ultimate decision or the rationality of inquiry supporting it. And therein lies a serious problem for Ho's theory, or any other theory of adjudication resting on the use of categorical belief: because adjudication *does* separate the regulation of the adequacy of inquiry (monitored generally by rules and standards applied by trial judges not acting as fact-finders) from the task of fact-finders, the fact-finders are not in a position to rely on ordinary categorical belief determinations regarding the ultimate facts controlling the resolution of adjudicated cases. The use of criteria of decision stated in terms of gradational or partial beliefs, whether or not conceived as probabilities, avoids this problem.

To be sure, I acknowledge that my arguments do not succeed in demonstrating that a categorical belief model of adjudicative fact-finding *cannot* be made to work successfully. What I have shown, however, is that Ho's model does not succeed and that the reasons it does not succeed cast serious doubt on the viability of any such model.[94] For good or ill, partial

---

[93] For an illustration of this separation, see the discussion of John Josephson's analysis of abduction in § 3.4.

[94] At one point, Ho toys with the idea of using Shackle's theory of surprise to construct a model of categorical belief. Id. at 143–51. Whatever heuristic value Shackle's theory may have in informing belief formation, because of the problems noted in the text I do not see how such a theory of categorical belief can succeed in the adjudicative context. Beyond that, I will not attempt a detailed discussion of the theory of surprise, except to note the irony in using Shackle's theory for this purpose. Shackle, believing that probability theory was inadequate for much practical decision making, developed an alternative theory, but it is nonetheless a theory of partial, not categorical, belief. Moreover, Shackle's theory

beliefs, those that can be graded using probabilities or some other gradational measure of epistemic warrant, seem to be built into the fabric of legal adjudication.

is embedded in a decision theory that is explicitly action oriented, addressed to rational investment decisions. See, e.g., Shackle (1969). As discussed in § 2.1, Ho insists that adjudicative fact-finding is theoretical reasoning, not one of "betting on the truth" by "acting on probabilities," but rather one of declaring justified beliefs. In these terms, although Shackle does not explicitly address adjudication, he would have placed himself squarely in the "betting on the truth" camp, even though he would not use conventional mathematical probabilities as his preferred tool.

6

Conclusion

In his famous treatise, Wigmore compared ordinary practical decision making with adjudication, in the course of which he made the following comment regarding both: "So far as mere logic is concerned, it is perhaps questionable whether there is much importance in the doctrine of burden of proof as affecting persons in controversy."[1] While I have the utmost respect for the work of this giant of jurisprudence, much of the present book, if successful, will have shown just how misleading this comment can be.

6.1 A Brief Summary

My inquiry has elucidated an understanding of the burdens of proof in terms of two distinct kinds of evidential "weight." On the one hand, an adjudicative tribunal is called on to assess weight in a sense that is comparative as between the two sides. The tribunal compares the support that the evidence gives to the claimant's case with that which the evidence gives to the opponent's case. This notion of weight I have called the "discriminatory power" of the evidence available to the tribunal, where it is understood that the evidence formally presented in court is assessed within the context of the general background information with which the tribunal legitimately approaches its task as well as the more case-specific, uncontroverted facts that are communicated to the fact-finder in numerous ways. Chapter 2 illustrated how the idea of discriminatory power can be developed. One powerful interpretive model, an adaptation of conventional decision theory, has identifiable strengths as well as some weaknesses. While it is largely agnostic about the process by which the fact-finder reaches its assessment, it does suppose that the outcome of that assessment can be captured by comparing an approximate probability or odds with a publicly stated standard. This judgment implements the law's policy regarding the allocation of the unavoidable risks of error.

---

[1] Wigmore (1981) § 2485 at 285.

On the other hand – and to a large degree independent of how one gives specific content to a theory of discriminatory power – the tribunal is called on to assess weight in a sense that is comparative only in a different way: this sense of weight is the same for each of the contending hypotheses, but it varies with the amount of evidence considered with respect to them. In this respect, the task of the tribunal is to ensure a practical optimization of the amount and quality of the evidence – the Keynesian weight of the evidence – as a condition on its final assessment of discriminatory power. Chapter 3 explained the importance of such optimization, examined some of the analytical tools that may be used to understand it, and detailed how the conflation of this enterprise with the assessment of discriminatory power, often expressed in terms of a holistic assessment of evidential weight, leads to persistent confusion, at least in the adjudicative context. Perhaps the most important feature of this practical optimization is that it does not contemplate a threshold minimum required degree of Keynesian weight other than that which is (or should have been) reasonably obtainable. What is reasonable will depend on the nature of the case, the amount in controversy, context-sensitive factors about the potential value of evidence to be acquired, and, of course, the costs of evidence acquisition. Here is the context in which, for any category of cases or even for each particular case, the law chooses how much accuracy it is worth pursuing.

In Chapter 4, I discussed the implications of disentangling these theoretically distinct adjudicative functions in the context of two great modern legal traditions – the civil law and the common law. I dwelt at much greater length on the adversarial system of the common law in part because the distinctive roles of fact-finder (including a jury when one is employed) and trial regulator (the judge acting not as fact-finder) that appear in the common-law system require greater precision about the respective roles of those agents in addressing discriminatory power and Keynesian weight. To recapitulate, the assessment of discriminatory power is primarily the role of the fact-finder, whereas the practical optimization of Keynesian weight is primarily the role of the parties under the supervision of the court. In lawyers' vernacular, discriminatory power is at home in the domain of the "burden of persuasion," whereas Keynesian weight finds its place with the "burden of production." This expansive notion of the burden of production embraces a wide variety of legal doctrines and gives them coherence as a pattern of tools used to regulate the degree of Keynesian weight in the evidence presented to the fact-finder.

Chapter 5 examined the connections between the foregoing ideas and the frequently suggested concern about tenacity of belief, or resilience of probability assessments. There is a connection between Keynesian weight and such notions, but the connection is contingent: increases in Keynesian weight necessarily increase expected certainty, but they do not necessarily increase resilience of probability assessments. Even when they do, there is no reason to insist on a certain degree of resilience, as a condition on an affirmative judgment, other than the resilience that results from an evidence package the Keynesian weight of which has been practically optimized. Moreover, any requirement of resilience would have to be enforced by the fact-finder who assesses the probability of the parties' claims, which – especially for a bifurcated tribunal – would place such a requirement at odds with the court's management of Keynesian weight. Similarly, any focus on tenacity of categorical belief as a condition on an affirmative judgment presupposes a criterion of decision that synthesizes both the costs of evidence acquisition and decisional error costs into the process of reaching categorical belief. Such a synthesis does not cohere well with the separation of responsibilities that the law actually employs. It gives too much responsibility and authority to the fact-finder and ignores the vital role of policy makers who set both the standards of discriminatory power and the conditions of Keynesian weight within which the fact-finder is to make its epistemic appraisal.

6.2 Further Applications of the Theory: International Tribunals

I have used the distinction between Keynesian weight and discriminatory power primarily to illuminate the functions of particular evidentiary rules, to clarify the proper roles of institutional actors, and to relate these to a proper understanding of the role of Keynesian weight in decision making. Both the modern civil law and the modern common law are systems of adjudication that, if properly executed, can do a good job optimizing Keynesian weight. But it should be clear that these insights can be extended to other decision-making contexts. In particular, the import of the foregoing discussion is that any type of fact-finding tribunal can be assessed on two distinct dimensions: how well it makes determinations of discriminatory power and how well it ensures a practical optimization of Keynesian weight as a prelude to the final assessment of discriminatory power. A tribunal may be relatively effective on one dimension and relatively ineffective on the other. International tribunals illustrate the point. Some international tribunals arguably do not fare well on either dimension. Consider, for example, the international criminal tribunals specially formed to try cases of genocide and other atrocities, which trace their origin to the trials following World War II. After the Nuremburg trials of Nazi leaders and the Tokyo trials of Imperial Japanese leaders, there was a gap of some 60 years before the modern era saw the formation of several courts of specialized subject-matter jurisdiction – such as the International Criminal Tribunal for the former Yugoslavia and the International Criminal Tribunal for Rwanda – as well as the creation of the permanent International Criminal Court. An important and detailed recent study of these largely adversarial courts by Nancy Combs reveals substantial defects both in the acquisition of useful evidence by prosecutors – a problem of Keynesian weight – and in the evaluation of the admitted evidence by the courts – a problem of discriminatory power.[2]

With regard to the former, Combs points to the inadequacy of investigation in many such cases attributable to an insufficiency of investigative resources and to the poor quality of the training of investigators, who must often work under very difficult conditions in foreign countries in the context of significant linguistic and cultural obstacles, as well as to the reluctance of courts to visit important locales and their failure to take serious action to suppress likely widespread perjury.[3] With regard to the latter – the courts' assessments of discriminatory power of the evidence they do have – Combs identifies a disturbing failure to take seriously the gross deficiencies in the eyewitness testimony on which these courts are generally forced to rely.[4] She argues that this cavalier, even "lackadaisical" attitude toward testimonial deficiencies reveals a pro-conviction bias arising from a judicial reluctance to delegitimize such courts by acquitting persons widely (and perhaps quite reasonably) believed to be guilty and from the selection of judges insufficiently rooted in a culture that takes the "proof beyond reasonable doubt" standard seriously.[5] The combined effect is to cast serious doubt on the fact-finding competence of these tribunals.[6]

Some other international tribunals, however, while not particularly bad at making determinations regarding discriminatory power, are still seriously hampered by inadequate development of an evidentiary base (Keynesian weight) on which to make such determinations. A fascinating example is the International Court of Justice (ICJ), at least in its more

---

[2] See Combs (2010).
[3] Id. at 274–85. On the issue of perjury, see also id. at 130–66.
[4] Id. at 11–166, 189–223.
[5] Id. at 225–35. Combs also points to the use of inferences from the defendant's position in the organization alleged to have orchestrated the crime, which has the potential to slide subtly into liability by mere association. Id. at 235–72, 335–9.
[6] Id. at 167–88.

recent activity. The ICJ, created by the United Nations, hears controversies between sovereign nations on matters ranging from border disputes to alleged violations of treaty obligations. Sitting without a lay jury, it resolves both questions of fact and questions of law. Importantly, it has jurisdiction over disputes only by the consent of the countries involved. This fact has affected its rules of evidence and how they are deployed. Fortunately, again, we have the benefit of a recent systematic study of the evidentiary procedures before the ICJ, this one by Anna Riddell and Brendan Plant,[7] that will allow me quickly to make the pertinent observations.

The ICJ was intended to incorporate aspects of both the inquisitorial and adversarial systems, and it is sometimes claimed that it incorporates the best elements of both.[8] The basis for this claim is the fact that while parties have primary control of the presentation of evidence, as in the adversarial common law, the Court has explicit authority to call on the parties for additional evidence, to question witnesses called by the parties, and to authorize the use of neutral experts to collect and analyze useful information, as in more inquisitorial systems.[9] Riddell and Plant argue, however, that the "best of both worlds" characterization is doubtful, that the attributes described are correct, but the reality of the workings of the Court reveal something quite different from what one might expect from such a description. They note several points: the Court's power to request additional evidence from parties is rarely used and cannot be enforced; the power to commission experts is rarely used, even when it would be very desirable; and the Court has no power to subpoena evidence from third parties.[10] So the reality of the Court's operation is that is depends almost entirely on what is voluntarily presented by the state parties. As Riddell and Plant conclude, "at times it appears that the Court represents an incoherent synthesis of incompatible influences."[11]

I would go further. For an adversarial system, there are some major defects. There is no compulsory discovery of evidence within the control of a party's opponent.[12] There are no generally applicable admissibility rules preferring alternative evidence to that which a party chooses to present.[13] And there is only scant recognition of a burden of production

---

[7] Riddell & Plant (2009).
[8] Id. at 38–9.
[9] Id. at 48–68.
[10] Id. at 62–3.
[11] Id. at 11.
[12] Id. at 59.
[13] Id. at 151–85. As so often is the case, the absence of admissibility rules is misleadingly attributed to the absence of a lay jury. See id. at 151 (quoting Roseanne (1985)) and at 197

or adverse inference by which the Court can induce a party to produce evidence within that party's exclusive control.[14] Consequently, adjudication before the ICJ would be more aptly called "adversarialism on steroids." And it is easy to anticipate the consequences. Much information, of great importance to the factual issues raised by the parties and well within the power of (at least one of) the parties to produce, never appears before the Court. Not surprisingly, the major criticism of the system leveled by commentators is its inadequacy in producing before the Court a reasonably complete package of evidence.[15]

This is not to say that the Court has done a great job of assessing the evidence that it *does* receive. Indeed, there have been trenchant complaints on this score over the years. Riddell and Plant make the case, however, that the Court has begun to recognize the importance of factual determinations, has become more willing to include in its judgments thorough evaluations of the evidence on hand, and has publicly stated various plausible principles by which its assessments are conducted.[16] Moreover, it is noteworthy that the harshest criticisms of the Court's assessments of factual issues relate to its reluctance to draw adverse inferences from a party's failure to present evidence within its control,[17] a criticism that relates as much to the failure to optimize Keynesian weight as to the failure to properly assess the discriminatory power of the evidence before the Court. Like so many of the limitations on the Court's powers noted earlier, this reluctance is attributable to the Court's overriding policy concern to respect the sovereignty, and to presume the good faith, of the state parties that appear before it. Thus, the ICJ's most serious evidential problems arise in contexts that reflect both a self-imposed lack of insight in the assessment of discriminatory power and a failure, whether or not for good reason, to use its powers effectively to practically optimize Keynesian weight.

As these studies illustrate, adjudicative systems can be assessed in terms of the quality of their fact-finding without overtly using the distinction between (let alone the terminology of) discriminatory power and

---

(quoting Valencia-Ospina (1999)). To be sure, since 1991, the Court has begun to be more transparent in the principles it uses to *assess* evidence (id. at 187–200), and the Court's articulations include, for example, warnings that it will attribute little weight to hearsay (id. at 195–7), which warnings presumably will have the desirable effect of discouraging parties from relying on hearsay to establish some fact, at least when this can be avoided.

[14] Id. at 81–5, 203–19.
[15] Id. at 77.
[16] Id. at 185–200.
[17] See id. at 116–19. See also Scharf & Day (2012),

Keynesian weight, though they become more clearly defined when understood with attention to this distinction. Such analysis yields practical recommendations that, once again, could be articulated without the help of the Keynesian weight vocabulary but that are more transparent when put in this context.

The importance of explicitness and clarity about the distinction between discriminatory power and Keynesian weight can be illustrated with reference to international tribunals and the conceptual structures and arguments that are used in connection with them. For example, in his interesting study of burdens of proof before a broad sampling of non-criminal international tribunals, Mojtaba Kazazi sets the stage for a consideration of the difficult issue of what standard of proof applies with the following analysis:

> [T]he trier of fact in an international proceeding might encounter three different situations with respect to the degree of proof in a given case:
>
> *First*, there is no evidence at all or the evidence is so meagre that it can be ignored.
> *Second*, the evidence produced in the case is so decisive and fully convincing that it proves beyond doubt the assertion of the claimant.
> *Third*, the evidence produced is neither meagre nor decisive, but its cogency could be categorized as lying somewhere between the first and second situations.
>
> Obviously, the first and second situations are not difficult to deal with, since they present two extreme and clear-cut cases. In the first situation the evidence could easily be characterized as insufficient, and in the second situation as conclusive, leading respectively to a dismissal or acceptance of the claim. The third situation, however, is the one that needs greater attention of the trier of fact in an international proceeding. For it requires a determination of the question of what degree of proof, short of being conclusive, may still be acceptable for satisfying the burden of proof.[18]

Clearly, this statement by an experienced international law judge contemplates a categorization of cases along one dimension of evidential weight, which he refers to as "degree of proof." The effect, however, is to mix together the two senses of weight discussed here. His first situation seems to indicate either a deficiency in Keynesian weight or one of discriminatory power, whereas his second situation arguably presents a case of strong discriminatory power that may, or may not, involve optimized Keynesian weight. Once one recognizes the two senses of weight involved, it is clear that the evidence in a case can be both exhaustively developed

[18] Kazazi (1996) at 326.

and yet indecisive, or it can be poorly developed yet decisive in terms of discriminatory power. To complete the taxonomy that forms the basis for his ensuing analysis, Dr. Kazazi needs not three categories along a single dimension but rather at least three along the dimension of discriminatory power (i.e., very weak, close, and very strong) and at least two (i.e., inadequately developed and adequately developed) along the dimension of Keynesian weight.

It is difficult to discern what effect this clarification would have had on Kazazi's particular analysis. His treatment of the standards of proof, such as proof by a preponderance of the evidence or proof beyond reasonable doubt, includes many uses of the terms *weight* and *weighty* that are ambiguous with reference to the distinction I have pressed in these pages.[19] Elsewhere, however, Kazazi reveals an astute perception of the difference. Recall, for example, my claim that in light of the importance of Keynesian weight, the burden of production in American adversarial trials (contrary to conventional articulations) has two components, one that looks to the question of whether the evidence will permit a reasonable fact-finder to decide the case either way and one that looks to the question of whether particular evidence should be produced by an appropriate party (§ 4.1.4). Because the international tribunals addressed by Kazazi do not use juries, the first component should fall away, and under the conventional view, the burden of production would essentially disappear as a distinct concept.[20] But Kazazi rightly says otherwise, noting that the burden of persuasion (which he calls the "burden of proof") and the burden of production can fall on different parties even in international adjudication precisely because of (what I have called) the second component of the production burden:

> As an example, if in order to prove its case the claimant relies on documents which are undoubtedly in the sole possession of the respondent, then it might be right to say that the claimant carries the burden of proof but the burden of presentation of evidence is on the respondent.[21]

---

[19] See id. at 343–52.

[20] Of course, as in American trials, a distinct "tactical burden" of producing evidence can shift back and forth during the presentation of evidence in accordance with the assessed discriminatory power at that moment. But this is simply a recognition by a party that if it does not present additional evidence, it is likely to lose.

[21] Id. at 37. It might be going too far to say that Kazazi perceives the excusable preference structure that rightly attends Keynesian weight (§ 3.3), but he does write, in regard to the effect of discharging a party's burden of production, that "even though a party has submitted *all the evidence possible*, the tribunal may still conclude that the burden of proof [i.e., persuasion] has not been discharged." Id. at 36 (emphasis added).

Moreover, he observes that the use of sanctions for nonproduction, while a very delicate matter when dealing with sovereign nations, is not limited to – that is, not identified with – the use of adverse inferences that can be drawn against the nonproducing party (a matter of what I have called "discriminatory power"). Rather, it is a tool to encourage parties to present "as much evidence as possible" (essentially what I have called "practically optimized" Keynesian weight) in accordance with their duty to cooperate in presenting a reasonably complete package of evidence to the tribunal.[22]

Another interesting example can be found in Combs's account of international criminal tribunals. Combs does not explicitly recognize the distinction I have pressed, which leads her into making an important but curiously articulated argument. Specifically, in an effort both to explain and to justify the decisions made by many international criminal tribunals, despite the problems she has identified, she uses the decision-theoretic model to make the plausible observation that the "beyond reasonable doubt" standard employed in such tribunals may not involve a uniform high level of probability and that these tribunals may have systematically different assessments of the costs of erroneous convictions and erroneous acquittals than is true in common domestic trials.[23] Thus Combs describes the blurred line between guilt and innocence in the context of crimes such as genocide and the likelihood that a defendant, though innocent of the particular version of the crime of which he or she is accused, has committed something closely akin to it.[24] And she points to a balance of reasons that plausibly suggests that the concern for acquittal of the guilty is higher in the context of such international crimes than in the context of domestic crimes.[25] In other words, she makes the case that adjudicators in international criminal trials do and perhaps should use a lower P^* than is common in domestic trials.

I do not here dispute Combs's general conclusion, but the analysis of previous chapters shows that one particular argument she deploys in support of it does not withstand scrutiny. The difficulty arises in the first reason that she gives in support of the claim that the international criminal tribunals often perceive lower costs of inaccurate convictions. She writes:

> First, there is a greater likelihood in an international case featuring reasonable doubt than a domestic case featuring reasonable doubt that the

---

[22] Id. at 308–22, 373–4.
[23] Combs (2010) at 343–64.
[24] Id. at 355–7.
[25] Id. at 357–9.

reasonable doubt arose as a consequence of investigatory failures rather than as a consequence of true evidentiary insufficiency....

[W]e can have much greater confidence in a domestic case than in an international case that the evidence the prosecution presents is the best evidence available. Consequently, when the evidence in a domestic case leaves any quantity of doubt in the mind of the fact finder, that doubt is more indicative that the defendant is in fact innocent [than, presumably, the same quantity of doubt would be for an international criminal defendant].[26]

This argument is rather hard to follow, but a sympathetic reading would run as follows: since the utilities and disutilities in the decision-theoretic model on which Combs relies do not depend on either the fact-finder's doubts about guilt or the sources thereof, Combs is here not explaining why international adjudicators use a lower P^*. Rather, her argument is about the quantity that is being compared with P^*, that is, $P(C|E)$, or, more specifically, about what goes into the probability of innocence, that is, $P(\text{not-}C|E)$. She argues that when adjudicators have doubt about the factual claims in a criminal trial, that doubt can arise from two distinct sources: "investigatory failures" and "true evidentiary insufficiency." The quantum of doubt that is, as a psychological or descriptive matter, compared by adjudicators with the "reasonable doubt" standard is the combination of these. However, only the latter kind of doubt is properly considered in deciding the guilt of the accused. As a consequence, although the "true evidentiary" value that is present in a case that is normatively sufficient for a verdict of guilt actually may be the same in typical international criminal trials as it is in typical domestic criminal trials, the *perceived* permissible doubt will depend on how much additional doubt is attributable to inadequate investigation. Because there is more doubt attributable to inadequate investigation for international cases, the total perceived doubt permissible for a conviction will be higher for international cases.

With the benefit of the foregoing study, one can identify both the strengths and weaknesses of this argument, if I have construed it correctly. Plainly, "inadequacy of investigation" is another way of expressing the inadequacy of Keynesian weight, and "true evidentiary" value is another way of expressing discriminatory power. So understood, Combs correctly perceives that there are two distinct kinds of doubt: doubt about the adequacy of investigation and doubt about the guilt of the accused. And Combs also correctly perceives that it is the latter that ought to be

---

[26] Id. at 353–5 (bracketed material added to complete the implicit comparative).

determinative of the verdict. Doubt about the adequacy of investigation may, if somehow combined with doubt about the defendant's factual innocence, present as a large quantum of doubt even though a conviction is appropriate.

But it is clear now that there is a serious confusion in this argument. Insofar as Combs endorses the idea that the doubt attributable to these two sources is commensurable, and thus can be combined into a single measure of aggregate doubt, the argument reflects the kind of holism that I rejected in Chapter 3 (§ 3.6). Of course, insofar as Combs is making a purely descriptive point, arguing that many adjudicators *think* that these two sources of doubt can be meaningfully combined, Combs may well be correct. After all, the holistic error is not an uncommon one.[27] The kind of adjudicator she describes is tempted to make the mistake against which Keynes and others warned – namely, to think that a (contextually assessed) deficiency in Keynesian weight, *vel non*, tells us something about the probability of innocence. It does not. Absent improper motives on the part of the investigators that might raise spoliation inferences, poor-quality investigation does not translate into increased probability of innocence. It only tells us that the decision maker needs to be better informed. What it takes to resolve such doubt, rationally speaking, is entirely different from what it takes to resolve doubts about the innocence of the accused. This difference is what compels Combs to emphasize, rightly, the normative role of "true evidentiary sufficiency"; it is this idea, after all, that determines whether the defendant is properly convicted by the fact-finder. But this seems to leave "investigatory failures" out in the juridical cold, so to speak. While much of Combs book is devoted to suggesting how investigatory methods are deficient and how they should be improved, she does not suggest a distinct role for the court in taking such deficiencies into account in rulings on the burden of proof. Imposing appropriate burdens of production on either the prosecution or the defense in relation to the practical optimization of Keynesian weight does not seem to be within Combs's contemplation.

Her argument on this point can be reconstrued as an argument that what would be an *inexcusable* deficiency of Keynesian weight in a domestic setting may be an *excusable* deficiency of Keynesian weight in the international criminal context. To be sure, Combs is somewhat ambiguous about whether or not the deficiencies of investigative efforts in the

---

[27] Then, too, the actual adjudicators involved may be capable of segregating these two kinds of doubt and keeping them in their proper analytical place.

international criminal context should be considered unavoidable and thus excusable. As noted earlier, at points she seems to say that such problems could be and should be significantly ameliorated by improved investigative techniques and stronger actions by the court to suppress perjury. But she also expresses great sympathy for the difficult circumstances within which the investigators must operate. This, of course, poses the important and difficult policy question. The argument might play out such that it allows us to accept as legitimate the verdicts of international criminal tribunals despite the relatively poor development of the evidence. But even if so, this does not affect either the appropriate standard of discriminatory power or whether it has been met in a particular case.

6.3 Postscript

From the macroscopic level of institutional assessment to the microscopic detail of analyzing particular evidential rules, the distinction between Keynesian weight and discriminatory power is fundamental to the understanding of decision making in general and adjudicative practices in particular. The experience of both municipal and international tribunals serves to illustrate both the usefulness of the distinction between discriminatory power and Keynesian weight and the critical importance of the development and assessment of procedures that will ensure the practical optimization of Keynesian weight. The felt imperative that Keynesian weight be thus optimized is revealed in all legal systems that take seriously the importance of factual accuracy in adjudication.

The importance of attending to the practical optimization of Keynesian weight is critical to those who contemplate afresh the construction of adjudicative procedures. For example, developing countries or other countries contemplating a major overhaul of existing adjudicative institutions are wise to remember that institutional arrangements must be designed to ensure not only that adjudicators are best positioned to assess the evidence that is placed before them but also that adjudicators are able to ensure that the evidence placed before them is as fully developed as cost and other legitimate constraints will allow. The choice between relatively inquisitorial and relatively adversarial procedures is driven by many things, not the least of which is history and institutional inertia. Regardless of a jurisdiction's choice in this regard, the theory developed here provides insight into how to proceed and what to avoid. For relatively inquisitorial systems, the critical factors include the development of (1) procedures to ensure that the investigating magistrate is apprised of the evidentiary leads known to the parties, (2) procedures to permit the investigating magistrate to pursue the leads encountered, and (3) procedures, including methods of training and appropriate appellate review, that emphasize to investigating magistrates the importance of a full but cost-sensitive development of the evidence relevant to the controlling issues. For relatively adversarial systems, the matter is obviously more complex. In particular, one should not be blinded by the supposed passivity of judges in an adversary system. Such passivity is only viable within an institutional arrangement that includes tools for optimizing Keynesian weight. Courts and legislatures must be sensitive to the inevitable limitations of the system of party-initiated disclosure or discovery and be ready to augment the effectiveness of that system with one or more of a variety of legal tools. An important step in rationalizing the use of such tools is seeing them as components of what I described earlier as an expansive notion of the burden of production.

No doubt a clear perception of the dual structure of decision making – separating the evidence-search problem from the ultimate decision problem – can be of assistance in legal contexts outside conventional adjudication before courts. One area of obvious importance is decision making by administrative agencies. The implications of the present work for agency decision making are best left to those with the appropriate expertise. I only observe that agencies must regularly contend with the distinct issue of how to regulate the flow of information to the agencies, much of it coming from interested parties, on the basis of which ultimate decisions are to be made. As in the international adjudication context, subtle differences in incentive structures with regard to the production of evidence can make a great deal of difference to the necessary framework for regulating Keynesian weight. In any event, it is important for institutional designers as well as those with decisional responsibility to be aware of the dual structure of fact-finding.

Unfortunately, no branch of the law seems to have had a good vocabulary for capturing the distinction I have pressed. In common-law adjudication, one consequence is that the felt imperative regarding Keynesian weight has been buried within the operation of many doctrines, sometimes including (perversely) those doctrines articulating requirements on the discriminatory power of evidence. I have tried to dispel the confusion that has resulted. Perhaps, despite the enormous inertia of legal doctrine and usage, the important distinction between discriminatory power and Keynesian weight will now gain wider acceptance. If so, the result will have been worth the effort.

REFERENCES

Material in brackets after each work indicates chapter and footnote where the work is cited in the text. For example, [(3: 1) (4: 12–16)] indicates that the work is cited in Chapter 3, footnote 1, as well as in Chapter 4, footnotes 12 through 16.

Abel & Marsh (1984). Charles F. Abel & Frank H. Marsh, *Punishment and Restitution: A Restitutionary Approach to Crime and the Criminal*, Greenwood Publishing. [(2: 81)]

Achinstein (2001). Peter Achinstein, *The Book of Evidence*, Oxford University Press. [(2: 53)]

Aitken & Taroni (2004). C. G. G. Aitken & Franco Taroni, *Statistics and the Evaluation of Evidence for Forensic Scientists* (2d ed.), Wiley. [(1: 26) (2: 228, 236–7)]

Allen (1986). Ronald J. Allen, A reconceptualization of civil trials, *Boston University Law Review* 66: 401–37. [(2: 192–3) (3: 10–11) (4: 107)]

(1991). Ronald J. Allen, The nature of juridical proof. *Cardozo Law Review* 13: 373–422. [(2: 192, 204, 226)]

(1994). Ronald J. Allen, Factual ambiguity and a theory of evidence. *Northwestern University Law Review* 88: 604–40. [(2: 202, 204)]

(1997). Ronald J. Allen, Rationality, algorithms, and juridical proof: a preliminary inquiry. *International Journal of Evidence & Proof* 1: 253–75. [(2: 32)]

(2000). Ronald J. Allen, Clarifying the burden of persuasion and Bayesian decision rules: a response to Professor Kaye. *International Journal of Evidence & Proof* 4: 246–59. [(2: 32)]

(2006). Ronald J. Allen, The narrative fallacy, the relative plausibility theory, and a theory of the trial. *International Commentary on Evidence* 3(1): 1–6. [(2: 219)]

Allen & Jehl (2003). Ronald J. Allen & Sarah A. Jehl, Burden of persuasion in civil actions: algorithms v. Explanations. *Michigan State Law Review* 4: 893–944. [(2: 200–1)]

Allen & Laudan (2008). Ronald J. Allen & Larry Laudan, Deadly dilemmas. *Texas Tech Law Review* 41: 65–92. [(2: 72)]

Allen & Leiter (2001). Ronald J. Allen & Brian Leiter, Naturalized epistemology and the law of evidence. *Virginia Law Review* 87: 1491–1550. [(2: 192, 203)]

Allen & Pardo (2007). Ronald J. Allen & Michael S. Pardo, The problematic value of mathematical models of evidence. *Journal of Legal Studies* 36: 107–40. [(2: 229)]

Allen & Stein (2013). Ronald J. Allen & Alex Stein, Evidence, probability and the burden of proof. *Arizona Law Review* 55: 557–602. [(2: 177)]

Alexander & Sherwin (2001). Larry Alexander & Emily Sherwin, *The Rule of Rules: Morality, Rules, and the Dilemmas of Law*, Duke University Press. [(2: 171)]

Amaya (2009). Amalia Amaya, Inference to the best legal explanation, in *Legal Evidence and Proof* (H. Kaptein, H. Prakken, & B. Verheij, eds.), Ashgate Publishing. [(2: 229)]

Anderson et al. (2005). Terence Anderson, David Schum, & William Twining, *The Analysis of Evidence* (2d ed.), Cambridge University Press. [(2: 247–8)]

Ayer (1957). A. J. Ayer, The conception of probability as a logical relation, in *Observation and Interpretation in The Philosophy of Physics* (S. Körner ed.), Dover. [(3: 98)]

Ball (1961). V. C. Ball, The moment of truth: probability theory and standards of proof. *Vanderbilt Law Review* 14: 807–30. [(2: 49)]

Barnett (1980). Randy E. Barnett, The justice of restitution. *American Journal of Jurisprudence* 25: 117–32. [(2: 81)]

Beardsley (1986). James Beardsley, Proof of fact in French civil procedure. *American Journal of Comparative Law* 34: 459–86. [(4: 6)]

Beebee & Papineau (1997). Helen Beebee & David Papineau, Probability as a guide to life. *Journal of Philosophy* 94(5): 217–43. [(2: 101) (3: 38)]

Bentham (1827). Jeremy Bentham, *Rationale of Judicial Evidence*, Hunt & Clark. [(3: 208)]

Bex & Walton (2010). Floris Bex & Douglas Walton, Burdens and standards of proof for inference to the best explanation, in *Legal Knowledge and Information Systems* (R. G. F. Winkels, ed.), IOS Press. [(2: 220) (3: 122)]

Blackburn (1980). Simon Blackburn, Review of "The probable and the provable." *Synthese* 44: 149–59. [(3: 94)]

Black (1999). *Black's Law Dictionary* (7th ed.), West Publishing Co. [(1: 19)]

Blackstone (1769). William Blackstone, *Commentaries on the Laws of England*, Oxford University Press. [(2: 66)]

Bolding (1960). Olof Bolding, Aspects of the burden of proof. *Scandinavian Studies in Law* 4: 9–27. [(1: 9) (2: 50) (5: 74–5)]

Brilmayer (1986). Lea Brilmayer, Second-order evidence and Bayesian logic. *Boston University Law Review*. 66: 673–91. [(1: 31) (3: 142) (4: 79–80, 177) (5: 3, 46)]

Brinkmann (2004). Moritz Brinkmann, The synthesis of common and civil law standard of proof formulae in the ALI/Unidroit principles of transnational civil procedure. *Uniform Law Review* (n.s.), 9: 875–91 [(1: 31) (3: 42) (4: 79–80, 177) (5: 3, 46)]

Brook (1985). James Brook, The use of statistical evidence of identification in civil litigation: well-worn hypotheticals, real cases, and controversy. *St. Louis University Law Journal* 29: 293–352. [(3: 13)]

Byrd (1989). Sharon Byrd, Kant's theory of punishment: deterrence in its threat, retribution in its execution. *Law & Philosophy* 8: 151–200. [(2: 182)]

Callen (1994). Craig R. Callen, Hearsay and informal reasoning. *Vanderbilt Law Review* 47: 43–113. [(4: 40)]

— (2003). Craig R. Callen, Rationality and relevancy: conditional relevancy and constrained resources. *Michigan State Law Review* 2003: 1243–1303. [(4: 40)]

Carnap (1950). Rudolf Carnap, *Logical Foundations of Probability*, University of Chicago Press. [(3: 207)]

Cheng (2009). Edward K. Cheng, A practical solution to the reference class problem. *Columbia Law Review* 109: 2081–105. [(2: 229)]

— (2012). Edward K. Cheng, Reconceptualizing the burden of proof. *Yale Law Journal* 122: 1254–79. [(2: 213, 260-2)]

Cheng & Pardo (2015). Edward K. Cheng & Michael S. Pardo, Accuracy, optimality, and the preponderance standard. *Law, Probability and Risk* 14: 193–212. [(2: 56, 179, 187)]

Cleary & Strong (1966). Edward W. Cleary & John W. Strong, The best evidence rule: an evaluation in context. *Iowa Law Review* 51: 825–48. [(4: 19-20, 22)]

Clermont (1987). Kevin M. Clermont, Procedure's magical number three: psychological bases for standards of decision. *Cornell Law Review* 72: 1115–56. [(2: 147)]

— (2009). Kevin M. Clermont, Standards of proof revisited. *Vermont Law Review* 33: 469–87. [(2: 242) (3: 196)]

— (2013). Kevin M. Clermont, *Standards of Decision in Law*, Carolina Academic Press. [(1: 15) (2: 42, 147-51, 154) (3: 187-90, 192-5) (5: 9)]

Clermont & Sherwin (2002). Kevin M. Clermont & Emily Sherwin, A comparative view of standards of proof. *American Journal of Comparative Law* 50: 243–75. [(1: 24) (2: 40) (3: 204) (4: 107) (5: 75)]

Cobb & Shenoy (2003). Barry R. Cobb & Prakash P. Shinoy, A comparison of methods for transforming belief function models to probability models, in *Symbolic and Quantitative Approaches to Reasoning with Uncertainty* (Thomas D. Nielsen & Nevin Lianwen Zhang, eds.), Springer. [(3:182)]

Cohen, J. (1977). L. J. Cohen, *The Probable and the Provable*, Oxford University Press. [(1: 32) (2: 109) (3: 4, 77, 82, 103-4) (4: 2)]

— (1981). L. J. Cohen, Subjective probability and the paradox of the gatecrasher. *Arizona State Law Journal* 1981: 627–34. [(3: 7-8)]

— (1985). L. J. Cohen, Twelve questions about Keynes' concept of weight. *British Journal for the Philosophy of Science* 37: 263–78. [(3: 3, 41, 93, 126, 136) (4: 15)]

— (1986). L. J. Cohen, The role of evidential weight in criminal proof. *Boston University Law Review* 66: 635–49. [(2: 46) (3: 80-1, 106) (4: 2)]

(1989). L. J. Cohen, *An Introduction to the Philosophy of Induction and Probability*, Oxford University Press. [(2: 109) (3: 3, 27, 41, 143, 166)]

(1992). L. J. Cohen, *An Essay on Belief and Acceptance*, Oxford University Press. [(2: 37)]

Cohen, N. (1985). Neil B. Cohen, Confidence in probability: burdens of persuasion in a world of imperfect knowledge. *New York University Law Review* 60: 385–422. [(2: 33) (3: 165) (4: 2) (5: 7–8, 10–12, 16, 19–21, 25–6, 28)]

(1987). Neil B. Cohen, Conceptualizing proof and calculating probabilities: a response to Professor Kaye. *Cornell Law Review* 73: 78–95. [(1: 38) (5: 12, 13–15, 18, 22, 51)]

Cohen, S. (2005). Stewart Cohen, Contextualism defended, in *Contemporary Debates in Epistemology* (Matthias Steup & Ernest Sosa, eds.), Blackwell. [(5: 89)]

Cohen & Bersten (1990). Stephen Cohen & Michael Bersten, Probability out of court: notes on "guilt beyond reasonable doubt." *Australasian Journal of Philosophy* 66: 229–40. [(4: 151)]

Combs (2010). Nancy Armoury Combs, *Fact-Finding without Facts: The Uncertain Evidentiary Foundations of International Criminal Convictions*, Cambridge University Press. [(6: 1–5, 22–5)]

Coons (1964). John E. Coons, Approaches to court-imposed compromise: the uses of doubt and reason. *Northwestern University Law Review* 58: 750–804. [(2: 5)]

Corman (1991). Calvin W. Corman, *Limitations of Actions* (Vol. I), Little, Brown. [(4: 94)]

Cox (1961). Richard T. Cox, *The Algebra of Probable Inference*, Johns Hopkins University Press. [(2: 97, 110)]

Damaška (1986). Mirjan Damaška, *The Faces of Justice and State Authority*, Yale University Press. [(4: 92)]

(1997). Mirjan Damaška, *Evidence Law Adrift*, Yale University Press. [(2: 141) (4: 23, 97)]

Davidson & Pargetter (1986). Barbara Davidson & Robert Pargetter, Weight. *Philosophical Studies* 49: 219–30. [(1: 31, 33) (3: 3, 12, 76) (5: 42)]

(1987). Barbara Davidson & Robert Pargetter, Guilt beyond reasonable doubt. *Australasian Journal of Philosophy* 65: 182–7.[(3: 62–3, 66, 72–4, 142, 205) (4: 2) (5: 44–5)]

De Finetti (1972). Bruno De Finetti, *Probability, Induction and Statistics*, Wiley. [(2: 156)]

DeKay (1996). Michael L. DeKay, The difference between Blackstone-like error rates and probabilistic standards of proof. *Law and Social Inquiry* 21: 95–132. [(2: 29, 34, 36, 67)]

Dershowitz (1996). Alan M. Dershowitz, Life is not a dramatic narrative, in *Law's Stories* (Peter Brooks & Paul Gewirtz, eds.), Yale University Press. [(2: 215)]

REFERENCES

Devitt & Blackmar (1977). Edward J. Devitt & Charles B. Blackmar, *Federal Jury Practice and Instructions* (3d ed.), West Publishing Co. [(2: 196)]

Devitt et al. (1987). Edward J. Devitt, Charles B. Blackmar, & Michael A. Wolff, *Federal Jury Practice and Instructions: Civil* (4th ed.), West Publishing Co. [(2: 196)]

Dunham & Birmingham (1989). Nancy J. Dunham & Robert L. Birmingham, On legal proof. *Australasian Journal of Philosophy* 67: 479–86. [(4: 91)]

Durlauf & Nagin (2011). Steven N. Durlauf & Daniel S. Nagin, Imprisonment and crime. *Criminology & Public Policy* 10: 13–54. [(2: 80)]

Dworkin (1986). Ronald Dworkin, *Law's Empire*, Harvard University Press. [(1: 37)]

Enderton (1977). Herbert E. Enderton, *Elements of Set Theory*, Academic Press. [(2: 126–8) (3: 127)]

Enoch et al. (2012). David Enoch, Levi Spectre, & Talia Fisher, Statistical Evidence, sensitivity, and the legal value of knowledge. *Philosophy & Public Affairs* 40(3): 197–224. [(5: 91)]

Fallis (2002). Don Fallis, Goldman on probabilistic inference. *Philosophical Studies* 109: 223–40. [(2: 246)]

Felix & Whitten (2011). Robert L. Felix & Ralph U. Whitten, *American Conflicts Law* (6th ed.), Carolina Academic Press. [(2: 42) (4: 95) (5: 52)]

Fine (1973). Terrence L. Fine, *Theories of Probability*, Academic Press. [(2: 93)]

Finkelstein & Fairley (1970). Michael O. Finkelstein & William B. Fairley, A Bayesian approach to identification evidence. *Harvard Law Review* 83: 489–517. [(2: 230)]

Fisher (2008). George Fisher, *Evidence* (2d ed.), Foundation Press. [(4: 54)]

Forer (1994). Lois G. Forer, *A Rage to Punish: The Unintended Consequences of Mandatory Sentencing*, Correctional Education Association. [(2: 80)]

Franklin (2001). James Franklin, Resurrecting logical probability. *Erkenntnis* 55: 277–305. [(2: 103, 164)]

(2006). James Franklin, Case comment – United States v. Copeland, 369 F. Supp. 2d 275 (E.D.N.Y. 2005): quantification of the "proof beyond reasonable doubt" standard. *Law, Probability & Risk* 5: 159–65. [(3: 165) (4: 2, 68, 84) (5: 53)]

Friedman (1992). Richard D. Friedman, Toward a partial economic, game-theoretic analysis of hearsay. *Minnesota Law Review* 76: 723–96. [(2: 206) (4: 55)]

(1996). Richard D. Friedman, Assessing evidence. *Michigan Law Review* 94: 1810–38. [(3: 12, 142) (4: 177)]

(1997a). Richard D. Friedman, Answering the Bayesioskeptical challenge. *International Journal of Evidence & Proof* 1: 276–91. [(2: 28, 202, 238) (3: 148–50)]

(1997b). Richard D. Friedman, Dealing with evidentiary deficiency. *Cardozo Law Review* 18: 1961–86. [(3: 147, 152)]

(2000). Richard D. Friedman, A presumption of innocence, not of even odds. *Stanford Law Review* 52: 873-87. [(2: 272-3)]

(2001). Richard D. Friedman, "E" is for eclectic: multiple perspectives on evidence. *Virginia. Law Review* 87: 2029-54. [(2: 219)]

(2003). Richard D. Friedman, Minimizing the jury over-valuation concern. *Michigan State Law Review* 4: 967-86. [(4: 52)]

Fuller (1968). Lon L. Fuller, *The Morality of Law* (rev. ed.), Yale University Press. [(2: 52)]

(1971). Lon L. Fuller, The adversary system, in *Talks on American Law* (Harold Berman, ed.), Vintage Books. [(4: 10)]

Gärdenfors (1993). Peter Gärdenfors, On the logic of relevance, in *Philosophy of Probability* (Jacques-Paul Dubucs, ed.), Kluwer Academic. [(4: 15)]

Gärdenfors & Sahlin (1982a). Peter Gärdenfors & Nils-Eric Sahlin, Unreliable probabilities, risk taking, and decision making. *Synthese* 53: 361-86. [(2: 158)]

(1982b). Peter Gärdenfors & Nils-Eric Sahlin, Reply to Levi. *Synthese* 53: 433-8. [(2: 159)]

Garnett (2012). Richard Garnett, *Substance and Procedure in Private International Law*, Oxford University Press. [(2: 42)]

Garrett (2011). Brandon L. Garrett, *Convicting the Innocent*, Harvard University Press. [(2: 42) (4: 99)]

Gemes (2007). Ken Gemes, Irrelevance: strengthening the Bayesian requirements. *Synthese* 156: 161-6. [(4: 15)]

Gershel (2010). Alan M. Gershel, A review of the law in jurisdictions requiring electronic recording of custodial interrogations. *Richmond Journal of Law and Technology* 16: art 9. [(4: 96)]

Gibbons & Katzenbach (2006). John J. Gibbons & Nicholas de B. Katzenbach (Commission Co-Chairs), *Confronting Confinement: A Report of the Commission on Safety and Abuse in America's Prisons*, Vera Institute of Justice. [(2: 79)]

Gigerenzer (2002). Gerd Gigerenzer, *Reckoning with Risk: Learning to Live with Uncertainty*, Penguin Books. [(2: 125)]

(2008). Gerd Gigerenzer, *Rationality for Mortals*, Oxford University Press. [(3: 101)]

Gigerenzer et al. (1999). Gerd Gigerenzer, Peter M. Todd, and the ABC Research Group, *Simple Heuristics That Make Us Smart*, Oxford University Press. [(2: 125) (3: 210)]

Gilbert (1754). Geoffrey Gilbert, *The Law of Evidence* (1st ed.), reprinted by Garland Publishing Co. (1979). [(4: 1)]

Gillies (2000). Donald Gillies, *Philosophical Theories of Probability*, Routledge. [(2: 94, 95-8, 103, 105, 108-9, 125, 164, 229) (3: 27, 122)]

Goldman (2002). Alvin Goldman, Quasi-objective Bayesianism and legal evidence. *Jurimetrics Journal* 42: 237-60. [(2: 243-6)]

Good (1966). I. J. Good, On the principle of total evidence. *British Journal for the Philosophy of Science* 17: 319-21. [(3: 38)]

(1968). I. J. Good, Corroboration, evolving probability, simplicity, and a sharpened razor. *British Journal for the Philosophy of Science* 19: 123–43. [(3: 134)]

Goodwin (2000). Jean Goodwin, Wigmore's chart method. *Informal Logic* 20(3): 223–43. [(2: 248)]

Gorelick et al. (1989). Jamie S. Gorelick, Stephen Marzen, & Lawrence Solum, *Destruction of Evidence*, Wiley Law Publications. [(4: 109)]

Griffin (2013). Lisa Kern Griffin, Narrative, truth, and trial. *Georgetown Law Journal* 101: 281–335. [(2: 253, 256)]

Haack (1993). Susan Haack, *Evidence and Inquiry*, Blackwell. [(2: 221) (3: 153, 156–7, 161)]

(2001). Susan Haack, An epistemologist in the bramble-bush: at the supreme court with Mr. Joiner. *Journal of Health Politics, Policy & Law* 26: 217–48. [(4: 127)]

(2003). Susan Haack, *Defending Science – Within Reason*, Prometheus Books. [(3: 167)]

(2008). Susan Haack, Proving causation: the holism of warrant and the atomism of *Daubert*. *Journal of Health and Biomedical Law* 4: 253–89. [(3: 153, 155, 160, 162)]

(2012). Susan Haack, The embedded epistemologist: dispatches from the legal front. *Ratio Juris* 25: 206–35. [(3: 158) (5:73)]

(2014). Susan Haack, *Evidence Matters: Science, Proof, and Truth in the Law*, Cambridge University Press. [(1: 17) (2: 126) (3: 159, 166) (4: 121, 133)]

Hacking (2001). Ian Hacking, *An Introduction to Probability and Inductive Logic*, Cambridge University Press. [(2: 103) (5: 4)]

Hale (1847). Matthew Hale, *History of the Pleas of the Crown* (1st American ed.) [1736], R. H. Small. [(2: 68)]

Hamer (2004). David Hamer, Probabilistic standards of proof, their complements and the errors that are expected to flow from them. *University of New England Law Journal* 1: 71–107. [(2: 73, 104)]

(2012a). David Hamer, Delayed complaint, lost evidence and fair trial: epistemic and non-epistemic concerns, in *Criminal Evidence and Human Rights* (P. Roberts and J. Hunter, eds.), Oxford University Press. [(4: 91)]

(2012b). David Hamer, Probability, anti-resilience, and the weight of expectation. *Law, Probability & Risk* 11: 135–58. [(4: 2) (5: 32–3, 38–9)]

Hamilton & Urahn (2010). Doug Hamilton & Susan K. Urahn (Directors), *Collateral Costs: Incarceration's Effect on Economic Mobility*, Pew Charitable Trusts. [(2: 77)]

Harman (1980). Gilbert Harman, Reasoning and evidence one does not possess. *Midwest Studies in Philosophy* 5: 163–82. [(2: 240) (3: 90)]

(1986). Gilbert Harman, *Change in View*, MIT Press. [(1: 27)]

Hart & McNaughton (1958). Henry M. Hart & John T. McNaughton, Evidence and inference in law. *Daedalus* 87: 40–64. [(2: 4) (3: 76)]

Hart (1961). H. L. A. Hart, *The Concept of Law*, Oxford University Press. [(2: 170) (4: 28)]

Hastie (1993). Reid Hastie, Algebraic models of juror decision processes, in *Inside the Juror: The Psychology of Juror Decision Making* (R. Hastie, ed.), Cambridge University Press. [(2: 90, 129, 274)]

Hay (1997). Bruce L. Hay, Allocating the burden of proof. *Indiana Law Journal* 72: 651–79. [(1: 13)]

Hay & Spier (1997). Bruce L. Hay & Kathryn E. Spier, Burdens of proof in civil litigation: an economic perspective. *Journal of Legal Studies* 26: 413–31. [(4: 180)]

Henderson (1971). G. P. Henderson, "Ought" implies "can." *Philosophy* 2: 101–12. [(3: 65)]

Herman-Stahl et al. (2008). Mindy Herman-Stahl, Marni L. Kan, & Tasseli McKay, *Incarceration and the Family: A Review of Research and Promising Approaches for Serving Fathers and Families*, United States Department of Health and Human Services, Office of Assistant Secretary for Planning and Evaluation. [(2: 78)]

Herzog (1967) Peter Herzog, *Civil Procedure in France*, Martinus Nijhoff. [(4: 9)]

Ho (2008). H. L. Ho, *A Philosophy of Evidence Law*, Oxford University Press. [(1: 5, 34) (2: 2, 12–15, 17–18, 140) (3: 12, 78, 165, 206) (4: 2, 77, 87, 142–3, 145–6, 150) (5: 63–72, 76–83, 85–9, 92)]

Holmes (1897). Oliver Wendell Holmes, The path of the law. *Harvard Law Review* 10: 457–78. [(2: 169) (4: 28)]

Horwich (1982). Paul Horwich, *Probability and Evidence*, Cambridge University Press. [(2: 16, 107, 110) (3: 163) (5: 3)

Howard-Snyder (2006). Frances Howard-Snyder, "Cannot" implies "not ought." *Philosophical Studies* 130: 233–46. [(3: 65)]

Howson & Urbach (1993). Colin Howson & Peter Urbach, *Scientific Reasoning: The Bayesian Approach* (2nd ed.), Open Court. [(2: 16)]

Imwinkelried & Garland (2004). Edward J. Imwinkelried & Norman M. Garland, *Exculpatory Evidence: the Accused's Constitutional Right to Introduce Favorable Evidence*, LexisNexis. [(4: 104)]

James & Hazard (1985). Fleming James, Jr. & Geoffrey C. Hazard, Jr., *Civil Procedure* (3d ed.), Little, Brown. [(4: 83)]

James (1940). George F. James, The role of the hearsay rule in a rational scheme of evidence. *Illinois Law Review* 34: 788–92. [(4: 55)]

Jaynes (2003). E. T. Jaynes, *Probability Theory: The Logic of Science*, Cambridge University Press. [(2: 110)]

Josephson (2001). John R. Josephson, On the proof dynamics of inference to the best explanation. *Cardozo Law Review* 22: 1621–43. [(3: 113–15, 117–18)]

Josephson & Josephson (1994). John R. Josephson & Susan G. Josephson, *Abductive Inference: Computation, Philosophy, Technology*, Cambridge University Press. [(3: 116, 119)]

Juslin et al. (2011). Peter Juslin, Håkan Nilsson, Anders Winman, & Marcus Lindskog, Reducing cognitive biases in probabilistic reasoning by the use of logarithm formats. *Cognition* 120: 248–67. [(2: 237)]

Kadane & Schum (1996). Joseph B. Kadane & David A. Schum, *A Probabilistic Analysis of the Sacco and Vanzetti Case*, Wiley. [(2: 152)]

Kadish & Kadish (1973). Mortimer R. Kadish & Sanford H. Kadish, *Discretion to Disobey*, Stanford University Press. [(4: 175)]

Kagehiro & Stanton (1985). Dorothy K. Kagehiro & W. Clark Stanton, Legal vs. quantified definitions of standards of proof. *Law and Human Behavior* 9: 159–78. [(2: 85)]

Kahneman (2011). Daniel Kahneman, *Thinking, Fast and Slow*, Farrar, Straus, & Giroux. [(2: 252)]

Kaplan, J. (1968). John Kaplan, Decision theory and the factfinding process. *Stanford Law Review* 20: 1065–92. [(2: 26, 49, 86)]

Kaplan, M. (1996). Mark Kaplan, *Decision Theory as Philosophy*, Cambridge University Press. [(2: 31)]

Kaplow (2011). Louis Kaplow, On the optimal burden of proof. *Journal of Political Economy* 119: 1104–40. [(2: 166)]

 (2012). Louis Kaplow, Burden of proof. *Yale Law Journal* 121: 738–859. [(2: 113, 166–8, 172, 176, 178, 180, 185, 187–91) (3: 201)]

 (2014). Louis Kaplow, Likelihood ratio tests and legal decision rules. *American Law and Economics Review* 16(1): 1–39. [(2: 166, 183)]

Kaplow & Shavell (2002). Louis Kaplow & Steven Shavell, *Fairness versus Welfare*, Harvard University Press. [(1: 38) (2: 48)]

Kaptein (2009). Hendrik Kaptein, Rigid anarchic principles of evidence and proof: anomist panaceas against legal pathologies of proceduralism, in *Legal Evidence and Proof: Statistics, Stories, Logic* (H. Kaptein, H. Prakken, & B. Verheij, eds.), Ashgate Publishing. [(1: 3)]

Karp (1994). David J. Karp, Evidence of propensity and probability in sex offense cases and other cases. *Chicago-Kent Law Review* 70: 15–35. [(3: 97)]

Kaye (1979a). David Kaye, The paradox of the gatecrasher and other stories. *Arizona State Law Journal* 1979: 101–9. [(3: 9) (4: 76)]

 (1979b). David Kaye, The laws of probability and the law of the land. *University of Chicago Law Review* 47: 34–56. [(2: 103)]

 (1981). David H. Kaye, Paradoxes, gedanken experiments and the burden of proof: a response to Dr. Cohen's reply. *Arizona State Law Journal* 1981: 635–45. [(3: 9)]

 (1982). David H. Kaye, The limits of the preponderance of the evidence standard: justifiably naked statistical evidence and multiple causation, 1982. *American Bar Foundation Research Journal* [now *Law and Social Inquiry*] 1982: 487–516. [(2: 212)]

 (1986). David H. Kaye, Do we need a calculus of weight, to understand proof beyond reasonable doubt? *Boston University Law Review* 66: 657–72. [(4: 2, 160)]

(1987). David H. Kaye, Apples and oranges: confidence coefficients and the burden of persuasion. *Cornell Law Review* 73: 54–77. [(5: 17)]

(1999). David H. Kaye, Clarifying the burden of persuasion: what Bayesian decision rules do and do not do. *International Journal of Evidence and Proof* 3: 1–28. [(2: 32–3) (3: 199)]

(2000). David H. Kaye, Bayes, burdens and base rates. *International Journal of Evidence and Proof* 4: 260–7. [(2: 32)]

Kaye et al. (2007). David H. Kaye, Valerie P. Hans, B. Michael Dann, Erin Farley, & Stephanie Albertson, Statistics in the jury box: how jurors respond to mitochondrial DNA match probabilities. *Journal of Empirical Legal Studies* 4: 797–834. [(2: 90)]

Kazazi (1996). Mojtaba Kazazi, *Burden of Proof and Related Issues: A Study of Evidence before International Tribunals*, Kluwer Law International. [(6: 18–22)]

Keynes (1921). John M. Keynes, *A Treatise on Probability*, Macmillan. [(1: 25) (3: 2, 26, 30, 33–5, 42, 125, 146) (4: 14)]

Kitai (2003). Rinat Kitai, Protecting the guilty. *Buffalo Criminal Law Review* 6: 1163–87. [(2: 70)]

Kleiger (1989). Estelle Fox Kleiger, *The Trial of Levi Weeks*, Academy Chicago Publishers. [(2: 68)]

Klonoff & Colby (1990). Robert H. Klonoff & Paul L. Colby, *Sponsorship Strategy: Evidentiary Tactics for Winning Jury Trials*, The Michie Company. [(2: 205, 267)(4: 23)]

Koehler (2002). Jonathan J. Koehler, When do courts think base rate statistics are relevant? *Jurimetrics Journal* 42: 373–402. [(3: 13)]

Koehler & Shaviro (1990). Jonathan J. Koehler & Daniel N. Shaviro, Veridical verdicts: increasing verdict accuracy through the use of overtly probabilistic evidence and methods. *Cornell Law Review* 75: 247–79. [(2: 239, 268) (3: 5, 70) (5: 40)]

Kovera et al. (1992). Margaret B. Kovera, Roger C. Park, & Steven D. Penrod, Jurors' perceptions of eyewitness and hearsay evidence. *Minnesota Law Review* 76: 703–22. [(4: 56)]

Kyburg (1983). Henry E. Kyburg, Jr., *Epistemology and Inference*, University of Minnesota Press. [(2: 160)]

LaFave (2003). Wayne R. LaFave, *Substantive Criminal Law* (2d ed.), West Publishing Co. [(1: 12) (2: 41)]

Lamperti (1996). John W. Lamperti, *Probability: A Survey of the Mathematical Theory* (2d ed.), Wiley. [(2: 94)]

Langbein (1985). John Langbein, The German advantage in civil litigation. *University of Chicago Law Review* 52: 823–66. [(4: 6)]

Laplace (1814). Pierre-Simon Laplace, *A Philosophical Essay on Probabilities* (English translation of the 6th French edition, 1951), Dover. [(2: 102) (3: 27)]

Laudan (2006). Larry Laudan, *Truth, Error, and Criminal Law*, Cambridge University Press. [(1: 5) (2: 46) (3: 191) (4: 102, 139)]

(2007). Larry Laudan, Strange bedfellows: inference to the best explanation and the criminal standards of proof. *International Journal of Evidence & Proof* 11: 292–306. [(2: 210) (3: 191)]

Laudan & Saunders (2009). Larry Laudan & Harry D. Saunders, Re-thinking the criminal standard of proof: seeking consensus about the utilities of trial outcomes. *International Commentary on Evidence* 7(2): 1–34. [(2: 72)]

Lee (1997). Thomas R. Lee, Pleading and proof: the economics of legal burdens. *Brigham Young University Law Review* 1997: 1–34. [(2: 62)]

Lempert (1986). Richard O. Lempert, The new evidence scholarship: analyzing the process of proof. *Boston University Law Review* 66: 439–77. [(2: 206) (3: 11) (4: 77–8)]

(1993a). Richard O. Lempert, The suspect population and DNA identification. *Jurimetrics* 34: 1–7. [(2: 229)]

(1993b). Richard O. Lempert, Civil juries and complex cases: taking stock after twelve years, in *Verdict: Assessing the Civil Jury System* (Robert E. Litan, ed.), Brookings Institution. [(4: 126)]

(1997). Richard O. Lempert, Of flutes, oboes, and the as if world of evidence law. *International Journal of Evidence and Proof* 1: 316–20. [(2: 238)]

(2001). Richard O. Lempert, The economic analysis of evidence law: common sense on stilts. *Virginia Law Review* 87: 1619–712. [(1: 13) (2: 83) (3: 131)]

Leubsdorf (1991). John Leubsdorf, Stories and numbers. *Cardozo Law Review* 13: 455–63. [(2: 206)]

(2010). John Leubsdorf, Evidence law as a system of incentives. *Iowa Law Review* 95: 1621–62. [(4: 108)]

(2013). John Leubsdorf, Preponderance of the evidence: some history, Research paper no. 149, Rutgers School of Law–Newark, ssrn.com/abstract = 2466127. [(1: 23)]

Levi (1980). Isaac Levi, *The Enterprise of Knowledge*, MIT Press. [(2: 155) (5: 61)]

(1982). Isaac Levi, Ignorance, probability and rational choice. *Synthese* 53: 387–417. [(2: 157)]

(1984). Isaac Levi, *Decisions and Revisions: Philosophical Essays on Knowledge and Value*, Cambridge University Press. [(2: 99)]

Levmore (1990). Saul Levmore, Probabilistic recoveries, restitution, and recurring wrongs. *Journal of Legal Studies* 19: 691–726. [(2: 15) (3: 6)]

Lillquist (2002). Erik Lillquist, Recasting reasonable doubt: decision theory and the virtues of variability. *University of California at Davis Law Review* 36: 85–196. [(2: 28, 87)]

Lilly et al. (2012). Graham C. Lilly, Daniel J. Capra, & Stephen A. Saltzburg, *Principles of Evidence* (6th ed.), West Publishing Co. [(4: 44, 82)]

Lipton (2001). Peter Lipton, What good is explanation? in *Explanation: Theoretical Approaches and Explanations* (G. Hon and S. S. Rakover, eds.), Kluwer Academic. [(2: 218, 221, 231, 238)]

REFERENCES

Livermore (1984). Joseph M. Livermore, Absent evidence. *Arizona Law Review* 26: 27–40. [(4: 163)]

Livingston (1969). J. Sterling Livingston, Pygmalion in management. *Harvard Business Review* 47: 81–9. [(2: 174)]

Locke (1690). John Locke, *An Essay Concerning Human Understanding* (originally published 1690-1700) (P. Nidditch, ed., 1975), Oxford University Press. [(2: 1) (3: 1) (5: 1)]

Logue (1995). James Logue, *Projective Probability*, Oxford University Press. [(1: 28) (2: 110) (3: 103) (5: 49–50)]

Marder (2005). Nancy S. Marder, *The Jury Process*, Foundation Press. [(2: 9, 132–3) (4: 137)]

Martin & Schum (1987). Anne W. Martin & David A. Schum, Quantifying burdens of proof: a likelihood ratio approach. *Jurimetrics Journal* 27: 383–402. [(2: 275)]

McBaine (1944). J. P. McBaine, Burden of proof: degrees of belief. *California Law Review*, 32: 242–68. [(2: 45, 146)]

McCormick (2013). *McCormick on Evidence* (7th ed., Kenneth S. Broun, gen. ed.), West Publishing Co. [(1: 2, 4, 6–7, 9, 24) (2: 47, 134, 143, 258, 270) (4: 62, 98, 172)]

McNaughton (1955). James McNaughton, Burdens of production of evidence: a function of the burden of persuasion. *Harvard Law Review* 68: 1382–91. [(4: 59)]

Meine et al. (1992). Peter Meine, Roger Park, & Eugene Borgida, Juror decision making and the evaluation of hearsay evidence. *Minnesota Law Review* 76: 683–701. [(4: 56)]

Mellor (2005). D. H. Mellor, *Probability: A Philosophical Introduction*, Routledge. [(2: 95, 103, 106–7, 111–12]

Milich (1992). Paul S. Milich, Hearsay antimonies: the case for abolishing the rule and starting over. *Oregon Law Review* 71: 723–79. [(4: 55)]

Miller (1956). George A. Miller, The magical number seven, plus or minus two: some limits on our capacity for processing information. *Psychological Review* 63: 81–97. [(2: 27)]

Miller et al. (1975). Richard L. Miller, Philip Brickman, & Diana Bolen, Attribution versus persuasion as a means for modifying behaviour. *Journal of Personality and Social Psychology* 31: 430–41. [(2: 174)]

Mitchell & Tetlock (2006). Gregory Mitchell & Philip E. Tetlock, An empirical inquiry into the relation of corrective justice to distributive justice. *Journal of Empirical Legal Studies* 3: 421–66. [(2: 51)]

Morgan (1933). Edmund M. Morgan, Instructing the jury upon presumptions and burden of proof. *Harvard Law Review* 47: 59–83. [(2: 45)]

(1937). Edmund Morgan, The jury and the exclusionary rules of evidence. *University of Chicago Law Review* 4: 247–58. [(4: 52)]

Mueller (1992). Christopher B. Mueller, Post-modern hearsay reform: the importance of complexity. *Minnesota Law Review* 76: 367–423. [(4: 54)]

Mueller & Kirkpatrick (2012). Christopher B. Mueller & Laird C. Kirkpatrick, *Evidence* (5th ed.), Wolters Kluwer Law and Business. [(2: 264–5)]

Murray & Stürner (2004). Peter L Murray & Rolf Stürner, *German Civil Procedure*, Carolina Academic Press. [(4: 9)]

Nagin (2013). Daniel S. Nagin, Deterrence in the twenty-first century. *Crime and Justice: A Review of Research* 42: 199–263. [(2: 179)]

Nance (1986). Dale A. Nance, A comment on the supposed paradoxes of a mathematical interpretation of the logic of trials. *Boston University Law Review* 66: 947–52. [(2: 197)]

(1988). Dale A. Nance, The best evidence principle. *Iowa Law Review* 73: 227–97. [(4: 31, 49, 55)]

(1990). Dale A. Nance, Conditional relevance reinterpreted. *Boston University Law Review* 70: 447–507. [(4: 43)]

(1991). Dale A. Nance, Missing evidence. *Cardozo Law Review* 13: 831–82. [(4: 33)]

(1992). Dale A. Nance, Understanding responses to hearsay: an extension of the comparative analysis. *Minnesota Law Review* 76: 459–72. [(4: 55)]

(1994). Dale A. Nance, Civility and the burden of proof. *Harvard Journal of Law and Public Policy* 17: 647–90. [(1: 9) (2: 55–6)]

(1995a). Dale A. Nance, A theory of verbal completeness. *Iowa Law Review* 80: 825–99. [(4: 16)]

(1995b). Dale A. Nance, Conditional probative value and the reconstruction of the federal rules of evidence. *Michigan Law Review* 94: 419–56. [(4: 43)]

(1996). Dale A. Nance, Verbal completeness and exclusionary rules under the federal rules of evidence. *Texas Law Review* 75: 51–129. [(4: 43)]

(1997). Dale A. Nance, Guidance rules and enforcement rules: a better view of the cathedral. *Virginia Law Review* 83: 837–937. [(2: 173, 181) (4: 30)]

(1998). Dale A. Nance, Evidential completeness and the burden of proof. *Hastings Law Journal* 49: 621–62. [(3: 142) (4: 33, 69, 71, 84, 162)]

(1999). Dale A. Nance, *Law and Justice: Cases and Readings on the American Legal System* (2d ed.), Carolina Academic Press. [(2: 28)]

(2001). Dale A. Nance, Naturalized epistemology and the critique of evidence theory. *Virginia Law Review* 87: 1551–1618. [(2: 202, 206, 208, 210, 223, 227, 236, 241)]

(2003). Dale A. Nance, Reliability and the admissibility of experts. *Seton Hall Law Review* 34: 191–253. [(3: 162) (4: 119, 127, 134)]

(2004). Dale A. Nance, Rethinking confrontation after *Crawford*. *International Commentary on Evidence* 2(1): 1–17. [(4: 75)]

(2006a). Dale A. Nance, *The Wisdom of Dallas County*, in *Evidence Stories* (Richard Lempert, ed.), West Publishing Co. [(4: 57)]

(2006b). Dale A. Nance, Rules, standards, and the internal point of view. *Fordham Law Review* 75: 1287-1316. [(2: 175) (4: 30)]

(2007a). Dale A. Nance, The reference class problem and mathematical models of inference. *International Journal of Evidence and Proof* 11: 259-73. [(2: 229)]

(2007b). Dale A. Nance, Allocating the risk of error: its role in the theory of evidence law. *Legal Theory* 13: 129-64. [(3: 89) (4: 2, 97)]

(2007c). Dale A. Nance, The inferential arrow: a comment on interdisciplinary conversation. *Law, Probability and Risk* 6: 87-95. [(2: 249)]

(2007d). Dale A. Nance, Juries and experts: some recent data from medical malpractice litigation. *International Society of Barristers* 42: 421-3. [(4: 126)]

(2008). Dale A. Nance, The weights of evidence. *Episteme: A Journal of Social Epistemology* 5(3): 267-81. [(1: 26)]

(2010). Dale A. Nance, Adverse inferences about adverse inferences: restructuring juridical roles for responding to evidence tampering by parties to litigation. *Boston University Law Review* 90: 1089-1146. [(3: 164) (4: 33, 110, 112, 155, 159, 161, 164, 173-4, 179, 181)]

Nance & Morris (2002). Dale A. Nance & Scott B. Morris, An empirical assessment of presentation formats for trace evidence with a relatively large and quantifiable random match probability. *Jurimetrics Journal* 42: 403-45. [(2: 230) (4: 126)]

(2005). Dale A. Nance & Scott B. Morris, Juror understanding of DNA evidence: an empirical assessment of presentation formats for trace evidence with a relatively small and quantifiable random match probability. *Journal of Legal Studies* 34: 395-444. [(2: 90, 230) (4: 126)]

Neff (2001). James Neff, *The Wrong Man*, Random House. [(4: 25)]

Nesson (1985). Charles Nesson, The evidence or the event? On judicial proof and the acceptability of verdicts. *Harvard Law Review* 98: 1357-92. [(2: 44)]

(1991). Charles Nesson, Incentives to spoliate evidence in civil litigation: the need for vigorous judicial action. *Cardozo Law Review* 13: 793-803. [(4: 21)]

Niedermeier et al. (1999). Keith E. Niedermeier, Norbert L. Kerr, & Lawrence A. Messé, Jurors' use of naked statistical evidence: exploring bases and implications of the Wells effect. *Journal of Personality and Social Psychology* 76(4): 533-42. [(3: 21-2)]

Nozick (1981). Robert Nozick, *Philosophical Explanations*, Harvard University Press. [(5: 61)]

Oaksford & Chater (2007). Mike Oaksford & Nick Chater, *Bayesian Rationality: The Probabilistic Approach to Human Reasoning*, Oxford University Press. [(2: 250)]

Okasha (2000). Samir Okasha, Van Fraassen's critique of inference to the best explanation. *Studies in the History and Philosophy of Science* 31: 691-710. [(2: 234)]

O'Donnell (1992). Rod O'Donnell, Keynes' weight of argument and Popper's paradox of ideal evidence. *Philosophy of Science* 59: 44-52. [(4: 15)]

O'Malley et al. (2006). Kevin F. O'Malley, Jay E. Grenig, & William C. Lee, *Federal Jury Practice and Instructions* (6th ed.), West Publishing Co. [(1: 15, 23, 29) (2: 51, 55, 131, 142, 263, 265-7) (4: 158, 170)]

Orloff & Stedinger (1983). Neil Orloff & Jery Stedinger, A framework for evaluating the preponderance-of-the-evidence standard. *University of Pennsylvania Law Review* 131: 1159-74. [(3: 6)]

Owens (2000). David Owens, *Reason without Freedom – The Problem of Epistemic Normativity*, Routledge. [(1: 27)]

Pardo (2007). Michael S. Pardo, Book review: On misshapen stones and criminal law's epistemology (reviewing Larry Laudan, *Truth, Error, and Criminal Law: An Essay in Legal Epistemology*). *Texas Law Review* 86: 347-83. [(4: 102)]

(2009). Michael S. Pardo, Second-order proof rules. *Florida Law Review* 61: 1083-1113. [(2: 225, 233) (3: 197)]

(2010). Michael S. Pardo, The Gettier problem and legal proof. *Legal Theory* 16: 37-57. [(5: 91)]

(2013). Michael S. Pardo, The nature and purpose of evidence theory. *Vanderbilt Law Review* 66: 547-613. [(2: 136, 211, 225, 233) (3: 197)]

Pardo & Allen (2008). Michael S. Pardo & Ronald J. Allen, Juridical proof and the best explanation. *Law and Philosophy* 27: 223-68. [(4: 11)]

Parisi (2002). Francesco Parisi, Rent-seeking through litigation: adversarial and inquisitorial systems compared. *International Review of Law and Economics* 22: 193-216. [(4: 11)]

Park et al. (2011). Roger C. Park, David P. Leonard, Aviva A. Orenstein, & Steven H. Goldberg, *Evidence Law: A Student's Guide to the Law of Evidence as Applied in American Trials* (3d ed.), West Publishing Co. [(1: 10) (2: 42)]

Peirce (1932). *The Collected Papers of Charles Sanders Peirce* (Vol. 2, C. Hartshorne & P. Weiss, eds.), Harvard University Press. [(3: 128)]

(1955). C. S. Peirce, Abduction and induction, in *Philosophical Writings of Peirce* (J. Buchler, ed.) [orig. pub. 1901]), Dover. [(3: 112)]

Pennington & Hastie (1991). Nancy Pennington & Reid Hastie, A cognitive theory of juror decision making: the story model. *Cardozo Law Review* 13: 519-57. [(2: 222)]

(1992). Nancy Pennington & Reid Hastie, Explaining the evidence: tests of the story model for juror decision making. *Journal of Personality and Social Psychology* 62: 189-206. [(2: 251)]

(1993). Nancy Pennington & Reid Hastie, The story model for juror decision making, in *Inside the Juror: The Psychology of Juror Decision Making* (Reid Hastie, ed.), Cambridge University Press. [(2: 222, 224)]

Picinali (2013). Federico Picinali, Two meanings of "reasonableness": dispelling the "floating" reasonable doubt. *Modern Law Review* 76: 845-75. [(2: 19, 88)]

Plantinga (1993). Alvin Plantinga, *Warrant and Proper Function*, Oxford University Press. [(2: 99, 107)]

Polinsky (1989). A. Mitchell Polinsky, *An Introduction to Law and Economics* (2nd ed.), Little, Brown. [(3: 59)]

Popper (1959). Karl R. Popper, *The Logic of Scientific Discovery*, Basic Books. [(4: 13)]

Posner (1998). Richard A. Posner, Rational choice, behavioral economics and the law. *Stanford Law Review* 50: 1551–75. [(1: 13) (2: 38)]

(1999). Richard A. Posner, An economic approach to evidence law. *Stanford Law Review* 51: 1477–1546. [(2: 271) (3: 141) (4: 54, 85–6)]

Priest & Klein (1984). George L. Priest & Benjamin Klein, The selection of disputes for litigation. *Journal of Legal Studies* 13: 1–55. [(2: 259)]

Rakos & Landsman (1992). Richard F. Rakos & Stephen Landsman, Researching the hearsay rule: emerging findings, general issues and future directions. *Minnesota Law Review* 76: 655–82. [(4: 56)]

Rao et al. (2002). Rajesh P. N. Rao, Bruno A. Olshausen, & Michael S. Lewicki, *Probabilistic Models of the Brain: Perception and Neural Function*, Bradford Books. [(2: 254)]

Rawls (1971). John Rawls, *A Theory of Justice*, Harvard University Press. [(1: 3)]

Redmayne (1999). Mike Redmayne, Standards of proof in civil litigation. *Modern Law Review* 62: 167–95. [(1: 4) (2: 28, 87)]

(2003). Mike Redmayne, Objective probability and the assessment of evidence. *Law, Probability and Risk* 2: 275–94. [(2: 105)]

(2008a). Mike Redmayne, Exploring the proof paradoxes. *Legal Theory* 14: 281–309. [(3: 5)]

(2008b). Mike Redmayne, Book review: Reviewing Larry Laudan, *Truth, Error, and Criminal Law: An Essay in Legal Epistemology*. *New Criminal Law Review* 11: 181–5. [(4: 102)]

Reichenbach (1949). Hans Reichenbach, *The Theory of Probability* (2d ed.), University of California Press. [(3: 49–51)]

Rescher (1976). Nicholas Rescher, *Plausible Reasoning: An Introduction to the Theory and Practice of Plausibilistic Inference*, Van Gorcum. [(3: 110)]

(1989). Nicholas Rescher, *Cognitive Economy: The Economic Dimension of the Theory of Knowledge*, University of Pittsburgh Press. [(3: 91–2, 209)]

(2009). Nicholas Rescher, *Ignorance: On the Wider Implications of Deficient Knowledge*, University of Pittsburgh Press. [(3: 68–9)]

Riddell & Plant (2009). Anna Riddell & Brendan Plant, *Evidence before the International Court of Justice*, British Institute of International and Comparative Law. [(2: 39–40) (4: 8) (6: 6–16)]

Risinger (1982). D. Michael Risinger, "Substance" and "procedure" revisited, with some afterthoughts on the constitutional problems of "irrebuttable presumptions." *UCLA Law Review* 30: 189–216. [(2: 42)]

Robertson & Vignaux (1995). Bernard Robertson & G. A. Vignaux, *Interpreting Evidence: Evaluating Forensic Science in the Courtroom*, Wiley. [(2: 228)]

Rosenne (1985). Shabtai Rosenne, *The Law and Practice of the International Court* (3d ed.), Martinus Nijhoff. [(6: 12)]

Rosenthal & Jacobson (1968). Robert Rosenthal & Lenore Jacobson, *Pygmalion in the Classroom: Teacher Expectation and Pupils' Intellectual Development*, Holt, Reinhart & Winston. [(2: 174)]

Runde (1990). Jochen Runde, Keynesian uncertainty and the weight of arguments. *Economics and Philosophy* 6: 275–92. [(3: 3, 129, 132)]

  (1994). Jochen Runde, Keynes after Ramsey: In defense of *A Treatise on Probability*. *Studies in the History and Philosophy of Science* 25: 97–124. [(3: 2)]

  (2000). Jochen Runde, Shackle on probability, in *Economics as an Art of Thought: Essays in Memory of G. L. S. Shackle* (Peter E. Earl & Stephen F. Frowen, eds.), Routledge. [(3: 99)]

Sahlin (1993). Nils-Eric Sahlin, On higher order beliefs, in *Philosophy of Probability* (Jacques-Paul Dubucs, ed.), Kluwer Academic. [(3: 53-7)]

Saks (2000). Michael J. Saks, The aftermath of *Daubert*: an evolving jurisprudence of expert evidence. *Jurimetrics Journal* 40: 229–41. [(4: 136)]

Salmon (1973). Wesley Salmon, *Logic* (2d ed.), Prentice-Hall. [(3: 207)]

Saltzburg (1978a). Stephen A. Saltzburg, The unnecessarily expanding role of the American trial judge. *Virginia Law Review* 64: 1–81. [(4: 176)]

  (1978b). Stephen A. Saltzburg, A special aspect of relevance: countering negative inferences associated with the absence of evidence. *California Law Review* 66: 1011–60. [(4: 157)]

Sanchirico (1997). Chris W. Sanchirico, The burden of proof in civil litigation: a simple model of mechanism design. *International Review of Law and Economics* 17: 431–47. [(3: 60)]

  (2008). Chris W. Sanchirico, A primary-activity approach to proof burdens. *Journal of Legal Studies*, 37: 273–313. [(1: 13)]

Sanders (1998). Joseph Sanders, *Bendectin on Trial: A Study of Mass Tort Litigation*, University of Michigan Press. [(4: 132)]

Saunders (2005). Harry D. Saunders, Quantifying reasonable doubt: a proposed solution to an equal protection problem. *ExpressO*; available at: http://works.bepress.com/harry_saunders/2 [(2: 87, 153)]

Scharf & Day (2012). Michael P. Scharf & Margaux Day, The International Court of Justice's treatment of circumstantial evidence and adverse inferences. *Chicago Journal of International Law* 13: 123–51. [(6: 16)]

Schauer (1991). Frederick Schauer, *Playing by the Rules: A Philosophical Examination of Rule-Based DecisionMaking in Law and in Life*, Oxford University Press. [(4: 81)]

  (2003). Frederick Schauer, *Profiles, Probabilities, and Stereotypes*, Harvard University Press. [(2: 269)]

Schauer & Spellman (2013). Frederick Schauer & Barbara A. Spellman, Is expert evidence really different? *Notre Dame Law Review* 89: 1–26. [(4: 126)]

Scheck et al. (2003). Barry Scheck, Peter Neufeld, & Jim Dwyer, *Actual Innocence: When Justice Goes Wrong and How to Make it Right*, Penguin (New American Library). [(5: 59)]

Schlesinger (1991). George N. Schlesinger, *The Sweep of Probability*, University of Notre Dame Press. [(2: 103) (4: 15)]

Schmalbeck (1986). Richard Schmalbeck, The trouble with statistical evidence. *Law and Contemporary Problems* 49: 221–36. [(5: 3)]

Schoemaker (1982). Paul J. H. Schoemaker, The expected utility model: its variants, purposes, evidence and limitations. *Journal of Economic Literature* 20: 529–63. [(2: 31)]

Schoeman (1987). Ferdinand Schoeman, Cohen on inductive probability and the law of evidence. *Philosophy of Science* 54: 76–91. [(3: 103, 203)]

Schuetz & Lilley (1999). Janice E. Schuetz & Lin S. Lilley (eds.), *The O. J. Simpson Trials: Rhetoric, Media and the Law*, Southern Illinois University Press. [(5: 57)]

Schum (1994). David A. Schum, *Evidential Foundations of Probabilistic Reasoning*, Wiley. [(1: 36) (2: 25, 117, 124, 254, 257) (3: 75, 105, 134, 154, 159, 169)]

Seigel (1992). Michael Seigel, Rationalizing hearsay: a proposal for a best evidence hearsay rule. *Boston University Law Review* 72: 893–950. [(4: 57)]

Shackle (1969). G. L. S. Shackle, *Decision, Order and Time in Human Affairs* (2nd ed.), Cambridge University Press. [(5: 94)]

Shafer (1976). Glenn Shafer, *A Mathematical Theory of Evidence*, Princeton University Press. [(2: 130) (3: 36, 168, 171, 173, 180)]

(1981). Glen Shafer, Constructive probability. *Synthese* 48: 1–60. [(2: 165)]

(1986). Glen Shafer, The construction of probability arguments. *Boston University Law Review* 66: 799–816. [(3: 36)]

Simon & Blaskovich (2002). Rita J. Simon & Dagny A. Blaskovich, *A Comparative Analysis of Capital Punishment*, Lexington Books. [(2: 75)]

Sinnott-Armstrong (1984). Walter Sinnott-Armstrong, "Ought" conversationally implies "can." *Philosophical Review* 93: 249–61. [(3: 65)]

Skyrms (1990). Bryan Skyrms, *The Dynamics of Rational Deliberation*, Harvard University Press. [(3: 39–40)]

(2000). Brian Skyrms, *Choice and Chance* (4th ed.), Wadsworth. [(3: 207)]

Smets (2005). Philippe Smets, Decision making in the TBM: the necessity of the pignistic transformation. *International Journal of Approximate Reasoning* 38: 133–47. [(3: 183)]

Smith (2010). Martin Smith, What else justification could be. *Noûs* 44: 10–31. [(3: 123)]

Sommer (1976). Robert Sommer, *The End of Imprisonment*, Oxford University Press. [(2: 80)]

Sowle (1994). Stephen D. Sowle, A regime of social death: criminal punishment in the age of prisons. *New York University Review of Law & Social Change* 21: 497–565 [(2: 80)]

Spottswood (2013). Mark Spottswood, The hidden structure of fact-finding. *Case Western Reserve Law Review* 64: 131–200. [(2: 254, 256)]

Starkie (1832). Thomas Starkie, *A Practical Treatise on the Law of Evidence* (4th ed., P. H. Nicklin & T. Johnson, eds.), reprinted in 2012 by Nabu Press. [(2: 69)]

Stein (1996). Alex Stein, The refoundation of evidence law. *Canadian Journal of Law and Jurisprudence* 9: 279-342. [(1: 15, 28, 31) (2: 11, 109, 114-15, 119) (3: 78)]

(2005). Alex Stein, *Foundations of Evidence Law*, Oxford University Press. [(3: 12, 25, 31, 79, 89, 107, 142, 197) (4: 2, 29, 97) (5: 29-30, 36-7, 40, 48)]

(2011). Alex Stein, The flawed probabilistic foundations of law and economics. *Northwestern University Law Review* 105: 199-260. [(2: 119-22, 125) (3: 43-4)]

Stier (1985). Robert H. Stier, Jr., Revisiting the missing witness inference: quieting the loud voice from the empty chair. *Maryland Law Review* 44: 137-76. [(4: 168)]

Stoffelmayr & Diamond (2000). Elisabeth Stoffelmayr & Shari Seidman Diamond, The conflict between precision and flexibility in explaining "beyond a reasonable doubt." *Psychology Public Policy and Law* 6: 769-87. [(2: 47)]

Stanovich (2011). Keith E. Stanovich, *Rationality and the Reflective Mind*, Oxford Unversity Press. [(2: 255)]

Strat (1990). Thomas M. Strat, Decision analysis using belief functions. *International Journal of Approximate Reasoning* 4: 391-417 [(3: 181, 186)]

Summers (1969). Robert S. Summers, Law, adjudicative processes, and civil justice, in *Law, Reason, and Justice* (G. Hughes, ed.), New York University Press. [(4: 107)

(1974). Robert S. Summers, Evaluating and improving legal process: a plea for "process values." *Cornell Law Review* 60: 1-52. [(3: 212)]

Swinburne (2001). Richard S. Swinburne, *Epistemic Justification*, Oxford University Press. [(2: 107, 110, 231) (3: 37, 65, 92, 102, 206)]

Tapper (1995). Colin Tapper, *Cross and Tapper on Evidence* (8th ed.), Butterworths. [(1: 8)]

Taruffo (2003). Michelle Tarfuffo, Rethinking the standards of proof. *American Journal of Comparative Law* 51: 659-77. (2: 35, 40) (4: 7)

Teply & Whitten (1994). Larry L. Reply & Ralph U. Whitten, *Civil Procedure*, Foundation Press. [(1: 20)]

Thayer (1898). James Bradley Thayer, *A Preliminary Treatise on Evidence at the Common Law*, Little, Brown (reprinted in 1969 by Augustus M. Kelley Publishers). [(4: 52)]

Tillers & Gottfried (2006). Peter Tillers & Jonathan Gottfried, United States v. Copeland, 369 F. Supp. 2d 276 (E.D.N.Y. 2005): a collateral attack on the legal maxim that proof beyond reasonable doubt is unquantifiable? *Law, Probability and Risk* 5: 135-73. [(2: 91, 152, 242)]

Toulmin (1958). Stephen Toulmin, *The Uses of Argument*, Cambridge University Press. [(3: 109)]

Tribe (1971). Lawrence Tribe, trial by mathematics: precision and ritual in the legal process. *Harvard Law Review* 84: 1329-93. [(2: 28-9) (4: 76)]

Troffaes (2007). Matthias C. M. Troffaes, Decision making under uncertainty using imprecise probabilities. *International Journal of Approximate Reasoning* 45(1): 17-29. [(2: 165)]

Twining (1984). William Twining, Evidence and legal theory. *Modern Law Review*, 47: 261-83. [(4: 107)]

(1985). William Twining, *Theories of Evidence: Bentham and Wigmore*, Weidenfeld & Nicolson. [(2: 144)]

(1990). William Twining, *Rethinking Evidence: Exploratory Essays*, Basil Blackwell. [(4: 107)]

Valencia-Ospina (1999). E. Valencia-Ospina, Evidence before the International Court of Justice. *International Law Forum du droit international* 4: 202-7. [(6: 12)]

Vidmar & Diamond (2001). Neil Vidmar & Shari Seidman Diamond, Juries and expert evidence. *Brooklyn Law Review* 66: 1121-80. [(4: 126)]

Walker (1996). Vern R. Walker, Preponderance, probability, and warranted factfinding. *Brooklyn Law Review* 62: 1075-1136. [(2: 276)]

(2001). Vern R. Walker, Theories of uncertainty: explaining the possible sources of error in inferences. *Cardozo Law Review* 22: 1523-70. [(4: 3)]

Walley (1991). Peter Walley, *Statistical Reasoning with Imprecise Probabilities*, Chapman & Hall. [(2: 145)

Walton (2002). Douglas Walton, *Legal Argumentation and Evidence*, Pennsylvania State University Press. [(1: 16) (3: 111, 120-122, 124)]

Weinrib (2011). Ernest J. Weinrib, Private law and public right. *University of Toronto Law Journal* 61: 191-211. [(2: 54)]

Weinstein & Dewbury (2006). Jack B. Weinstein & Ian Dewsbury, Comment on the meaning of "proof beyond reasonable doubt." *Law, Probability and Risk* 5: 167-73. [(2: 47, 85)]

Wells (1992). Gary L. Wells, Naked statistical evidence of liability: is subjective probability enough? *Journal of Personality and Social Psychology* 62: 739-52. [(3: 14-18, 23)]

Whitebread & Slobogin (2008). Charles H. Whitebread & Christopher Slobogin, *Criminal Procedure* (5th ed.), Foundation Press. [(4: 20, 147)]

Whitman (2008). James Q. Whitman, *The Origins of Reasonable Doubt: The Theological Roots of the Criminal Trial*, Yale University Press. [(2: 43) (4: 169)]

Wigmore (1913). John H. Wigmore, *The Principles of Judicial Proof*, Little, Brown. [(2: 247)]

(1937). John H. Wigmore, *The Science of Judicial Proof* (3d ed.), Little, Brown. [(1: 1) (2: 247-8) (3: 108)]

(1970). 3 John H. Wigmore, *Evidence in Trials at Common Law (Wigmore on Evidence)* (Chadbourn rev. 1970), Little, Brown. [(4: 99)]

(1972). 4 John H. Wigmore, *Evidence in Trials at Common Law (Wigmore on Evidence)* (Chadbourn rev. 1972), Little, Brown. [(4: 51)]

(1978). 7 John H. Wigmore, *Evidence in Trials at Common Law (Wigmore on Evidence)* (Chadbourn rev. 1978), Little, Brown. [(4: 101)]

(1981). 9 John H. Wigmore, *Evidence in Trials at Common Law (Wigmore on Evidence)* (Chadbourn rev. 1981), Little, Brown. [(1: 11) (2: 270) (4: 176) (6: 1)]

(1983). 1A John H. Wigmore, *Evidence in Trials at Common Law (Wigmore on Evidence)* (Tillers rev. 1983), Little, Brown. [(1: 35) (4: 4)]

Wright et al. (1982). Charles Alan Wright, Arthur R. Miller, & Edward H. Cooper, *Federal Practice and Procedure* (2d ed.), West Publishing Co. [(2: 65)]

Zamir & Ritov (2012). Eyal Zamir & Ilana Ritov, Loss aversion, omission bias, and the burden of proof in civil litigation. *Journal of Legal Studies* 41: 165–207. [(2: 59, 61)]

INDEX

adjudication as practical
   reasoning, 16–20
adjudicative facts
   distinguished from legislative facts, 2
   ultimate facts, 1, 22
admissibility rules, 203, 213,
   215–27, 296
adversarial duty and privilege, 192–3
adversarial versus inquisitorial
   procedures
   consideration of Keynesian weight, 303
   international tribunals, 296
   standard of discriminatory power, 27–9
   taking of evidence, 186–8
adverse inferences (spoliation), 198,
   233, 236–43, 297
allocation
   burden of persuasion, 3
   burden of producing specific
     evidence. *See* § 4.3
   initial burden of production, 4
analysis of evidence. *See* §§ 2.4 & 3.4
   Bayesian vs. explanatory, 84–91
   descriptive theories of, 93–5
   graphical, 91–3
   tools of informal reasoning, 140–7

background information, 95–101
   contestable non-case-specific, 97
   prior odds, 95–7
   uncontested case-specific, 98
Bayes's rule. *See* analysis of evidence;
   background information
belief functions, 167–78
   Bayesian versus non-Bayesian, 170
   decision making, 170–8
   evidential completeness, 168–70

Bernoulli's theorem, 253
best evidence principle, 196–200
best explanation, inference to. *See*
   inference to the best explanation
burden of persuasion
   metaphor of weight, 7–8
   models of. *See* discriminatory
     power
   versus burden of production, 2
burdens of proof
   burden of producing specific
     evidence. *See* Chapter 4
   persuasion versus production, 1

complementarity and Keynesian weight
   (paradox of negation), 166–7
completeness
   evidential. *See* evidence
   verbal, doctrine of, 196
conditional relevance, 196
confidence intervals, 254
conjunction, paradox of, 74–8
constitutional requirements, 12,
   20–1, 215
contextualism, 284–90
corroboration rules, 214

damages, proof of, 157
decision theory
   and discriminatory power. *See* § 2.2
   and Keynesian weight, 120n48
deontological constraints
   standard of discriminatory power,
     31–5
   standard of Keynesian weight, 135
   standard of discriminatory power,
     69–72

descriptive, prescriptive, and
    interpretive theory, 11
discovery
    and relevance, 188–92
    sanctions related to, 193–4
discriminatory power. *See* Chapter 2
    characterized as weight, 7–8
    civil cases, standard for, 32–6, 40–2,
        170–8
    criminal cases, standard for,
        36–40, 170–8
    decision-theoretic model, 21–63
    distinguished from Keynesian
        weight, 8, 157
    inference to the best
        explanation, 79–84
    relative plausibility theory, 73–9
    using to regulate primary
        conduct, 64–73

embarrassment costs, 273
endowment effect (loss aversion), 35
enforcement costs, 36, 39
epistemic warrant
    holistic theories of, 156–67
    relation to probability. *See*
        probability
equipoise, default rule for, 3, 24, 63, 255
evidence
    weight of. *See* weight of evidence
evidence, nature and sources of
    background information, 95–101
    formally introduced, 22
expected certainty, 266–7

fact-finder, role of
    bifurcation of court, 13
    monitoring Keynesian weight. *See* § 4.2
    practical versus theoretical
        reasoning, 18–20
    probability assessments, 18–20, 27,
        42–63
    setting standard for discriminatory
        power, 40–2
    use of background information.
        See § 2.5
    use of categorical beliefs. *See* § 5.3
finality. *See* promptness and finality
free evaluation of evidence, 55–7

gestalt holism and Keynesian weight,
    161–5
goals of adjudication
    Keynesian weight's relation to.
        See § 3.8

hearsay rule, 196, 233n150
Holmesian "bad man" cynicism,
    65–71, 192–3

indifference, principle of, 47, 112
inference to the best explanation,
    79–88, 140–4
informal reasoning, theories of.
    See § 3.4
    as criteria of decision, 137–40
    as inferential tools, 140–7
inquisitorial procedures. *See* adversarial
    versus inquisitorial procedures
international tribunals, 294–303
    criminal courts, 294–5, 300–3
    International Court of Justice, 295–300
interpretive theory, 11

jury as fact-finder. *See* fact-finder, role of
juror credulity, 196–201
jury notice, 97

Keynesian weight
    adequacy of. *See* § 3.3
    articulated by Keynes, 111
    belief functions, theory of. *See* § 3.7
    chosen, not merely assessed, 115
    comparative nature, 9, 113, 117–19
    distinguished from discriminatory
        power, 8
    effects on discriminatory power
        as limit, 137
    epistemic risk, relation to, 123
    gestalt holism, relation to, 161–5
    goals of adjudication, relation to.
        See § 3.8
    higher order probabilities, 120
    informal reasoning, relation to.
        See § 3.4
    international tribunals, evidence
        before. *See* § 6.2
    need for a theory of, 9–11
    practical optimization, 135

preferential versus strict
    standard, 132
quantification of. See § 3.5
quantitative versus qualitative
    changes in, 113
responsibility for. See Chapter 4
stakes, relation to, 135
synthetic holism, relation to, 158–61
tenacity of belief, relation to. See
    Chapter 5
tradoffs with discriminatory
    power, 156–8
value of increasing, 114–17, 264–7

legislative facts, 2
loss aversion (endowment effect), 35

maximin decision rule, 60–3

naked statistical evidence
    civil context, 104–11, 206–9
    criminal context, 125–9
negation and Keynesian weight
    (complementarity), 166–7

omission bias, 34, 161
original recording rule, 196–9

paradox of ideal evidence, 189n13
paradoxes of probabilistic proof standards
    conjunction of elements, 74–8
    negation and complementarity, 166–7
personal knowledge rule, 196
practical optimization, 135
practical reasoning
    adjudication as, 16–20
preferential versus strict standards, 132
prescriptive, descriptive, and
    interpretive theory, 11
prior odds and background
    information. See § 2.5
probability. See § 2.2.2
    causitive, 50–3
    credal, 44
    empirical, 43
    epistemic, 43
    epistemic warrant, relation to, 48–9,
        54–5, 161–5
    epistemological, 45

logical, 44
mathematical, 43
measurement of, 44–5
naive frequentism, 49–50
objectivity, aspects of, 47
past events, 45
positivistic error, 45
principle of indifference, 47
rationalist, 43
second-order uncertainty. See § 2.2.3
subjective, 44
probative value, 96
promptness and finality, 17, 121, 166,
    261, 287

relevance, 188–90
reliability of expert testimony, 221–7
resilience. See tenacity of belief
risk avoidance, 123–4

Second-order uncertainty. See § 2.2.3
    confused with Keynesian weight,
        120–2, 253–64
    imprecision, 58–9
    lower probabilities and
        equipoise, 62–3
    maximin decision rule, 60–3
    probabilities about
        probabilities, 59–60
spoliation of evidence. See adverse
    inferences
stability of verdicts. See § 5.2
stakes of decision, 135
standard of proof, 1
    discriminatory power, relation to. See
        discriminatory power
    Keynesian weight, requirements of.
        See Keynesian weight
    strict vs. preferential standards, 132
Succession, Rule of, 112
surprise, theory of, 290n94
suspension of judgment. See
    promptness and finality
synthetic holism and Keynesian
    weight, 158–61

tenacity of belief, 11
    categorical or gradational belief, 251
    contextualism, 284–90

tenacity of belief (*cont.*)
  knowledge and commitment, 280–2
  resilience of probability, relation to. *See* § 5.1
  security of judgments. *See* § 5.2
theoretical reasoning
  fact-finding as, 18–20

ultimate facts, 16, 22
uncontested case-specific facts, 98

verdicts, nature and effect of, 16

weight of evidence, diverse meanings of, 7–9, 11, 89, 111, 148–56, 168
Wells effect, 108–10

Lightning Source UK Ltd.
Milton Keynes UK
UKHW010802200119
335875UK00016B/376/P